# INTRODUCTION TO SYSTEM
# PROGRAMMING

A.I.P.C. Studies in Data Processing
General Editor: Richard Goodman

1. Some Commercial Autocodes. A Comparative Study
   E. L. Willey, A. d'Agapeyeff, Michelle Clark, Marion Tribe and B. J. Gibbens.

2. A Primer of ALGOL 60 Programming
   E. W. Dijkstra

3. Input Language for Automatic Programming
   A. P. Yershov, G. I. Kozhukhin and U. Voloshin

4. Introduction to System Programming
   Edited by Peter Wegner

5. ALGOL 60 Implementation. The Translation and Use of Algol 60 Programs on a Computer
   B. Randell and L. J. Russell
   With a Foreword by E. E. Dijkstra

A.P.I.C. Studies in Data Processing
No. 4

# INTRODUCTION TO SYSTEM PROGRAMMING

Proceedings of a Symposium
held at the London School of Economics
July, 1962

*Edited by*
## PETER WEGNER
*London School of Economics*
*University of London, England*

*Published for*
THE AUTOMATIC PROGRAMMING INFORMATION CENTRE
Brighton College of Technology, England
*by*

1964
ACADEMIC PRESS
LONDON AND NEW YORK

ACADEMIC PRESS INC. (LONDON) LTD.
Berkeley Square House
Berkeley Square
London, W.1

*U.S. Edition published by*
ACADEMIC PRESS INC.
111 Fifth Avenue
New York, New York 10003

Second printing 1965

Third printing 1965
Fourth printing 1969

*Library of Congress Catalog Card Number:* 64–14228

SBN: 12 741450 9

PRINTED IN GREAT BRITAIN BY
T. & A. CONSTABLE LTD., HOPETOUN STREET
PRINTERS TO THE UNIVERSITY OF EDINBURGH

# CONTRIBUTORS

A. d'AGAPEYEFF, *Computer Analysts and Programmers Ltd., London, England.*
(p. 199)

W. H. BURGE, *Univac Division of Sperry Rand Corp., New York, U.S.A.*
(p. 294)

D. GABOR, *Imperial College, London, England.* (p. 313)

S. GILL, *International Computers and Tabulators Ltd., London, England.*
(pp. 10 and 214)

J. C. HARWELL, *Honeywell Controls Ltd., London, England.* (p. 178)

C. A. R. HOARE, *Elliott Bros. (London) Ltd., London, England.* (p. 156)

D. HOWARTH, *International Computers and Tabulators Ltd., London, England.*
(p. 227)

E. HUMBY, *International Computers and Tabulators Ltd., London, England.*
(p. 166)

D. H. R. HUXTABLE, *The English Electric Company Ltd., Stoke-on-Trent,
England.* (p. 137)

J. K. ILIFFE, *International Computers and Tabulators Ltd., London, England.*
(pp. 256 and 276)

D. P. JENKINS, *Royal Radar Establishment, Malvern, Worcestershire, England.*
(p. 283)

D. MORRIS, *Electrical Engineering Laboratories, The University, Manchester,
England.* (p. 249)

J. A. NASH, *I.B.M. United Kingdom Ltd., London, England.* (p. 239)

I. C. PYLE, *Atomic Energy Research Establishment, Harwell, Berkshire,
England.* (pp. 38 and 86)

B. RANDELL, *The English Electric Company Ltd., Atomic Power Division,
Whetstone, near Leicester, England.* (p. 122)

P. WEGNER, *London School of Economics and Political Science, London,
England.* (pp. 1, 20, 73 and 101)

M. WOODGER, *National Physical Laboratory, Teddington, Middlesex, England*
(p. 56)

v

# PREFACE

The papers in this volume are based on lectures delivered at a one-week symposium on programming held at the London School of Economics. Lecturers were drawn from the principal British programming research groups, and the present volume is representative of current thought in this field in Britain.

The earlier chapters in this volume are introductory, and later ones are intended to be more detailed expository accounts of specific topics in system programming. The volume as a whole is experimental, seeking to develop a nucleus of material which might in future become the basis of a science of programming. It is hoped that the reader will carry away with him a sense of excitement appropriate to the emergence of a new subject, and that the book as a whole will have a coherence transcending the individual papers of which it is composed. Finally, this volume should be useful as a textbook for students of system programming who wish to gain an overall picture of the subject.

The papers in this volume are grouped into the following seven parts.

1. An introductory paper discussing various alternative theoretical approaches to the topic of programming.

2. Three papers on FORTRAN and ALGOL, which are intended both as expository papers for those unfamiliar with these languages, and as an introduction to the papers on implementation which follow.

3. Two papers on the implementation of FORTRAN-like compilers which incidentally throw some light on the structure of the FORTRAN language.

4. Four papers on the implementation of ALGOL-like compilers which indicate a number of alternative approaches to ALGOL implementation, and, by implication, emphasize structural features of ALGOL which call for implementation techniques differing from those used in FORTRAN (i.e. Block structure, arrays with dynamic bounds, and potentially recursive procedures).

5. Three papers on commercial languages and compilers, which include descriptions of COBOL, Rapidwrite and FACT, and an introduction to techniques of commercial compilation.

6. Three papers on programming systems with special emphasis on time sharing; including a general survey, and descriptions of the Atlas and Stretch supervisory systems.

7. Five papers on various topics in advanced programming, including syntactic analysis, addressing techniques, continuous evaluation, list programming, and stack techniques.

Finally, there is an Appendix, which consists of a thought-provoking talk by Professor Gabor on 'The Future of Computers.'

The Editor would like to acknowledge the editorial assistance of J. K. Iliffe who efficiently co-ordinated the galley proof stage of the editing.

PETER WEGNER

*London School of Economics and Political Science,*
*London, England*
  *January* 1964

# CONTENTS

*Page*

Contributors . . . . . . . . . . . . . . . . . . . . . v

Preface . . . . . . . . . . . . . . . . . . . vii

Introduction. P. WEGNER . . . . . . . . . . . . . . 1

## PART ONE. GENERAL SURVEY

1. Programming Systems and Languages. S. GILL . . . . . . . . 10

## PART TWO. PROGRAMMING LANGUAGES

2. FORTRAN, ALGOL and COBOL. P. WEGNER . . . . . . . . 20
3. An Outline of FORTRAN. I. C. PYLE . . . . . . . . . . 38
4. An Introduction to ALGOL 60. M. WOODGER . . . . . . . . 56

## PART THREE. FORTRAN IMPLEMENTATION

5. Intermediate Languages and Programming Systems. P. WEGNER . 73
6. Implementation of FORTRAN on Atlas. I. C. PYLE. . . . . . . . 86

## PART FOUR. ALGOL IMPLEMENTATION

7. An Introduction to Stack Compilation Techniques. P. WEGNER . 101
8. The Whetstone KDF9 Algol Translator. B. RANDELL . . . . . . 122
9. On Writing an Optimizing Translator for ALGOL 60 . . . . . .
    D. H. R. HUXTABLE . . . . . . . . . . . . . . . . 137
10. The Elliott ALGOL Programming System. C. A. R. HOARE . . . . 156

## PART FIVE. COMMERCIAL LANGUAGES AND COMPILERS

11. I.C.T. COBOL Rapidwrite. E. HUMBY . . . . . . . . . . . 166
12. Programming in Honeywell FACT. J. C. HARWELL . . . . . . . 178
13. An Introduction to Commercial Compilers. A. d'AGAPEYEFF . . 199

## PART SIX. PROGRAMMING SYSTEMS

14. Introduction to Time-Sharing. S. GILL . . . . . . . . . . . 214
15. The Atlas Supervisor Program. D. HOWARTH . . . . . . . . 227
16. Time-Sharing Aspects of the Stretch Computer. J. A. NASH . . . . 239

# CONTENT

## PART SEVEN. ADVANCED PROGRAMMING TECHNIQUES

17. The Use of Syntactic Analysis in Compilers. D. MORRIS . . . . 249
18. The Role of Addressing in Programming Systems. J. K. ILIFFE . . 256
19. Continuous Evaluation. J. K. ILIFFE . . . . . . . . . . . 276
20. List Programming. D. P. JENKINS . . . . . . . . . . . . 283
21. Interpretation, Stacks and Evaluation. W. H. BURGE . . . . . . 294

## APPENDIX

The Future of Computers. D. GABOR . . . . . . . . . . . 313

# INTRODUCTION

## P. WEGNER

*London School of Economics and Political Science, London, England*

This introduction attempts to summarize the content of each of the chapters in this volume. It should help readers to obtain an overall picture, before being caught up in the details.

### PART ONE. GENERAL SURVEY

The first chapter is quite a subtle one. It gives the impression of being tentative and incomplete, and in this respect it faithfully reflects the state of the subject matter being described. Dr Gill regards the computer as an empty black box with latent structure which can be supplied with instructions and data to make it behave to suit particular circumstances. A programming system can be regarded as an initial layer of programs which enable the computer to accept and deal with a sequence of problems and data, in suitable problem and data languages. However, the present rigid distinction between program translation and data manipulation (execution) might well disappear in future programming systems, as indicated in Chapter 19.

Next, the suitability of programming languages for problem statement and communication, and their efficiency in the sense of information theory are considered. Various aspects of language structure such as name-value distinctions, program segmentation and data specification are also discussed.

Finally, the author considers salient features of compilers and programming systems, such as the number of passes over the data, and the specification of compilers in a metalanguage. Some of the tasks performed by supervisory routines, such as sequencing of jobs, error diagnosis, and log-keeping, are enumerated.

### PART TWO. PROGRAMMING LANGUAGES

Chapter 2, which is an introduction to the third and fourth discusses, within the framework of a single paper, FORTRAN, ALGOL and COBOL. It consists of a set of graduated examples in each of the languages.

The twenty FORTRAN examples introduce fixed and floating point variables, expressions and statements, consider the order of evaluation of arithmetic expressions, and continue with examples of subscripted variables, arrays, the *IF* statement, the *DO* statement, *DO* loops, *DIMENSION* and comment statements, *FORMAT* statements, and input-output statements. The final examples include complete subroutines, a subroutine call, and a main program involving input, output and a simple computation.

The seventeen ALGOL examples introduce identifiers, assignment statements, declarations, Boolean variables operators and values, relational operators and conditional statements. For statements, compound statements, blocks, procedures and functions are then introduced. The difference between declarations and specifications, and between calls by value and calls by name is discussed, and recursion is illustrated by a recursive summation procedure which makes use of Jensen's device.

The eight COBOL examples illustrate the identification division, environment division, data division and procedure division of a simple file updating program.

Chapter 3 consists of a more detailed and rigorous exposition of FORTRAN. An example of a FORTRAN main routine and subroutine is introduced, and the constituents occurring in these routines are used to illustrate the subsequent discussion. The concepts and constituents considered include variables, values and domains, names and their scopes, constants, arrays, functions, expressions, arithmetic statements, flow of control, loops, subroutine calls, complete routines, arguments of functions, input and output values of arguments, *COMMON* storage, input-output statements, and input-output formats.

Chapter 4 is a reprint of Mr Woodger's paper on ALGOL 60 in the *Computer Journal*, and is included here for purposes of reference. ALGOL 60 is presented as a machine-independent language for specifying the processes of computation. Simple variables, assignment statements, declarations, arrays, labels, blocks, functions and procedures are introduced. Following some examples of ALGOL programs, the metalanguage of the ALGOL report (Backus normal form) is introduced, and syntactic definitions of most of the more important constituents of ALGOL are given.

PART THREE. FORTRAN IMPLEMENTATION

Chapter 5 is concerned with the structure of the intermediate language and the programming system associated with FORTRAN II. The process of translation, loading and execution of a program consisting of independently translated routines is described. The characteristics of the intermediate language, which permits flexible communication between the independently translated routines, is then considered. The block structure of FORTRAN and ALGOL are briefly compared. In a final section the organization of the FORTRAN Monitor System is discussed.

Chapter 6, on Atlas FORTRAN, consists of two parts, the first concerned with general strategy and the second with specific details of the compiler. The compiler itself is written in FORTRAN. This permits the compiler to be translated into an object program on any computer which accepts FORTRAN, such as, for example, the 7090. The resulting object program can then be used on the 7090 to translate FORTRAN source programs into the intermediate language required for the Atlas computer. In particular, the compiler itself can be translated into the Atlas intermediate language.

When all the above operations have been performed on the 7090, the Atlas intermediate language version of the FORTRAN compiler can be run on Atlas merely by providing a loader from the intermediate language to Atlas machine language.

Within the FORTRAN compiler itself, compiling-machine dependent features and target-machine dependent features are specifically indicated by defining three classes of routines referred to respectively as machine independent, compiling-machine dependent and target-machine dependent routines.

The extensions to FORTRAN II available in Atlas FORTRAN are described, including Boolean and relational operations, simultaneous assignment to several variables as in ALGOL, mixed expressions with real and integer variables, generalized array subscript expressions, a *FOR* statement with more general subscripts than the *DO* statement, a *PUBLIC* declaration for global symbols, and a *PARAMETER* declaration for symbolic dimensions to be defined at load time by a *DEFINE* statement.

The second part of the chapter discusses the main sections of the compiler. Section 1 makes an initial analysis of each source language routine, recording information from declarations in tables, and editing executable statements into standard forms. The second section performs translation of these instructions into unoptimized symbolic machine language. The third section deals with optimization of *DO* and *FOR* loops. The fourth section deals with optimization of *IF* and *GO TO* statements. Finally the fifth section merges the output of the three previous sections, producing an intermediate language *BAS* program and a storage map.

PART FOUR. ALGOL IMPLEMENTATION

Chapter 7 uses the Burroughs Compiler Game to illustrate the basic principles of compilation and execution through the use of a stack. Following an introduction to reverse Polish notation, a specific ALGOL program (for finding the maximum element of a matrix) is broken down into its constituents, and the rearrangement of constituents required for representation in reverse Polish notation is presented. The translation of arithmetic expressions is described, using a stack controlled by an operator hierarchy table. Next, the author describes the Burroughs Compiler Game, illustrating by means of a concrete example how stack techniques can be extended to permit compilation of a subset of ALGOL and COBOL. The main steps in the translation of the above mentioned ALGOL program are then indicated, and translation of a simple COBOL program is also discussed. A final section describes the Burroughs B5000 machine language, and gives the actual machine language instructions for the above ALGOL and COBOL programs. The detailed analysis of a specific ALGOL and COBOL program should be useful to the beginner. However, it should be stressed that the translation algorithm works only for a very primitive subset of ALGOL and COBOL.

Chapters 8, 9 and 10 are concerned with three approaches to ALGOL translation. Chapter 8 describes a rapid, one-pass translator for the KDF9 which is executed interpretively, while Chapter 9 demonstrates an optimizing translator for the same computer designed to permit rapid object program execution. Both compilers accept full ALGOL 60 with the exception of dynamic **own** arrays and integer labels, and require obligatory specification for all parameters. The two compilers will be compatible, and it is anticipated that the interpretive translator will be used for program checking and that the optimizing translator will be used for final translation before the production run.

The ALGOL translator described in Chapter 8, translates ALGOL 60 to an intermediate language for an "ideal" computer. This intermediate language consists of a fairly simple set of stack operations, somewhat similar to those of Burroughs B5000 machine language illustrated in chapter 7. The stack itself consists (during execution of the program) of an elaborate pushdown list which permits references to quantities stored at any depth by means of a system of links. The basic constituent of this push-down list is the record of activation of an ALGOL block or procedure. Each record contains two links. These link it respectively to the block from which it was activated (dynamic link), and to the most recent activation of the next textually enclosing block (static link). The dynamic link is used for purposes of entry to and exit from the block during execution, while the static link is used to locate quantities whose scopes are valid in the current block.

Following the description of stack organization in the object program, the intermediate language representation of parameters, arrays, labels and switches, and for statements is briefly discussed.

The author then discusses the translation program; indicating the basic translation process using stacks and a priority system, the translation of conditional statements, the use of a name list during translation for evaluation of names, the use of chaining for evaluation of forward references in one-pass translation, the use of state variables to keep track of the context of certain otherwise ambiguous constituents, storage allocation in the object program, and code procedures. The final section considers communication between the ALGOL program and programmer.

Chapter 9 describes an optimizing translator for ALGOL 60. It makes use of hardware features of the KDF9, such as index registers and the sixteen-word stack (nesting accumulator), to produce more efficient object programs; and tries to perform storage allocation and other housekeeping functions during translation rather than execution. However, in contrast to FORTRAN, ALGOL 60 requires dynamic storage allocation during execution for arrays with dynamically varying bounds, and for recursive procedures, and some provision for storage allocation during execution must therefore be made.

The organization of the stack during execution is discussed. Whereas the basic unit of storage in Chapter 8 relates to activation of the ALGOL block, the basic stack unit of Chapter 9 relates only to the potentially recursive procedure (program level), reflecting the fact that dynamic storage allocation for recursive procedures is a difficult storage allocation problem in an ALGOL compiler. Within each program level, fixed storage, relative to the beginning of the program level, is assigned to links, parameters, locally declared scalar quantities, array definition quantities, and pointers to constituent blocks. Space for arrays is assigned following the fixed storage area every time the program level is entered. This permits relative addresses of local scalar variables to be fixed during translation relative to the base address of the program level.

Since array references would in this scheme require computation of the storage mapping function on every reference to the array, special facilities for prior computation of all or part of the storage mapping function and for **for** loop optimization have been provided.

The methods of **for** loop optimization, and of classification of procedures into non-recursive and potentially recursive are discussed in some detail. The final sections discuss the use of KDF9 index registers (Q-stores), the nesting accumulator, and the partial result store for quantities which are required in an order other than last-in-first-out.

In Chapter 10 on the Elliott ALGOL system, simple variables are assigned addresses by the translator in the same way as would be done by a symbolic assembly program. Array allocation is performed by use of a dynamic stack, space being assigned every time the declaration is encountered, and being relinquished on exit from the block. The compiler does not perform automatic **for** loop optimization, but special ALGOL procedures are available by means of which the user can achieve effective **for** loop optimization. Arithmetic expressions are translated by a "compile arithmetic expression" routine, which is recursively entered. The above organization makes activation of recursive procedures more difficult than when all variable information is stored in a stack. A special push-down procedure for implementation of recursive procedures is provided. Recursive procedures may not have parameters called by name other than labels and arrays.

PART FIVE. COMMERCIAL LANGUAGES AND COMPILERS

Chapter 11 deals with COBOL and Rapidwrite. COBOL is introduced principally in order to indicate the superiority of the Rapidwrite approach to the specification of commercial programs. After an introduction which explains the characteristics of commercial problems and the historical development of commercial languages, some of the features of a specific COBOL program are analysed in greater detail. The way in which inessential verbiage may be eliminated by the Rapidwrite approach is then considered.

A Rapidwrite program is written on a series of forms on which only the essential information regarding the environment and data division is filled in. The procedure division is written, one statement to a punched card, and a different type of card is available for each type of statement. The abbreviated information is punched and input into the computer. For purposes of output, a verbose program complete with all the verbiage of required COBOL can be produced by the computer, with the aid of a dictionary of "noise" words The final section considers the translation of Rapidwrite programs into other languages, by supplying dictionaries of noise words and data names in the required language.

Chapter 12 deals with the FACT programming system. FACT data descriptions are specified on a "file outline form", and permit nested "secondary" data groups which can occur an arbitrary number of times for each occurrence of the higher level group. The source program is specified in a language similar to that of COBOL. Basic statements are grouped into paragraphs which may be named. Boolean conditions are represented by "definitions" which may also be named. A number of examples of FACT programming are given, and the "card description form" and "report generator form" are described. The "sort generator" facilities of FACT are described and illustrated with an example. File maintenance procedures are discussed. The final section deals with FACT segmentation and with the FACT programming system.

Chapter 13 is a widely ranging discussion of the factors which must be considered in writing a commercial compiler. A compiler is defined as a program which enables the machine to accept programs in an artificial language. The desired characteristics of the artificial language, and the effect which these characteristics have on the design of the compiler are then considered (e.g. data declarations, input-output formats, data fields which vary dynamically in length, time and space efficiency, character codes, and requirements of the operating system such as debugging facilities and storage allocation). Techniques of associating structures defined by data declarations with corresponding data references are discussed.

One of the drawbacks of existing commercial languages is that they were designed before the advantages of systematic nesting of expressions, procedures and data structures had been realized. As a result, it is difficult to apply stack techniques in implementing these commercial languages.

The properties of commercial compilers for large and small computers, and the potentialities of time sharing of packing and unpacking with processing are discussed. The author concludes with the remark that the current difficulties in implementation of commercial compilers are due to the fact that the wrong kind of language is being implemented. The right kind of language will result both in greater ease of use and in greater ease of implementation.

## PART SIX. TIME SHARING PROGRAMMING SYSTEMS

Chapter 14 is an introduction to time sharing. Basically, a computer must execute a set of activities in order to solve a problem. Although some activities must wait for the completion of others before they can be initiated, there is almost always some degree of arbitrariness about the sequence in which activities are to be performed. This permits certain independent activities within a given problem such as input-output and computation, to proceed in parallel. However, in order to ensure that serial operation is resumed when it becomes necessary, interlocks between autonomously operating activities are required. Parallel activities may share equipment in the control unit, and may even share common storage registers when in the "read only" mode.

Time sharing between programs on an instruction by instruction basis requires that each time-shared program has its own set of memory and special registers. When time sharing involves relatively infrequent interchanges of program, a single set of special registers dumped on every program interchange is sufficient. Even dumping is unnecessary if program interchange is restricted to points at which information in special registers is known to be redundant, or if restart points having this property can be established.

Time sharing between programs is most efficient when programs are independent and becomes successively more involved the more that programs are interdependent. Current languages are sequential in structure, and it is very difficult to disentangle necessary sequential relationships from arbitrary ones. The author feels that source languages which explicitly differentiate between necessarily sequential activities and parallel activities will come increasingly to the fore, since areas of advanced programming such as heuristic exploration of the solution space are inherently parallel in nature.

Chapter 15 describes the Atlas supervisor program. The Atlas computer has elaborate interlock, lock-out, and interrupt hardware which facilitates writing of a time-sharing supervisory program. In addition to a two-level core-drum store, there is a fixed read-only store for routines of special status (extracodes), such as supervisory routines, a "V-store" accessible only to supervisor routines which contain the "state" information required for interrupts and interlocks, and a subsidiary store which is used as workspace by the supervisor.

There are three modes of operation, referred to respectively as "main control", "extracode control" and "interrupt control". Main control is the normal mode of operation during execution of a problem program. However, main control can transfer control to extracode control when execution of an extracode routine is required, and can be interrupted by interrupt control when peripheral equipment requires attention or when the clock causes a scheduled interruption. Interrupt control checks on the cause of interrupt, initiates any action that is urgent because of real time considerations, and passes control to extracode control if more elaborate action is required. Three of the index registers serve as respective control registers for main, extracode and interrupt control.

The system of priorities between interrupt and extracode routines is elaborate, interrupt routines having priority over extracode routines, and extracode routines being divided into four priority groups.

The interrupt and extracode system is described in some detail, and the overall organization of the system to optimize all branches of the computing system is considered. Time sharing between a computer-limited problem, an input-output-limited problem, and a long "background" problem is discussed. The final pages consider the input-output well technique for extending the effective random access memory.

Chapter 16, which deals with time sharing aspects of the Stretch computer, is divided into two sections, dealing respectively with hardware features of Stretch and with the Stretch supervisory control system. The section on hardware considers the general layout of the computer, core storage, CPU and input-output exchange organization, and the interrupt system. The supervisory system, called the master control program (*MCP*), is concerned with automatic operation, job sequencing, control of program and machine errors, system input and output, and problem program input and output. It examines the input stream of problems up to twenty jobs ahead in order to determine input requirements. Data input and output for problem programs is processed in parallel with the execution phase by an

B

elaborate system of interrupts and programmed interlocks. Normally, problems are processed in sequence in the order of input. However, a by-pass mode is available for high priority runs which want to jump the queue.

Although *MCP* is a relatively unsophisticated supervisory program, it took thirty-four man-years to write.

PART SEVEN. ADVANCED PROGRAMMING TECHNIQUES

Chapter 17 deals with the use of syntactic analysis in compilers. After a brief introduction to syntactic analysis, a number of alternative schemes for the implementation of syntactic analysis are discussed. Basically, all methods scan the input string and apply rules specified by a set of recursive meta-syntactic formulae to recognize successive syntactic constituents. The scheme used for the Atlas compiler is then described in greater detail. This scheme converts the input text into tree structures, using the *PHRASE* and *FORMAT* definitions of the metalanguage. The resulting trees are converted to target-machine language by means of *ROUTINE* definitions which use the tree representation produced by the syntactic analysis as an input parameter, and produce machine language instructions as output.

Chapter 18 considers the role of addressing in programming systems. Concepts such as name, address, location number, and operand are defined, and the representation of an operand by a symbolic address is analysed. Scopes, defining the context in which a symbolic address may be used as the name of an operand, are associated with symbolic addresses in order to avoid ambiguity. *Routine* boundaries are seen to be natural boundaries for the purpose of delimiting scope. The "scope rules" of FORTRAN and ALGOL are discussed, and the ALGOL scope rules are elaborated in some detail. The role of symbolic addressing in the case of data structures and operating systems is considered, special attention being devoted to the question of when a symbolic address should be translated into a machine oriented representation.

Alternative forms of machine addressing are considered, including the implicit address, truncated address, relative address, modified address, block address, indirect address, immediate address and associative machine address.

Following a discussion of symbolic addresses and machine addresses, the process of translation from symbolic to machine addresses is discussed. Mapping on to a single level store is considered, including the use of special fast registers, such as B-registers. In the case of mapping on to a multiple-level store, problems of lockout, priority, and dynamic relocation are considered. Dynamic mapping on to a stack is compared with dynamic mapping on to variable length segments using an index, and the implications for communication between independently compiled routines are considered. The final section enumerates conflicting factors which must be considered in the design of an addressing system.

Chapter 19, which is concerned with continuous evaluation, considers a form of organization of a programming system in which evaluation is performed during translation whenever the values of all required quantities are defined. Every variable has associated with it a "state indicator" which specifies whether that variable is undefined, numerically defined, or defined in terms of formal variables or parameters. During translation an operator with one or more undefined arguments is translated into a sequence of machine language instructions, while an operator with all arguments numerically defined is immediately applied to its arguments.

Continuous evaluation is facilitated by specification of the program in terms of a number of definition sets—analogous to FORTRAN subroutines, ALGOL procedures or jobs or documents in a programming system. The translation—evaluation phase can be applied in parallel to each of the definition sets, thus permitting parallel execution of those parts of a program which do not require sequential execution. Two simple examples of continuous evaluation are given, and suggestions are made for further development of the concept.

Chapter 20, which is concerned with list programming, discusses particularly the relation between the LISP and ALGOL languages. After an introduction to the idea of lists, and to their representation in a sequential computer memory, the primitive operations of LISP are introduced. Some of the standard LISP functions are then defined as procedures in an ALGOL-like language, and the relation between their representation in LISP and ALGOL is discussed. LISP is seen to be a functional rather than a command language, involving functions all of whose parameters are called by value. Whereas ALGOL separates procedure definitions and procedure call, LISP permits a procedure definition to occur at any point at which a procedure call is permitted. The ALGOL counterparts of the LISP procedures **length, append** and **maplist** are discussed in some detail. The principal difficulty of implementing list processing within ALGOL is that of storage allocation for lists. However, the embedding of list processing primitives in ALGOL would permit efficient manipulation of both numerical data and lists, and would greatly facilitate the definition of flexible list processing procedures by mixing functional and command constructions.

Chapter 21 throws some interesting light on the processes of interpretation, stack manipulation, and evaluation. The first section, which describes a general interpretive programming system, called GIPSY, indicates that the basic elements required for an interpretive open-ended programming system are simple and few in number. The second part discusses the tree representation of arithmetic formulae. The correspondence between tree representation and representation in a stack is developed in some detail. A generalized function concept is then introduced, consisting of any set of connected points of the tree, and methods are introduced for shrinking the tree so that this function is represented by a single point.

The material on stacks and evaluation is developed by analogy with concepts originally developed for LISP. The $\lambda$ notation of Church is introduced for defining the context of formal parameters, and stack operations for a stack with nested "context delimiters" are developed. An interesting algorithm is discussed for transforming a function specified in $\lambda$ notation into its tree representation.

# 1. PROGRAMMING SYSTEMS AND LANGUAGES

## S. GILL

*International Computers and Tabulators Ltd., London, England*

Mathematically, programming is based on some very simple premises—deceptively simple in fact. Basically, all that is assumed is a computer with a certain instruction code; and it is the programmer's job to load it with instructions which cause it to display the sort of behaviour required in particular circumstances. Yet if one follows up any logical development of this subject, one is led very quickly into ideas which are, in many ways, very similar to some of the ideas explored by mathematical logicians in the 1930's, '40's and '50's, and clearly the subject can be taken a good deal further yet. As a serious study it bears all the signs of being hardly out of the cradle, yet, as an industry, it is already something to be reckoned with. It is not usually taken into account by the economic experts, to whom the computing business usually means computer manufacturing, not programming. Of course, it is rather difficult to obtain an estimate of the amount of work that is going on in computer programming, because it is mixed up with so many other different activities. It is probable that in this country it has already passed the £1m a year mark, and in the United States it must be at least approaching, if it has not already passed, a billion dollars a year. Just to take one simple example, the compiler program for the FACT language on the Honeywell 800 is said to consist of some 223,000 instructions. (Perhaps they were not all written by hand, but obviously a lot of work has gone into that single project.)

Few of those engaged in it realize the mathematical subtlety of the work on which they are spending so much money. Certainly a minority of those who are responsible for administering the job do. On the other hand, few of those who study the subject in the universities (and there are not many of them) seem to realize what industry really needs. A collection of miscellaneous and assorted ideas is not of much value in this work. Every important program used in industry has to be documented thoroughly, often from several different points of view; it has to be taught, and understood by dozens or hundreds of people; it has to be maintained in varying circumstances, perhaps for a range of related but different machines; and it has to be defended against 'improvements', maybe for several years. Under these circumstances, quite a lot of bright ideas are just not worth having. The ideas that are adopted and embodied in a big program have to be carefully considered, to make sure that they are going to stand up to this sort of treatment.

What is needed above everything else is a coherent overall picture of the subject, a framework on which new ideas can be hung, so that one can judge just how bright an idea really is. At the moment it is probably fair to say that we are not very near yet to getting such an understanding.

*Programming Systems*

What is a programming system? A computing machine is a device which has a prescribed manner of behaviour—a behaviour pattern if you like, although we must not be misled into thinking of a behaviour pattern here as the sort of thing that psychologists deal with, because the behaviour pattern of a computer must of course be very strictly prescribed, that is, we must know just what it is going to do under particular circumstances. A computer may perhaps be a special-purpose machine, which is fed with data and which is to produce results or behave in a way depending on that data. But of more interest is a general-purpose computer which, before it can answer a particular problem, must be fed with a program telling it how to deal with the data. It is this composite system, consisting of the computer together with the program, that is fed with the data.

In some circumstances we may find it convenient to consider the data itself as made up of two parts. We may call the first batch of data Data 1, and when that has been inserted then the system is ready to deal with Data 2. Now Data 1 may have quite a lot of the attributes of the sort of things that we think of as computer programs. It may be a list of steps to be followed in dealing with Data 2, so that in fact we are in the situation where the computer plus the first program can be thought of as a computer which accepts another program which gets it into a state to accept some data. Very often you can think quite usefully of other levels in this business too. You might be able to think of the first program as being in two layers, one of which is perhaps a set of subroutines, which added to the original design of the computer provides a rather more powerful system, for which you write the rest of the program.

We start, therefore, with a simple system, a computer, and we add to it, layer by layer, more programs for behaviour specification, and so gradually elaborate the system. The actual form that these layers take varies considerably. Commonly, however, one can distinguish two main layers of program.

A computer is usually fed with certain programs that we call the 'system programs', which broadly speaking extend the computer so that although it still looks like a general purpose computer, it has several desirable features that the engineers did not put into the actual hardware. These programs form the first layer, and when we talk about a programming system we are usually thinking of this layer. We add to this a problem program which, in general, we think of as something that is specific to a particular kind of task and which merely tells the machine how to accept the data, which is usually numerical and does not have anything in the nature of a program about it.

Usually the problem program is processed by a system program called a 'compiler', before the data is available. No more logical manipulation is then performed on it until its actual 'execution', which cannot occur until the whole of the data is available. Now this also is perhaps being too rigid. One can conceive a situation in which whatever part of the data may arrive first can be absorbed into the system, and some logical manipulation can be performed within the system in order to 'prepare' it for the remaining part of the data (see Chapter 11).

The main point of interest in a programming system, if it is to accept programs, is the language in which these programs are to be submitted. There are of course several other features which are of interest too: for example, what facilities it provides for finding mistakes in these programs; what facilities it provides for keeping control of the equipment attached to the computer; automatic log-keeping of computer activities; perhaps automatic scheduling of jobs as they are submitted, and so on. But the one on which most attention has been focused is the language in which the problem program is to be submitted.

*Programming Languages*

There are many conflicting requirements of a programming language, and that is one reason why movements to establish common programming languages have run into difficulties. We obviously want a language that is easily learnt, that is easy to use once you have learnt it, and easy for other people to follow if they have to go through your program afterwards, and one that does not require a really enormous compiler to produce a reasonably efficient execution of the job on the computer.

You can look at the subject of programming languages from a lot of different viewpoints. You can look at it from the viewpoint of information theory, which tells you a few rather obvious things, and in this case nothing particularly useful. It tells you for example that for efficient coding you should use concise representations of things that you are going to want to say frequently; but you can in fact overdo this. If you go to great lengths to pick out operations that you are going to need to perform frequently, and to find concise methods of coding them all, you may discover that you have made your language too specialized. There may be some jobs which look at first sight to be just the sort of thing for which your language is designed, but then for some reason or other you find that the particular concise codes available in the language are not quite applicable. So you have got to allow perfectly general expressions, just as in a more primitive system, and you may then find that there are a great many alternative ways of saying the same thing. Often there is not much to choose between them, and the programmer is left trying to make arbitrary decisions on very little basis. The language is no longer very efficient because you have allowed too many alternative expressions.

In any case, in practice the coding efficiency of the program is not really of great importance. The volume of information to be handled in the form of programs is usually smaller than the volume of the data. One interesting thing which information theory tells us is that if we have redundancy in a code, we should choose this in order to enable us to detect errors if possible. In fact on a primitive level we all do this. We choose, for example, parity checked codes, at least for numerical information. To some extent we try to choose our program notations so that simple failures on the part of the equipment preparing the program will lead to an obviously incorrect program, which can be detected by the input routine. Nowadays, however, the problems of dealing with errors made by the equipment for preparing tape or cards are pretty well understood, and they do not usually give us a lot of trouble. Troublesome are the logical mistakes made by the programmer in planning the job, and in writing his program, and it is really impossible for the machine to protect itself against all of these. If you produce a system that will allow you to describe very general problems to the machine, then you are necessarily making it possible to write an enormous variety of programs. This means that it is going to be fairly easy to choose the wrong problem, or to write the wrong program. There is no safeguard against this except simply making the system more specialized so that it assumes the sort of problem you want to perform without having to be told.

Information efficiency, therefore, does not get us very far. We must dig a bit more deeply and consider the *structure* of the language. The simplest form of program structure is the form that the machine itself accepts, namely a series of instructions in code. We write these down, one after another, with the idea that the computer is to interpret each one as some operation to be performed, and is to execute them all in the sequence in which they are presented, except of course for occasional jumps which lead it from one part of the program to another. Each of these instructions has a certain structure, which in the simplest case (single address code) comprises a function part which defines the type of operation that is to be performed, and an address part, which is a numerical parameter associated with the function, usually the store address of an operand or perhaps a number which itself takes some part in the job. We may have a rather more elaborate structure than this; for example the address may itself be composite, and may contain a '*B*-address' through which the machine finds a number which is to be added to the main part of the address before using it. The structure of the function may also be more elaborate, and there may be two or three address parts. There may even be instructions of different lengths. On a large scale you may break up your string of instructions into subroutines, each of which can essentially play the part of a single instruction within a higher level of language.

The modern scientific programming languages, like FORTRAN, ALGOL and so on, will allow you to write single statements which have an even more elaborate structure than this. They may have a function on to which are attached one, two or more parameters. Each of these parameters may itself be a further function with further parameters, and so on. This is simply the kind of generalization that we allow ourselves in ordinary algebraic expressions, where we can write, for example,

$$y = x + z$$

but we can equally well write, for example, $AP$ instead of $z$, thus:

$$y = x + AP$$

Furthermore $P$ itself may be some expression such as the square root of $Q$, and $x$ also may be replaced by some other expression. This kind of 'nesting' of expressions which we allow ourselves in ordinary algebra can now be included in the more recent scientific programming languages. Nevertheless these languages still consist of a string of statements to be obeyed one after another in the program, similar to the machine instructions.

We are are beginning to break away from this also; in some of the programming systems now being designed we are not restricted to saying that the instructions must be in some particular sequence depending only on the program and the data given, but the machine may in fact choose its own sequence, or, if it is able to do so, it may do two different things at the same time. In the old-fashioned type of program, we had instructions called 'jump' or 'branching' instructions, which selected one of two sequences to be followed according to some criterion. But some of the more recent systems will contain instructions that will say to the machine, 'both of these things need doing, in whichever sequence you like or perhaps both together'. This leads to a lot of other ramifications which cannot be discussed here, but it is something which is going to be increasingly important in the future (see p. 222).

Another complication in programming languages that we have to watch out for, if we are not familiar with it already, is the distinction between the name of a quantity and its value. Now this is something that we are all familiar with intuitively. When we write for example the expression '$x + 2$' we know perfectly well that $x$ is the name of a number and 2 is the value of a number. Since we always use different kinds of symbols for the names of numbers and for the numbers themselves, we do not lead ourselves into any confusion. If we wanted to be really explicit we ought I suppose to write, say, $V(x)$ for the value of the number whose name is $x$, but we do not bother with that because we have the convention that since $x$ is a letter it must be a name. But when we are talking about other things than numbers we do have to be rather careful about this. In fact this distinction arises in ordinary machine programming, where for the names of quantities we use the addresses of store positions, which are of course numbers. To take an example from the Pegasus code, we can have an instruction such as

$$34\ 2\ 00$$

where *00* is the function part and *34* is an address part, and *2* is the address of an accumulator. What this says is, 'load the contents of register *34* into accumulator *2*'. The instruction

$$34\ 2\ 40$$

says 'load the *number 34* into accumulator *2*'. It is essentially the same function, but we have used a different function code which indicates that the address part is to be interpreted in a slightly different way. In the first case *34* is the *name* of an operand, in the second case it is the *value* of an operand. More recently, people have tended to take this distinction out of the function part, where it does not really belong, and to associate it with the address. When we come to consider more powerful languages like ALGOL, COBOL and so on, we still have to be careful to see that this distinction is properly made between names and values. This is particularly important in business work, where the information being handled is often itself alphabetical and the names that are used to describe the items of information are also.

In fact, names give trouble in other ways too. One has to see that the same name does not get used for two different things in a way that will lead to confusion. You may in fact want to allow the same name to be used for different items, so long as a distinction can still be kept between these items. This is perhaps because you may want to put together parts of a program written independently or on two different occasions, and you want to make sure that if the same name does happen to have been used for two different purposes, the machine does not assume that this name must necessarily refer to the same item throughout. There are other cases in which you want to use the same bit of program in more than one context, and it is necessary to tell the system that a name being used in this program is to be interpreted as referring to one item on one occasion and to another item on another occasion. In fact the meaning of every name that you write down must depend on the context in some way, and the business of explaining to the system exactly what context is to be applied in interpreting a particular name is something that must be thought out very carefully in designing a programming language. ALGOL, for example, has some very specific rules about the meaning to be attached to the names in various parts of the program.

Another general trend which is worth noting is the tendency to design a programming language so that the various things that a programmer has to decide when planning a program are separated wherever possible in the program that he writes. Often when you are trying to write a program you have to stop and think rather carefully about how you are going to arrange this or that, about how you are going to file a particular item, how you are going to group items together, etc., and when you have made one of these agonizing decisions you very often find that it is necessary to jot it down very quickly in the margin because you are going to refer to this decision several times at other points in the program. Conversely, what you write at any moment may depend on decisions made half-an-hour or a couple of weeks beforehand. Obviously it would be better, if possible, to design the language so that, having made a decision of this kind, you can embody it quickly in some statement which you write down as part of the program and which you then don't have to repeat. The system will take that one statement and automatically incorporate the information which it contains wherever it is relevant to the program.

As a simple example of what I am talking about here, one of the first things that happened when we broke away from machine coding was that, instead of referring to every item of stored data by means of its particular numerical address, we simply used a symbol such as $P$. Many references to this item could then be made, independently of any decision about where the item was actually located. This decision was made separately, e.g. simply by labelling the address concerned with the label $P$, or by means of a statement called a 'directive' or 'declaration'; or by letting the system decide for itself. Having done that, we did not have to go through the program again and incorporate these decisions all over the place; the system did that for us. The idea has probably been taken furthest in the commercial programming languages like COBOL, where the program is separated into several parts. One part is called the 'procedure division', and this is the part corresponding to the ordinary program as we used to know it – the definition of the procedure to be followed. We also have the 'data division' in which we describe the data that we are working on; this corresponds to the directives or declarations, although the data part of commercial programs has got very much more involved since these ideas began. Nowadays the programmer is asked to state what kind of items he is referring to; if they are alphabetical, how many characters they ought to be allowed; if they are numerical what their ranges are, and so on.

In fact one of the trends today is towards letting the programmer talk about more and more varied kinds of item. The primitive system itself, the computer, usually simply handles words of a particular length, and performs a certain set of operations which are described as operations on fixed-point numbers. If we want to produce a system in which the programmer can call for operations on other kinds of information, such as floating-point numbers, or alphabetical items, and so on, then we have to get the system to find a suitable correspondence between the actual stored information in the machine and the information that we want it to handle, and to interpret the program accordingly. This kind of thing has now been extended to include, for example, list structures – something that will be discussed later. To represent these in the machine we usually put each element into a different word and include with it an address telling us where the next element is to which it is attached.

There are several things that affect the way that a program is executed, without affecting the results obtained, and which the programmer would therefore prefer not to have to specify. Thus, in most of the advanced programming languages, the programmer does not have to specify exactly where the items to which he refers are to be stored. Obviously the system must make a number of decisions like this within itself in order to get the job done. Some of these decisions may be rather difficult ones to make, and you may find these getting reflected back directly or indirectly into the language; i.e. the language may call on the programmer to make certain arbitrary decisions in order to make the job easier for the system.

What, in fact, are the decisions which are likely to give the system quite a job to do if they are left to it entirely? The main ones, I think, are in the business of laying out the store; not merely in deciding which word is to be placed where – that is not so difficult – but in such things as, for example, the packing of short items into one word or the spreading of long items over several words. First of all, the system must decide where to put these items in the store, and how to associate them together; and secondly, it must decide how to operate on them. This often accounts for a large part of compilers; thus the FACT compiler which I mentioned earlier for the Honeywell 800 has nearly a quarter of a million instructions, a great many of which are concerned with making these decisions about how to pack and unpack items of information.

Another aspect of storage use which either the system or the programmer has got to deal with at some stage is that of different levels of storage available in the system. Many computers have two or even more levels of storage, of different speeds and different sizes, with different facilities for operating on information in each, and in order to get a big job done some decisions have to be made about which bodies of information are going to be kept in which level and when they are going to be transferred from one level to another. A lot of past programming systems required statements from the programmer saying where the information had to be put. The MERCURY AUTOCODE, for example, virtually left this decision to the programmer by presenting him with two different types of variables with different kinds of names which he had to use in the appropriate manner, and the system then merely took the different kinds of variables as things to be stored in two different levels of the store. But more recent systems have tried to do all this for the programmer, or at least to give him a great deal of help with it. To some extent they have been successful, to some extent unsuccessful. In fact since they may not always be successful, they often include an escape route by allowing a programmer still to give some indication to the system to help it solve this problem.

Another aspect which I have touched on already is the problem of deciding exactly in which sequence the machine is to carry out the various steps that are going to be necessary in performing a calculation. The kind of program with which we are most familiar is one which states quite explicitly a particular sequence of operations to be carried out; but we are beginning to break away from that now. We are beginning to allow programmers to leave decisions about sequence to the system, and we may perhaps go a long way in this direction in the future. This will have a marked effect on programming languages.

At a low level, the hardware very often finds itself making very quick decisions about the precise sequence of operations, even when the program is purely serial. In a very big machine like Stretch for example, which we shall be hearing about later, the processing part of the machine – the control, arithmetic units and so on – is so powerful that it can be doing two or three different things at once. So it looks at a short stretch of program and tries to arrange that, as far as possible, it can be preparing to execute one or two fresh instructions while it is extracting the operand for the previous one, performing the arithmetic for the one before that, and possibly storing the result from the one before that.

So we have a situation where we have clung to what is beginning to look like rather an old-fashioned kind of notation in which the program specifies a serial sequence of steps, but the system (which is powerful enough to do several things at once) has to try and put these into some semi-parallel form in order to make the best use that it can of its own logical power. Doing so is complicated by the need to observe the possible appearance of several conditions which, although unremarkable in a serial program, call for special action when parallel operations are attempted.

## Compilers

So much for programming languages. Now I must say a few words about the compiler, which is the part of the programming system that translates programs from their original language into machine language. Compilers are often classified as one pass, two pass, three pass compilers and so on. These are terms which are most relevant in cases where the program is large compared with the internal storage system, so that the entire program cannot be held within the machine while it is being translated from source to machine language. What one usually does then is to keep it on magnetic tape and simply scan it repeatedly, performing a further translation on it at each stage, and the number of times that it has to be scanned in order to get the complete translation done is called the number of passes.

This term might also be applicable in cases where it is not necessary to keep it on the magnetic tape, because there is room for the whole program inside the machine. Even then a compiler may be organized in such a way that it scans through the program being interpreted from beginning to end (or from end to beginning) a certain number of times, and it may still be described as a two, or a three or a four pass compiler. But many compilers do not work in this kind of way. The NEBULA compiler on Orion, for example, will not make clearly distinguishable complete passes through a program; the number of semi-passes that it makes may be very large.

If a compiler does make a clear number of passes, then obviously in between two passes the program is still there in some form or other; in fact, it is in an intermediate language, between the source language and the final language. This subject of intermediate languages in which programs are held during their translation is therefore one of interest.

Another is the language in which the compiler itself is written. Compilers are such enormous things that one rarely writes them in machine language any more, and one can choose, in the same way as in the writing of any program, between various possible languages in which it might be written. It is important to distinguish between the language in which a compiler is written, and the languages to which, through which, and from which it compiles. It may happen in some cases that the language from which it compiles is the same as the language in which the compiler itself is written, but this is not necessarily so.

In considering the best language in which to write a compiler, we are effectively considering a system designed to accept compilers, i.e. a system to which the compiler itself acts as data. The purpose of this data is to select the required compiler from among conceivable compilers (i.e. compilers which accept various source languages or produce various machine languages), and so really what we want to be able to write as our compiler is simply a definition of the source language or of the machine language or both. We want to have a system into which we could feed, for example, a definition of a source language, so that having supplied that definition we would now have an effective compiling system into which we could feed the source language itself.

In fact what this system has to accept is what mathematicians call a metalanguage, that is a language which is used for describing languages. This kind of approach has been explored by several people both here and in America. Various kinds of meta-languages have been devised, and various means for building systems that will accept these languages.

Another aspect of compilers is the question of diagnostics: how the system is going to enable us to find mistakes in the programs that go into it. Finding mistakes is always, and probably always will be, a considerable part of programming.

## Scheduling and Supervisor Routines

Mistake diagnosis really goes beyond the compiler itself, because some mistakes are only apparent when the job is executed, so that we must rely on other routines in the system that will provide diagnostic information during or after the execution of a job.

These routines are in turn connected with the procedures used for feeding problems into the system and keeping track of the results.

These procedures are particularly critical in the case of a very big machine like Atlas or Stretch, where the machine may be handling quite a large number of medium sized jobs during an hour, so that the task of log-keeping and booking of jobs onto the machine, which is normally done nowadays by a girl sitting at a desk, will have to be done almost entirely by the computer, because otherwise one would need fifty girls and fifty desks. We shall hear something later about the supervisor routine which is being written for Atlas to do this kind of thing, and which itself raises some interesting problems in the programming of processes which cannot be described simply as a number of operations to be performed in series.

I am afraid that all I have done is to touch rather haphazardly on a series of topics, but I have tried to point out some of the ideas that have been arising in this subject so that you will at least know what to look out for.

# 2. FORTRAN, ALGOL AND COBOL

## P. WEGNER

*London School of Economics and Political Science, London, England*

### Introduction

This paper is concerned with the three problem orientated languages FORTRAN, ALGOL and COBOL. In each case the language is largely independent of any particular computer, and is designed to permit the computer user to specify his problem in a language that is natural to the problem being solved. FORTRAN and ALGOL are mathematical languages, being most suited to the specification of mathematical problems. COBOL is a language suited to the specification of business and commercial problems, particularly when the problems involve the processing and updating of large files of information.

Consider the problem of setting a variable equal to the sum of two variables $X$ and $Y$. This operation is specified in FORTRAN by the arithmetic statement

$$Z = X + Y$$

The above statement has exactly the same form as a mathematical equation. However, there is an important difference between a mathematical equation and a FORTRAN arithmetic statement. A mathematical equation states that the values of the expressions occurring on the left and right hand sides are equal for all values of the variables, whereas a FORTRAN arithmetic statement indicates that a computational step is to be performed which sets the value of the variable on the left hand side equal to the value of the expression on the right hand side. The difference is clearly brought out by the formula

$$N = N + 1$$

If this statement is considered as a mathematical equation it leads to a contradiction. However, a FORTRAN statement of this form indicates that the new value of the variable $N$ is one greater than the previous value.

ALGOL specifies arithmetic statements in a form that is basically similar to FORTRAN, both languages being based on mathematical notation. However, ALGOL is a more precise and consistent language than FORTRAN. In the case of arithmetic statements, the greater precision manifests itself by an explicit notation to take account of the asymmetry between left and right hand sides in specifying a computational step. The above two FORTRAN statements would be specified in ALGOL by

$$Z := X + Y;$$

and
$$N := N + 1;$$

The $=$ sign of FORTRAN is represented in ALGOL by an $:=$ sign (read "becomes"). The extra colon may be regarded as a pointer indicating replacement (compare with ←). Both the FORTRAN statement and the ALGOL statement may be regarded as an operation of replacement, i.e. $X = Y$ or $X := Y$ should be read as 'replace $X$ by $Y$', or more precisely as 'replace the value of the variable $X$ by the value of the expression $Y$'.

In COBOL, arithmetic expressions are specified in ordinary language rather than algebraically. Thus the statement $Z = X + Y$ can be written in COBOL as

$$COMPUTE\ Z\ EQUALS\ X\ PLUS\ Y.$$

or  $$COMPUTE\ Z = X + Y.$$

or  $$ADD\ X\ TO\ Y\ GIVING\ Z.$$

A typical COBOL application would be that of weekly updating of a file of information on salaries to date for each of a number of individuals. In this case there might be two entries for each individual called *SALARY-TO-DATE* and *WEEKLY-SALARY*. Updating could be performed by the COBOL statement *ADD WEEKLY-SALARY TO SALARY-TO-DATE GIVING SALARY-TO-DATE*.

The above statement presupposes some information about the structure of the file being updated. The principal structural difference between commercial languages like COBOL and mathematical languages like FORTRAN and ALGOL is not the superficial difference in the appearance of arithmetic statements, but an additional facility in commercial languages for the explicit description of files. Commercial languages like COBOL lay special emphasis on the separation of program description from data file description.

The characteristics of each of the above three languages will now be exhibited by means of examples.

### 1. Examples from FORTRAN

A FORTRAN program consists of one or more routines each of which consists of a number of FORTRAN statements. The examples below illustrate some of the rules for writing FORTRAN statements, routines and programs.

*Example 1.1*  Fixed Point Arithmetic Statement

$K = 5$ This statement sets the variable whose name is $K$ equal to the value *5*. $K$ is an example of a fixed point variable. *5* is an example of a fixed point number (integer). The statement $K = 5$ is an example of a fixed point arithmetic statement.

*Example 1.2*  Floating Point Arithmetic Statement

$X = X + 5.0$ This statement increments by five the value of the variable $X$. The previous value of the variable $X$ is destroyed. $X$ is an example of a floating point variable and *5.0* is an example of a floating point number. A number is taken to be floating point when it contains a decimal point (e.g. *5.0*) and fixed point otherwise (e.g. *5*).

*Example 1.3*   Mixed Arithmetic Statements

Mixed expressions are not allowed in FORTRAN.

The expressions $K + 5.0$, $X + K$ and $X + 5$ are illegal since each contains both fixed and floating point quantities.

However, mixed *statements* are allowed in FORTRAN. A mixed statement is one containing either a fixed point left hand side and floating point right hand side or a floating point left hand side and a fixed point right hand side.

In the former case the floating point expression on the right hand side is truncated to the next lower integer

Thus

$$K = 3.8$$

causes the integer value *3* to be assigned to the fixed point variable *K*.

In the latter case the fixed point result is converted to floating point form. Thus

$$X = 3$$

causes the fixed point variable *3* to be converted to floating point form and assigned to *X*.

*Example 1.4*   Order of Evaluation of Arithmetic Expressions

The order of evaluation of arithmetic expressions is the same as for ordinary algebraic notation.

Multiplication and division are performed before addition and subtraction.

$R = X + Y * Z$      This statement is evaluated by determining the product of *Y* and *Z* and adding the result to *X*.

$R = 3.0 + 4.0 * 5.0$    This statement sets the value of *R* to *23*.

Exponentiation (which is indicated by $**$) is carried out before any other arithmetic operation. Thus $Z^2$ is written in FORTRAN as $Z**2$.

$R = X + Y*Z**2$      This statement may be written in mathematical notation as

$$x + yz^2.$$

Expressions in parentheses are evaluated as a unit before the application of operations outside the parentheses.

$R = (A + B) * C$      This statement is evaluated by adding *A* to *B* and multiplying the result by *C*.

$R = (2.0 + 3.0) * 4.0$    This statement sets the value of *R* to *20*.

Functions are applied to their arguments before the application of arithmetic operations.

$R = SINF(X + Y) ** 2$      This statement may be written in mathematical notation as $\sin^2(X + Y)$.

Apart from the above rules of priority, expressions are evaluated in a left to right order.

$R = X - Y + Z$   The order of evaluation in the first statement is
$R = (X - Y) + Z$   indicated by the parenthesis in the second statement.

$R = 3.0 - 4.0 + 5.0$   This statement sets the value of $R$ to $4$.

$R = X/Y * Z$   This statement sets $R$ to the result of dividing $X$ by $Y$ and multiplying the result by $Z$.

$R = 3.0/4.0 * 5.0$   This statement sets the value of $R$ to $15/4 = 3.75$.

*Example 1.5*   *IF* Statement

$IF(E)$ 10, 15, 20   This statement (*IF* statement) permits three way conditional branching, dependent on the value of the arithmetic expression in parentheses. The expression in parentheses is followed by three numbers separated by commas which represent statement labels of other statements in the program. The *IF* statement branches to the statement having the first label if the expression in parentheses is negative, to the statement having the second label if the expression is zero and to the statement having the third label if the expression is positive. This particular *IF* statement branches to the statement whose label is *10* if the floating point variable $E$ is negative, to the statement whose label is *15* if $E$ is zero and to the statement whose label is *20* if $E$ is positive.

*Example 1.6*   Absolute Value Computation

  $IF(ALPHA)$ 10, 15, 15   These three statements replace the variable
10   $ALPHA = - ALPHA$   $ALPHA$ by its absolute value. The third state-
15   $CONTINUE$   ment (*CONTINUE* statement) is used merely as a dummy statement for purposes of attaching a label.

*Example 1.7*   FORTRAN Variables

  Names of FORTRAN variables may be up to six alphanumeric characters in length. Fixed point variables must begin with one of the letters $I, J, K, L, M, N$.

  Examples of fixed point variable names: $I, I5, INDIA$.

  Floating point variables must begin with any letter other than $I, J, K, L, M, N$.

  Examples of floating point variable names: $A, A5, AFRICA$.

  Variable names starting with a numerical digit or having more than six characters are illegal.

  Examples of illegal variable names: $5, 5A, AMERICA$.

*Example 1.8*   Subscripted Variables

  Elements of a vector, matrix or three dimensional array may be represented by subscripted variables.

$R = X(I)$   This statement sets $R$ equal to the $i$th element $X_i$ of the vector $X$.

$R = A(I,J)$   This statement sets $R$ equal to the $ij$th element $A_{ij}$ of the matrix $A$.

2

*Example 1.9*   Vector Arithmetic

As an example of a vector consider the weekly salary of an employee. Let the salary in the *i*th week be denoted by the *i*th element of a vector called *WEEKLY,* having *52* elements. Assume that the cumulative salary to date is represented by the variable *TOTAL.*

$TOTAL = TOTAL + WEEKLY (15)$   This statement adds the salary earned in the *15*th week to the cumulative salary.

*Example 1.10*   *DO* Statement

$TOTAL = 0.0$
$DO\ 10\ I = 1,52$
10   $TOTAL = TOTAL + WEEKLY (I)$

Accumulate the *52* elements of the vector weekly to find the total yearly salary.

The *DO* statement specifies repetition of the statement whose label is *10* for values of the variable *I* starting with *1* and moving by increments of *1* to *52*. A repetitive execution sequence under the control of a *DO* statement is frequently called a *DO*-loop. In this case the *DO*-loop is repeated *52* times, the variable *I* taking successively the values *1, 2 . . . 52.*

*Example 1.11*   Dimension Statement

$DIMENSION\ WEEKLY (52)$   This statement specifies that the dimension (number of elements) of the vector *WEEKLY* is *52*.

*Example 1.12*   Comment Statement

$C\ THIS\ IS\ A\ COMMENT$   A statement having an initial *C* is treated as a comment. Comments are used to assist persons trying to understand the action of the program by describing the computation verbally.

*Example 1.13*   Read Statement with Format Statement

$READ\ 100,\ M,\ X$
100   $FORMAT\ (I5, F10.4)$

These two statements cause read-in of a card from the card reader containing a fixed point variable *M* in columns *1* through *5* and a floating point variable *X* in columns *6* through *15*. The word *READ* in the first statement specifies card reader input. The number *100* is the label of a *FORMAT* statement specifying the format of the card. Following the label there is a list of variable names which should match format codes in the list inside the parentheses of the FORMAT statement. In this case the FORMAT statement specifies a five digit integer field (*I5*) in columns *1* through *5* of the card and a ten digit floating point number with four decimal places (*F10.4*) in columns *6* through *15* of the card. For example, the digits *37* in columns *4* and *5* of the card would be read in as the integer *37*, and the digits *352* in columns *11, 12* and *13* would be read in as the floating point number *3.52.*

*Example 1.14*   Read Input Tape Statement

    *READ INPUT TAPE 5, 100, M, X*  These two statements read
*100   FORMAT (I5, F10.4)*                from magnetic tape number *5*
                                            a card image of exactly the
same form as in the previous example. Since card images are normally
transferred to tape by off-line card-to-tape conversion equipment before
being input into the computer, this form of input statement is more common than the previous one.

*Example 1.15*   Print Statement

    *PRINT 100, M, X*      This statement prints one line on the on-line
*100   FORMAT (I5, F10.4)*      printer in the same format as the last two
                                    examples. Thus if the value of *M* were *37*
then the digits *37* would be printed in columns *4* and *5* of the line and
if the value of *X* were *3.52* then the characters *3.52* would be printed in
columns *10, 11, 12* and *13* of the line. Note that the decimal point, which
need not be punched explicitly on input, appears automatically on output, thus leading to an asymmetry between the effect of the FORMAT statement on input and output.

*Example 1.16*   Write Output Tape Statement

    *WRITE OUTPUT TAPE 6, 100, M, X*  These two statements form
*100   FORMAT (I5, F10.4)*                a printer line image on
                                           magnetic tape number *6* for
subsequent off-line printing by tape-to-printer conversion equipment or
punching by tape-to-punch conversion equipment. Off-line output of data
is much more common than on-line output.

*Example 1.17*   Addition Subroutine

    *SUBROUTINE ADD (A, N, SUM)*  This set of statements is a com-
    *DIMENSION A(100)*            plete subroutine for finding the
    *SUM = 0.0*                   sum of the first *N* elements of
    *DO 6 I = 1, N*               the vector *A*. The first statement
*6   SUM = SUM + A(I)*          (*SUBROUTINE*      statement)
    *RETURN*                      specifies that the statements
    *END*                         which follow but precede the
                                     next *END* statement constitute
a subroutine called *ADD* having three parameters. The *DIMENSION*
statement specifies that the dimension *N* of *A* cannot exceed *100*. The third,
fourth and fifth statements perform the summation (see example *1.10*).
The *RETURN* statement specifies return to the calling program. The *END*
statement specifies the end of the subroutine.

*Example 1.18*   *CALL* Statement

*CALL ADD (WEEKLY, 52, TOTAL)*  This statement (*CALL* statement)
                                      is used to initiate the subroutine
*ADD*. Its effect will be to form the sum of the first *52* elements of the vector
*WEEKLY*, i.e. to compute the total salary for *52* weeks as in example *1.10*.

Note that the parameters in the subroutine *ADD* are bound variables. Their names are irrelevant to the calling routines and only their order of specification is important. The bound variables of a subroutine definition are frequently called 'formal parameters'. The actual names or values of the formal parameters are defined by 'actual parameters' when the subroutine is called.

*Example 1.19*    Find the Largest Element of a Matrix

```
      SUBROUTINE MAX(A, M, N, Y, K, L)
      DIMENSION A(50, 50)
      Y = 0.0
      DO 10 I = 1, M
      DO 10 J = 1, N
      IF (A(I,J) − Y) 10, 10, 15
   15 Y = A(I,J)
      K = I
      L = J
   10 CONTINUE
      RETURN
      END
```

This subroutine finds the largest element of an *M* by *N* matrix *A* of non-negative elements, and stores the largest element *Y* and the indices *K* and *L* of the largest element. The subroutine has six parameters, three of which are input parameters and three output parameters. The *DIMENSION* statement specifies that neither *M* nor *N* is greater than *50*. The body of the example is a double *DO*-loop with a conditional statement to determine whether the current matrix element is larger than the previously obtained largest element.

*Example 1.20*    Complete Addition Program with Input and Output

```
      DIMENSION A(100)
      READ INPUT TAPE 5, 100, (A(I), I = 1, N)
  100 FORMAT (6F10.4)
      SUM = 0.0
      DO 6 I = 1, N
    6 SUM = SUM + A(I)
      WRITE OUTPUT TAPE 6, 100, SUM
      END
```

This program reads in a vector of *N* numbers, computes the sum, and prints it out. The *FORMAT* statement specifies that the numbers are punched 6 to a card as *10* digit floating point numbers with *4* decimal places. This is an example of a *FORTRAN* main program without any subroutines.

The above examples should be sufficient to give a general picture of the FORTRAN language. The ALGOL language will be discussed next. Since ALGOL is similar to FORTRAN, and since there are no input-output facilities to be discussed, the discussion of ALGOL will be somewhat shorter than the discussion of FORTRAN.

## 2. Examples from ALGOL

An ALGOL program consists of a sequence of ALGOL statements and declarations organized into blocks. The ALGOL language will be introduced by means of examples.

*Example 2.1*  Assignment Statements

The ALGOL Assignment Statement is the counterpart of the FORTRAN arithmetic statement.

$K := 5$;     This assignment statement sets the value of the variable *K* to 5.

$X := X + 5$;     This assignment statement increments the value of the variable *X* by 5.

The variable names *K* and *X* are referred to in ALGOL as identifiers. Statements are normally terminated by a semicolon.

*Example 2.2*  Integer and Real Variables

The FORTRAN terms fixed point and floating point are replaced in ALGOL by the terms integer and real. In FORTRAN it was necessary to introduce two types of numbers and two types of variables, leading to considerable complications in notation. This difficulty is avoided in ALGOL by means of declarations which specify for each identifier whether it is integer or real. The numbers in an expression are always assumed to be converted to a type that is compatible with the identifiers in the expression.

**integer** $K$; **real** $X$;     The two declarations on the first line specify that
$K := 5$; $X := X + 5$;     the identifier *K* is of type integer and that the
identifier *X* is of type real. The number 5 in the first assignment statement is therefore left as an integer and the number 5 in the second assignment statement is converted to a real (floating point) number. The declarations **integer** and **real** are underlined because they represent basic ALGOL symbols. The fact that **integer** has 7 letters and **real** has 4 letters is irrelevant to the representation of these symbols. They could be represented on a special ALGOL keyboard by single keys, and are basically single characters which happen to be represented by more than one alphabetic character.

*Example 2.3*  Boolean (logical) Variables

Boolean variables are two valued variables used to represent truth or falsity of a condition. The two values of a Boolean variable are represented by the basic ALGOL symbols **true** and **false**. Boolean variables are introduced by the declaration **Boolean**. The operators $\wedge$ (logical and), $\vee$ (logical or) and $\neg$ (logical not) may be used to operate on Boolean variables

**Boolean** $A, B, C$;     The declaration declares *A*, *B* and *C* to be Boolean.
$C := A \wedge B$     The subsequent assignment statement sets *C* to the
value **true** if both *A* and *B* have the value **true** and to the value **false** otherwise.

*Example 2.4*  Conditions

A condition is either true or false and therefore has a Boolean value. However the condition may be truth or falsity of a relation between arithmetic variables

$A \leqslant B$  This condition has the value **true** whenever the value of the variable *A* is less than or equal to the variable *B* and **false** otherwise.

The symbol $\leqslant$ is an example of a relational operator. *A* relational operator has arithmetic expressions as input and produces Boolean values as output. The following six relational operators are permitted in ALGOL:

$$\leqslant, <, =, \neq, >, \geqslant.$$

*Example 2.5*   Conditional Statements

The ALGOL conditional statement is the counterpart of the FORTRAN *IF* statement.

**if** $X = 0$ **then** $Y := Y + 1$ **else** $Y := Y - 1$;   A conditional statement consists of the basic ALGOL symbol **if** followed by a condition (in this case $X = 0$). If the condition is satisfied then the statement following the basic symbol **then** is executed. If the condition is not satisfied then the statement following the basic symbol **else** is executed. In this case $Y$ is incremented by $1$ when $X = 0$ and decremented by $1$ otherwise.

*Example 2.6*   Absolute Value Computation

**if** $X < 0$ **then** $X := -X$;   This conditional statement which computes the absolute value of $X$ is simpler in form than the previous one, the **else** having been omitted. When the **else** is omitted the statement following the **then** is executed if the condition is satisfied and skipped otherwise.

*Example 2.7*   **for** Statement

The ALGOL **for** statement is the counterpart of the FORTRAN *DO* statement.

$SUM := 0$;            The first statement sets the variable $SUM$ to zero.
**for** $I :=$            The second statement is a **for** statement which
   $1$ **step** $1$ **until** $N$ **do**      specifies execution of the assignment statement
$SUM := SUM + A[I]$;   which follows for values of the variable $I$ starting with $1$ and moving by increments of $1$ to $N$. The two statements compute the sum of the first $N$ elements of the vector $A$. The part of the **for** statement preceding the assignment statement is called a **for** clause.

*Example 2.8*   Comments

Comments can be inserted into ALGOL programs just as they are inserted into FORTRAN programs.

**comment** This is a comment;   Comments are introduced following a semicolon by the basic ALGOL symbol **comment**. The text following this symbol is terminated by the first semicolon that is encountered.

*Example 2.9*   Input and Output

ALGOL does not contain any explicit input or output facilities. However, formatless input and output statements for reading and punching paper tape are used frequently for purposes of illustration. This example also introduces the **go to** statement which is used to transfer out of sequence, and the concept of a label.

```
real A, B, C;
LOOP:  READ (A, B);
          if A = 0 then go to END;
          C := A + B;
          PUNCH(C);
          go to LOOP;
   END:
```

This ALGOL program reads two floating point numbers $A$ and $B$, and, if $A \neq 0$, computes their sum, and punches the result $C$. Then control is transferred to the statement whose label is $LOOP$, (i.e. the $READ$ statement) and the process of reading and testing is repeated. The $READ$ statement is an example of a labelled statement. If $A = 0$ control is transferred to the statement labelled $END$ and the process is terminated.

*Example 2.10*   Compound Statements

A sequence of statements can be treated as a single statement by enclosing them by the special ALGOL symbols **begin, end** which act as statement parentheses.

```
begin
   K := 3;
   L := 4;
   M := 5
end
```

The sequence of three assignment statements enclosed by **begin** and **end** are treated as a single statement. This is an example of a compound statement.

Compound statements are used when it is desired to assign values to more than one variable in an **if** or **for** statement, since the range of effect of a condition or a **for** clause is only a single statement.

*Example 2.11*   Blocks

A block is a sequence of declarations followed by statements enclosed by **begin** and **end**. If there are no declarations, the block is a compound statement. Variables declared within a block may be used only within that block and have no meaning outside the block.

```
begin real K;
   K := X;
   X := Y;
   Y := K
end
```

This program interchanges the values of the variables $X$ and $Y$. The variable $K$ is declared within the block, and cannot be used outside the block. It is said to be local to the block. The block is said to define the scope of the variable $K$. The variables $X$ and $Y$ must be declared in an outer block which encloses the given block.

The significance of declarations is best understood by considering the question of storage allocation during execution. In machine-oriented terms, the declaration **real** $K$; serves to reserve a temporary storage register for the variable $K$ at the point of entry to the block. This storage register is relinquished on exit from the block. In general, a declaration serves to reserve storage space during execution for the quantities declared. The space is requisitioned at the moment that the block is entered, by executing the **begin** defining the beginning of the block and is relinquished on exit from the block by executing the **end**.

*Example 2.12*   Procedures

The ALGOL procedure is the counterpart of the FORTRAN subroutine. A procedure is defined by a procedure declaration, which consists of the ALGOL symbol **procedure** followed by a procedure identifier, followed by a list of formal parameters in parentheses, followed by a value specification for formal parameters called by value, followed by *specifications* for formal parameters, followed by a single statement which constitutes the body of the procedure.

**procedure** $ADD(A, N, SUM)$;
   **value** $N$; **integer** $N$; **array** $A$; **real** $SUM$;
   **begin integer** $I$;
    $SUM := O$;
    **for** $I := 1$ **step** $1$ **until** $N$ **do**
    $SUM := SUM + A[I]$
   **end** $ADD$

This procedure declaration defines a subroutine for the addition of $N$ elements of the vector $A$. The value part of this procedure specifies that the *value* of $N$ on entry to the procedure is used during execution. In the case of the parameters $A$ and $SUM$, the procedure uses the *name* of the corresponding identifiers for computation. The parameter $N$ is said to be called by value and the parameters $A$ and $SUM$ are said to be called by name.

The specifications **integer** $N$; **array** $A$; **real** $SUM$; specify the *types* of the formal parameters $A$, $N$, $SUM$.

Specifications differ from declarations in that they do not assign storage space, but merely serve to identify the types of the formal parameters. Specifications are optional in pure ALGOL for parameters called by value, but are frequently obligatory in implementation of ALGOL since they make the task of translation easier and lead to more efficient object programs.

*Example 2.13*   Procedure Statement

$ADD(WEEKLY, 52, TOTAL)$   This is an example of a procedure call which sums the *52* elements of the vector *WEEKLY* and stores the result as the quantity named *TOTAL*.

*Note on Call by Value and Call by Name*

The distinction between call by value and call by name may best be illustrated by considering the question of storage allocation. Assume that the procedure is represented by a compact block of program during execution. Then a call by value reserves a register for the formal parameter within the block of program which constitutes the procedure in the same way as a declared variable, and results in all references to the parameter called by value to refer to this internal register. Actual parameters called by value are evaluated once on entry to the procedure, and stored in the reserved register for use during execution of the procedure.

A call by name causes all references to the parameter to refer to memory registers determined by the calling program. Actual parameters called by name are evaluated at each occurrence within the procedure. If execution of a given procedure, $A$, involves execution of other secondary procedures which modify actual parameters of the procedure call to $A$, then on returning to $A$ after execution of the secondary procedures, parameters called by name will be used in their modified form, whereas the parameters called by value, having been stored locally on entry to the procedure $A$, will not be affected by modification of the actual parameters.

*Example 2.14*   Functions

A procedure for computing a single value can have the same name as the value which is computed. Such a procedure is called a function, and the corresponding procedure identifier with its parenthesized list of actual parameters is called a function designator.

**procedure** $SUM(A, N)$;
  **value** $N$; **integer** $N$; **array** A;
  **begin integer** $I$; **real** $X$;
    $X := 0$;
    **for** $I := 1$ **step** $1$ **until** $N$ **do**
    $X := X + A[I]$;
    $SUM := X$
  **end** $SUM$

This procedure is the same as the procedure *2.12* except that it has a value (assigned to a variable of the same name as the procedure within the procedure itself) which defines the value of the function $SUM$. Note that the variable $SUM$ cannot be used during accumulation since in an expression of the form

$$SUM := SUM + A[I]$$

the variable $SUM$ appearing on the right-hand-side would be interpreted as a recursive activation of the procedure (see Example 2.17).

*Example 2.15*   Use of Function in Arithmetic Expression

A function can be used as a variable in an arithmetic expression.

$X := Y + SUM(WEEKLY, 52)$

This statement assigns to $X$ the result of adding the sum computed by the procedure $SUM$ to the variable $Y$.

*Example 2.16*   Find the Largest Element of a Matrix

**procedure** $MAX(A, M, N, Y, K, L)$;
  **value** $M, N$;
  **integer** $K, L, M, N$; **array** $A$;
  **real** $Y$;
  **begin integer** $I, J$;
    $Y := 0$;
    **for** $I := 1$ **step** $1$ **until** $M$ **do**
    **for** $J := 1$ **step** $1$ **until** $N$ **do**
    **if** $A[I, J] > Y$ **then**
    **begin** $Y := A[I,J]$;
      $K := I$;
      $L := J$
    **end**;
  **end** $MAX$

This procedure is the counterpart of the FORTRAN subroutine of example 1.19 A comparison of the two programs brings out some of the differences between the two languages. The ALGOL procedure requires declarations of variables local to the procedure, but does not require a dimension declaration for $A$ since $A$ is defined outside the procedure. The ALGOL procedure does not require the care in naming of variables that is required in FORTRAN procedures. ALGOL notation for **for** statements is more general than that for FORTRAN $DO$ statements, but it **is** more laborious when the entire generality is not required. The restriction of the scope of **for** and **if** to single statements results in frequent use of **begin** and **end** in ALGOL programs thus leading to greater length of programs. This restriction also results in less frequent use of labels in ALGOL programs than in FORTRAN programs. Finally, the meanings of non local ALGOL variables are determined by the physical embedding of the procedure in outer ALGOL blocks, so that the procedure cannot be stacked away on cards or tape as an independent building block of a larger program. This latter drawback is a serious one.

*Example 2.17.*   Recursion and Jensen's Device

Finally, an example of a recursive procedure will be given. A recursive procedure is one which is defined in terms of itself. Consider for instance the following recursively defined summation procedure:

$$\sum_{i=L}^{M} f_i = f_L + \sum_{i=L+1}^{M} f_i$$

i.e. the sum of a series $f_i$ from a lower limit $L$ to an upper limit $M$ is defined as the first element $f_L$ plus the sum of the remaining terms.

Corresponding to the above mathematical statement, we can define a recursive procedure *SIGMA* whose parameters include the lower and upper bounds $L$, $M$ and whose backbone would be of the form

$$SIGMA(L,M) = f_L + SIGMA(L+1,M)$$

However, a test for termination when $L > M$ is required. Furthermore, the function $f$ which is to be summed, and the index $i$ over which the function is to be summed must also be specified as formal parameters of the procedure. The complete summation procedure can be specified in ALGOL as follows:

```
real procedure SIGMA(i,L,M,f); value L, M; integer i, L, M;
real f;
begin i := L;
SIGMA := if L > M then 0 else f + SIGMA(i, L+1, M,f)
end
```

In order to evaluate the sum of the first three elements of a vector $x_i$ the following procedure call would be used

$$SIGMA\ (i,1,3,x[i])$$

This call would activate the procedure *SIGMA* recursively with successive values *1, 2, 3, 4* of the second parameter. At the fourth recursive call we have the expression

$$x[1] + x[2] + x[3] + SIGMA\ (i, 4, 3, x[i]) = x[1] + x[2] + x[3] + 0$$

since $SIGMA = 0$ for $L > M$.

The parameter $i$ in the above expression is required in order to permit explicit reference to the index $i$ in the function $f$. The use of a parameter $i$ as the dummy variable of a second parameter is referred to as Jensen's device. Jensen's device is essentially a convenient technique for specifying a parameter which varies at successive levels of activation of a recursive procedure, or for supplying an explicit function as parameter.

## 3. Examples from COBOL

COBOL is a business oriented language. Its facilities for expressing sequences of instructions by means of procedures are not as elegant as those of FORTRAN or ALGOL. However, COBOL has special facilities for environment description and data description.

The COBOL language has four divisions corresponding to four different categories of information:

1. Identification Division
2. Environment Division
3. Data Division
4. Procedure Division

The identification division contains programmer and program identification.

The environment division specifies the equipment being used. It contains a description of the computer, the memory size, and the input output units required. It associates input-output channels with each stream of information. A stream of information is called a file.

The data division describes the structure of data files manipulated or created by the object program. Files consist of one or more records belonging to one or more record types. A record contains one or more entries. Each entry may be the name of a numeric or alphanumeric data element, or the name of a lower level entry which itself contains several entries. The data division of a file specifies the structure of a file in terms of records and entries.

The procedure division specifies the program to be executed. The procedure division of COBOL is similar in structure to mathematical languages such as FORTRAN and ALGOL. Procedures are written as sequences of sentences (corresponding to statements in FORTRAN or ALGOL). Sentences may be combined into paragraphs, and paragraphs may be combined into sections.

*Example 3.1*   Identification Division

```
000100   IDENTIFICATION  DIVISION.
000200   PROGRAM-ID.  PAYROLL.
000300   AUTHOR.  JOHN SMITH.
000400   DATE WRITTEN.  JULY 2, 1962.
000500   DATE COMPILED.
000600   NOTE.  THIS EXAMPLE
000700          INDICATES THE KIND
000800          OF INFORMATION IN THE
000900          IDENTIFICATION DIVISION.
```

This is a typical example of the content of the identification division. The first line contains the heading *IDENTIFICATION DIVISION*. The second line specifies the program identification. The third line identifies the programmer. The fourth line indicates the date written. The fifth line specifies that the date on which the program is compiled is to be inserted during compilation. The sixth and subsequent lines are general remarks. Each line begins with the six digit sequence number. The sequence numbers are specified as integers in the fourth digit to permit subsequent insertion of sequence number if required.

Sequence numbering is required in all four divisions of a COBOL program, and presupposes that input is prepared in fixed length records such as punched cards. If the logical unit of information is longer than a single physical record, as in the case of the remarks card above, the continuation is indicated by an indentation of *4* characters.

*Example 3.2*   Environment Division

```
000100   ENVIRONMENT DIVISION.
000200   CONFIGURATION SECTION.
000300   SOURCE COMPUTER.  ANDROMEDA
000400   MEMORY SIZE 16384 WORDS.
000500   OBJECT COMPUTER.  URSAMAJOR
000600   MEMORY SIZE 32768 WORDS.
000700
000800   INPUT-OUTPUT SECTION.
000900   FILE CONTROL.
001000   SELECT INPUT-SALARIES ASSIGN TO TAPE-1;
001100   SELECT WEEKLY-SALARIES ASSIGN TO TAPE-2;
001200   SELECT OUTPUT-SALARIES ASSIGN TO TAPE-3;
001300
001400   INPUT-OUTPUT CONTROL.
001500   SAME RECORD AREA FOR INPUT-SALARIES, OUTPUT-
001600         SALARIES.
```

This is a typical example of the environment division. The configuration section specifies a source computer called *ANDROMEDA* for compilation, with *16384* words of memory; and an object computer called *URSAMAJOR* for execution, with *32768* words of memory. The file control section specifies input-output equipment for each file of input and output information. The input-output control specifies that records of the files *INPUT-SALARIES* and *OUTPUT-SALARIES* share the same memory area.

*Example 3.3*   Data Division

```
000100   DATA DIVISION.
000200   FD  INPUT-SALARIES; BLOCK CONTAINS 15
000250        CHARACTERS;
000300        LABEL RECORDS ARE STANDARD;
000400        DATA RECORDS ARE EMPLOYEE.
000500        01 EMPLOYEE; SIZE IS 15 CHARACTERS.
000600        02 NUMBER; SIZE IS 5 CHARACTERS;
000700           CLASS IS NUMERIC.
000800        02 SALARY-TO-DATE; SIZE IS 10 CHARACTERS;
000900           CLASS IS STERLING.
001000
001150   FD  WEEKLY-SALARIES; BLOCK CONTAINS 15
001100        CHARACTERS;
001200        LABEL RECORDS ARE STANDARD;
001300        DATA RECORDS ARE EMPLOYEE.
001400
001500        01 EMPLOYEE; SIZE IS 15 CHARACTERS.
001600        02 NUMBER; SIZE IS 5 CHARACTERS;
001700           CLASS IS NUMERIC.
001800        02 WEEKLY-SALARY; SIZE IS 10 CHARACTERS;
001900           CLASS IS STERLING.
002000
002100   FD  OUTPUT SALARIES; BLOCK CONTAINS 15
002150        CHARACTERS;
002200        LABEL RECORDS ARE STANDARD;
002300        DATA RECORDS ARE EMPLOYEE.
002400
002500        01 EMPLOYEE; SIZE IS 15 CHARACTERS
002600        02 NUMBER; SIZE IS 5 CHARACTERS;
002700           CLASS IS NUMERIC.
002800        02 SALARY-TO-DATE; SIZE IS 10 CHARACTERS;
002900           CLASS IS STERLING.
003000
```

This example contains a description of 3 files. Each file description starts with the characters *FD* (file description) followed by the file name, followed by some general information about the file. In this case each of the files has the same structure. Each file consists of records of a single type with two words of 5 and 10 characters. The first word in each case is an employee number. The second word is a 10 digit sterling quantity (i.e. 2 digits each for shillings and pence, and 6 digits for pounds). Records and entries have level numbers associated with them. Records always have a level number *01*. An entry of a record which is the name of a data element has the level *02*. If an entry is the name of a list of entries, the list of entries named has a level number one lower than the entry which names the list.

The examples below are all from the COBOL procedure division.

*Example 3.4*   File Setup

> *OPEN INPUT INPUT-SALARIES, WEEKLY-SALARIES, OUTPUT OUTPUT-SALARIES.*

This COBOL sentence sets up the input files *INPUT-SALARIES* and *WEEKLY-SALARIES*, and the output file *OUTPUT-SALARIES*. All files must be opened before they are used.

*Example 3.5*   Record Input

> *READ INPUT-SALARIES RECORD; AT END GO TO ENDING.*

This COBOL sentence makes available a single record from the file named *INPUT-SALARIES* and tests to see whether the final record has been reached. If so control is transferred to the sentence whose label is *ENDING*. Otherwise control continues in sequence. The COBOL system automatically marks the end of a file with a special marker so that a test for the end of the file can be performed automatically.

*Example 3.6*   Arithmetic sentence

The following sentences indicate alternative ways to add *WEEKLY-SALARY* to *SALARY-TO-DATE* and store the result in *SALARY-TO-DATE*.

3.6.1   *ADD WEEKLY-SALARY TO SALARY-TO-DATE GIVING SALARY-TO-DATE*
3.6.2   *ADD WEEKLY-SALARY TO SALARY-TO-DATE*
3.6.3   *COMPUTE SALARY-TO-DATE = WEEKLY-SALARY PLUS SALARY-TO-DATE*
3.6.4   *COMPUTE SALARY-TO-DATE = WEEKLY-SALARY + SALARY-TO-DATE*

The first word of each of the above operations is a COBOL verb. COBOL verbs specify the type of operation to be performed. The variable names *SALARY-TO-DATE* and *WEEKLY-SALARY* are nouns. The connectives *BY*, *PLUS*, *TO*, *GIVING*, =, +, are COBOL operators. Some operators such as *TO* above must be qualified by a verb (e.g. *ADD*) in order to determine their effect uniquely.

*Example 3.7*   Conditional Statement

> *IF NUMBER OF INPUT-SALARIES IS UNEQUAL TO NUMBER OF WEEKLY-SALARIES GO TO ERROR.*

This COBOL sentence tests to see whether the entry *NUMBER* in the file *INPUT-SALARIES* is unequal to the entry *NUMBER* in the file *WEEKLY-SALARIES*. If so control is transferred to the sentence whose label is *ERROR*. Otherwise the next sentence in sequence is executed.

*Example 3.8*   Updating Procedure

```
000100   START.  OPEN INPUT INPUT-SALARIES, WEEKLY-
000200        SALARIES. OUTPUT OUTPUT-SALARIES.
000300   UPDATE.  READ INPUT-SALARIES, WEEKLY-SALARIES;
000400     AT END GO TO ENDING.  IF NUMBER OF
000500     INPUT-SALARIES IS UNEQUAL TO NUMBER OF
000600     WEEKLY SALARIES GO TO ERROR.  ADD
000700     WEEKLY-SALARY  TO  SALARY-TO-DATE  OF INPUT-
000800     SALARIES. WRITE EMPLOYEE OF OUTPUT-SALARIES.
000900     GO TO UPDATE CLOSE.
```

This procedure assumes that the identification, environment and data descriptions of examples 1, 2, 3 have been given. It reads one record from each of the two files *INPUT-SALARIES* and *WEEKLY-SALARIES*, updates the file *INPUT-SALARIES*, and writes out the updated file *OUTPUT-SALARIES* which, according to example 2, has been declared to have the same record area as the file *INPUT-SALARIES*. The updating process is repeated for all records in the file *INPUT-SALARIES*.

# 3. AN OUTLINE OF FORTRAN

I. C. PYLE

*Atomic Energy Research Establishment, Harwell, England*

## 1. Introduction

The first point which I wish to emphasize is that a *program* written in FORTRAN consists of a collection of *routines*, which are physically disjoint. They are translated separately into an intermediate binary language, and at a later stage are combined by a loader to form an executable program. This process can be illustrated diagrammatically thus:

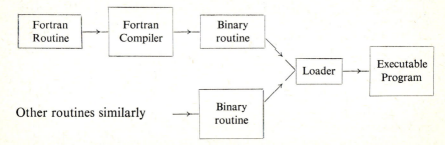

The routines have to be presented to the computer in some hard form, which is usually punched cards. If there is a suitable input channel the computer could accept paper tape input. There is no inherent difference, because "lines" of information are assembled as they would be printed, and these line images are processed by the compiler.

Here is an example of a complete FORTRAN program, to compute and print $\sqrt{(a_1^2 + a_2^2 + \ldots + a_n^2)}$ where $a_1$, $a_2$, etc. are provided as data. It consists of two routines (a main routine and a subroutine) which contain various types of statement: i.e. declarations and instructions, including input/output statements with format specifications, and a *DO* loop to control the repetitive execution of a group of statements.

```
C       MAIN ROUTINE
        DIMENSION A (1000)
        READ INPUT TAPE 2, 100, N, (A (I), I = 1, N)
100     FORMAT (I5/(7F10.0))
        CALL SUMSQ (A,N, TOTAL)
        S = SQRTF (TOTAL)
        WRITE OUTPUT TAPE 3, 103, N, S
103     FORMAT (I10, F15.5)
        CALL EXIT
        END
```

```
      SUBROUTINE SUMSQ(VECTOR, NUMBER, SUM)
      DIMENSION VECTOR (1000)
      X = 0.
      DO 5 I = 1, NUMBER
      X = X + VECTOR (I) ** 2
 5    CONTINUE
      SUM = X
      RETURN
      END
```

As will be seen from the example, a routine consists of a simple sequence *statements*. (There are no compound statements.) Each statement begins on a new line, and may extend over several lines. A special mark (a character other than blank or '*0*' in column 6) indicates that the current line is a continuation. A routine may contain *comments*, which are to be printed with the routine but otherwise ignored. Each comment must be on one separate line, and indicated by a special mark (*C* in column 1). The first line in the example is a comment.

The operations in FORTRAN are designed principally to describe numerical calculations, but may be used for quite general work in a computer. Statements are either executable (instructions which specify operations to be carried out), or non-executable (declarations which specify the properties of names used).

Although some statements look like algebra, there is an important difference; they are dynamic, expressing the process of computation, rather than static, expressing relations. Thus the statement

$$I = I + 1$$

is completely legitimate, meaning that the expression $I + 1$ is to be evaluated and assigned as the new value of the variable $I$. The equals sign means "is to be given the value of" rather than "has the same value as".

The dialect of FORTRAN which is mainly described here is called FORTRAN II. This is the version which has been widely used up to the present. New dialects are now being introduced, principally FORTRAN IV and also Atlas FORTRAN. Some of the differences will be mentioned in passing.

## 2. Variables, Names and Values

The fundamental quantities in FORTRAN are called variables, which are identified by their *names*. Each variable can take any *value* within a certain *domain*, and the value may be changed during the computation. A statement involving variables is to be treated in the same way, regardless of the actual values which the variables currently have. Some instructions allow the current values of variables to be tested, and thus determine subsequent action.

Names, which identify variables and other objects in FORTRAN, consist of up to six characters (letters or digits), of which the first is a letter. The choice of names is left to the programmer, except for certain standard functions.

Thus in the above example, the variables are called

A, N TOTAL, S, VECTOR, NUMBER, SUM, X, I.

The name *SQRTF* denotes a standard function (square root). Some others are described in Section 4.

It is possible for several names to identify the same object, and for the same name in different contexts to identify different objects. Each name has the same meaning throughout the routine in which it occurs: it cannot be used to identify more than one object in one routine. But in different routines, the same name may be used to identify different objects. The region through-out which the name identifies the same object (i.e. has the same meaning) is called the *scope* of the name.

When we speak of "the object (variable, array, function, etc.) $X$" we really mean "the object whose name in this context is $X$". Similarly "the value is $X$" or "there are $N$ equations" really refer to the current value of the variable whose name in this context is given.

The values which a variable can take all lie within a particular domain. The domains normally used in numerical work are *REAL* (floating point numbers having a finite accuracy in a large but finite range) and *INTEGER* (integers lying in a finite range, usually used for counting). Another domain of interest is *COMPLEX* (in which the real and imaginary parts are separately in the domain *REAL*). The finite accuracy and range of the *REAL* domain is sometimes inadequate, and extended multiple precision domains may be needed to improve the situation.

Non-numerical domains which are useful are *LOGICAL* (containing only two values *.TRUE.* and *.FALSE.*) and *TEXT* in which the values are characters (letters, digits etc.). It is sometimes possible to treat a sequence of logical variables or characters together as a single variable.

The *mode* of a variable is the domain in which its values lie. There is a convention that the name of a variable indicates its mode, according to the initial letter: *I, J, K, L, M,* or *N* for *INTEGER*, the other letters normally for *REAL*, but can be used for the other modes. Thus, in the above example

N, NUM, I are INTEGER

A, TOTAL, S are REAL

This convention must be adhered to in FORTRAN II, but can be overridden in the new dialects.

### 3. Arrays

An array is identified by its name, whose initial letter indicates the mode of the members (all of which should be of the same mode). For example, all the numbers $a_i$ in the example are *REAL*, and they are grouped in the array *A*.

Individual members of the array are specified by the array name followed by a list of subscripts, separated by commas, and enclosed in parentheses. The subscripts must have *INTEGER* values. In the dialects FORTRAN II and FORTRAN IV, the allowed forms of subscripts are typified by:

$$2, I, J + 3, K - 4,$$
$$5 * L, 6 * M + 7, 8 * N - 9$$

The number of subscripts, and the range of values which they may take (lower and upper bounds) are fixed properties of the array. An array with one subscript represents a vector; one with two subscripts a matrix. Three dimensional arrays are also allowed. An isolated variable may be thought of as an array with no subscripts: it represents a scalar.

These properties are associated with the array name by specifying its *dimensions*. If we think of the array as a multi-dimensional cuboid, we give the ordered set of lengths in the different dimensions. The lower bound for subscript values is always 1; the specified lengths are the upper bounds. Thus in the example we have in the main routine

$$DIMENSION \ A \ (1000)$$

which specifies that $A$ is an array name, that one subscript is to be expected, and that the values of the subscript should lie in the range 1 to 1000. It is the programmer's responsibility to obey this rule: there is no dynamic checking.

Properties of several arrays may be declared in the same statement, e.g.

$$DIMENSION \ B(5, 10, 20), \ RAD \ (50), \ ITEM \ (500, 3)$$

specifying that $B$, $RAD$, and $ITEM$ are array names, using three, one and two subscripts respectively, with the given upper bounds. The declaration of the properties of an array must always precede any instruction which refers to an element of it.

## 4. Functions

A *function* is a subsidiary calculation which produces a value as its result. The result may depend on the current values of some variables (scalars or arrays), or on other functions or subroutines. These are its *arguments*. A *function call* is a reference which activates the subsidiary calculation, after making certain substitutions to specify the actual objects to be used as arguments. Although the principal action is to produce a result, there is no prohibition on other action occurring.

The primitive arithmetic functions of addition, subtraction, multiplication, division and exponentiation of *REAL* and *INTEGER* variables are written like algebra, with a special sign between the variables concerned. The signs used are $+$, $-$, $*$ (crossed to avoid confusion with $x$), $/$ (treated as inverse multiplication) and $**$ respectively. In FORTRAN II and FORTRAN IV, the variables which they combine must be of the same mode, except that a *REAL* variable can be exponentiated by an *INTEGER* variable. Mixed modes have to be prohibited because the primitive functions do not work with variables having values in different domains. In Atlas FORTRAN, more powerful primitive functions are available, and this rule is dropped.

Apart from the above arithmetic functions, functions are identified by their names, whose initial letter indicates the mode of the result. The modes of the arguments need not be the same as the mode of the result, but each of the quantities specified as an actual argument should be of the mode which the subsidiary calculation expects for that argument. The number of arguments is usually a fixed property of the function.

There are several types of function, of which the most important are standard functions, and private functions defined by the programmer. The names of these functions have the same meaning throughout a whole program; they are not limited to a routine.

Standard functions in FORTRAN II have an F after the stem of their name, and the result is presumed to be an *INTEGER* if and only if the name begins with the letter *X*. (This unusual convention is an historical accident.) The values of the arguments are supplied on entry to the subsidiary calculation. Some of the standard functions are:

| | |
|---|---|
| *ABSF (X)* | absolute value. |
| *FLOATF (I)* | value in *REAL* domain corresponding to *INTEGER* argument |
| *SQRTF (X)* | square root |
| *EXPF (X)* | exponential |

The way in which a programmer defines his own functions will be described later. The name must not end in *F*, and the mode of the result is presumed to be an *INTEGER* if and only if the initial letter of the function name is *I, J, K, L, M* or *N* (the usual FORTRAN convention).

The information supplied on entry to the subsidiary calculation is effectively a simple name for each argument. It is not necessarily the name of a variable with a value, but may be an array or a function.

The following three examples of function calls refer to private functions which respectively carry out a straightforward computation, do a more sophisticated list processing operation, and output a number.

| | |
|---|---|
| *SUM 1 (VECT, N)* | produce the sum of the first *N* members of the array *VECT*. |
| *ISITIN (WORD, LIST)* | search the array *LIST* (it defines its own length, *L*) for a word equal to *WORD*. Give the result $I (> 0)$ if it is the $I^{th}$, $- L - 1 (< 0)$ if it is not in the list. |
| *QPRINT (X)* | Output the value of *X* in a standard format, and produce the same value as result. |

## 5. Constants

Numerical constants are written using the ordinary decimal notation. A scale factor (integral power of *10*) may be included after the letter *E*. Constants in the domain *INTEGER* are written with digits alone. Those in the *REAL* domain have a decimal point or scale factor. Thus:

*1, 2, 37, 1066,* are *INTEGER,*

*.5, 2.718, 25., 1962.8,* are *REAL;*

*3.14159, .314159E1, 314.159 E − 2, 314159E − 5*

are different ways of writing the same constant.

A constant is treated like a variable, which is given the appropriate value before starting the calculation.

## 6. Expressions

Several kinds of statement may contain expressions, which are written like algebra, and cause the current values of the appropriate elements to be combined in the specified ways. An element in an expression may be a constant, a simple variable, an array variable, a subexpression or a function call, e.g. (respectively)

$$2.352, SCALAR, MATRIX (I, J), (U + V * W - X),$$
$$SQRTF (X(I) ** 2 + Y(I) ** 2)$$

The elements may be combined thus

$$U + V * W - X$$
$$(I - J) * L$$
$$S/T (I,J) + X(I) * Y(J)$$

A subexpression is written like an expression and enclosed in parentheses. A function call is written as the function name, followed by a list of arguments in parentheses; each argument may be an expression. Thus, subexpressions may themselves contain subexpressions, and arguments of function calls may contain function calls, and so on.

The value of a subexpression or argument expression is calculated in advance and then treated as the value of a variable which effectively replaces it. Thus each expression is reduced to an arithmetic combination of variables. These are treated in the conventional order, first exponentiation, then multiplication and division, and finally addition and subtraction as illustrated in Chapter 2.

The order of evaluation of subexpressions is illustrated by the following example:

$$A/B - ( (C(I) ** D) \quad ** E + COSF (2.0 * \quad (F + G) ) )$$

In the above example, the expression is represented in the form of an upside down tree. The tree representation of arithmetic expressions is further discussed in Chapter 21.

## 7. Arithmetic Statements

The fundamental instruction in a calculation assigns a new value of a variable. This is called an Arithmetic Statement, (although it need not involve any arithmetic). It causes a value to be obtained (in general by evaluating an expression), and then given to a specified variable. A scalar or a single member of an array may be changed in one statement.

As pointed out in the introduction, a variable may be involved in the expression and then have its value changed: no contradiction is implied. Here are some examples of arithmetic statements:

$X = 0.$
$X = X + VECTOR(I) ** 2$
$S = SQRTF(TOTAL)$
$B(I, J) = A(I,J) + X(I) * Y(J)$
$XZ = QPRINT(ZZ*YZ ** 2 - 1)$
$D = ABC(E, ABC(F - G, H))$

Note that an argument of a function may involve the function itself. No problem of recursion arises because the arguments are always worked out in advance. Thus the last example above is interpreted as:

$W1 = F - G$
$W2 = ABC(W1, H)$
$D = ABC(E, W2)$

## 8. Flow of Control

The order in which the instructions are executed is important. We say that control flows (or is sent) from one instruction to another.

The instructions of a routine are normally obeyed in the order in which they are written, but some instructions explicitly specify which is to be obeyed next, allowing the written sequence to be broken. Statements in the routine may be identified by means of *statement numbers*, written as integers in the margin on the same line as the beginning of the statement (card columns 1 to 5). There is a dummy instruction

*CONTINUE*

which allows a statement number to be defined at a particular point, but itself causes no action.

Control is sent unconditionally to a specified instruction by the unconditional *GO TO* statement, e.g.

*GO TO 50*

Until another successor is explicitly defined, the specified instruction and those written after it are executed in order.

There are several ways of sending control to one of a number of statements. In all cases, there is a list of possible successors, one of which is chosen each time the statement is executed.

In the computed *GO TO* statement, the successor is chosen according to the value of a variable: control is sent to the appropriate member of a list of possible successors, e.g.

  *GO TO (5, 5, 7, 1, 21, 1), JUMP*

If the variable *JUMP* currently has the value *4*, control is sent to statement number *1*. The variable acts rather like a subscript, and must be of mode *INTEGER*; its lower bound is *1*, its upper bound is the number of successor specified. If the instruction is executed with the variable outside the allowed range, the program gets out of control: there is no check.

In the arithmetic *IF* statement, the successor depends on the sign of an expression: the expression is evaluated, and control passes to the first, second or third possible successor (there must be three) according as the value is negative, zero or positive, e.g.

  *IF (X − Y) 10, 11, 12*

If the current value of *X* is less than that of *Y*, the result of evaluating the expression is negative, so control goes to statement number *10*.

The form of this statement is rather unconventional: it is an ingenious notation to avoid the need for special relational operator symbols ($<$ $\leqslant$ $\neq$, etc.) in a limited character set. All six relations can be obtained by putting the same statement numbers in two of the three possible successor positions.

The expression is written according to the usual rules: it may be a simple variable or even a constant. Thus to replace *X* by its absolute value we could write

```
     IF (X) 10, 15, 15
10  X = − X
15  CONTINUE
```

This will give the same effect as

  *X = ABSF (X)*

There are other statements which specify successors (assigned *GO TO* and special *IF*s for testing machine indicators) which are less important.

### 9. Loops

A group of instructions can be repeated a number of times by setting up a *loop*. The *DO* statement specifies the statement number of the last of the group of instructions to be repeated, and defines the values which the *index* of the loop is to take. Thus

```
    DO 5 I = 1, NUMBER
    X = X + VECTOR (I) ** 2
5  CONTINUE
```

causes the instructions after the *DO* statement until statement number *5* (which is usually a *CONTINUE*, but may specify calculation) to be executed repeatedly while *I* takes the values *1, 2, 3 .... NUMBER*.

The parameters (*1* and *NUMBER*) may be constants or variables. If increments of the loop index other than *1* are required, a third parameter is specified. The parameters must be positive and of mode *INTEGER*.

The loop is always begun. It may contain instructions which send control out of the loop, breaking off the repetitions. Whenever the end of the loop is reached, the index is incremented; if it is then less than or equal to the final value, control is sent back to the beginning of the loop, otherwise control flows out of the loop.

The loop may contain another *DO* statement and inner loop, which is executed repeatedly for each repetition of the outer loop. Several loops may specify the same statement as their last. For example, to search a matrix for the element with greatest absolute value, we would have

```
    Y = 0.
    DO 5 I = 1, M
    DO 5 J = 1, N
    IF (ABSF(A(I,J)) − Y) 5, 5, 4
 4  Y = ABSF (A(I,J))
    K = I
    L = J
 5  CONTINUE
```

### 10. Subroutine Calls

As mentioned in the introduction, a program consists of a number of logically separate sections called routines. The rules for writing complete routines are described in Section 11. The order in which routines occur has no relation to the order of execution: they always activate one another by explicit reference.

A routine is identified by its name, which has the same meaning throughout, the program. A routine may have arguments, which may influence its action and may be influenced by it. Each routine defines a particular part of the calculation to be performed and is activated from another routine by an explicit *subroutine call* statement e.g.

```
    CALL SUMSQ (A, N, TOTAL).
```

This instruction causes the subroutine *SUMSQ* to be activated, with substitutions made as specified by the arguments: thus *VECTOR* in the subroutine is replaced by *A* and so on. Since *SUM* is replaced by *TOTAL*, this subroutine call causes the sum of squares of the first *N* members of the vector *A* to be calculated, and the value assigned to the variable *TOTAL*. On completion of the subroutine, the activating routine is resumed.

A calculation may therefore be organized by a main routine calling a sequence of subroutines in order thus:

```
    CALL ADD 1(SALARY, 15, TOTAL)
    CALL TEXT (8, 8H TOTAL =)
    CALL PRINT (TOTAL, 5, 3)
    CALL LINE
```

These subroutines respectively add together the first *15* elements of the array *SALARY*, putting the sum in *TOTAL*; output the sequence of *8* characters specified; output the current value of *TOTAL*; and print the output on a separate line.

There need not be any arguments in a subroutine call; an argument may be the name of a variable, array or routine, or an expression which may be just a constant. All arguments are effectively replaced by simple names before activating the subroutine. An expression is evaluated in advance, and its value given to a generated variable whose name effectively replaces it. An array may be identified by its name or its first element: an array element is given a simple name, which may be regarded as a scalar or an array name. A constant is similarly treated as a simple name. A constant of mode *TEXT* is written as a sequence of characters, preceded by the character count and the letter *H*.

Here is another subroutine call statement:

$$CALL\ RUKU\ (SUBR,\ Y,\ F,\ G,\ H,\ X,\ N,\ DX)$$

This advances by one step (*DX*) the integration of the differential equations

$$\frac{dY(I)}{dX} = F(I) \text{ for } I = 1, N$$

using the Runge-Kutta-Gill process. The argument *SUBR* denotes a subroutine which is called by *RUKU* to evaluate the derivatives *F* for the *N* equations, with independent variable *X* and dependent variables in the array *Y*. The arrays *G* and *H* are used as working space.

If a routine name (e.g. *SUBR*) is used as an argument, and is not used in a function call or subroutine call elsewhere in the same routine, then a declaration must be made to distinguish it from a scalar. The form of this declaration in FORTRAN II is

$$F\ SUBR$$

(the *F* in column 1) but in new dialects of FORTRAN it is

$$EXTERNAL\ SUBR$$

## 11. Complete Routines

In previous sections we have described how to write the statements which constitute the body of a routine (apart from input/output, which is described in Section 15). We now show how to build this body into a complete routine.

There are three types of routine, which are activated in different ways. The basic type is a *subroutine*, which just carries out a section of the program. This is activated by an explicit subroutine call in another routine. A *function* also carries out a section of the program, but in addition produces a scalar value as its 'result'. The routine is activated when a reference to the function (a function call) occurs in an expression; the result of the function is subsequently used in the evaluation. The third type is a *main routine* which must always be present. This is activated by the loader to begin execution of the program.

The type of the routine, its name, and a list of 'dummy' arguments are specified in a declaration which must be the first physical statement of the routine, e.g.

> *SUBROUTINE ADD 1 (A, N, SUM)*
> *FUNCTION SUM 1 (A, N)*

A main routine is identified by a null declaration. In other words, if the first statement is not one of the above, then the routine is taken to be a main routine. The last physical statement of every routine must be the declaration

> *END*

Whenever a routine is activated, control begins at the first written instruction, and continues according to the standard rules until it comes to the instruction

> *RETURN*

This defines the logical end of the routine: when the instruction is encountered during execution, the routine which activated it is resumed.

Although routines are physically disjoint, there is no limit to the depth to which they may activate each other. However, a routine may not activate itself (either directly or indirectly) unless no return is expected.

## 12. Arguments

The 'dummy' arguments written in the routine declaration may be used like other names throughout the routine. Each time the routine is activated, they will be treated as synonymous with the names provided in the calling instruction. They are effectively replaced, each time the routine is entered, by a 'prologue' which is executed before obeying the first instruction.

There is no checking during this replacement: it is the programmer's responsibility to see that the actual arguments supplied are consistent with the uses made of the dummy arguments, in number, mode, and type. When an argument is an array name, the routine must declare the properties associated with the dummy name. These are normally the same as those of actual arrays used as arguments, which are consequently all of the same size and shape. However, the length in the last dimension may differ: in particular, vectors of different lengths may be used. Thus, for vectors, a length of 1 may be conventionally specified in the routine. Inside a function routine, the routine name is used like a scalar. The value of this scalar on returning is the 'result' of the function.

Here are some examples of complete routines:

```
FUNCTION QPRINT (X)
CALL LINE
CALL PRINT (X, 0, 8)
QPRINT = X
RETURN
END

SUBROUTINE SET (I, J)
I = J
RETURN
END

  SUBROUTINE ADD 1 (A, N, SUM)
  DIMENSION A (1)
  SUM = 0.
  DO 6 I = 1, N
6 SUM = SUM + A (I)
  RETURN
  END
```

### 13. Input and Output Values

Since each reference to an argument in the routine requires action in the prologue to replace it, the programmer may take steps to reduce the number of references in the interest of speed. It is useful to distinguish arguments which are scalars, in which the value on entry to the routine or on exit from it (or both) may be significant.

If there is an output scalar which is specially important, the routine can be made a function, of which this is the result. There is then no corresponding argument. Otherwise, the values may be copied from the arguments into private variables at entry, or vice versa at exit. The body of the routine then uses the private variables, and no adjustment is needed during execution. This is worth doing if there are more than three references to the variable.

For example, we may convert *ADD 1* into a function (because *SUM* is significant on output):

```
  FUNCTION SUM 1(A, N)
  DIMENSION A (1) `
  SUM 1 = 0.
  DO 6 I = 1, N
6 SUM 1 = SUM 1 + A (I)
  RETURN
  END
```

or we could leave it as a subroutine but copy only the output value of *SUM* into the argument:

```
    SUBROUTINE ADD 2 (A, N, SUM 2)
    DIMENSION A (1)
    SUM = 0.
    DO 6 I = 1, N
  6 SUM = SUM + A (I)
    SUM 2 = SUM
    RETURN
    END
```

If there were more references to $N$ we could replace the second dummy argument by $N1$ and put

$$N = N1$$

at the beginning. This makes $N$ a normal variable, whose initial value is set to that of $N1$.

### 14. Common

The treatment of arguments is such that a routine can be called on different occasions to carry out a calculation using quite different sets of variables. In many circumstances, this flexibility is not needed: the routine may be activated several times, but always the same variables are concerned.

In this case the replacements effected by the prologue are clearly unnecessary; a better way of communicating values between routines is by use of *common* variables.

The normal variables of a routine are private, and are protected from interference by other routines, unless they are explicitly specified as arguments. But the declaration

```
    COMMON A1, B1, X1
```

makes the names $A1$, $B1$, $X1$, in this routine identify the first three common variables, which are accessible to all routines. If another routine contains

```
    COMMON A2, B2, X2
```

then these names in this routine will similarly identify the first three common variables, i.e. the same variables as the names $A1$, $B1$, $X1$ in the first routine. Note that the correspondence is by position in the *COMMON* declaration rather than by name.

An array name may occur in a *COMMON* declaration; it is equivalent to specifying as many scalars as there are elements in the array. Thus

```
    COMMON F1, G1, H1
    DIMENSION G1 (5)
```

defines names usable in this routine for the first seven common variables. Another routine might use different names, and even different groupings, thus

```
    COMMON C2, E2
    DIMENSION C2 (3) E2 (4)
```

Then the names referring to the common variables are as follows

| Common variable number | In first routine | In second routine |
|:---:|:---:|:---:|
| 1 | F1 | C2(1) |
| 2 | G1(1) | C2(2) |
| 3 | G1(2) | C2(3) |
| 4 | G1(3) | E2(1) |
| 5 | G1(4) | E2(2) |
| 6 | G1(5) | E2(3) |
| 7 | H1 | E2(4) |

Of course, the above example is not typical; one usually has identical COMMON and DIMENSION declarations in all routines, so the names are the same throughout.

For example, the array SALARY might be in common. We could then further improve the efficiency of ADD2:

```
   SUBROUTINE ADD 3 (N, SUM 3)
   COMMON SALARY
   DIMENSION SALARY (100)
   SUM = 0.
   DO 6 I = 1, N
 6 SUM = SUM + SALARY (I)
   SUM 3 = SUM
   RETURN
   END
```

The same could be done with the function SUM 1.

## 15. Input/Output

Fortran contains powerful input/output facilities, which are implemented by hidden library routines controlled by the programmer's instructions. The controlling statements usually come in pairs, one specifying the variables whose values are to be input or output and the other specifying the external format of these values.

For example, a simple input instruction and format specification would be

```
     READ INPUT TAPE 2, 200, N, M
 200 FORMAT (2I5)
```

This will cause N and M to be given the respective values of two decimal integers on input tape number 2, each occupying five character positions. A typical line of input for this is

>     bbbb5bb100

where the letter $b$ denotes a blank space.

To output the values, the statements would be

>     WRITE OUTPUT TAPE 3, 300, N, M
>     300    FORMAT (4HbbN = I5, 4H,bM = I5)

This would give the following output line

>     bbN = bbbb5,bM = bb100

We could in fact have used the input format statement (number *200*) to give output of the numbers alone, but it is good programming practice to put explanatory information with the numbers output.

There are really three parts to the information in an input/output statement: the equipment to be used, the external form of the information and the internal form of the information. The word(s) at the beginning specify the nature of the external medium, and of course whether it is input or output. For on-line equipment the words are

>     READ      (card reader)
>     PRINT     (line printer)
>     PUNCH     (card punch)

Because input and output of cards and line printing are relatively slow processes, the usual method is now to use an auxiliary off-line computer to copy information between cards and tape or from tape to printer, and use magnetic tape input and output at the main computer. For these the instructions contain an integer (constant or variable) to specify the tape number, thus

>     READ INPUT TAPE M
>     WRITE OUTPUT TAPE N

where $M$ and $N$ have conventional values for the installation.

For input and output of data and results, the external arrangement of the information is specified by a *FORMAT* statement, which is written separately, and referenced by its statement number. For auxiliary storage of variables which are only to be read back by the computer, the external arrangement of the information is irrelevant (it is in binary words), and instruction beginning

>     READ TAPE I
>     WRITE TAPE J

are used.

The internal arrangement of the information is specified by a list of variable names, whose values are to be input or output. There can be any number of

variables in such a list, either specified individually or in an implied loop:
e.g.

> , $X, Y(5), Z(L)$
> , $(A(I), I = 1, 4)$ equivalent to , $A(1)$ , $A(2)$ , $A(3)$ , $A(4)$
> , $(I,(C(I,J), J = 1, N), B(I), I = 1, M)$

### 16. Input/Output in the New Dialects

There are some changes in notation for the new dialects of FORTRAN, and
generalizations of meaning appropriate to more advanced computers.

The notational change is to substitute for the rather lengthy statement

> *WRITE OUTPUT TAPE 3, 100*

the shorter statement

> *WRITE (3, 100)*

and similarly

> *READ (2, 101)* for *READ INPUT TAPE 2, 101*

also

> *READ (5)* for *READ TAPE 5*
> *WRITE (6)* for *WRITE TAPE 6*

The semantic change is based on the advent of time-sharing computers,
which can do their own 'off-line' processing. The statements no longer specify
actual input/output equipments, but identify 'streams' of information which
are separately input and output.

There is one principal input stream (containing the program followed by
its data) which is read by the instruction

> *READ*

not followed immediately by a parenthesis. Similarly there is one principal
output stream for printing, for which we use

> *PRINT*

An auxiliary output stream is reserved for information which is to be subsequently read mechanically; this is specified by

> *PUNCH*

All other input and output streams are numbered (the correspondence
between the numbers used and the actual equipment used is set up by the
operating system on the computer) and specified by the generalized

> *READ (N, FMT)*
> *WRITE (M, FMT)*

instructions.

## 17. Formats

The rules for writing format specifications are quite distinct from the rest of
FORTRAN. One thinks of an image of the external line scanned from left to
right; the processing to be carried out during this scan is specified by code
sequences in the format specification. A field is a group of adjacent characters
treated together.

Thus *I5* means that the next field consists of 5 characters which represent
a decimal integer. For output, the next variable is taken from the list, and its
current value is converted to decimal. For input, the characters are collected
to form a binary integer, whose value is given to the next variable in the list.
An integer before the code letter means that there are as many adjacent fields of
the same form. Similarly, *F6.1* means that the next field consists of 6 characters, which represent a real number in decimal form, with 1 digit after the
decimal point.

Headings and other constant text can be output among the numbers by
including a constant of mode *TEXT* in the specification. The letter *H* after an
integer means copy as many following characters (spaces and commas
included) from the format specification into the line image. Variable text can
be handled using *A*-type conversion. The next variable in the list should be of
mode *TEXT*: characters are copied from it to the line image for output, vice
versa for input.

Items can be spaced out by using code *X*: *8X* means space over the next *8*
character positions (this produces spaces on output, ignores character on
input). The end of a line is denoted by a / or the end of the format specification.

One level of parentheses can be used, preceded by an integer, to denote
repetition of a group of fields. The whole specification is enclosed in parentheses.

If the lists comes to an end in the middle of a format specification, the rest
of the specification is abandoned: the next reference to it will start at the
beginning. If the list contains more variables than the format specifies, then
the last part of the specification is repeated indefinitely (from the right-most
left parenthesis with its associated count).

The following example is rather more complicated:

> *WRITE OUTPUT TAPE 3, 102, IP, CASE,*
> *X   (((PAGE (I, J, K), I = 1, 3), J = 1, 2), K = 1, NL)*
> *102   FORMAT (5H1PAGE, I5, 10H FOR CASE , A6 /*
> *X    2(8X, 3F6.1, 8X))*

If the current values of the variables are as follows

> *IP = 7*
> *CASE = 4H ICP*
> *PAGE (1, 1, 1) = 111.0*
> *PAGE (1, 1, 2) = 112.0*

>          etc.

and $NL = 5$

then the page of output produced by this would be

PAGE   7 FOR CASE   ICP
   111.0 211.0 311.0  121.0 221.0 321.0
   112.0 212.0 312.0  122.0 222.0 322.0
   113.0 213.0 313.0  123.0 223.0 323.0
   114.0 214.0 314.0  124.0 224.0 324.0
   115.0 215.0 315.0  125.0 225.0 325.0

The character at the beginning of each line is treated specially: 1 starts a new page, space is normal, for single spacing.

## 18. Conclusion

The word FORTRAN has at least four different meanings. I have been using it as the name of the source language in which routines may be written. It is also sometimes applied to the compiler which translates these routines into the intermediate binary language.

Third, it is used to mean the FORTRAN MONITOR SYSTEM (FMS) which includes the compiler and loader, and controls the processing and execution of jobs on the computer. Fourth, it is used for the underlying philosophy of independent treatment of routines, on which much of the total system is based.

The development of FORTRAN has covered a period of several years, and not all the present features were available in early systems. A brief summary of the stages it has gone through should spotlight the important features which programmers find convenient.

The original FORTRAN I did not allow subroutines: all the program had to be compiled together. The algebraic language was a great advance from machine language coding, but it forced programs to be monolithic and inflexible. Then FORTRAN II introduced the subroutine facilities, but still separated compilation from execution. This was a great improvement, and really marked the beginning of FORTRAN as a powerful system. Manufacturers other than IBM started providing FORTRAN compilers. Finally, the FORTRAN MONITOR SYSTEM emerged, giving an even more marked improvement, as compilation and execution could be combined, and complete jobs prepared by the programmer away from the computer, to be run without any need for manual intervention.

# 4. AN INTRODUCTION TO ALGOL 60

## M. WOODGER

*National Physical Laboratory, Teddington, England*

## 1. Introduction*

### 1. Purpose

ALGOL 60 is a formal symbolic language for expressing processes of computation (*algorithms*).

The order code for any individual computer is, in fact, such a language—it has a 'syntax' or set of rules specifying what are meaningful combinations of symbols, and a 'semantics' or set of rules specifying the meanings of these combinations, that is to say the action taken by the computer when the orders are executed.

Such 'machine languages' are burdened with details of the particular structure, arithmetic facilities, input-output and storage arrangements of the computer concerned. The purpose of ALGOL 60 is to provide a language for the expression of computation processes to the extent that they are independent of these details, and in a form which can be translated automatically, into any particular machine code, by a suitable translator program written for the computer concerned. The 'machine oriented' details of the computation are to be embodied in the translator rather than in the ALGOL 60 program.

A second use of ALGOL 60 is for expressing processes of computation in a form suitable for human consumption. Whereas an unbroken sequence of symbols of a few different sorts is satisfactory for input to a computer, legibility requires a display on the printed page, and a variety of forms of expression which will reflect the natural subdivision of the process. To accommodate these varying requirements there are three forms of ALGOL 60: it is defined in a form known as the *reference language* (employing a total of 116 basic symbols but in a linear fashion); it is used as input to translators in an appropriate *hardware representation* (employing, e.g., 5-bit characters on punched paper tape); and it is used in publications in the form of *publication language*. The latter admits the use of suffixes ($a_{i,j}$ corresponding to $a[i, j]$ in the reference language), exponents ($a^3$ corresponding to $a\uparrow3$), Greek letters, spaces, and line groupings of characters. Apart from such relatively trivial differences the three forms of ALGOL 60 are identical in content.

Words printed in bold type such as **begin** represent single basic symbols. In the typescript of an ALGOL 60 program these would be underlined.

### 2. Subject-Matter

The computing processes described deal principally with ordinary real

---

*Chapter 4 is a reprint of the article which appeared originally in the *Computer Journal*, 3, 2 July 1960.

numbers, integers, and arrays of these. The real numbers are of necessity approximated digitally, but how this is done is not expressed.

In order to avoid reference to particular storage locations a notation is introduced for variable quantities in store, and it is important to be clear as to its precise significance. A letter, or a string of letters or decimal digits of which the first is a letter, is called an *identifier*. An identifier may be used in an ALGOL 60 program as a *simple variable*. This means that the program, when ultimately translated and run on a computer, will associate a particular storage location with that identifier. The number held in this store at any stage in the calculation is called the *current value* of the variable. An instruction or *statement* in the ALGOL 60 program which contains this identifier calls either for the use of this number in calculation or for its replacement by the result of calculation—the latter is referred to as 'assignment of a value to the variable'.

### 3. Calculation Rules

The course of the computation process described by the ALGOL 60 program may be visualized as a succession of assignments of values to variables. The program expresses rules for the calculation of these assigned values, and these rules take a variety of forms. The simplest rules are provided by ordinary algebraic expressions compounded from simple variables and numerical (decimal) constants by the usual symbols for addition, subtraction, multiplication and division. If $E$ denotes such an expression, the instruction in ALGOL 60 which calls for the assignment of the current value of $E$ to a variable $V$ is written

$$V := E.$$

$E$ may well contain $V$ itself; for example, the assignment statement $V := V + 1$ increases the current value of $V$ by 1.

To indicate that the variable $V$ is to be treated as a real variable (say), rather than as an integer or other 'type' of quantity, a *type declaration* **real** $V$ is used. A succession of type declarations for the variables employed, followed by a succession of assignment statements, each statement and declaration being separated from its neighbours by a semicolon (;), and the whole being enclosed between the 'statement brackets' **begin** and **end**, would constitute a simple ALGOL 60 program.

### 4. Arrays

Large blocks of numerical data are commonly treated as *arrays*, the elements of which are specified by sets of integers. The number of integers in such a set is the 'dimensionality' of the array. Thus a matrix $A$ is a two-dimensional array for which a set of two integers, the row number $i$ and column number $j$, is used to single out a particular element. This element is denoted by the suffixed symbol $A_{ij}$. If the elements of a matrix $A$ of $n$ columns are stored in consecutive locations row by row, the position number of element $A_{ij}$ relative to $A_{11}$ as number 0 is $(i - 1)n + (j - 1)$, and this rule for finding the $(i, j)$ element must be available to the computer whenever the value of this element is called for.

An array is in effect a function of a number of integer variables, the values of the function being explicitly listed (stored) and the values of the variables being used to locate the function value in the list (store). This may be contrasted with the situation with an algebraic expression, which is effectively a function of the variables it contains. In that case no function values are stored, but the values of the variables are used to calculate the function value by a formula. A formula can generally be used for arbitrary values of the arguments. An array, on the other hand, is limited, for reasons of storage, in each of its dimensions. ALGOL 60 deals only with arrays whose dimensions are independent, i.e. generalized rectangular arrays, and in particular only those employing consecutive integer suffix values. The extent of an array is specified by the lower and upper limiting values of each of its suffixes, and this information for each array, together with the type of its elements, is provided by an *array declaration*.

Each element of an array may be assigned a value independently of the others. The general form of such an assignment statement is

$$V[E, E, \ldots, E] := F$$

or in 'publication language' ALGOL 60 (which permits the use of suffixes instead of square brackets)

$$V_{E, E, \ldots, E} := F.$$

Here $V$ is a *subscripted variable* (the identifier naming the array); each $E$ (a *subscript*) is an expression whose current value is used to locate the appropriate element of the array, and $F$ is the expression whose current value is to be assigned to that element.

## 5. Constituents of a Program

The basic constituents of an ALGOL 60 program are thus *statements* which are executed as instructions in the order in which they are written and have the effect of assigning values to certain variables, and *declarations* which are not themselves executed as instructions but provide information necessary to the execution of the statements following them.

There is a third (unnamed) category of constituents which corresponds to the control or 'red tape' instructions in machine language. These make it possible

(i) to break off a sequence of calculations and start again somewhere else in the program (the 'jump' or *go to* statements);

(ii) to skip certain statements in a sequence if certain conditions are not satisfied (*conditional* statements); and

(iii) to repeat the next statement for a succession of values of a variable (the *for* statements).

Since no reference is made to storage locations of the ALGOL 60 statements themselves, they have to be *labelled* to be identified as destinations for *go to* statements. Any identifier or unsigned integer may be used as a label, written in front of the statement labelled and separated from it by a colon (:).

Sequences of statements may be combined within the statement brackets **begin** and **end** to form *compound statements*, which again may be labelled.

## 6. *Blocks and Declarations*

Each identifier used in an ALGOL 60 program, other than as a label, is introduced by a declaration which gives information concerning it, and which is referred to by the translator when executing the statements in which the identifier appears. This declaration is written (possibly with others) following the **begin** symbol of some compound statement (possibly the whole program). A compound statement containing declarations in this way is called a *block*, and each declaration is valid only for the block to which it is attached. This means that each identifier *I* is 'local' to the block *B* for which it is declared, in the sense that on exit from *B* either via the **end** (on completion of the last statement in *B*) or on execution of a *go to* (jump) statement leading outside *B*, *I* has no longer the declared significance and may be used afresh in a new declaration to denote some entirely different thing. Alternatively, if the block *B* is itself a component statement of a larger block *A* for which *I* was already declared, then, while *B* is being executed, *I* has the local significance declared for *B* but on exit to *A* it reverts to the significance it had when *B* was entered, its value (if a variable) remaining unaffected by passage through *B*. Identifiers used in *A* and not declared for *B* retain their significance within *B*. Thus every block automatically introduces a new level of nomenclature.

Labels are automatically 'local' to the blocks in which they are used, so that a jump into a block from outside is not possible—that would by-pass the governing declarations.

A declaration *D*, attached to a block *B* and governing an identifier *I* representing a variable or array, may be prefixed with the symbol **own**. This has the effect that on re-entering *B* the value of the variable (or values of the array elements) is as it was left at the previous exit from *B*.

## 7. *Functions and Procedures*

We have noted that an algebraic expression can be considered as a rule for evaluating a function, the constituent variables in the expression being the arguments of the function. More generally, the same is true of any ALGOL 60 program if we single out one of the variables to which the program assigns a value as being the value of the function. ALGOL 60 provides for the definition of a function in this way, giving it a name and indicating the variables concerned, and for using its name (followed by a parenthesized list of expressions to be used as its arguments) as a constituent of algebraic expressions elsewhere, i.e. as a 'function designator'. A notation is also provided for defining as a 'procedure' any ALGOL 60 program even when its effect is not simply the assignment of a value to a single variable. In this case the procedure name (followed by a parenthesized argument list as before) appears not as part of an algebraic expression but as a statement—a 'procedure statement'—in the program. Both functions and procedures are introduced and defined by *procedure declarations* which comprise the defining block of program or statement (the 'procedure body') prefixed by the symbol **procedure**, the name of the procedure (any identifier), and details regarding which identifiers in it are to be treated as the arguments or 'parameters' and how they are to be used when the procedure is called. A type declaration in front of the symbol **procedure** indicates that a function is being defined and gives the type of its value.

For example the procedure declaration

$$\textbf{real procedure } sumsq \ (P, \ Q, \ R, \ S);$$
$$sumsq := P^2 + Q^2 + R^2 + S^2$$

might be used to define the function designator appearing in a statement such as

$$y := T^2 + sumsq \ (a - m, \ b - m, \ c - m, \ d - m)/3.$$

When this statement is executed the effect is as if *sumsq* represented a simple variable to which a value was first assigned by *substituting* the 'actual parameters' $a - m, b - m, c - m, d - m$ respectively for the 'formal parameters' $P, Q, R, S$ in the procedure body and then executing the resulting assignment statement. $T^2 + sumsq/3$ is then calculated and its value assigned to $y$.

It should be noted that the letters $P, Q, R, S$ (in general any identifiers) bear no relation to other identifiers outside the procedure body and do not represent 'variables'—they are used simply to mark positions for substitution in the procedure body, and for this reason are called 'formal parameters'.

A simple example of a procedure statement is

$$TEST \ (b^2 - 4 \times a \times c, L1, L2, L3)$$

which might be used as a three-way discrimination using current values of variables $a, b, c$ to continue the program at statements labelled $L1, L2$ or $L3$ according as $b^2 - 4 \times a \times c$ is positive zero or negative. The procedure declaration defining *TEST* (which must appear in the head of a block in which the above statement appears) could be as follows:

$$\textbf{procedure } TEST \ (a, P, Z, N); \textbf{ if } a > 0 \textbf{ then go to } P \textbf{ else if}$$
$$a = 0 \textbf{ then go to } Z \textbf{ else go to } N.$$

This illustrates also a simple form of conditional statement. If $B$ represents some condition which may or may not be currently satisfied, and $S, T$ represent statements, the effect of

$$\textbf{if } B \textbf{ then } S \textbf{ else } T$$

is the same as that of $S$ if $B$ holds, and is the same as that of $T$ if $B$ does not hold. The statement

$$\textbf{if } B \textbf{ then } S$$

has no effect (is skipped) if $B$ does not hold.

## 8. *Standard Functions*

It is recommended in the Report that the following identifiers should be reserved for standard functions which may be available with a particular translator without explicit declaration, through the use of a library of subroutines. $x$ denotes the current value of the expression $E$.

| | |
|---|---|
| *abs* $(E)$ | the modulus (absolute value) of $x$ |
| *sign* $(E)$ | $\left. \begin{array}{l} +\ 1 \text{ if } x > 0 \\ \phantom{+\ }0 \text{ if } x = 0 \\ -\ 1 \text{ if } x < 0 \end{array} \right\}$ of type **integer** |
| *entier* $(E)$ | the integral part of $x$ (largest integer not greater than $x$), of type **integer** |
| *sqrt* $(E)$ | square root of $x$ |
| *sin* $(E)$ | sine of $x$ |
| *cos* $(E)$ | cosine of $x$ |
| *arctan* $(E)$ | principal value of arctangent of $x$ |
| *ln* $(E)$ | natural logarithm of $x$ |
| *exp* $(E)$ | exponential function of $x$. |

## 9. *Input and Output*

The input of data and the output of results have been excluded from detailed consideration in the reference language, but it is intended that suitable procedures be available with individual translators which will perform these functions. These procedures would be referred to by name in the ALGOL program and might require as parameters information concerning the layout of data on the external medium, i.e. information not expressible in the language. For this purpose arbitrary strings of ALGOL 60 symbols may be entered as actual parameters of procedures through the use of two special 'string quotes' symbols, and the body of a procedure declaration may be expressed in machine code while the heading remains expressed in ALGOL 60 for reference.

### 2. Examples

Before indicating the full generality of the various categories of symbolism provided in ALGOL 60 we give first some elementary examples.

*1.* The following procedure declaration defines *max* $(a, n)$ as the function whose arguments are a vector (one-dimensional array) $a$ of $n$ elements, and the integer $n$, and whose value is the modulus of the largest component of the vector.

```
    real procedure max (a, n);
L1: begin real m; m := 0; L2: for i := 1 step 1 until n do
L3: begin real x; x := aᵢ; if x < 0 then x := − x; if x > m then m :=
        x end;
L4: max := m end.
```

This illustrates a simple kind of 'for' statement—the statement labelled $L2$

causes the statement $L3$ to be executed $n$ times with $i$ taking the values 1, 2, ... $n$ in turn, before proceeding to statement $L4$. The labels are superfluous in this case since no *go to* statement is used.

It is worth noting that one cannot eliminate $m$ and write the procedure body simply as

$L1$: **begin** *max* $:= 0$; $L2$: **for** $i := 1$ **step** 1 **until** $n$ **do**
$L3$: **begin real** $x$; $x := a_i$; **if** $x < 0$ **then** $x := -x$; **if** $x > max$ **then**
     $max := x$ **end end**

because wherever the identifier *max* appears other than on the left of an assignment statement—in this case in the condition $(x > max)$—it calls into use the procedure *max* itself, which is not the intention here.

2. To illustrate the use of the above procedure declaration by a function designator in an algebraic expression, suppose we have a matrix $B$ of $r$ rows and $c$ columns and we wish to normalize its rows to have largest elements unity (where the rows have at least one non-zero element). We could write:

**for** $i := 1$ **step** 1 **until** $r$ **do**
1: **begin array** $a[1 : c]$; **for** $j := 1$ **step** 1 **until** $c$ **do** $a_j := B_{i,j}$;
   **for** $j := 1$ **step** 1 **until** $c$ **do**
   **if** $max\,(a, c) \neq 0$ **then** $B_{i,j} := B_{i,j}/max\,(a, c)$ **end**.

Here an array $a$ local to the block labelled 1 has been introduced and a copy of the current $i$th row of $B$ assigned to it simply in order to have a one-dimensional array to use as actual parameter of *max*. $a$ is defined by the array declaration **array** $a[1 : c]$ as being one-dimensional with suffix values ranging from 1 to $c$, and because no 'type' is indicated, the type **real** is understood (a special convention for array declarations). $B$ could have been introduced by a declaration of the form

**array** $B\,[1 : r, 1 : c]$.

3. The following example from the ALGOL 60 report illustrates a more general form of the heading of a procedure declaration.

**procedure** *Innerproduct* $(a, b)$ *order:* $(k, p)$ *Result:* $(y)$;
**value** $k$;
**integer** $k, p$; **real** $y, a, b$;
**begin real** $s$; $s := 0$;
**for** $p := 1$ **step** 1 **until** $k$ **do** $s := s + a \times b$;
$y := s$ **end** *Innerproduct*

The formal parameters of this procedure are $a, b, k, p, y$, and could have simply been listed between a single pair of parentheses in the first line. The convention used here is that any separating comma ('parameter delimiter') may be replaced without effect on the program by a string of letters followed by a colon and enclosed between reversed parentheses thus

$)$ *order:* $($

By this means the various parameters may more easily be recognized by the reader.

The last line illustrates a similar convention that the symbol **end** may be followed, without effect, by any sequence of symbols not containing **end** or **else** or a semicolon.

The second line of the declaration is known as the 'value part,' and has been absent from the examples given earlier. It indicates those parameters which are to be 'called by value' rather than 'called by name' as hitherto. This means that at a procedure call these formal parameters in the procedure body are *not* to be replaced by the actual parameters but are to be treated in the execution of the procedure as if they were identifiers local to the procedure body, representing variables or arrays to which were initially assigned the current values of the actual parameter expressions.

The third line of the declaration is called the 'specification part' and provides in general information concerning the kinds and types of admissible actual parameters.

In this example the 'running variable' $p$ of the 'for' statement has deliberately been made one of the parameters so that it may also appear as a suffix in the actual parameter expressions substituted for $a$ and $b$. Thus a particular procedure statement employing this procedure to form the inner product of a vector $B$ of order 10 and a vector defined by fixing the first and third suffix of a three-dimensional array $A$ might be

$$Innerproduct\ (A\ [t, P, u],\ B[P],\ 10,\ P,\ Y)$$

Of course the procedure could also be abused (presumably successfully) by writing $Innerproduct\ (C, D, n, i, E)$ to have the same effect as

$$E := n \times C \times D$$

in which $C$, $D$ and $n$ are simple variables, the last a positive integer.

By omitting the parameter $y$, replacing the last assignment statement by $Innerproduct := s$, and preceding the symbol **procedure** by **real** this procedure declaration would be changed into a definition of $Innerproduct$ as a function designator.

### 3. Syntax

In order to describe precisely what combinations of symbols are meaningful in ALGOL 60, a special notation is used which is best explained by an example. Given that the symbol ⟨letter⟩ names any one of the fifty-two lower or upper case Latin letters, and that ⟨digit⟩ names any one of 0, 1, ... 9, we can define the name ⟨identifier⟩ by the formula

$$⟨identifier⟩ ::= ⟨letter⟩ \mid ⟨identifier⟩ ⟨letter⟩ \mid ⟨identifier⟩ ⟨digit⟩$$

in which the vertical strokes may be read 'or'. This is to be read as saying that an identifier is either a letter or is an identifier followed by a letter or is an identifier followed by a digit. It defines the notion of identifier recursively. Thus $V23a$ is an identifier because $V23$ is one, $V23$ because $V2$ is, and $V2$

because the single letter $V$ is. This corresponds with the verbal definition in Section 1.2 above as 'a letter or a string of letters or decimal digits of which the first is a letter'.

In general, the juxtaposition of names in these 'metalinguistic formulae' is used to name the juxtaposition of the sequences of symbols named, and any ALGOL 60 symbol appearing is used to name itself. Thus examples of sequences named by $+\langle\text{digit}\rangle \cdot \langle\text{digit}\rangle$ would be $+ 3\cdot7, + 0\cdot0, + 9\cdot9$.

In the next section the full extent of the more important means of expression in ALGOL 60 will become apparent.

## 4. Syntax of Expressions

### 1. Numbers

Constant numbers are expressed in ALGOL 60 in the decimal notation with sign, integral part, decimal point, fractional part, and finally a signed power of ten to be used as a scale factor. The exponent of 10 is brought down to the level of the text by using a special suffix symbol $_{10}$ for the radix, and this and various parts of the general form may be omitted when superfluous, e.g.

$$-1\cdot083_{10}-02, \quad \cdot7300, \quad +_{10}7.$$

The precise definition in several steps is as follows:

$\langle\text{unsigned integer}\rangle ::= \langle\text{digit}\rangle \mid \langle\text{unsigned integer}\rangle\langle\text{digit}\rangle$
$\langle\text{integer}\rangle ::= \langle\text{unsigned integer}\rangle \mid +\langle\text{unsigned integer}\rangle \mid$
    $-\langle\text{unsigned integer}\rangle$
$\langle\text{decimal fraction}\rangle ::= \cdot\langle\text{unsigned integer}\rangle$
$\langle\text{exponent part}\rangle ::= {}_{10}\langle\text{integer}\rangle$
$\langle\text{decimal number}\rangle ::= \langle\text{unsigned integer}\rangle \mid \langle\text{decimal fraction}\rangle \mid$
    $\langle\text{unsigned integer}\rangle\langle\text{decimal fraction}\rangle$
$\langle\text{unsigned number}\rangle ::= \langle\text{decimal number}\rangle \mid \langle\text{exponent part}\rangle \mid$
    $\langle\text{decimal number}\rangle\langle\text{exponent part}\rangle$
$\langle\text{number}\rangle ::= \langle\text{unsigned number}\rangle \mid +\langle\text{unsigned number}\rangle \mid$
    $-\langle\text{unsigned number}\rangle$

### 2. Variables

$\langle\text{simple variable}\rangle ::= \langle\text{identifier}\rangle$
$\langle\text{array identifier}\rangle ::= \langle\text{identifier}\rangle$

Although strictly speaking redundant, these definitions help to convey part of the meaning at the same time as the structure is defined.

$\langle\text{subscript list}\rangle ::= \langle\text{arithmetic expression}\rangle \mid \langle\text{subscript list}\rangle,$
    $\langle\text{arithmetic expression}\rangle$
$\langle\text{subscripted variable}\rangle ::= \langle\text{array identifier}\rangle [\langle\text{subscript list}\rangle]$
$\langle\text{variable}\rangle ::= \langle\text{simple variable}\rangle \mid \langle\text{subscripted variable}\rangle$

### 3. Function Designators

$\langle\text{actual parameter}\rangle ::= \langle\text{string}\rangle \mid \langle\text{expression}\rangle \mid \langle\text{array identifier}\rangle \mid$
    $\langle\text{switch identifier}\rangle \mid \langle\text{procedure identifier}\rangle$

Strings are not discussed in this article. Switches are defined under 4.7.

⟨letter string⟩ ::= ⟨letter⟩ | ⟨letter string⟩⟨letter⟩
⟨parameter delimiter⟩ ::=, | )⟨letter string⟩ : (
⟨actual parameter list⟩ ::= ⟨actual parameter⟩ | ⟨actual parameter list⟩
  ⟨parameter delimiter⟩⟨actual parameter⟩
⟨procedure identifier⟩ ::= ⟨identifier⟩
⟨function designator⟩ ::= ⟨procedure identifier⟩ |
  ⟨procedure identifier⟩(⟨actual parameter list⟩)

## 4. Simple Arithmetic Expressions

⟨adding operator⟩ ::= + | −
⟨multiplying operator⟩ ::= × | / | ÷
⟨primary⟩ ::= ⟨unsigned number⟩ | ⟨variable⟩ | ⟨function designator⟩ |
  (⟨arithmetic expression⟩)
⟨factor⟩ ::= ⟨primary⟩ | ⟨factor⟩ ↑ ⟨primary⟩
⟨term⟩ ::= ⟨factor⟩ | ⟨term⟩⟨multiplying operator⟩⟨factor⟩
⟨simple arithmetic expression⟩ ::= ⟨term⟩ | ⟨adding operator⟩⟨term⟩ |
  ⟨simple arithmetic expression⟩⟨adding operator⟩ ⟨term⟩

The operators $+$, $-$, $\times$ have the conventional meaning and yield expressions of type **integer** when both operands have type **integer**, otherwise **real**.

The operator $/$ denotes division, to be understood as a multiplication of the preceding term by the reciprocal of the following factor, the result having always type **real**.

The operator $\div$ also denotes division, but is restricted to operands of type **integer** and yields the integral part of the quotient, defined by

$$m \div n = sign\ (m/n) \times entier\ (abs\ (m/n))$$

The operator $\uparrow$ denotes exponentiation, the preceding factor being the base and the following 'primary' the exponent. If the exponent is a positive integer $i$ the result is a product of $i$ equal factors of the same type as the base, if a negative integer then the result is the reciprocal of such a product and of type **real**, or is undefined if the base is zero, while if the exponent is zero the result is unity of the same type as the base. If the exponent $r$ is of type **real** and the base $a$ is positive the result is $exp\ (r \times ln\ (a))$ of type **real**; if $a$ is zero the result is zero of type **real** for positive $r$, and otherwise is undefined.

The sequence of operations in evaluating an expression is from left to right subject to the usual use of parentheses and to the following rules of precedence between the operators, which are reflected in the syntax above:

first:         ↑
second:    × / ÷
third:        + −

## 5. Boolean Expressions

These are used chiefly to express conditions for use in conditional statements and, as introduced below, in conditional expressions. For these purposes a condition is essentially a two-valued thing, it either holds or does not hold, and one can manipulate conditions as two-valued variables by the algebra of logic, i.e. Boolean algebra, which is available as part of ALGOL 60. A variable may be declared to have type **Boolean**, and its value is then either **true** or **false** (these being basic symbols). Such a variable may be assigned the current value of a Boolean expression just as in ordinary arithmetic. A function designator may have type **Boolean**, and one can have a Boolean array.

The simplest conditions are relations of equality or inequality between arithmetic expressions. From any condition we can derive the reverse condition by preceding it by the logical negation sign $\neg$, and from any two conditions we can derive, by the logical operators $\wedge$ (and), $\vee$ (or), $\supset$ (implies) and $\equiv$ (equivalent), compound conditions expressing respectively that both hold, that at least one holds, that either the first does not hold or the second does or both, and that they either both hold or both do not hold.

For example:

**if** $(a > b + 1) \vee (a < b - 1)$ **then   go to** $L$.

This is equivalent to

**if** $\neg$ $abs\,(a - b) \leqslant 1$ **then   go to** $L$

and also to

$B := abs\,(a - b) \leqslant 1$; **if** $\neg$ $B$ **then   go to** $L$

which illustrates the 'calculation' of a condition.

The sequence of operations in evaluating a Boolean expression follows the rules for arithmetic expressions, with the rules of precedence extended thus:

4th: $<\ \leqslant\ =\ \geqslant\ >\ \neq$
5th: $\neg$
6th: $\wedge$
7th: $\vee$
8th: $\supset$
9th: $\equiv$

so the condition in the first example above could be written without parentheses as $a > b + 1 \vee a < b - 1$.

The syntax built up following this order of precedence is as follows:

⟨relational operator⟩ ::= $<\ |\ \leqslant\ |\ =\ |\ \geqslant\ |\ >\ |\ \neq$
⟨relation⟩ ::= ⟨arithmetic expression⟩⟨relational operator⟩⟨arithmetic expression⟩
⟨logical value⟩ ::= **true** | **false**
⟨Boolean primary⟩ ::= ⟨logical value⟩ | ⟨variable⟩ |
   ⟨function designator⟩ | ⟨relation⟩ | (⟨Boolean expression⟩)
⟨Boolean secondary⟩ ::= ⟨Boolean primary⟩ | $\neg$ ⟨Boolean primary⟩
⟨Boolean factor⟩ ::= ⟨Boolean secondary⟩ |
   ⟨Boolean factor⟩ $\wedge$ ⟨Boolean secondary⟩

⟨Boolean term⟩ ::= ⟨Boolean factor⟩ | ⟨Boolean term⟩∨⟨Boolean factor⟩
⟨implication⟩ ::= ⟨Boolean term⟩ | ⟨implication⟩ ⊃ ⟨Boolean term⟩
⟨simple Boolean⟩ ::= ⟨implication⟩ | ⟨simple Boolean⟩ ≡ ⟨implication⟩

## 6. Conditional Expressions

These provide a method (due to J. McCarthy) for selecting one of a sequence of expressions $E_1$, $E_2$, . . . according to the current values of a corresponding sequence of conditions (Boolean expressions) $B_1$, $B_2$, . . . If $B_k$ is the first condition to hold, i.e. to have the value **true,** then the value of the following conditional arithmetic expression is that of $E_k$, regardless of whether or not $B_{k+1}$, $B_{k+2}$, . . . , or $E_{k+1}$, $E_{k+2}$, . . . are even defined.

**if** $B_1$ **then** $E_1$ **else if** $B_2$ **then** $E_2$ **else** . . . **else** $E_n$

In particular $E_1$, $E_2$, . . . may themselves be Boolean expressions.

This enables us to complete the syntax of arithmetic and Boolean expressions as follows:

⟨if clause⟩ ::= **if** ⟨Boolean expression⟩ **then**
⟨Boolean expression⟩ ::= ⟨simple Boolean⟩ |
   ⟨if clause⟩ ⟨simple Boolean⟩ **else** ⟨Boolean expression⟩
⟨arithmetic expression⟩ ::= ⟨simple arithmetic expression⟩ | ⟨if clause⟩
   ⟨simple arithmetic expression⟩ **else** ⟨arithmetic expression⟩

Discontinuous functions are naturally expressed as conditional expressions.

For example

*sign* $(E)$ is equivalent to

**if** $E > 0$ **then** 1 **else if** $E = 0$ **then** 0 **else** $- 1$

and *abs* $(E)$ is equivalent to

**if** $E < 0$ **then** $- E$ **else** $E$

## 7. Switches, Designational Expressions

Just as an arithmetic expression is a rule for obtaining a numerical value, so a designational expression is a rule for obtaining a designation of a statement, i.e. a label. The only such expression so far introduced is simply a label itself, but we now provide a notation—the 'switch'—for using any arithmetic expression whose value is a positive integer to select one from a list of labels (or again in general designational expressions). This is in some ways analogous to a one dimensional array. Whereas an array declaration merely specifies size, shape and type of values, a *switch declaration* actually exhibits the list of values. The designational expression whose value is the $k$th label in this list is written like a suffixed variable with $k$ as suffix and the switch identifier as identifier.

For example, if the switch $S$ were defined by the declaration

**switch** $S := L, P, 4, L$

then the 'switch designators' $S[1]$ and $S[4]$ and $S[3 + 1 \uparrow 1]$ have each as value the label $L$. These may themselves appear in *go to* statements within the block to which the switch declaration is attached, or as entries in other switch declarations.

Finally, one can have conditional designational expressions just as in the case of arithmetic and Boolean expressions, and the full syntax is as follows:

⟨label⟩ ::= ⟨identifier⟩ | ⟨unsigned integer⟩
⟨switch identifier⟩ ::= ⟨identifier⟩
⟨switch designator⟩ ::= ⟨switch identifier⟩[⟨arithmetic expression⟩]
⟨simple designational expression⟩ ::= ⟨label⟩ | ⟨switch designator⟩ |
   (⟨designational expression⟩)
⟨designational expression⟩ ::= ⟨simple designational expression⟩ |
   ⟨if clause⟩ ⟨simple designational expression⟩ **else** ⟨designational expression⟩ |
   sion⟩ |
⟨expression⟩ ::= ⟨arithmetic expression⟩ | ⟨Boolean expression⟩ |
   ⟨designational expression⟩

## 5. Syntax of Statements

### *1. Assignment Statements*

The only new point here is the provision for simultaneous assignments such as

$$a[b[1,\ 1]] := x := b[1,\ 1] := 3 \times x$$

which assigns the current value of $3 \times x$ to a certain element of the one-dimensional array $a$ (depending on the current value of $b_{1,1}$), to $x$ itself, and then to $b_{1,1}$. (All variables here must be integers.)

If the expression assigned is $E$ of type **real**, the variables may be of type **integer** and then the value assigned to them is that of *entier* $(E + 0 \cdot 5)$.

⟨left part⟩ ::= ⟨variable⟩ :=
⟨left part list⟩ ::= ⟨left part⟩ | ⟨left part list⟩⟨left part⟩
⟨assignment statement⟩ ::= ⟨left part list⟩ ⟨arithmetic expression⟩|
   ⟨left part list⟩ ⟨Boolean expression⟩

### *2. Go to Statements*

⟨go to statement⟩ ::= **go to** ⟨designational expression⟩

### *3. Dummy Statements*

⟨dummy statement⟩ ::= ⟨empty⟩
⟨empty⟩ names the 'empty' sequence of symbols.

A dummy statement is simply a blank—nothing is written. Its only purpose is to place a label. A *go to* statement which is simply to lead out of a compound statement to the following one can refer to a labelled dummy statement before the **end**, thus:

**begin** . . .; **if** $x < 0$ **then go to** $END$; . . .; $END$: **end**.

## 4. *Procedure Statements*

These are syntactically identical with function designators (4.3 above) but are used as statements instead of as expressions.

⟨procedure statement⟩ ::= ⟨procedure identifier⟩ | ⟨procedure identifier⟩
(⟨actual parameter list⟩)

The actual parameter list might be absent, e.g. in the case of a procedure which simply sounded an alarm; the procedure itself would then be in machine code.

## 5. **For** *Statements*

A "for clause" causes the statement $S$ which it precedes to be executed zero or more times, and performs an assignment of a value to a 'controlled variable' $V$ immediately before each execution. The 'for list' defines these consecutively assigned values. An element of this list which is an arithmetic expression causes the assignment of its current value to $V$ and a single execution of $S$. An element of the form $A$**step**$B$**until**$C$ where $A$, $B$, $C$ are arithmetic expressions causes the assignment of the current values of $A$, $A + B$, $A + 2B$, ... to $V$ and corresponding execution of $S$, the operation terminating as soon as $V - C$ has the same sign as $B$ (this test being made just prior to each execution, so that $S$ is never executed if initially $A - C$ and $B$ have equal signs). An element of the form $E$**while**$F$ where $E$ is an arithmetic expression and $F$ a Boolean expression causes the assignment of the current value of $E$ prior to each execution, this being repeated until the current value of $F$ is **false**, the test being made prior to each execution as above. This additional facility enables the number of times a loop is executed to be made to depend on the results of calculation without the necessity of writing a special test instruction.

If $S$ is left by a *go to* statement, interrupting the execution of the *for* statement, the then current value of $V$ continues to be available outside; otherwise $V$ is treated as local to the *for* statement.

⟨for list element⟩ ::= ⟨arithmetic expression⟩ | ⟨arithmetic expression⟩
**step** ⟨arithmetic expression⟩ **until** ⟨arithmetic expression⟩ |
⟨arithmetic expression⟩ **while** ⟨Boolean expression⟩
⟨for list⟩ ::= ⟨for list element⟩ | ⟨for list⟩, ⟨for list element⟩
⟨for clause⟩ ::= **for** ⟨variable⟩ := ⟨for list⟩ **do**
⟨for statement⟩ ::= ⟨for clause⟩ ⟨statement⟩ | ⟨label⟩: ⟨for statement⟩

The last definition shows that *for* statements may be repeatedly labelled. This is true of all kinds of statement, as will be seen.

## 6. *Conditional Statements, Compound Statements, Blocks*

The following completes the syntax of statements:

⟨basic statement⟩ ::= ⟨assignment statement⟩ | ⟨go to statement⟩ |
⟨dummy statement⟩ | ⟨procedure statement⟩ | ⟨label⟩ : ⟨basic statement⟩

⟨unconditional statement⟩ ::= ⟨basic statement⟩ | ⟨for statement⟩ | ⟨compound statement⟩ | ⟨block⟩
⟨if statement⟩ ::= ⟨if clause⟩ ⟨unconditional statement⟩ | ⟨label⟩ : ⟨if statement⟩
⟨conditional statement⟩ ::= ⟨if statement⟩ | ⟨if statement⟩ **else** ⟨statement⟩
⟨statement⟩ ::= ⟨unconditional statement⟩ | ⟨conditional statement⟩
⟨compound tail⟩ ::= ⟨statement⟩ **end** | ⟨statement⟩; ⟨compound tail⟩
⟨compound statement⟩ ::= **begin** ⟨compound tail⟩ | ⟨label⟩ : ⟨compound statement⟩
⟨block head⟩ ::= **begin** ⟨declaration⟩ | ⟨block head⟩; ⟨declaration⟩
⟨block⟩ ::= ⟨block head⟩; ⟨compound tail⟩ | ⟨label⟩ : ⟨block⟩

## 6. Syntax of Declarations

⟨declaration⟩ ::= ⟨type declaration⟩ | ⟨array declaration⟩ | ⟨switch declaration⟩ | ⟨procedure declaration⟩

### 1. Type Declarations

⟨type list⟩ ::= ⟨simple variable⟩ | ⟨simple variable⟩, ⟨type list⟩
⟨type⟩ ::= **real** | **integer** | **Boolean**
⟨local or own type⟩ ::= ⟨type⟩ | **own** ⟨type⟩
⟨type declaration⟩ ::= ⟨local or own type⟩ ⟨type list⟩

### 2. Array Declarations

⟨lower bound⟩ ::= ⟨arithmetic expression⟩
⟨upper bound⟩ ::= ⟨arithmetic expression⟩
⟨bound pair⟩ ::= ⟨lower bound⟩ : ⟨upper bound⟩
⟨bound pair list⟩ ::= ⟨bound pair⟩ | ⟨bound pair list⟩, ⟨bound pair⟩
⟨array segment⟩ ::= ⟨array identifier⟩[⟨bound pair list⟩] | ⟨array identifier⟩, ⟨array segment⟩
⟨array list⟩ ::= ⟨array segment⟩ | ⟨array list⟩, ⟨array segment⟩
⟨array declaration⟩ ::= **array** ⟨array list⟩ | ⟨local or own type⟩ **array** ⟨array list⟩

### Examples

**array**$a,b,c[7:n,2:m],s,u[-2 \times r:10]$

declares three matrices $a$, $b$, $c$ and two vectors $s$ and $u$.

**own Boolean array** $peter3[1 + (\text{if } n \geqslant 0 \text{ then } n \text{ else } 0):20]$

declares a vector called $peter3$ with elements each either **true** or **false**, the definition of the lower bound of its suffix involving a conditional arithmetic expression.

### 3. Switch Declarations

⟨switch list⟩ ::= ⟨designational expression⟩ | ⟨switch list⟩, ⟨designational expression⟩
⟨switch declaration⟩ ::= **switch** ⟨switch identifier⟩ := ⟨switch list⟩

## 4. *Procedure Declarations*

⟨formal parameter⟩ ::= ⟨identifier⟩
⟨formal parameter list⟩ ::= ⟨formal parameter⟩ | ⟨formal parameter list⟩ ⟨parameter delimiter⟩ ⟨formal parameter⟩
⟨formal parameter part⟩ ::= ⟨empty⟩ | (⟨formal parameter list⟩)
⟨identifier list⟩ ::= ⟨identifier⟩ | ⟨identifier list⟩, ⟨identifier⟩
⟨value part⟩ ::= ⟨empty⟩ | **value** ⟨identifier list⟩;
⟨specifier⟩ ::= **string** | ⟨type⟩ | **array** | ⟨type⟩ **array** | **label** | **switch** | **procedure** | ⟨type⟩ **procedure**
⟨specification part⟩ ::= ⟨empty⟩ | ⟨specifier⟩ ⟨identifier list⟩; | ⟨specification part⟩ ⟨specifier⟩ ⟨identifier list⟩;
⟨procedure heading⟩ ::= ⟨procedure identifier⟩ ⟨formal parameter part⟩; ⟨value part⟩ ⟨specification part⟩
⟨procedure body⟩ ::= ⟨statement⟩ | ⟨code⟩
⟨procedure declaration⟩ ::= **procedure** ⟨procedure heading⟩ ⟨procedure body⟩ | ⟨type⟩ **procedure** ⟨procedure heading⟩ ⟨procedure body⟩

### 7. Classification of Basic Symbols

As stated earlier the Reference language embraces 116 basic symbols.

⟨basic symbol⟩ ::= ⟨letter⟩ | ⟨digit⟩ | ⟨logical value⟩ | ⟨delimiter⟩
⟨delimiter⟩ ::= ⟨operator⟩ | ⟨separator⟩ | ⟨bracket⟩ | ⟨declarator⟩ | ⟨specificator⟩
⟨operator⟩ ::= ⟨arithmetic operator⟩ | ⟨relational operator⟩ | ⟨logical operator⟩ | ⟨sequential operator⟩
⟨arithmetic operator⟩ ::= $+$ | $-$ | $\times$ | $/$ | $\div$ | $\uparrow$
⟨logical operator⟩ ::= $\equiv$ | $\supset$ | $\vee$ | $\wedge$ | $\neg$
⟨sequential operator⟩ ::= **go to** | **if** | **then** | **else** | **for** | **do**
⟨separator⟩ ::= , | . | $_{10}$ | : | ; | := | ⊔ | **step** | **until** | **while** | **comment**
⟨bracket⟩ ::= ( | ) | [ | ] | ' | ' | **begin** | **end**
⟨declarator⟩ ::= **own** | **Boolean** | **integer** | **real** | **array** | **switch** | **procedure**
⟨specificator⟩ ::= **string** | **label** | **value**

The separator ⊔ denoting a space and the brackets ' and ' are used in forming strings used as parameters of procedures. The separator **comment** is used to introduce explanatory text in an ALGOL 60 program without affecting the meaning of the program; the convention is used that

; **comment** ⟨any sequence of basic symbols not containing a semicolon⟩;
is equivalent to a single semicolon.

### 8. Example

**procedure** *Bisection(F)initial*: (*x*1,*d*1)*precision*: (*d*0) *result bounds*: (*xP,xL*);
   **comment** *Finds bounds xP and xL (with difference less than d0) for a zero of the function F(x) at which its derivative is positive. Evaluates F(x) at x1, x1 + d1 and then at equispaced values of x until the zero is passed (indicated by b =* **true**) *when it is located by the method of repeated bisection, xP being the final*

*value and xL the previous value the other side of the zero*; **value** $d0$; **real** $xL$, $xP$;
**real procedure** $F$; **begin Boolean** $a$, $b$, $c$; **real** $x$, $d$;

> $a := b :=$ **false**; $x := x1$; $d := d1$;
> $A : c := sign(F(x)) = sign(d)$;
> $b := c \wedge a \vee b$;
> **if** $c \wedge a$ **then** $xL := x - d$;
> $a :=$ **true**;
> **if** $b$ **then** $d := d/2$;
> **if** $c$ **then** $d := - d$;
> **if** $abs(d) \geqslant d0$ **then begin** $x := x + d$; **go to** $A$ **end**;
> $xP := x$ **end** *Bisection*

This process has been used for non-linear eigenvalue problems in which the largest part of the calculation is the evaluation of the function $F(x)$, and this function involves empirical data so that its derivative is not available. The Boolean variable $a$ is used to distinguish the first passage through the sequence of instructions (when it has the value **false**). The formula for the Boolean variable $b$ is equivalent to $b := (c \wedge a) \vee b$ by the precedence rules for the logical operators. This shows that once $b$ has been assigned the value **true** it will 'stick' at that value—indicating that the required zero of $F(x)$ has been 'bracketed'. The part $c \wedge a$ ensures that this will not happen on the first step (when insufficient information is available for this decision). $c =$ **true** indicates (when $a$ is **true**) that addition of $d$ to $x$ will move it farther from the required zero, i.e. that the sign of $d$ is to be changed.

## Acknowledgement

This article is published with the permission of the Director of the National Physical Laboratory.

## REFERENCES

1. P. NAUR (Ed.) (1960). Report on the Algorithmic Language ALGOL 60. *Comm. A.C.M.* **3**, 299-314, and *Numerische Mathematik* **2**, 106-136.
2. P. NAUR (Ed.) (1963). Revised report on the Algorithmic Language ALGOL 60. *Computer J.* **5**, 4, 349-367.

# 5. INTERMEDIATE LANGUAGES AND PROGRAMMING SYSTEMS

P. WEGNER

*London School of Economics and Political Science, London, England*

## 1. Introduction

This chapter is concerned with intermediate languages and with programming systems. These two topics appear to be unconnected, and indeed their subject matter is quite different. The connection between the two topics is one of philosophy rather than one of subject matter. Thus, when the subject of automatic programming is approached from the point of view of information flow, the study of information flow during the process of translation leads to the concept of intermediate languages, and the study of information flow as successive problems are processed by the computer, leads to the idea of a programming system.

Of the two subjects, the programming system is the more fundamental one. The programming system approach is concerned with ironing out all bottle-necks in the use of the computer, taking into account all classes of users, operators, service engineers and any other conceivable person or circumstance that might impinge on the overall efficiency of computer operation. The overall efficiency is measured in terms of the total 'throughput' of problems through the computer.

The computer is regarded as a hydra-headed monster which accepts a number of streams of input information, performs computations, and produces a number of streams of output information. In the most general case input-output and computation can be overlapped, and the problem of efficient computer usage takes on the characteristics of the job-shop scheduling problem (i.e. the problem of performing, in minimum time, a number of jobs, each of which requires processing by each of a number of machines in a specified order). This problem will be considered in subsequent papers on time sharing. The problem considered here is the much simpler one of processing in strictly sequential order a single input stream consisting of a sequence of jobs.

The approach towards the design of a programming system developed here is essentially that embodied in the FORTRAN Monitor System, which is currently used more widely than any other programming system.

The basic unit processed by a programming system is called the job. The programming system is designed to facilitate processing of successive jobs by the computer.

Jobs normally consist of a program and the data upon which the program operates. The program is initially written in a problem-oriented source language such as FORTRAN, ALGOL or COBOL. When a given job is processed, the source language program must be translated into machine language before execution. In a simple minded programming system the processing of a single job would consist of two stages, called respectively the translation stage and the execution stage. The mode of operation of such a programming system is indicated in Fig. 1.

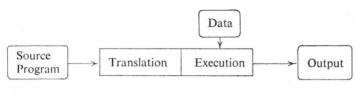

Fig. 1

The above mode of operation is convenient for small simple jobs. However, in the case of a large job, it is convenient to split a job into component parts (corresponding to subproblems of the problem which is being solved) and to program each component independently of other components. The technique of decomposing a complex problem into component subproblems and of specifying the solution of the complex problem in terms of the solution of its subproblems is probably the single most important technique in the armoury of the problem solver, and enables him to decrease by an exponential factor the amount of work required to obtain the solution. The importance of an analogous technique to facilitate the programming of complex problems cannot therefore be overestimated.

The components of a job which correspond to subproblems will here be called *routines*. Every program consists of one or more routines which specify the problem to be solved. For maximum independence of routines it is desirable that routines be programmed completely independently of each other even when intercommunication between the routines is involved. Furthermore, since the different parts of a given program might require different source languages for convenient programming, it is desirable that independently programmed routines in different source languages should be able to communicate with each other.

It is evident that the central problem of a programming system organized into routines is that of providing flexible means of intercommunication between routines while at the same time preserving complete independence at the programming stage. This is achieved by identifying those features of the language required for intercommunication between routines and distinguishing them from those features required for computation.

During translation of a routine those features required for intercommunication must be preserved since the intercommunication cannot be accomplished until all routines which intercommunicate with a given routine have also been translated. However those features that are independent of intercommunication can be translated independently of other routines. In general a routine corresponds to a well-defined subproblem, and its communication with the larger program is restricted both in the number of references and the kind of references. The bulk of a routine can therefore be translated independently of other routines.

The above approach to translation results in translation from the source language to a language which preserves untranslated those features of the source language required for communication. This language is called the intermediate language. The translation process therefore proceeds in two stages. The first, which involves translation from a source language to the intermediate language is called the translation stage. The program which performs the translations is called a compiler. The second, which involves translation from the intermediate language to the computer machine language, and setting up of communication links is called the loading stage. The corresponding translation program is called a loader.

A programming system which is organized along the above lines processes a job by first translating all source language routines to the intermediate language, then loading all routines required for execution of the given job, and finally initiating execution of the job.

When source language routines may be in one of a number of source languages, a translation program from each source language to the intermediate language must be available. However the resulting intermediate language routines will be indistinguishable from each other, except possibly for special information specifically designed to identify the original source language. The loader need not therefore concern itself with the original source language in which the routine is written, and loads all intermediate routines irrespective of race, creed, colour, country of origin or source language.

The translation process for the three source languages FORTRAN, ALGOL and COBOL is illustrated in Fig. 2.

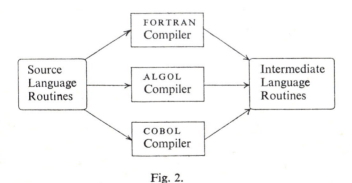

Fig. 2.

The loading and execution process is illustrated in Fig. 3. It is assumed that the loader loads intermediate language routines that have just been translated, previously translated routines available in a private program file, and library routines available in a library file.

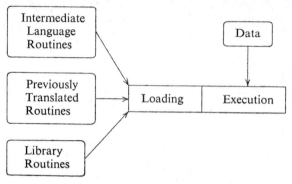

Fig. 3

## 2. Communication in the Intermediate Language

A routine which forms a component unit in the statement of a problem for computer solution, must communicate with its environment. The facilities for communication between routines are strongly reflected in the intermediate language, since they are the principal portions of the source language not translated during the translation stage.

The class of intermediate languages considered here inevitably makes some assumption about type of computer and organization of routines.

Assume that the computer has sequential memory structure, that routines form compact blocks in the memory, and that the number of memory locations for each constitutent within the routine is known at translation time. This permits relative addresses relative to the beginning of the routine to be assigned to all internal cross references.

Each routine may communicate with any other routine. In addition to routines, there are data blocks, which also form compact blocks in memory. Data blocks are characterized by the fact that they do not normally initiate references to other blocks, but are merely referred to. The communication between three routines $R1$, $R2$, $R3$, and two data blocks $D1$, $D2$ is illustrated in Fig. 4.

Communication between blocks will be of two principal kinds.

1. Reference to an item of information in another routine or in a data block. This form of communication will be characterized by the instruc-

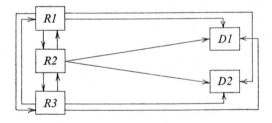

Fig. 4

tion '*FETCH A*' where *A* is the name of an item of information external to the routine.

Transfer of control to another routine. The form of communication will be characterized by the instruction *GO TO A*, where *A* is the name of an instruction sequence external to the routine.

In both cases *A* is a label attached to information external to the routine, and the value of *A* will eventually be the memory location in which the information is stored in the computer. However the value of *A* is not available at translation time, since it occurs at an arbitrary point in an independently programmed routine. Routines in the intermediate language therefore store references to external symbols in symbolic form, both in the program which uses the external reference and in the program in which it is defined. At load time the value of all uses of a symbol can be determined by matching with defined symbols.

Consider first the form of storage of external symbol *definitions*. For each symbol *defined* in a given routine and *used* externally, an indicator is required to indicate that the value of the symbol will be required during the loading stage by some other routine, and should therefore be retained in the intermediate language. Symbols defined in a given routine but used in another routine will be called 'public symbols'. The value of a public symbol may be specified as a relative memory location, relative to the beginning of the routine. Each routine will contain a symbol table of public symbols and their values in the intermediate language. Such a table has been called a 'definition table'.

Now consider the *use* of external symbols. The value of an external symbol cannot be determined at translation time. The symbol must therefore be retained in its symbolic form together with a note of all points in the routine in which it is used. For each external symbol of a routine there will therefore be an associated list of relative addresses specifying the uses of the symbol in that routine. This information is stored in a table called the 'use table' (*1*) (*2*). Figure 5 illustrates a definition table entry and a use table entry with three uses at the internal relative locations *R1, R2 and R3*.

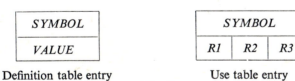

|   | Definition table entry |  | Use table entry |
|---|---|---|---|

Fig. 5

Every intermediate language routine contains a definition table, a use table, and a routine body, as illustrated in Fig. 6.

During the loading process all entries in the definition table are accumulated by the loader into a single symbol table, called the 'loader symbol table'. Since all external symbols must be defined in some routine available to the loader, the loader symbol table should contain all symbols occurring in the use table of any routine. The value of each symbolic entry in the use table can

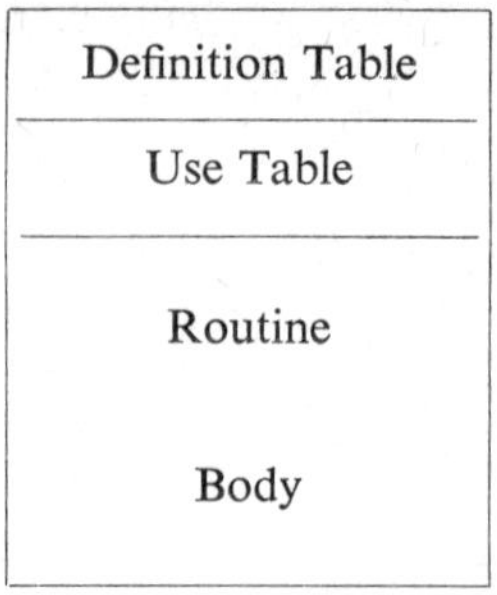

| |
|---|
| Definition Table |
| Use Table |
| Routine |
| Body |

Fig. 6

therefore be found by table look up in the loader symbol table, and can be substituted for all its occurrences in the routine body.

The process described above permits data cross references and external transfers of control to be dealt with adequately in principle. However, the use table is clumsy in format, requiring an entry for every use of an external symbol in the routine. The subsequent physical substitution of a value for each symbol during the loading stage is also unaesthetic.

Multiple substitutions at load time for a given external symbol can be avoided by channelling all references to a given external symbol through a single location in a special communication region of the routine. Direct substitution at load time of the value of the external symbol for all its occurrences, can be replaced by a single substitution of the symbol in the communication region, and indirect reference through the communication region whenever the symbol is used. The use of a communication region for references to external symbols is illustrated in Fig. 7. Indirect address reference is indicated by a * following the operation code.

The communication region technique outlined above has been adopted for FORTRAN routines on the 7090. The communication region is called the transfer vector. During translation, the external symbol is stored directly in the transfer vector location, and all references to the external symbol are replaced by indirect references to the transfer vector location. At load time all symbols in the transfer vector are replaced by their values, by means of table look-up in the loader symbol table.

Although the communication region scheme permits greater economy at load time, than direct substitution, it still requires more substitutions than necessary when a given public symbol is used in more than a single routine. In this case the communication region technique requires substitution of the value of the public symbol in the communication region of each of the routines which use the symbol. Multiple substitution in communication regions can be avoided by introducing a global communication region for all routines, and channelling all external cross references through the global communication region.

This approach has been adopted in the GENIE system, where the global communication region is called the value table. The value table contains

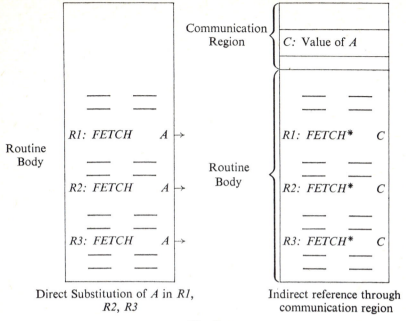

Fig. 7

the symbolic names of all public symbols, and a location in which the value of each symbol can be inserted. All references to a public symbol are channelled through a single location in the value table.

The value table technique involves two stage indirect addressing for external symbol references, the first through local communication regions and the second through a global value table. Every entry in the value table is the potential root of a tree whose nodes of depth 1 are entries in local communication regions and whose end points (of depth 2) are the points in the routine body at which the external symbol is used. A value table entry used in each of two routines at each of three different points is illustrated in Fig. 8.

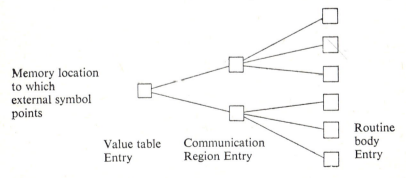

Fig. 8

The value table technique does not reduce the number of load time substitutions. Links in each communication region to the value table must be set up at load time as before, since the number of entries in the value table, and therefore their location, can only be determined at load time. However once the links from local communication regions to the value table have been set up, any change in the value of a public symbol can be accomplished by a single substitution in the value table. Thus if the set of locations in which a routine operates must be changed during the run, then an adjustment of values in the value table of public symbols defined in that routine will permit the program to run in its new configuration.

More generally, indirect addressing structures in the intermediate language which tie a large number of references to a given parameter or quantity to a single occurrence of its value, permit an effective change of value of all references to be accomplished merely by changing the single quantity. Indirect addressing structure effectively superimposes a programmed memory structure on the sequential memory of the computer.

The above discussion indicates some of the considerations in designing an intermediate language that permits more flexible intercommunication between routines. The requirements of the source language to permit communication in the intermediate language will now briefly be considered. These are principally of two kinds.

1. The source language should indicate which symbols defined within a routine are external, so that a definition table can be constructed. In principle a symbol table of all symbols in the routine could be retained in the intermediate language. This is in fact done when subsequent source language debugging of the routine is required. However for purposes of communication, the loader has to load all symbol tables of all routines at load time. If each symbol table contained internal as well as external symbols, the composite symbol table from all routines would be unduly long, perhaps exceeding the total available memory space. The search time to set the communication links would also be longer than necessary.

2. The source language should indicate which symbols used within a routine are defined outside the routine. This is not strictly necessary since all undefined symbols within a routine can be assumed to be defined elsewhere. However, explicit specification permits external symbols to be distinguished from symbols undefined due to an error on the part of the programmer.

Source language facilities for the specification of external symbols will now be indicated in the case of FORTRAN and FAP.

In FORTRAN the only kind of symbolic cross reference between routines is that of subroutine calling. A *SUBROUTINE* statement automatically indicates that the corresponding subroutine name is defined outside the subroutine. A *CALL* statement automatically implies that the name of the subroutine called is an externally defined symbol, and a place for this symbol is reserved in the communication region of the routine.

Thus the statement

SUBROUTINE ADD(A, N, SUM)

specifies incidentally that the symbol ADD will be used externally and should be entered in the definition table. The statement

CALL ADD(A, N, SUM)

specifies incidentaily that the symbol ADD is defined outside the routine in which the statement occurs. A location in the communication region (transfer vector) is therefore reserved for this symbol.

It should be noted that in the case of this subroutine call, the single symbolic cross reference ADD permits the names or values of the three parameters A, N, SUM to be transmitted between the two routines. These parameters are specified by FORTRAN in locations that are fixed relative to the point of symbolic cross reference, i.e. A is specified in the first location relative to the instruction transferring control to the ADD routine, and N and SUM are specified in the 2nd and 3rd relative locations. Since the subroutine ADD will have available to it the address of the instruction from which it was called, it has access to information specified relative to the point of call. In general, a single symbolic cross reference can transmit an arbitrary amount of auxiliary information specified relative to the point of symbolic cross reference.

In FAP public symbols are defined by the declaration (control operation)

ENTRY.

Thus the control operation

ENTRY A

indicates to the translation program that the symbol A defined in the current routine is used in some other routine and should therefore be entered into the use table.

Externally defined symbols are indicated by the marker $. Thus

CLA∗ $A (Clear and Add indirect)

indicates that the symbol A is defined externally, and gives rise to an indirect address reference to a location in the communication region.

### 3. ALGOL Blocks and Procedures

In the ALGOL source language the nearest concept to that of the routine is that of the block or procedure. The units of program which correspond to subproblems are procedures, and for many purposes procedures can be programmed autonomously. However, ALGOL procedures do not possess the same degree of independence of each other as routines of the type discussed above.

The context of an ALGOL block or procedure is determined by the context in which it is physically embedded. Every symbol in ALGOL is introduced by means of a declaration, which defines the range of program over which it can be used. A symbol which is declared within a given block or procedure has no meaning outside that block. Thus use of a symbol external to a block in which it is declared is not possible. If a symbol is to be used for purposes of communication between blocks it must be declared in a block that textually encloses all blocks that use the symbol. The requirement of physical insertion of a block into an outer block for purposes of communication with other blocks is a real impediment to truly independent manipulation of blocks.

The fact that there are no global symbols permits the compiler writer to do away with value tables and communication regions. The structure of the source language encourages implementers to translate ALGOL programs all in one piece directly to machine language, setting up all possible communication links at translation time and providing a mechanism for allocating storage during execution to information which requires dynamic storage allocation. Alternatively, a number of ALGOL implementers have implemented partial translation to an intermediate language that is subsequently obeyed interpretively. In this case the nested structure of ALGOL blocks permits all communication to be performed by indirect address chains within a stack. Every block while it is executed uses the next available area in the stack, which contains link information (i.e. the stack location of the block from which it was called, the stack location of the physically enclosing block, the return address and other information), information about formal parameters, and a stack that is used for working storage. In this interpretive mode the stack is effectively a communication region both for linkage between blocks currently being executed and for the data being processed. When a block has been processed it is removed from the stack. Linkage is set up afresh every time the block is executed.

The strictly nested block structure of ALGOL gives rise to certain economies in implementation and execution since, in the absence of global symbols, an explicit global symbol table can be dispensed with. However, this is achieved at the price of inflexibility in program segmentation. Furthermore the writing of an ALGOL subprogram which is a routine in a program containing other source languages is inconceivable with the present structure of ALGOL.

Global symbols and independent routines could be introduced relatively painlessly by introducing a declaration *common* for common (global) data, by introducing the declarations *public* and *external* for definition and use within a routine of global symbols, and by introducing a declaration *routine* analogous to the declaration *procedure* which would permit use of global symbol declarations and global symbols. The introduction of the declaration *routine* would permit the declaration *procedure* to be used in its previous sense so that compatibility would not be destroyed. Routines introduced by a *routine* declaration would be translated independently of each other into an intermediate language similar to that of Section 2. Library subroutines would normally be introduced by a *routine* declaration, thus providing a technique within ALGOL of defining reserved symbols.

## 4. Programming Systems

The design of a programming system is strongly affected by the approach adopted to the design of the intermediate language. In the case of a large system designed to handle complex sequences of operations segmentation is virtually imperative. Segmentation of a program into physical blocks can be accomplished by hardware as in the case of Atlas. Logical segmentation can also be helped considerably by hardware such as indirect address facilities, stacks etc.

The class of programming systems considered here accept as input a sequence of jobs stacked on a sequentially accessed input medium such as a magnetic tape. Each job consists of a sequence of routines followed by data. The routines may be in any source language for which a compiler is available, or in the intermediate language. Auxiliary inputs from the library file, and private program file, or a private data file, may be requested by the job. Figure 9 illustrates input of a sequence of 4 jobs, and the structure of a single job containing routines in FORTRAN, FAP and the intermediate language, and some data.

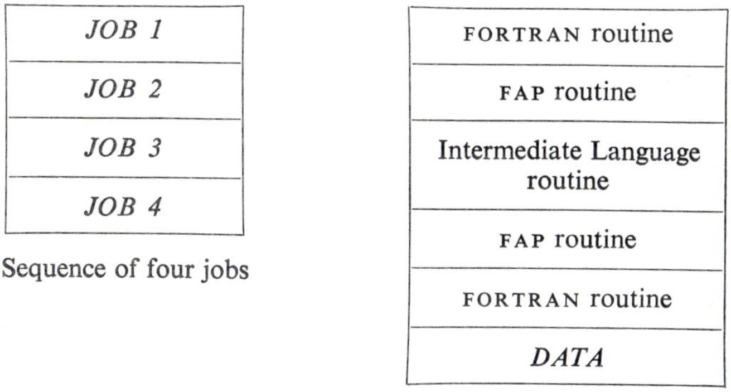

| JOB 1 |
| JOB 2 |
| JOB 3 |
| JOB 4 |

Sequence of four jobs

| FORTRAN routine |
| FAP routine |
| Intermediate Language routine |
| FAP routine |
| FORTRAN routine |
| DATA |

Job consisting of five
routines and data

Fig. 9

When the programming system processes a given job it translates routines into the intermediate language, and then, if all routines are available, it loads the intermediate language routines, establishes the linkages, and initiates computing. Since the data follows the program, it is ready to be read in as required by the program.

The programming system permits the user to exercise control over the execution of jobs by means of a vocabulary of commands. This vocabulary of commands is called the *control language*. Control languages are relatively simple languages since they are concerned not with arithmetic and logical manipulation but with information flow.

This section is concerned with outlining the bare essentials of a simple control language. The control language facilities used for purposes of illustration will be those of the FORTRAN Monitor System (*FMS*). Some source language debugging facilities available in the *FMS* will also be discussed. It will be assumed that the input is of punched card format, and card column numbers will be used in describing the *FMS* control language.

A system handles automatically a sequence of jobs to be run on the computer. Automatic handling requires careful identification of jobs so that they can be distinguished from each other, a clear indicator to mark the start of the job for purposes of automatic accounting by the monitor system, and a display for the benefit of the machine operator, indicating the current job that is being processed. In a typical control language the above would be accomplished by a job card containing the word *JOB* followed by identification information determined by the conventions of the computer installation. In the case of the *FMS* system the job card is merely the first card in the job deck.

*FMS* control language cards are distinguished from other cards by having a * (asterisk) in column 1 of the card. The job card has a * in column 1 and identification information on the remainder of the card according to the specification of the particular computer installation. Any card with a * in column 1 is printed for display purposes so that the operator automatically has access to the job identificators on the on-line printer.

When there are several source languages, control language cards are required to specify the source language of each routine to be compiled. In the case of the FMS system, a card with a * in column 1 and the words FAP punched in columns 7 — 9 indicates that the source language is FAP. In the absence of a FAP card, the routine is assumed to be in FORTRAN. Intermediate language cards are recognized by a special configuration of punches produced by the computer.

If the set of routines which constitute a job are to be executed it is necessary in the *FMS* system to include a card with a * in column 1 and the characters *XEQ* punched after column 7. This card must be included immediately after the job card for the given job.

Since data cards are indistinguishable in format from program cards an indicator is required to indicate the end of program input and the beginning of data input. This is accomplished by means of a card with a * in column 1 and the word DATA punched in columns 7 to 10.

The four control language cards described above having the following format

* Identification
* FAP
* *XEQ*
* *DATA*

The above four types of control language cards are sufficient to perform the basic operations within a programming system. The *FMS* system contains about fifteen other control language words concerned principally with special forms of output (e.g. FAP listing of FORTRAN programs, punching of card output). There is also a facility for organization and execution of successive segments of a program that cannot fit into memory simultaneously (chain link facility).

The degree of control available at the control language level is different for different programming systems. In the *FMS* system control is only possible with respect to sequencing jobs through the computer. Other programming systems for FORTRAN and FAP, such as Bell Telephone Laboratories system (*BTL*), permit more direct intervention at the control language level. For instance, the BTL system permits planting constants into the middle of the program, planting of snapshort dumps and dumping of the content of tapes.

More specialized programming languages such as those for linear programming, or statistics, include higher level subroutines in the control language vocabulary. Thus in most linear programming systems the style of output and the number of conditions over which solutions are required can be specified by control language vocabulary. In statistical systems, words such as CORRELATION, REGRESSION and FACTOR ANALYSIS can be part of the control language, and the control language can be used to specify, for instance, that a correlation analysis is to be performed followed by a factor analysis.

A programming system is concerned not only with information flow but also with access to information in the computer at intermediate and final stages of the computation. Unscheduled output for purposes such as program testing is obtained by means of debugging facilities. Ideally it is desirable to permit symbolic debugging in the source language.

Symbolic debugging is basically a process of inverse translation from machine language back into a symbolic source language. This is not normally possible, since the information which specifies the symbolic form of the source language is not normally available. However, sufficient information to permit a large degree of inverse translation may be obtained by retaining a symbol table of all symbolic cross references (internal and external) and a symbol table of all data locations.

In the case of symbolic debugging of FORTRAN within the *FMS* system the symbol table contains statement labels, data names local to the routine, *COMMON* data names, and a pointer to the beginning of working storage.

The symbol table permits specification of source-language-statement-numbers at which dumping is to occur, and the specification by name of the variables to be dumped. The debugging information is specified on control language cards with a * in column 1 and the word *DUMP* followed by the debugging information starting in column 7. Debugging cards are placed at the end of the program section and are interpreted by the loader. Monitoring instructions are physically inserted into the program at load time at points where debugging is to take place. The debugging can therefore be specified at load time and the system automatically inserts debugging sequences specified in the source language into the object program.

Prior to the availability of the above debugging facilities, dumping was accomplished by inserting a subroutine call to a dumping routine into the source program. The decision regarding the information to be dumped had therefore to be made at the translation stage.

The above description covers only the simplest type of programming system. A number of other chapters will deal with more complex programming systems.

# 6. IMPLEMENTATION OF FORTRAN ON ATLAS

I. C. PYLE

*Atomic Energy Research Establishment, Harwell, England*

*Part I: General Strategy*

## 1. Introduction

The general approach adopted in designing the Atlas Fortran compiler is one of machine independence, rather than language independence. The compiler is tied closely to the FORTRAN source language, but only loosely to the Atlas computer. This means that the compiler could work with very trivial changes on virtually any computer which has a Fortran system, and it could be fairly easily modified to produce target programs for any computer. Of course, it is quite a large program, and would need a reasonably large computer to work efficiently. One of the points which should be mentioned initially is that there is no sophisticated treatment of two level storage problems; it is presumed that the relevant computers have large enough stores for this not to be serious.

Since a Fortran compiler treats routines, not whole programs, we do not think it is necessary to be able to process large pieces of program. Various tables of finite size are used during compilation; if one gets filled, the compiler will give up and tell the source of programmer to break up the routine into smaller sections. We intend to keep all the tables in the main store of Atlas, so there will be no time lost because of transfers to and from tape.

## 2. Writing in FORTRAN

A compiler is, after all, just a large and rather complicated program, which can be written in any convenient language. We chose to write in FORTRAN for a variety of reasons, some subjective (we like it), but most objective.

The first point is that the compiler can then be run on any computer which understands FORTRAN. This is particularly important for a compiler for a new computer, since it can be thoroughly tested before the new computer arrives, without having to resort to simulation. We expect that our compiler will be checked out well before the N.I.R.N.S. Atlas is ready.

The other reason is not peculiar to our compiler, but is simply related to its size. Any program as large as this would get out of hand without a firm, but flexible framework. FORTRAN source language is far preferable to a symbolic machine language, and the Fortran Monitor System provides the programming system within which we can work.

Routines are written and compiled independently, then combined on loading to form the program. This arrangement makes it easy for us to change routines in the compiler during testing and, after we have got it working, to improve either facilities provided or efficiency of operation. It also makes it very easy to produce different versions of the compiler for different computers, in association with the Atlas Fortran project, routines are being written to compile for the Orion.

The only disadvantage which arises through writing in FORTRAN is that tables of small integers can be stored only one number per word, because packing and unpacking are awkward. The consequent limitation on available storage is accepted.

### 3. Programming System

In preparing a FORTRAN system for a new computer, it is not sufficient to provide a compiler alone, there has to be a library of routines which can be used by compiled routines. These will control input/output, and evaluate mathematical functions. In addition, there has to be at least a loader, to combine routines and initiate execution, but preferably a programming system which will control the processing of the various routines of a job.

The design of the programming system, especially the intermediate language used for communicating routines to the loader, is important, and influences the compiler and the source language, because of the facilities which can be provided.

The programming system to be used on the N.I.R.N.S. Atlas is called Hartran; it will provide facilities familiar to users of the Fortran Monitor System. The intermediate language used in the Hartran system is called BAS (Binary and Arbitrarily Symbolic). The information is principally in relocatable binary, but there is sufficient symbolic content to allow very flexible communication between independently compiled routines. A full description is given elsewhere (Curtis and Pyle, 1962). It is slightly more flexible than the BSS language used in IBM Fortran (IBM, 1958), the differences mainly being connected with storage of arrays.

The target language of the compiler is BAS; routines are output in this form, so that they can be loaded on several occasions without re-compilation. The use of BAS as target language allows us to generalize the FORTRAN source language slightly (PARAMETER and PUBLIC, described later).

### 4. Two Level Storage Problems

Most computers (and Atlas is no exception) have several types of internal store, of different sizes and accessibilities. In general, the most accessible stores are the smallest. Consequently, information has to be moved from one type of store to another at various stages of a calculation. The two-level storage problem is to determine the best times for these transfers. We do not know of any general solution of this problem.

Two level storage problems arise in two distinct contexts on Atlas, but fortunately the hardware of the machine renders them relatively unimportant and a simple treatment is acceptable.

(i) There are a number (eighty) of special registers called B-registers, which can be used to modify the addresses of instructions. These are used to

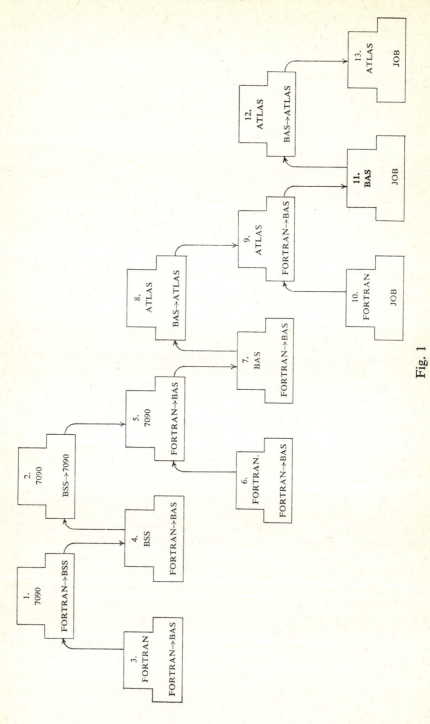

Fig. 1

reference locations which vary during execution (array elements, or dummy variables; ordinary variables are relocated on loading, and not changed during execution). The problem is, what happens if more than eighty such variable locations are needed?

Our solution is to treat the B-registers as private to each routine, and assign one for each variable location in the routine. We can insist that the total used in the routine is less than eighty. We have never seen a routine which needs more than twenty; anyway, a large routine can always be broken down. Thus there is no limit to the total number used in a program.

In order that a routine should not disturb the B-registers of the routine which activates it, it must store the contents of all the B-registers it needs before changing them, and put them back before returning. (If there is no return, then they need not be saved.) This transfer on entry to and exit from subroutines introduces an inefficiency of a few per cent, which is accepted. (ii) The main store of Atlas (core and drums) is large; of order 100 K. Thus few programs will need to use magnetic tape as a backing store. For those which do, instructions are provided for the programmer to use, to control transfers to and from tape.

In the basic system there are instructions for manipulating tapes (searching and transferring blocks of information). The Hartran system allows the programmer to specify how his large program is to be divided into chapters, and how variables are to be arranged in blocks. Library routines are provided to transmit chapters and blocks, but the programmer has to decide when to use them.

### 5. Transfer to Atlas

At first sight there seems to be a snag in the method described, because until the compiler is there, the Atlas cannot understand FORTRAN. How then are we to get the compiler in?

The solution is based on the fact that the compiler is written in its own language, so we can use a "bootstrapping" technique, starting with another computer for which a Fortran compiler already exists: e.g. the IBM 7090. We run the Atlas Fortran compiler on this computer (as for testing) and feed it with a copy of itself (see Fig. 1). The output is a translated version of the compiler, which can then be loaded into Atlas. The compiler then operates under the Hartran programming system, just like any other FORTRAN program.

In this diagram, a box represents a program. At the top is the name of the language it is expressed in, which may be an external language or the machine language of a computer executing it. At the bottom is a description of the program; for translation programs we specify the input and output languages. A loader is like a translation program, except that the output language is the appropriate machine language.

Boxes 1 and 2 represent programs which already exist: the Fortran compiler and loader for the 7090. BSS is the name of the intermediate language used in the IBM Fortran. Box 3 represents the Atlas Fortran compiler, which we are writing. It translates from FORTRAN into the BAS intermediate language. Boxes 4 and 5 represent programs which are produced automatically, giving a version of the Atlas Fortran compiler which runs on the 7090. Box 6 is a copy of box 3, which is input to the new compiler. Box 7 represents the program which is output, from the 7090, in a form ready for transfer to Atlas.

At this stage, we need an Atlas, and a loader, which has to be written and input independently using some primitive method. Box 8 represents the BAS loader for Atlas. Box 9 represents the ultimate form of the compiler, in Atlas. A job whose program is written in FORTRAN (box 10) may then be input, and converted to BAS (box 11). Box 12 is the same as box 8, the BAS loader, which combines the routines of the job and initiates execution (box 13).

## 6. Machine Dependence

It will be clear from the above discussion that we rely on the fact that it is not necessary for a compiler to run on the machine for which it produces output: compilation and execution need not be carried out on the same machine. We refer to the compiling machine and the target machine: initially we use the IBM 7090 and the Atlas; eventually both will be Atlas.

There are inevitably some machine dependent features in the compiler. Naturally we keep these to a minimum, and to make the system easily adaptable for different machines, we take all machine dependent features into separate routines. Then a version for a different computer can be made by writing logically equivalent routines, and giving them the same names. The structure of the compiler is machine independent although the contents of the individual routines may vary.

We classify routines according to their machine dependence: they are either machine independent, or target machine dependent, or compiling machine dependent. The machine independent part of the compiler is concerned with analysing the source routine and carrying out general optimization. This is described in more detail below.

Target machine dependent routines are concerned with the synthesis of instructions in target language. Since the repertoire of instructions is machine dependent we do not try to produce output in a machine independent form. Instead, we send control to an appropriate routine. Thus the names of routines can be thought of as an UNCOL (Universal Computer Oriented Language). For example, when an unconditional transfer is required, we enter a subroutine called *JUMP*. The Atlas version of this subroutine compiles a TRA instruction; the Orion version compiles a two-address 75 instruction. The instruction repertoire may also lead us to do some special optimization which is target machine dependent.

For example, on Atlas, subtraction may be slower than addition, even if the accumulator is first to be negated (but not if it is to be cleared). We therefore permute the elements of the expression, subject to the algebraic rules of associativity and commutativity, to arrange that subtract ($SU$) operations are avoided if possible, and replaced by clear and subtract ($CS$) or negate and add ($NA$).

Thus

$$A = B + C - D * E$$

is compiled as

    FCS  D
    FMP  E
    FAD  B
    FAD  C
    STO  A

i.e. $(-D) * E + B + C \rightarrow A$

and

$$I = J + K - L - M$$

is compiled as

    XCA L
    XAD  M
    XNA  J
    XAD  K
    STO  I

i.e. $-(L + M) + J + K \rightarrow I$

Compiling machine dependent routines are concerned with the compiler's own input and output. Initialization of the various tables is also compiling machine dependent.

The compiler consists of several sections which must be brought into the working store as they are needed. These correspond to chain links in the Fortran Monitor System, or to chapters in Mercury Autocode. The organization of chapters depends on the compiling machine, so this is another compiling machine dependent feature.

When the compiler is first written compiling for Atlas on the 7090, we need the machine independent routines, and target dependent routines for Atlas, but compiling machine dependent routines for the 7090. Later, we must prepare compiling dependent routines for the Atlas, and use these when we transfer the compiler to Atlas.

## 7. Extensions to FORTRAN Source Language

At the beginning of the Atlas Fortran project, it was decided that the FORTRAN II source language used on the IBM 704,709,7090 is somewhat restrictive, and that because of the ease of modification of FORTRAN programs, a small number of changes would be acceptable if (i) any features removed are replaced by better ones, (ii) most routines would need no change at all, and, (iii) where changes are needed, the places are easy to find.

Similar changes are being proposed by IBM for FORTRAN IV, and there is a close similarity between the dialects.

As an example of a proposed change, logical expressions can be written using the operations $.NOT.$, $.AND.$, $.OR.$, $.GT. (>)$, $.GE. (\geq)$, $.EQ. (=)$, $.NE.$ $(\neq)$, $.LE. (\leq)$, $.LT. (<)$ and variables of mode $LOGICAL$. An $IF$ statement can test a logical expression or a logical variable.

The following extensions are only in Atlas Fortran.

(i)   The values of several variables can be changed in one statement, e.g.

$$X, Y, Z = EXPR$$

(ii) An expression may contain elements of mixed modes *REAL* and *INTEGER*, e.g.

$$2 * X$$

(iii) A subscript may be an expression, e.g.

$$A ( I + J, K (L) )$$

(iv) We wish to remove some of the restrictions in the *DO* statement, e.g. that the increment must be positive, and the body is always executed at least once. Instead of altering the meaning of the *DO* statement, and introducing incompatibilities, we thought it better to introduce a new statement with different semantics. The principal difference between the new *FOR* statement and the *DO* statement is that the body will not be executed if the parameters are the "wrong" way round, e.g.

$$FOR \ I = 10, 1, 1$$

Further extensions could probably be also allowed for *DO* statements, without incompatibility: e.g. allowing expressions in the parameter positions, and taking account of the sign of the index. A *REPEAT* statement can be used instead of a numbered statement to end the loop.

The above changes are all notational: the same effect can be obtained in FORTRAN II by breaking up the statements into a number of simpler steps.

A more powerful change is concerned with communication between routines by "hidden parameters". The declaration

$$PUBLIC \ A$$

specifies that the name A in this routine represents the same thing as the name A in any other routine which specifies it to be *PUBLIC*. (In the absence of any declaration, the name is private; a *COMMON* declaration sets up correspondence by position in the common list, rather than by name). The implementation of *PUBLIC* is a feature of the BAS loader; the compiler has only to record symbolic information in the target routine.

Another change associated with the BAS loader concerns storage assignment for arrays. This can now be parameteric, and fixed at load time rather than compile time. For example,

$$PARAMETER \ I, J$$

allows us to have

$$DIMENSION \ X \ (I, J)$$

$$PUBLIC \ Y \ (I, J)$$

where these are actual arrays (not dummies; FORTRAN IV allows adjustable dimensions for dummy arrays, but otherwise insists on constants).

No storage is assigned on compilation, but on loading we can have a directive such as

*DEFINE I = 20, J = 50*

before the routine, and appropriate storage will be assigned.

## 8. Optimization

The level of optimization at which we aim is only slightly higher than that in IBM FORTRAN. We do the same elimination of common subexpressions, so that repetitions in an expression will be evaluated once only. The subscript analysis is rather more complicated as the allowed form for subscript has been generalized. References to members of an array are written as the array name followed by a list of subscripts in parentheses. Each subscript may be an expression (i.e. similar in form to a function argument). A single working subscript is derived by combining the expressions in a "storage mapping function" which depends on the dimensions of the array. Then the array is interpreted as a vector, the working subscript giving the position of the desired element.

The simple minded approach, used in compilers which do not optimize, is to evaluate the storage mapping function each time a reference is made. This is satisfactory if the subscript forms are very simple (of the form $I + 2$) but becomes time-consuming if multi-dimensional arrays and full expressions in subscripts are allowed.

Optimization of subscripts is based on the assumption that there are (statistically) more references to each array element than there are definitions of the dependent variables. Consequently, we aim to calculate the subscripts at points of definition, rather than on use.

Since it would not be feasible to recognize points of definition of functions or arrays, we classify subscripts as they are met according to their form. "Slow" subscripts contain array elements or functions. These are not optimized: they are evaluated on use. "Fast" subscripts contain no element more complicated than an integer scalar. These are optimized: evaluated on definition.

The definition of a subscript might be by an explicit change of value of a dependent variable, or by a controlling loop. During the scan of the source routine all value changes of integer scalars are noted, and a push-down list of current loops is maintained.

Fast subscripts which occur in a loop might or might not depend linearly on the index of the loop. Those which do are initialized before the loop begins, and incremented for each repetition. If they depend non-linearly on the index, they are evaluated at the beginning of every cycle.

*Part II: Some Details of the Compiler*

## 9. Outline of the Compiler

The compiler is divided into a number of sections which are executed in sequence for each source routine. The first five sections produce instructions in a symbolic machine language (like ASP) and the final section converts the routine into BAS. After describing the major sections in outline, we will give more detail about some of the processing carried out.

Section 1 reads in the routine one line at a time, and analyses each source statement. During the scan information is recorded in tables for later use. These concern the modes of identifiers, values of constants, fast subscripts, loops, flow of control, and storage assignment.

Before processing each line of the source routine, a printed copy is output for the programmer. If any error is discovered, an extra line is output, giving information about the error: usually it will come under the line containing the error.

This section is completed on reading the END card in the source routine. No further cards are read: all the information needed subsequently is obtained from the tables.

Section 2 deals with expressions which were analysed in Section 1. Symbolic machine instructions are produced and there is a considerable amount of local optimization (i.e. within each statement). Addition and multiplication and the logical operations 'or' and 'and' are assumed to be commutative, and the compiler permutes variables in order to improve the efficiency of the target program. Subscripts are stripped, and either evaluated with the statement or recorded as fast for evaluation on definition. Common subexpressions in a statement are recognized to avoid recalculation.

Section 3 deals with loops in the routine, arising from *DO* and *FOR* statements. Instructions are compiled to initialize and increment linearly dependent subscripts.

The processing of this section is carried out sequentially for each loop in the routine, in backwards order of the *DO* or *FOR* statements. This means that innermost loops are always treated first.

Each (fast) subscript which is used in the body of the loop is classified as linear or non-linear in the loop index. It is treated here only if it is linear. The subscript will be evaluated incrementally, and the initial value and increment must be set before the loop begins. The initial value and increment are then regarded as subscripts, and will be similarly treated in the next outer loop, if any.

Section 4 analyses the flow of control through the routine resulting from *IF* and *GO TO* statements. The object of this is to discover the points of definition of those subscripts which are not controlled by a loop. These result from changes to the values of dependent variables. Instructions are compiled to evaluate the subscripts at the appropriate points.

These three sections produce symbolic instructions in separate streams, with internal reference numbers attached to indicate their desired positions in the target routine.

Section 5 merges the outputs of the earlier sections, using the internal reference numbers as keys.

During the merge, each instruction address is compared with the list of dummy arguments (formal parameters) of the routine, in order to know what adjustments will be necessary during execution. This produces the body of the

PINC: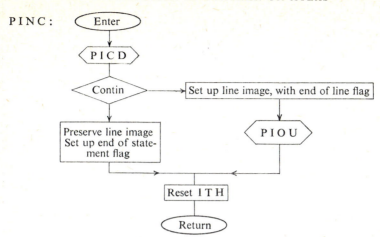

PICD: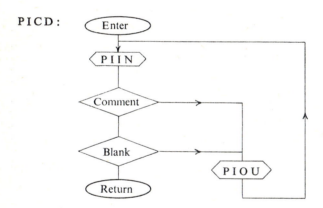

CIBS: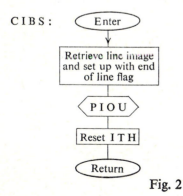

Fig. 2

target routine, after which the prologue and epilogue are compiled, for linking this routine with its caller, and then the tables of constants used by the routine, and storage for its own variables.

The relative locations of all parts of the routine are determined in this section (as in the first pass of an assembly program) and Section 6 produces the BAS routine by making the appropriate substitutions.

A storage map is printed, giving a list of indentifiers used, with their modes, types, and locations assigned, together with other information which might be useful to the programmer. If any errors were detected, explanatory messages will be printed. This arrangement allows comments to be made about possible errors, without suspending compilation.

## 10. Input of Statements

Compiling machine dependent routines are used to read in a line (PIIN) and output a copy of it (PIOU). These are used by machine independent routines PICD, which checks whether the line is a comment or blank, PINC, which sets up a continuation if there is one, and CIBS, which sets up the first line of each statement. The structure of the input section is shown in Fig. 2.

Whenever a scan reaches the end of line flag, routine PINC is activated to find a continuation. If there is none, an end of statement flag is set up to trigger off final processing of the statement.

There can be any number of continuation lines for each statement. This means that the first line of each statement is always read in before the previous statement is finished. Routine CIBS retrieves this line and sets it up at the beginning of each statement.

The only exception is the *END* statement, which defines the physical end of the routine. We do not allow this to have any continuations, and will never read beyond the end of line flag.

## 11. Scanning Procedure

As an example of the scanning technique used, we give the routine for collecting an unsigned decimal integer. This is used in processing *DIMENSION* statements, and for the successor statement numbers in *IF* and *GO TO*. It is written as a function, whose value is that of the integer read (see Fig. 3).

The scanning is carried out using a pointer ITH and an array IST, in common. The array represents the contents of the current card, successive elements being integers which represent the characters on the card. The code used is based on the Atlas internal code, using integers in the range 1 to 63. A particular number (6) is put after the last card character, indicating the end of the card. Similarly code number 7 is used to indicate the end of the statement. The integers 16 to 25 represent the decimal digits 0 to 9.

The routine is entered with ITH pointing at a digit, and the scan is to accumulate the integer which it introduces. Spaces (code 1) and erases (code 63) are to be ignored, end of line flag (code 6) and $\pi$ or $ (code 11) to bring in a new line. The different types of character are distinguished quickly by

```
      FUNCTION INTEG(J1)
C     THIS ROUTINE COLLECTS AN UNSIGNED DECIMAL INTEGER.
      COMMON ITH, IST
C     THE STANDARD COMMON IS NOT GIVEN IN FULL.
      DIMENSION IST(72)
      J = IST(ITH) - 16
 1    ITH = ITH + 1
      I = IST(ITH)
      GO TO (1,4,4,4,4,2,4,4,4,4,2,4,4,4,4,
C     1 IS SPACE, 6 IS EOL, 11 IS $ OR PI, REMAINDER ARE PUNCTUATION.
     1     3,3,3,3,3,3,3,3,3,3,4,4,4,4,4,4,
C     16 TO 25 ARE DECIMAL DIGITS, REMAINDER ARE PUNCTUATION.
     2     4,5,5,5,5,5,5,5,5,5,5,5,5,5,5,5,
C     32 IS PUNCTUATION, REMAINDER ARE LETTERS.
     3     5,5,5,5,5,5,5,5,5,5,5,5,5,5,4,1),I
C     62 IS ERROR, 63 IS ERASE, REMAINDER ARE LETTERS.
 3    J = J * 10 + I - 16
      GO TO 1
 2    CALL PINC
      GO TO 1
 5    CONTINUE
 4    ITH = ITH - 1
      INTEG = J
      RETURN
      END
```

Fig. 3

means of the 63-way computed *GO TO*, controlled by the current character.

In this computed *GO TO*, statement number 1 advances the scan (ignoring the current character;), 2 brings in a continuation, 3 accumulates the integer, and 4 and 5 terminate the scan (4 is for punctuation, 5 for letter, but since both act in the same way we could have used the same number for both). At the end, ITH has to be stepped back one character, because the end of the scan is only recognized when it has gone one character too far.

## 12. Classification

The type of each statement is determined by a preliminary scan of its first line. This scan stops on reaching the end of the line (or a Hollerith constant), and does not bring in continuations. Consequently, we require the source statement to have sufficient information on its first line.

The preliminary scan distinguishes three statement classes, by looking for parentheses (to determine the "level"), commas, and the equals sign. Arithmetic statements are identified by an equals sign and no subsequent comma at level zero (i.e. not enclosed in parentheses). Loop statements (*DO* and *FOR*) are identified by an equals sign and at least one subsequent comma at level zero. Other statements have no equals sign at level zero.

Statements in the last two classes are distinguished by comparing the beginning of the line with a dictionary of key words (e.g. *IF*, *CALL*, *GO TO*, *READ*). Some types are further classified by comparison with a subsidiary dictionary (e.g. for *READ* we may have *INPUT TAPE*, *INPUT*, *TAPE*, *DRUM*). The dictionary search routine stops the scan if the source character "." is met. This allows abbreviations, e.g. "*DIM.*" for "*DIMENSION*".

The reason why a preliminary scan is needed is that the key words are not reserved identifiers: variables can be called *IF*, *GO TO*, *DO5I* etc., and occur at the beginning of an arithmetic statement. There is an important difference between

$$DO5I = 1,3$$

and

$$DO5I = 1.3$$

(although the second is probably a mistake, it is quite legal, and we do not attempt to catch it!)

## 13. Expressions

Arithmetic statements, *DO*, *FOR*, *IF* and *CALL* statements may involve expressions, which are analysed by a standard group of routines. At present we use a method similar to the IBM method, described by Sheridan (1959), but as a direct consequence of this symposium we might well use Dijkstra's stack method (Dijkstra, 1961).

The difference concerns the treatment of parentheses. The problem is that the natural algebraic order is not the right order for computing. Different techniques are used to get the right order.

In Sheridan's method, instructions are compiled in the algebraic order, but tagged with numbers representing the computing order. At the end of the expression, the instructions have to be sorted.

In Dijkstra's method, the algebraic order is converted into computing order (reversed Polish) by the use of a stack to hold incomplete subexpressions. Instructions are compiled in the correct order as soon as a subexpression is completed.

The difference would not be serious if all expressions were fully bracketed. However, we must also build in the standard algebraic rules of precedence, by which

$$X + Y * Z$$

is taken to mean

$$X + (Y * Z)$$

and not

$$(X + Y) * Z$$

Sheridan treats this by putting extra parentheses around every operator, according to its priority (1 for **, 2 for *, 3 for +). Thus the above expression is treated as

$$(((( X ))) + ((( Y )) * (( Z ))))$$

This process produces a high proportion of redundant subexpressions, which have to be removed.

A further disadvantage is that every subexpression must be enclosed by a number of parentheses, equal to the maximum possible priority. We must keep this maximum priority low (4) to avoid an excessive number of redundant subexpressions.

Dijkstra compares the priority of the current operator with that at the top of the stack before adding to it. This avoids producing redundant subexpressions, and also removes the need for restricting priorities, allowing us to use more levels in the hierarchy.

## 14. Conclusion

We do not intend to implement the whole of the system described in the first instance. In order to get a working compiler more quickly, we will produce a simplified preliminary version, which will have none of the subscript optimization.

This will be done by changing the criterion for recognizing fast subscripts. All subscripts will be treated as slow, and consequently evaluated with the statements in which they are used, rather than on definition. The processing of Sections 3 and 4 is then unnecessary, only rudimentary versions will be put in. By this means, and by accepting some further limitations on the complexity of a source routine to be treated, we will produce a compiler which can process itself, giving a form ready to go to the Atlas.

Once an Atlas compiler produced in this way is working, the immediate aim of the present work will be achieved and the missing sections can be grafted in as they become available, to improve the efficiency of the target routines. The compiler could then be put through itself again.

### REFERENCES

1. A. R. CURTIS and I. C. PYLE (1962). A proposed Target Language for Compilers on Atlas. *Computer J.* **5**, 100.
2. E. W. DIJKSTRA (1961). Making a Translator for Algol 60. *APIC Bull.* No. 7, and Algol-60 Translation, *Algol Bull. Suppl.* No. 10.
3. *IBM* (1958). Reference Manual Fortran II, Form C28-6000-1.
4. P. SHERIDAN (1959). The Arithmetic Translator-Compiler of the IBM Fortran Automatic Coding System. *Comm. A.C.M.* **2**, No. 2.

# 7. AN INTRODUCTION TO STACK COMPILATION TECHNIQUES

*The Burroughs Compiler Game*

## P. WEGNER

*London School of Economics and Political Science, London, England*

### 1. Introduction

This chapter discusses the use of stacks in program compilation from an elementary point of view, and illustrates the use of stacks by detailed analysis of one ALGOL and one COBOL program. Section 2 is an introduction to the use of reverse Polish notation in the representation of arithmetic expressions. Section 3 analyses a program written in a dialect of ALGOL in terms of its constituents, and describes the way in which the constituents might be rearranged into reverse Polish notation. Section 4 is concerned with the use of stacks and operator hierarchies for compilation. Section 5 describes the Burroughs Compiler Game and illustrates its use in compilation of the ALGOL program introduced in Section 3. Section 6 illustrates the use of the Burroughs Compiler Game for the compilation of a COBOL program. Section 7 discusses the limitations on ALGOL and COBOL syntax of programs which can be compiled with the aid of the Burroughs Compiler Game. The appendix discusses the machine language of the Burroughs B5000, which includes a stack in its hardware, and permits operations on the stack in machine language. The machine language instructions into which the ALGOL and COBOL programs of sections 5 and 6 are translated, are also given in the appendix.

The programs which can be compiled by application of the rules of compilation of the Burroughs Compiler Game (see Fig. 1 and Table 2) are very restricted. However the detailed analysis of compilation of these programs throws some light both on the essential simplicity of the compilation process and on the structure of the ALGOL and COBOL languages.

### 2. Polish Notation

Polish notation was developed by the Polish mathematician J. Lukasiewicz as a "normal form" for the representation of formulae in logic. Polish notation permits an unambiguous sequential specification of the order of evaluation of logical and arithmetic expressions without requiring the use of parentheses. It is for this reason that it has been found useful as a *normal form* for computer-oriented mathematical languages.

The particular form of Polish notation most frequently used in formula translation is called reverse Polish notation. The basic characteristic of reverse Polish notation is that of putting an operator *after* the operands upon which it operates. Thus $A + B$ would be written in reverse Polish notation as $AB+$.

In the case of an expression with a number of two-operand operators, the result of an operation on two operands is a single operand which may be operated upon by subsequently applied operators. For instance, the expression

$$A + B \times C \qquad (1)$$

requires first the application of the multiplication operator to the two operands $B$ and $C$, producing an intermediate result $R$, and then the application of the addition operator to the operands $A$ and $R$.

The formula (1) would be written in Polish notation as

$$ABC \times + \qquad (2)$$

When this formula is scanned at execution time, the multiplication operator $\times$ can be applied to the two preceding operands $B$ and $C$ immediately it is encountered. The operator $+$ can then be applied to the operand $R$ resulting from the $\times$ operation, and the operand $A$. In general, Polish notation permits the application of operators to their operands immediately they are encountered in a sequential scanning process.

Polish notation also permits the representation without parentheses of a formula normally requiring parentheses. For instance, the formula

$$(A + B) \times C \qquad (3)$$

would be represented in Polish notation as

$$AB + C \times \qquad (4)$$

Polish notation can be extended to statements as well as expressions. For instance, the statement

$$X \leftarrow A \qquad (5)$$

which sets the value of the variable $X$ equal to the value of the variable $A$, is written in Polish notation as

$$XA \leftarrow \qquad (6)$$

and $\qquad\qquad X \leftarrow A + B \times C \qquad (7)$

is written as $\qquad\qquad XABC \times + \leftarrow \qquad (8)$

The use of Polish notation can be extended from simple arithmetic formulae to complete programming languages such as ALGOL. The next Section illustrates the transformation into Polish notation of a program written in a dialect of ALGOL, here referred to as "Burroughs ALGOL."*

### 3. A Sample ALGOL Program

*1. The* ALGOL *Program*

The characteristics of Burroughs ALGOL may be illustrated by considering the program below, which finds the largest element $A[I, J]$ of a two-dimensional

---

* "Burroughs ALGOL" is here used as a shorthand for "The ALGOL dialect used in the Burroughs Compiler Game". The term does not relate to versions of ALGOL actually available on any computers.

array $A$ of dimension $M \times N$, and notes the indices $I$ and $J$ of the largest element as the variables $K$ and $L$. The program consists essentially of a double loop preceded by some declarations which specify the kinds of variable occurring in the program. The variable $Y$ specifies the largest element yet found at an intermediate stage in the calculation, and specifies the largest element in the matrix at the end of the calculation. Since $Y$ is initialized to 0.0, it is assumed that the largest element is $\geq 0.0$.

*Sample Program for the Burroughs Compiler Game*

```
BEGIN
REAL ARRAY A [ , ];
REAL Y;
INTEGER I, J, K, L, M, N;
Y ← 0.0;
FOR I ← 1 STEP 1 UNTIL M DO
FOR J ← 1 STEP 1 UNTIL N DO
IF A [I, J] > Y THEN BEGIN
Y ← A [I, J]; K ← I; L ← J END END
```

The first line of the program contains the operator *BEGIN*, which indicates the beginning of an ALGOL statement. In this case, the *BEGIN* indicates the beginning of the statement constituting the whole program. Every *BEGIN* operator must have a matching *END* operator. A *BEGIN* operator with its corresponding *END* operator may be regarded as a pair of matching parentheses.

The next three declarations are type declarations, indicating the types of the variables occurring in the program. Thus $A$ is an array, $Y$ is a real (floating point) variable, and the other variables are integers.

The line $Y \leftarrow 0.0$ initializes the variable $Y$ to zero.

The next line is an ALGOL "*FOR* clause" which specifies execution of the next statement for $M$ values of the variable $I$, starting with 1 and moving by increments of 1 to $M$. The statement following the *FOR* clause contains a second, inner *FOR* clause followed by a conditional statement.

The conditional statement causes the statement enclosed by the *BEGIN* and *END* operators to be executed whenever the relation $A[I, J] > Y$ following the *IF* operator is true. This latter relation is an example of a Boolean relation, having a value which is either *TRUE* or *FALSE*. (It should be noted that square parentheses are used to enclose subscripts of an array. Square parentheses may be distinguished from the round parentheses used in defining the order of evaluation of arithmetic expressions.)

## 2. Constituents of the Program

Sufficient terminology has been introduced above to permit a more general discussion of the translation process for the dialect of ALGOL under consideration.

An ALGOL source program consists of a string of basic symbols, where the basic symbols may belong to one of the following four classes:

1. Operands.
2. Operators.
3. Declarators.
4. For Clause.

Operands may be array elements, real operands, integer operands or just literal numbers.

Operators include arithmetic operators, relational operators, logical operators, parentheses, and control words such as *IF*, *THEN*, etc. The five operators ) *END* ] [ ; require special treatment by the translator. All other operators can be dealt with in a standard way.

Declarators specify the type of operands in the program.

The *FOR* clause is split into three constituents, *FOR 1*, *FOR 2*, *FOR 3*. In the first *FOR* clause of the above example, the constituents would respectively be

> *FOR I ← 1*
> *STEP 1*
> *UNTIL M DO*

During translation on a computer, successive constituents of the source program are scanned and dealt with individually, either being placed directly in the target string, or being stored in a temporary storage area, pending information about subsequent constituents. In the compiler game, the splitting of a program into its basic constituents is accomplished by specifying each constituent on a separate card. The sample program above is decomposed into the 43 constituents indicated in Table 1.

## 3. The Polish String Program

The constituents of the source program retain their identity in the target program although some of the constituents, such as matching parentheses, are discarded. The target language program consists of 28 of the original 43 constituents, and two markers ↓, in the following order:

1. *Y 0.0 ←*
2. *FOR I ←1*
3. *UNTIL M DO*
4. *FOR J ← 1*
5. *UNTIL N DO*
6. *IJ, A↓Y >*
7. *Y IJ, A ↓ ←*
8. *K I ←*
9. *L J ←*
10. *IF*
11. *STEP 1*
12. *STEP 1*

TABLE 1. Constituents of the Sample Program

| Number of Constituent | Constituent | Type of Constituent | Hierarchy if an Operator (or a FOR 2) |
|---|---|---|---|
| 1 | *BEGIN* | *OPERATOR* | 0 |
| 2 | *REAL ARRAY A* [ , ]; | *DECLARATOR* | |
| 3 | *REAL Y* | *DECLARATOR* | |
| 4 | *INTEGER I, J, K, L, M, N* | *DECLARATOR* | |
| 5 | *Y* | *OPERAND* | |
| 6 | ← | *OPERATOR* | 6 |
| 7 | *0.0* | *OPERAND* | |
| 8 | ; | *OPERATOR* | 1 |
| 9 | *FOR I = 1* | *FOR 1* | |
| 10 | *STEP 1* | *FOR 2* | 1 |
| 11 | *UNTIL M DO* | *FOR 3* | |
| 12 | *FOR J = 1* | *FOR 1* | |
| 13 | *STEP 1* | *FOR 2* | 1 |
| 14 | *UNTIL N DO* | *FOR 3* | |
| 15 | *IF* | *OPERATOR* | 2 |
| 16 | *A* | *OPERAND* | |
| 17 | [ | *OPERATOR* | 10 |
| 18 | *I* | *OPERAND* | |
| 19 | , | *OPERATOR* | 7 |
| 20 | *J* | *OPERAND* | |
| 21 | ] | *OPERATOR* | 7 |
| 22 | > | *OPERATOR* | 6 |
| 23 | *Y* | *OPERAND* | |
| 24 | *THEN* | *OPERATOR* | 3 |
| 25 | *BEGIN* | *OPERATOR* | 0 |
| 26 | *Y* | *OPERAND* | |
| 27 | ← | *OPERATOR* | 6 |
| 28 | *A* | *OPERAND* | |
| 29 | [ | *OPERATOR* | 10 |
| 30 | *I* | *OPERAND* | |
| 31 | , | *OPERATOR* | 7 |
| 32 | *J* | *OPERAND* | |
| 33 | ] | *OPERATOR* | 7 |
| 34 | ; | *OPERATOR* | 1 |
| 35 | *K* | *OPERAND* | |
| 36 | ← | *OPERATOR* | 6 |
| 37 | *I* | *OPERAND* | |
| 38 | ; | *OPERATOR* | 1 |
| 39 | *L* | *OPERAND* | |
| 40 | ← | *OPERATOR* | 6 |
| 41 | *J* | *OPERAND* | |
| 42 | *END* | *OPERATOR* | 1 |
| 43 | *END* | *OPERATOR* | 1 |

The first line above contains $Y \leftarrow 0.0$ in Polish notation.

The second and third line contain the *FOR 1* and *FOR 3* constituents of the outer *FOR* clause, the matching *FOR 2* constituent being the last line of the program. The fourth and fifth line and the penultimate line contain respectively the *FOR 1*, *FOR 3* and *FOR 2* constituents of the inner *FOR* statement.

The sixth line contains the Boolean conditional relation $A[I, J] > Y$ in Polish notation. Note that in Polish notation, the indices of arrays precede the array name, and that the array name is followed by a marker $\downarrow$. The marker $\downarrow$ can be regarded as a special operator which finds the address of the array element $A[I,J]$.

The seventh line contains the arithmetic statement $Y \leftarrow A[I,J]$; in Polish notation.

The eighth and ninth lines contain the statements $K \leftarrow I$; and $L \leftarrow J$; in Polish notation.

The tenth line contains the operator *IF*, indicating the point to which control should be transferred when the Boolean condition of line six is not met.

It should be noted that constituents in the target program have retained their identity, but that all parentheses, including the matching parentheses *BEGIN* and *END*; have been discarded. Separators, such as *THEN* and ; have also been discarded.

## 4. Stacks and Operator Hierarchies

The translation from mathematical notation to reverse Polish notation can be illustrated by considering the two expressions

$$A - B + C$$

and

$$A + B \times C$$

whose representation in reverse Polish is respectively

$$AB - C+$$

and

$$ABC \times +$$

In both cases, the order of the operands $ABC$ is the same in the source and target strings. In the first case, the order of operators is also preserved, while in the second case, the order of the operators is reversed. The relative displacement of operators with respect to operands is determined by the fact that each operator must have its arguments immediately preceding it. The argument of an operator is either an operand, or a reverse Polish string of operators and operands, which leads to a single value upon execution. Thus in the first case the arguments of $-$ are $A$ and $B$, and the arguments of $+$ are $C$ and $AB-$. In the second case, the arguments of $\times$ are $B$ and $C$, and the arguments of $+$ are $A$ and $BC \times$.

The required order reversal of operators and relative displacement of operators and operands can be accomplished simply by associating a hierarchy number with each operator and storing operators temporarily in an operator stack with last-in-first-out properties (i.e. at any given time only the most recent operator introduced into the operator stack is available for manipulation). The elements in this kind of store are ordered in the order of recency of entry into the store, so that we may refer to the first (top), second − − nth elements in the store. When an item is entered into this kind of store it is entered into the "top" of the store, pushing down all previously entered elements by one position, so that the previously top element becomes the second element and the previously nth element becomes the $n + 1$th element. When an item is removed from the store, all items are pushed up one position, so that the previously second element becomes the top element, and the previously nth element becomes the $n − 1$th element. Stores with a last-in-first-out structure have been variously called stacks, push-down lists, cellars and nesting stores. The term stack is used by the designers of the Burroughs Compiler Game.

## 1. Stacks (push-down lists)

The use of a stack in formula translation can best be illustrated by the following model due to Dijkstra. Assume that the source language constituents are to be moved by railway from a source point $A$ to a target point $B$, either by a direct route or by a route which involves waiting at an intermediate point $S$ in a shunting yard with only one track so that only the constituent which has arrived most recently is free to leave. These two methods of moving from $A$ to $B$ are sufficient to permit translation from mathematical notation to reverse Polish notation in a single sequential scan over the source program.

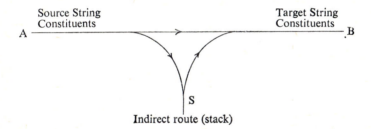

Fig. 1. Shunting yard model of stack.

During translation, operands are normally transferred directly to the target string, and operators are transferred initially to the operator stack $S$. The decision whether an operator is to be transferred from the stack to the target string depends on the relative hierarchy between the operator at the top of the stack (which is a previously encountered operator of the source string) and the current operator of the source string.

When the hierarchy of the current operator of the source string is less than, or equal to, the operator at the top of the stack, then the operator at the top of the stack can be entered into the target string. In the case of the expression

$$A - B + C$$

the hierarchy of $+$ is equal to the hierarchy of $-$. Therefore when the operator $+$ is encountered in scanning the source string (with $AB$ as the partial target string and $-$ in the operator stack) then, since the current source operator $+$ has the same hierarchy as the operator $-$ at the top of the stack, the operator $-$ can be inserted into the target string, giving the partial target string $AB-$ and leading eventually to the reverse Polish target string $AB-C+$.

When the hierarchy of the current source string operator is greater than the hierarchy of the operator at the top of the stack, then the source string operator will occur in the target string before the stack operator. This change of order is accomplished by inserting the source string operator into the top of the operator stack. Thus, in the case of the expression

$$A + B \times C$$

the hierarchy of the $\times$ is greater than the hierarchy of the $+$. Therefore, when the operator $\times$ is encountered in scanning the source string (with $AB$ as the partial target string and $+$ in the operator stack) the $\times$ is inserted into the top of the stack. The $\times$ will subsequently be inserted into the target string before the $+$ leading to the reverse Polish target string $ABC \times +$.

The following table defines the hierarchy numbers of those operators which occur in the subset of ALGOL that can be compiled by the compiler game.

TABLE 2. Operator Hierarchy Table

| Hierarchy Numbers | 0 | 1 | 2 | 3 | 4 | 5 | 6 | 7 | 8 | 9 | 10 |
|---|---|---|---|---|---|---|---|---|---|---|---|
| ALGOL Operators | ( | ; | IF | ∨ | ∧ | ¬ | = | , | − | × | [ |
| | BEGIN | END | ELSE | THEN | | | ≠ | ] | + | ÷ | |
| | ↓ | ) | STEP | GO TO | | | ← | | | / | |
| | | | | | | | < | | | | |
| | | | | | | | ≤ | | | | |
| | | | | | | | > | | | | |
| | | | | | | | ≥ | | | | |

This table is copied from a table given by Burroughs. However, the hierarchies of Boolean operators are wrong and should be ignored.

Now consider the translation of the following slightly more complex source string:

$$BEGIN\ E \leftarrow A \times B + C \times D\ END$$

into the reverse Polish target string

$$EAB \times CD \times + \leftarrow$$

The target string contains the operands $E\ A\ B\ C\ D$ and the operators $\times + \leftarrow$ which have respective hierarchy numbers 9, 8, 6 (see the hierarchy table in Fig. 3). The source string operators $BEGIN$ and $END$ which have hierarchy numbers 0 and 1, do not appear in the target string since they serve as statement parentheses, and reverse Polish is a parentheses free notation.

During translation, successive constituents of the source string are scanned from left to right. Table 3 indicates the contents of the operator stack and target string at successive stages of the translation process.

TABLE 3. Translation of $BEGIN\ E \leftarrow A \times B + C \times D\ END$

| Constituent Number | Current Constituent | Operator Stack | Target String |
|---|---|---|---|
| 1 | BEGIN | | |
| 2 | E | BEGIN | |
| 3 | ← | BEGIN | E |
| 4 | A | BEGIN ← | E |
| 5 | × | BEGIN ← | EA |
| 6 | B | BEGIN ← × | EA |
| 7 | + | BEGIN ← × | EAB |
| | | BEGIN ← | EAB× |
| 8 | C | BEGIN ← + | EAB× |
| 9 | × | BEGIN ← + | EAB × C |
| 10 | D | BEGIN ← +× | EAB × C |
| 11 | END | BEGIN ← +× | EAB × CD |
| | | BEGIN ← + | EAB × CD × |
| | | BEGIN ← | EAB × CD × + |
| | | BEGIN | EAB × CD × +← |
| | | | EAB × CD × +← |

Initially, BEGIN is entered into the operator stack and E is entered into the target string. Then the hierarchy of the operator ← is compared with that of the operator BEGIN at the top of the stack, and since the hierarchy of ← is greater than that of BEGIN the ← is placed above the begin at the top of the operator stack, as indicated in line 4.

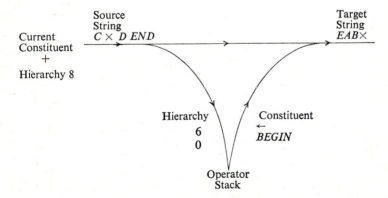

Fig. 2. Partially translated source string.

*A* is then entered into the target string (line 5) and $\times$ is placed above $\leftarrow$ at the top of the operator stack. *B* is then placed in the target string and, since the operator $\times$ at the top of the operator stack has a higher hierarchy than the source program constituent $+$, the operator $\times$ is moved from the stack to the target string. The current contents of the source string, operator stack and target string are exhibited in Fig. 2.

Having moved the operator $\times$ from the stack to the target string, the operator $+$ is compared with the new operator at the top of the stack. Since the hierarchy of $+$ is greater than the hierarchy of $\leftarrow$, $+$ is moved on top of $\leftarrow$ at the top of the operator stack. Then *C* is moved to the target string, $\times$ is moved to the operator stack (since its hierarchy is greater than $+$) and *D* is moved to the target string. When the operator *END* is reached the source string stack and target string appear as follows:

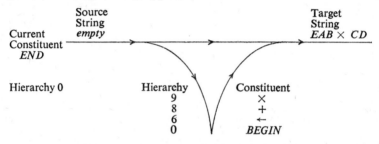

Fig. 3. Partially translated source string.

The operators $\times$ $+$ and $\leftarrow$ are now moved to the target string, resulting in the complete target string

$$EAB \times CD \times + \leftarrow$$

Finally, when the *END* operator encounters the *BEGIN* operator in the stack, a special action is initiated which results in the discarding of the *BEGIN* and *END* operations, leaving an empty stack.

The above procedure indicates in detail the process of translation from mathematical notation to reverse Polish notation. It is interesting to note that the shunting yard model can also be used also to describe the process of execution.

In this case successive operands are automatically introduced into the stack until an operator is encountered. The operator then assumes that it takes its operands from the top of the stack. The operators $+$, $-$, $\times$ and $/$ operate on the two top elements of the stack and place the resultant value at the top of the stack. Since the size of the stack is reduced by two because the operator requires two operands and increased by one when the operator plants the resultant value, the net effect of a binary arithmetic operator is that of reducing by one the number of elements in the stack. The operator $\leftarrow$ stores the value of the top element of the stack in the location specified by the second element of the stack, and reduces by two the number of elements in the stack.

The steps involved in execution of the reverse Polish string

$$EAB \times CD \times + \leftarrow$$

will now be briefly indicated.

The operands *E*, *A* and *B* are entered successively into the top of the stack. Then the operation × is applied to the two top operands in the stack producing a resultant element (say *R1*) in the stack. *C* and *D* are then entered into the stack. At this point the source string and the stack contain the following information.

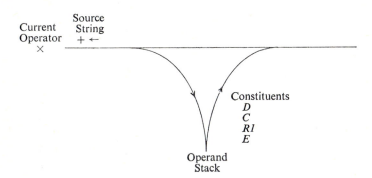

Fig. 4. Partially executed object string.

The operator × is now applied to *C* and *D* to produce a value, say *R2*. Then the operator + is applied to *R1* and *R2* to produce a value, say *R3*. Finally, the operator ← is applied to store the value of *R3* in the location *E*.

It is evident that the use of the stack during execution is much simpler than the use of the stack during translation. During execution there is no need to consider hierarchies, and no need to worry about the output string. In the Burroughs B 5000, execution of a program in reverse Polish notation is performed more or less along the lines indicated above.

## 5. ALGOL Compilation

The Compiler Game is played on a board which contains a flow diagrammatic algorithmic specification of the actions to be taken in scanning successive constituents of the course program (see Fig. 1), a set of data storage areas, on which the cards representing constituents can be placed, and a set of hierarchy tables, which correspond to the compiler tables in an actual compiler.

The flow diagrammed algorithm specifies for each constituent the action that is to be taken. Constituents are split into the three categories, operands, operators and "other", where other includes declarators and *FOR* statements. Operators are split into normal operators for which the procedure

112 P. WEGNER

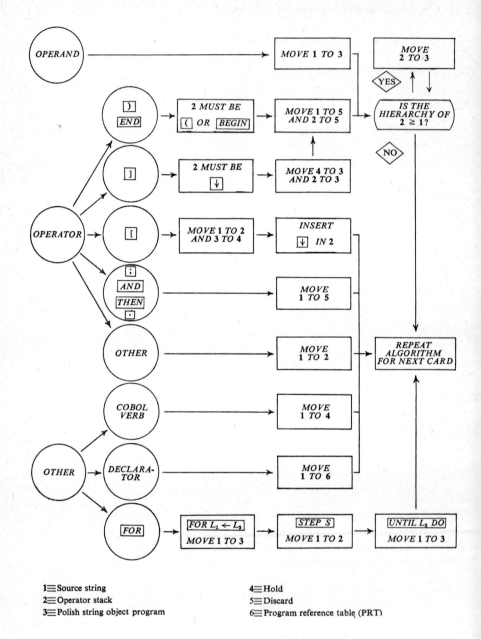

Fig. 5. Flow diagram of the compiler. (Used in the Compiler Game for manual compilation.)

outlined in Section 4 holds and four special classes of operators for which special actions are required.

The following five storage areas are designated on the board.

1. Source String: Corresponding to the input medium.
2. Operator Stack: Corresponding to the operator stack described in Section 4.
3. Polish String Object Program: The reverse Polish notation object program is accumulated in this section.
4. Hold: This is an auxiliary stack required for temporary array storage in the subset of ALGOL which can be compiled.
5. Program Reference Table: The program reference table is a communication region through which programs communicate with their data. Declarators and labels are moved to the program reference table so that they can be referred to when the corresponding names occur in the ALGOL program.

In addition to the above five memory areas, there is also a discard pile onto which source language constituents which do not appear in the source program are discarded.

Initially, the source language program is represented by a deck of cards containing one card for each source language constituent. Each card specifies the constituent number (in order of occurrence in the source string) the name of the constituent, whether it is an operand, operator, declarator or **for** statement and, if it is an operator, the hierarchy number. The following is a typical card representing a constituent:

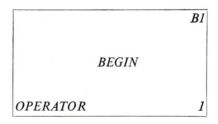

This card is the first card *B1* of program *B*, it represents the constituent *BEGIN*, it is an operator, and it has the hierarchy 1 (right hand lower corner).

Compilation proceeds by examining successive cards in the source string and moving them to the memory areas indicated on the algorithm part of the board.

Operands are moved directly to the target string (as indicated in Section 4). Since an operand is always followed by an operator, the hierarchy comparison between the source string operator and stack operator is performed on an operator which follows an operand immediately after shifting the operand to the target string. A hierarchy test at this point leads to some difficulty, since there is no opportunity to test for special operators before performing the hierarchy comparison. This leads to artificial hierarchy numbers which are different from those which would be assigned if special operators were dealt with before the hierarchy comparison is made.

The method of hierarchy comparison described above ensures that when an operator is encountered in the source string, all operators in the operator stack whose hierarchy entitles them to be moved to the target string will already have been moved. A normal (other) operator is therefore moved to the operator stack without further hierarchy testing. Special actions are performed for special operators.

Declarators are always moved directly to the program reference table.

A *FOR* clause consists of three constituents. The first and third constituents are moved directly to the target string, and the second constituent is moved to the operator stack and subsequently treated as an operator of hierarchy 1.

The compilation of the sample program of Section 3 by means of the rules of Fig. 1 is summarized below.

1. The first *BEGIN* operator is placed in the operator stack.

2. The next three constituents which define all operands of the program are stored in the program reference table.

3. The statement $Y \leftarrow 0.0$ is translated to Polish notation as described in section 4.2. The ; terminating this and subsequent statements is discarded.

4. The two *FOR* clauses are translated by placing the *FOR 1* and *FOR 3* parts directly in the target program and storing the *FOR 2* part in the operator stack for subsequent insertion at the termination of the *FOR* loop.

5. The Boolean conditional relation is translated into Polish notation, the operator *IF* being stored in the operator stack for subsequent insertion.

6. The *THEN* is discarded.

7. The three statements between the *BEGIN* and *END* operators are translated to Polish notation.

8. The *IF* operator is inserted to indicate the end of the conditionally executed statement.

9. The *FOR 2* operators are inserted to indicate the end of respective *FOR* loops.

10. Finally, the final *END* statement is matched with the initial *BEGIN* statement indicating that the translation procedure has been completed.

## 6. COBOL Compilation

The Burroughs Compiler game permits processing of both ALGOL programs and COBOL procedure descriptions using the same algorithm and the same memory organization. All that is required is a special hierarchy table for COBOL operators, and the addition of facilities to process COBOL verbs and one or two COBOL constituents that are not in ALGOL. Table 4 gives the hierarchy table used for COBOL operators, and a list of COBOL verbs.

The following COBOL program which is a portion of an accounts receivable routine will be analysed in detail.

*UPDATE-MASTER. IF ACCOUNT-NUMBER EQUALS ACCOUNT-NUMBER-OF-MASTER ADD INCREMENT TO COUNTER GIVING COUNTER AND GO TO PROCESS-MASTER. GO TO NEW-ACCOUNT.*
*PROCESS-MASTER. SUBTRACT AMOUNT-PAID FROM AMOUNT-RECEIVABLE GIVING AMOUNT-RECEIVABLE. MOVE DATE-OF-CRS TO DATE-OF-CUSTOMER-ACCOUNT.*

TABLE 4. COBOL Operators and Verbs

| | 0 | 1 | 2 | 3 | 4 |
|---|---|---|---|---|---|
| O | ( | ) | *GIVING* | *(ADD) TO* | × |
| P | | : | = | *(SUBTRACT) FROM* | *(MULTIPLY) BY* |
| E | | *IF* | *GO TO* | *(ADD),* | / |
| R | | . | *EXCEEDS* | + | *(DIVIDE) INTO* |
| A | | *OTHERWISE* | *AND* | − | |
| T | | | *EQUALS* | | |
| O | | | *(MOVE) TO* | | |
| R | | | *IS GREATER THAN* | | |
| S | | | *IS LESS THAN* | | |

The following COBOL verbs are permitted:

*ADD*
*MULTIPLY*
*DIVIDE*
*SUBTRACT*
*MOVE*
*COMPUTE*

This routine consists of two paragraphs labelled respectively *UPDATE-MASTER* and *PROCESS-MASTER*. The first paragraph contains two sentences of which the first is a conditional statement and the second is a *GO TO* statement. The conditional statement tests the account number of the current item against the account number of the master file. If the account numbers match the item is part of the current account being processed, and is processed by the paragraph *PROCESS-MASTER*. Otherwise the item belongs to a *NEW-ACCOUNT* and control is transferred to a portion of the program which initiates a new account. The *PROCESS-MASTER* paragraph consists of two simple arithmetic sentences which are concerned with updating of the account. The individual constituents of the COBOL program together with their types and hierarchies are indicated in Fig. 5.

TABLE 5

| Number of Constituents | Constituent | Type of Constituent | Hierarchy of Operator (or COBOL Verb) |
|---|---|---|---|
| 1 | UPDATE-MASTER | LABEL (DECLARATOR) | |
| 2 | IF | OPERATOR | 1 |
| 3 | ACCOUNT-NUMBER | OPERAND | |
| 4 | EQUALS | OPERATOR | 2 |
| 5 | ACCOUNT-NUMBER-OF-MASTER | OPERAND | |
| 6 | ADD | VERB | 2 |
| 7 | INCREMENT | OPERAND | |
| 8 | (ADD) TO | OPERATOR | 3 |
| 9 | COUNTER | OPERAND | |
| 10 | GIVING | OPERATOR | 2 |
| 11 | COUNTER | OPERAND | |
| 12 | AND | OPERATOR | 2 |
| 13 | GO TO | OPERATOR | 2 |
| 14 | PROCESS-MASTER | OPERAND | |
| 15 | . | OPERATOR | 1 |
| 16 | GO TO | OPERATOR | 2 |
| 17 | NEW ACCOUNT | OPERAND | |
| 18 | . | OPERATOR | 1 |
| 19 | PROCESS-MASTER | LABEL (DECLARATOR) | |
| 20 | SUBTRACT | VERB | 2 |
| 21 | AMOUNT-PAID | OPERAND | |
| 22 | (SUBTRACT) FROM | OPERATOR | 3 |
| 23 | AMOUNT-RECEIVABLE | OPERAND | |
| 24 | GIVING | OPERATOR | 2 |
| 25 | AMOUNT-RECEIVABLE | OPERAND | |
| 26 | . | OPERATOR | 1 |
| 27 | MOVE | VERB | 2 |
| 28 | DATE-OF-CRS | OPERAND | |
| 29 | (MOVE) TO | OPERATOR | 2 |
| 30 | DATE-OF-CUSTOMER-ACCOUNT | OPERAND | |
| 31 | . | OPERATOR | 1 |

The reverse Polish string program has the following form:

ACCOUNT-NUMBER  ACCOUNT-NUMBER-OF-MASTER  EQUALS
INCREMENT COUNTER (ADD) TO COUNTER GIVING
PROCESS-MASTER GO TO
IF
NEW-ACCOUNT GO TO
AMOUNT-PAID AMOUNT-RECEIVABLE (SUBTRACT) FROM
AMOUNT-RECEIVABLE GIVING DATE-OF-CRS DATE-OF-
CUSTOMER-ACCOUNT (MOVE) TO

It should be noted that the reverse Polish target string contains no labels or verbs. Labels have been noted in the program reference table and are available when required. Verbs determine the mode of interpretation of certain operators. Their effect is indicated by qualifying the affected operators by the verb names enclosed in parentheses.

The first line of the Polish string above is the Boolean condition of the *IF* statement. The scope of this condition, which is indicated by the operator *IF* on the fourth line, is an arithmetic statement and a *GO TO* statement. The fifth line contains the *GO TO* statement to be executed when the condition is not satisfied.

The sixth and seventh line contain the two arithmetic statements which constitute the paragraph *PROCESS-MASTER*.

### 7. Limitations on Syntax

*1. Limitations on* ALGOL *Syntax*

The subset of ALGOL 60 which can be compiled using the compiler game is extremely limited, and may be approximately defined as follows:

1. Assignment statements with the exception of
   (a) Conditional assignment statements
   (b) Subroutine references
   (c) Procedure references
   (d) Exponentation
   (e) Boolean variables and Boolean assignment statements
   (f) Multiple assignment statements
   (g) Unary $+$ and $-$
2. *FOR* statements using the *FOR* $I \leftarrow L_1$ *STEP S UNTIL* $L_2$ *DO* structure (where $I$, $L_1$, $S$, $L_2$ are simple variables)
3. *IF* statements
4. The declarations *REAL, INTEGER, ARRAY*
5. *GO TO* statements (excluding conditional designational expressions)
6. Compound statements
7. Single or multiple subscription of variables (excluding conditional subscript expressions.

*2. Limitations on* COBOL *Syntax*

1. Imperative statements using the following verbs in conjunction with the verb *GIVING*: *ADD, SUBTRACT, MULTIPLY, DIVIDE*
2. Imperative statements using the verb *MOVE*
3. *GO TO* statements
4. The *COMPUTE* verb and associated arithmetic expressions
5. *IF* statements, using the test construction only (e.g. *IF GROSS-PAY IS GREATER THAN 100.00 GO TO A-5*)

### 8. Acknowledgement

Acknowledgement is made to the Burroughs Corporation as the source of the compiler game and of a helpful accompanying manual.

## Appendix

*B5000 Machine Language*

The B5000 word length is 48 bits. B5000 instructions are called syllables. Syllables are 12 bits long, being stored 4 to a computer word.

The machine language is built around the fact that operators find their operands in a stack. Binary arithmetic operators take their two arguments from the two top locations of the stack and store their result in the top of the stack. Operands are obtained by specifying a 10 bit address in a 'program reference table'. The program reference table may contain either an operand or a 'data descriptor' which specifies an operand belonging to a more complex data structure such as an array.

There are four types of syllable, which are distinguished by two binary bits. The remaining 10 bits in each syllable specify a literal, an address in the program reference table, or an operation. The function of the above four types of syllable are as follows:

1. *Literal Syllable (LT)*. This type of syllable causes the positive 10 bit integer contained in its low order bits to be put into the stack. Literals which appear in the stack may be used to index descriptions in the program reference table.

2. *Operand Call (OC)*. This type of syllable causes an operand specified by a descriptor in the program reference table to be transferred to the stack. The descriptor is specified by a 10 bit address, and may be indexed by a literal previously entered into the stack.

3. *Descriptor Call (DC)*. This type of syllable causes the address of an operand specified by a descriptor in the program reference table to be transferred to the stack. The descriptor is specified by a 10 bit address and may be indexed by a literal previously entered into the stack.

4. *Operator (OP)*. This type of syllable causes the operation specified by the 10 low order bits of the syllable to be performed.

The use of the above four types of syllables will be illustrated by the following simple example:

$X(10) = S(5) + T(7)$    Add the 5th element of the array $S$ to the 7th element of the array $T$ and store the result as the 10th element of the array $X$.

The program for this computation is as follows:

| | |
|---|---|
| *LT* 5 | Literal 5 to top of stack. |
| *OC* S | Operand call $S$ indexed by literal 5. $S(5)$ to top of stack. |
| *LT* 7 | Literal 7 to top of stack. Push down $S(5)$. |
| *OC* T | Operand call $T$ indexed by 7. $T(7)$ to top of stack. |
| *OP* + | Perform + operations on two top stack elements. $S(5) + T(7)$ to top of stack. |
| *LT* 10 | Literal 10 to top of stack. Push down $S(5) + T(7)$. |
| *DC* X | Descriptor call $X$ indexed by 10. Address of $X(10)$ to top of stack. |
| *OP Store* | Store 2nd element of stack in the address specified by the top element, i.e. $S(5) + T(7) \rightarrow X(10)$. |

The B5000 machine language programs corresponding to the ALGOL and COBOL programs described in sections 3 and 6 are given in Figs. 7 and 8, and can be deciphered with the aid of the following mnemonics.

*XCH*    Exchange first and second elements in the stack.

*STD*    Store descriptor, i.e. store 2nd element in the stack in the location specified by the first.

*SND*    Send, i.e. store the second element in the stack in the location specified by the first and leave the value in the top of the stack.

*GTR*    Greater than. Set branch indicator if 2nd location of the stack is greater than the top location.

*CBF*    Conditional Branch Forward. Branch to the location specified in the program reference table if the conditional branch indicator is on, and switch off branch indicator. The program reference table address is specified in the top location of the stack.

*DD($A_i$)*    Data Descriptor $A_i$. This specifies a row descriptor for rows $A_i$ of the matrix $A_{ij}$.

*MDV*    Matrix Descriptor Value. This operation computes the effective address of the matrix element specified by operands at the top of the stack, and obtains the value of the matrix element.

*LEQ*    Less than or equal to. Set branching indicator if the 2nd location of the stack is less than or equal to the top location of the stack.

*UBB*    Unconditional Branch Backward. Branch unconditionally to the location specified in the program reference table. The program reference table address is specified in the top location of the stack.

*UBF*    Unconditional Branch Forward. Same as *UBB*.

*PROBLEM B*
ALGOL Program

Y      0.0      ↓

| LT:Y | LT:O.O | OP:XCH | OP:STD |

FOR J ← 1
    UNTIL N DO

| LT:J | OP:SND | OC:N | OP:GTR |

>      Y

| LT:S | OP:CBF | LT:Y | OC:I |

L      J

| OP:STD | LT:L | OC:J | OP:XCH |

↓

STEP 1

| OC:I | LT:1 | OP:ADD | LT:1 |

FOR I ← 1

| LT:1 | LT:1 | OP:SND | OC:M |

I

| LT:K2 | OP:CBF | OC:I | OC:DD(A₁) |

J      A↓

| OC:DD(A₁) | OC:J | OP:MDV | OP:XCH |

↓

| OP:STD | OC:J | LT:1 | OP:ADD |

IF STEP 1

| OP:SND | LT:L1 | OP:UBB |

UNTIL M DO      FOR J ← 1

| OP:GTR | LT:KI | OP:CBF | LT:1 |

J      A↓      Y

| OC:J | OP:MDV | OC:Y | OP:LEQ |

K      I

| OP:STD | LT:K | OC:I | OP:XCH |

↓

| LT:J | OP:SND | LT:L | OP:UBB |

| | | |

PROBLEM C
COBOL Program

ACCOUNT-NUMBER    ACCOUNT-NUMBER-OF-MASTER    EQUALS    INCREMENT

OC:A    LT:S2  OC:B    OP:NEQ ‖ LT:S1  OP:CBF    OC:C

COUNTER  (ADD) TO  COUNTER  GIVING  PROCESS-MASTER  GO TO  IN NEW-ACCOUNT

OC:D  OP:ADD  DC:D  OP:STD  LT:S3  OP:UBF  LT:S4

GO TO  AMOUNT RECEIVABLE  AMOUNT-PAID  (SUBTRACT) FROM  AMOUNT-RECEIVABLE

OP:UBF  OC:F  OC:E  OP:SUB  DC:F

GIVING  DATE-OF-CRS  DATE-OF-CUSTOMER-ACCOUNT  (MOVE) TO

OP:STD  OC:G  LT:S5  DC:H  OP:STD

# 8. THE WHETSTONE KDF9 ALGOL TRANSLATOR

## B. RANDELL

*The English Electric Company Ltd., Atomic Power Division, Whetstone, England*

## 1. Introduction

Past experience with computers and translation schemes at the Atomic Power Division has shown that users' requirements of an automatic programming scheme are to some extent conflicting. On the one hand the price paid for ease of writing and testing in a convenient language must be small, and, particularly for large or frequently used programs, the final running efficiency must be high. The first objective requires extremely fast translation—the second requires a large sophisticated translator with consequent increase in translation time. Possible solutions to this problem are, firstly, to have a compromise scheme, perhaps capable of varying degrees of sophistication, or secondly to satisfy the two requirements with two translators.

The second solution has much to recommend it, and has indeed been chosen. A team at the Data Processing Division is working on a large multi-pass optimizing translator, with the aim of producing as efficient a running program as possible. In parallel a smaller translator is being developed at Whetstone, due to be ready as quickly as possible after completion of the prototype KDF9, in which great stress has been laid on speed of translation, and on ease of communication between object program and programmer. This separation of translators enables each scheme to pursue its own objectives to the full, and allows the writers of the large scheme more time to pursue their goal of run time efficiency.

Naturally the two schemes are to have complete compatibility, and should enable a user to test a new program quickly and efficiently, and then recompile it to get an efficient running program. Both schemes will accept full ALGOL 60, with only the following restrictions: 1. no dynamic own arrays; 2. no integer labels; 3. obligatory specifications for all parameters.

The Whetstone translator takes advantage of the fact that due to the high speed of operation of the KDF9 computer, there is considerable scope for utilizing the time spent during input of a program. This leads naturally to the development of a scheme for strict one-pass translation of an ALGOL program, so that the object program is complete, ready to be obeyed, almost immediately after the reading of the ALGOL ceases.

## 2. The KDF9 Computer

Very little mention need be made of the KDF9 computer on which this translation scheme is being implemented. The basic machine configuration needed is an 8k core store, paper tape input/output, monitor typewriter, and two magnetic tape units. Each word of core storage is of 48 bits, made up of six 8-bit syllables. Only within the translation routine and the subroutines that make up the run time control routine is full use made of the rather novel nesting-store accumulator, which thus need not be considered in this paper.

Although the KDF9 is a binary machine the normal method of preparing machine code programs will be in User Code, an alphanumeric assembly language.

For a more complete description of the KDF9 and its User Code, see references 1 and 5.

## 3. The Object Program

At an early stage in the project, the author and a colleague, Mr L. J. Russell, met Dr Dijkstra, of the Mathematical Centre, Amsterdam, who, with Mr Zonneveld, was joint author of the extremely successful ALGOL translator for the Centre's X1 computer. Later, at the invitation of Dr Dijkstra, a most pleasant week was spent at the Mathematical Centre discussing translation techniques (Randell and Russell, 1962).

The object program generated by the Whetstone translator is a development of that of the X1 translator. Thus the object program consists of a set of operations, with parameters where necessary, which use the remaining core storage as a stack (Dijkstra, 1960) containing all the currently available declared quantities. The stack system is a natural consequence both of the block structure of ALGOL and of the fact that recursive calls can be made on procedures. The object program is obeyed interpretively at run time by a control routine, which performs the normal arithmetic and logical operations, dynamic storage allocation of arrays, and all the necessary stack manipulation operations.

The requirements of parallel declarations and one-pass translation have their effect on the design of the object program, which must be capable of being partially generated as the ALGOL is read in, and then completed when any previously missing declarations are found.

### 1. Arithmetic Expressions

The method of using a stack for the evaluation of an arithmetic expression is quite straightforward, and has been described by Dijkstra (1961a). Essentially any necessary operands are copied from their positions in the working storage section of the stack, into the top position of the stack, with information as to type, etc. All arithmetic operations work on the top one or two stack positions. Stack positions which contain a value, an address or a label, and information pertaining to the quantity, occupy a double-word of storage, called an accumulator, whereas the type and meaning of any quantity in working storage is always known at translation time, and can thus be given implicitly in any operations referring to it. The precedence of operations implied in an arithmetic expression is given explicitly by a re-ordering of operations into 'Reverse Polish' in the object program.

### Example

$x := i + y;$        ($x$, $y$ of type **real**, $i$ of type **integer**)

This is re-ordered into the Reverse Polish form

$x, i, y, +, :=$

This bears a close resemblance to the actual object program which is generated. In fact, in the object program the above identifiers are represented by 'Take Result' or 'Take Address' operations, each with a parameter used to find the location assigned to the identifier.

Thus the above statement is translated into

| TRA | $x$ | (Take Real Address) |
|-----|-----|---------------------|
| TIR | $i$ | (Take Integer Result) |
| TRR | $y$ | (Take Real Result) |
| $+$ |     | (Add) |
| ST  |     | (Store) |

(The identifiers $x$, $i$, $y$, here represent stack addresses).

The extent of the stack is always given by a counter $AP$, the Accumulator Pointer, counting in units of one word. $AP$ always indicates the first free store after the end of the stack, i.e. the store into which the next quantity to be stacked would be placed.

Then in the above example, if $AP$ is originally, say 12, the detailed action of the operation is:

| TRA | $x$ | Address of $x$ set in Stack [12] and a bit pattern meaning 'real address' in Stack [13]. Two added to $AP$. |
|-----|-----|---------------------|
| TIR | $i$ | Value of $i$ set in Stack [14], 'integer result' in Stack [15], two added to $AP$. |
| TRR | $y$ | Value of $y$ set in Stack [16], 'real result' in Stack [17], two added to $AP$. |
| $+$ |     | Examines positions $AP-3$, $AP-1$ (i.e. 15, 17) does the necessary conversion of $i$ in Stack [14], sets the result $i + y$ in Stack [14], 'real result' in Stack [15] and decreases $AP$ by two. |
| ST  |     | Works on top accumulator (a result) and the next accumulator (an address) does any necessary type conversions, performs the storage, and decreases $AP$ by four. |

## 2. Procedures and Blocks

At any point during the execution of the object program the stack will contain for each procedure: 1. an accumulator space for a resulting procedure value; 2. link data; 3. parameters; 4. declared scalars, labels, array words; 5. array storage; and 6. anonymous intermediate results. Apart from the procedure value accumulator, and the parameters, a block is treated as a procedure, and in what follows the two terms are used interchangeably.

Thus a recursive activation of a procedure will be shown by more than one such set of stacked information. The link data performs a double purpose— to provide access to the declared variables in the last activation of every procedure, and to provide a means of unravelling a set of nested procedure calls, through every activation of each procedure. Declared variables in stacked working storage are addressed relative to the starting position of the stack information pertaining to the block in which they are declared (this position is called $PP$ – the procedure pointer). Since the amount of link data is fixed, the addresses, relative to $PP$, of parameters and declared variables can be assigned at translation time. Thus the first function of the link data (providing access to declared variables) requires a scheme for finding the value of $PP$ for the last activation of each procedure, which can then be used with the relative address, to form the actual stack address of a declared variable. The second function of the link data is performed quite simply by maintaining a list of successive values of $PP$, for each activation of each procedure. (This list is called the dynamic chain, whilst the list of $PP$'s for the last activation of each procedure is called the static chain.) At any stage only the current procedure, and its surrounding procedures, are of any interest. A Block Number ($BN$), starting at one for the main program level, is allocated for each lexicographic level of block or procedure. Thus the static chain has one value of $PP$ for each level of the program, up to the current level. For the sake of efficiency the static chain is duplicated in a vector called $DISPLAY$. Then reference to any declared variable is by means of a dynamic address $(n, p)$, where $n$ is the lexicographic level of the block in which the declaration occurs, and $p$ is the stack address of the variable relative to the $PP$ of the block. The dynamic address is evaluated as '$DISPLAY [n] + p$'. It would be possible to find the appropriate $PP$ without using $DISPLAY$, by just working back down the static chain in the sets of stacked link data until the right level was encountered, but this is obviously inefficient.

The dynamic chain is rather more complicated as it is this mechanism that allows the stack to be restored to its original condition after exit from a procedure.

Taking an example of a block $a$ containing a procedure call on a procedure $b$ declared in a block $c$.

When the call is made the next available accumulator (indicated by $AP$) is left for a possible result from the procedure and after completion of the entry to the procedure the stack is:

Core No.

| | | |
|---|---|---|
| | 0⎫ 1⎭ | Procedure Value Accumulator |
| $APa, PPb$: | 2 | $PPc$ Static Chain |
| | | $PPa$ Dynamic Chain |
| | 3 | $BNb, WPb$ Block Number, Working Storage Pointer |
| | | $FP$ Formal Pointer |
| | 4 | $RAa$ Return Address |
| | | $LINK$ User Code Link |
| | 5⎫ 6⎭ | 1st Formal Parameter |
| | 7⎫ 8⎭ | 2nd Formal Parameter |

Core No.
    9      1st Working Store
    10      2nd Working Store
    11      3rd Working Store

*WPb, APb*: 12

In this example of a procedure with two parameters and three working stores, core numbers have been given arbitrarily from zero.

The ruling value of *PP* after entry to procedure *b* indicates the start of the link data, and is equal to the value of *AP* before entering procedure *b* from procedure *a*. The dynamic chain, in the second half of core 2, is the value of *PP* ruling during procedure *a*. The block number and amount of working space of the procedure *b* are known at translation time, and are given as parameters to the object program operation which performs the entry to the procedure for storage in the link data. The static chain is the *PP* of the block containing the procedure *b*, i.e. of the one with a block number one less than that of *b*. This could be found by working down through the chained link data, but in fact can be obtained directly from the vector *DISPLAY*. The new value of *PP* is added to *DISPLAY* at the position given by the block number of *b*. The formal pointer is originally set to indicate the first formal parameter accumulator, and is used in processing the parameters at a procedure call. The remaining link data consists of a return address and a User Code link. When a procedure is left the return address is used to reset the object program counter. The User Code link indicates the place within the control routine from where a procedure was called. Control is returned to this point, to finish any necessary functions of the control routine before calling for the next object program operation (as given by the reset object program counter).

This system for using a stack for procedures, possibly recursive, is fairly straightforward—the main complication is in ensuring that *DISPLAY* always contains a copy of the static chain. Whenever the validity of *DISPLAY* is in doubt it must be checked against the actual static chain given in the sets of stacked link data. This must be done on all formal procedure calls, and on leaving any procedure, normally or by a go to statement.

*Example*

```
begin integer i;
      procedure Q;
Q1 : begin real x;
          . . . . .
      Q2 : begin real y;
                . . . . .
                y : = 0;
                . . . . .
            end;
          . . . . .
      end;
      . . . . .
```

*P1* :   **begin real** *a*;

      . . . . .

   *P2* :   **begin real** *b*;

         . . . . .

      *P3* :   **begin real** *C*;

            . . . . .
               *C* : = *0*; *Q*
            **end**
         **end**
      **end**
   **end**

In this example, where dots indicate further statements, indentation has been used to show the various levels. Each block has been labelled, so as to indicate the level at which the label occurs, and the fact of being part of procedure *Q* or of the main program. It should be noted that a procedure whose body is itself a block only causes a single change in level.

The system of dynamic and static chaining, and the associated vector *DISPLAY* are illustrated using the above labels. For this purpose the main program is assumed to have the label *PROGRAM*.

*i.* At the assignment of zero to *C* only the blocks labelled *PROGRAM*, *P1*, *P2* and *P3* have been activated. The static and dynamic chains coincide, chaining together the four sets of link data in the stack, which correspond to the above four activations of blocks. Four entries have been made in display.

$$DISPLAY \ [1] = PROGRAM$$
$$DISPLAY \ [2] = P1$$
$$DISPLAY \ [3] = P2$$
$$DISPLAY \ [4] = P3$$

Here the labels in fact indicate stack addresses – the values of *PP* for each activation of each block.

*ii.* However, at the assignment of zero to *y*, in the call of procedure *Q* in block *P3*, the situation is more complicated. Six blocks have been activated, but only three (*PROGRAM*, *Q1* and *Q2*) are currently valid, in the sense of having declarations which could pertain to the situation at the statement '*y* : = *0*'. Thus the stack must still contain activations of blocks *P1*, *P2* and *P3*, hidden under the activations of blocks *Q1* and *Q2*.

As a result the dynamic chain links together, in order,

*PROGRAM, P1, P2, P3, Q1* and *Q2*

(this list, read from right to left, gives the complete set of blocks to be unravelled by working out through the various **end**'s),

whilst the static chain only links together

*PROGRAM, Q1* and *Q2*

Therefore at this time *DISPLAY*, which must mirror this static chain, contains only three entries

> *DISPLAY* [1] = *PROGRAM*
> *DISPLAY* [2] = *Q1*
> *DISPLAY* [3] = *Q2*

### 3. Parameters

On entry to a procedure the parameter operations in the object program are processed to set up the formal parameter accumulators in the stack, following the link data. For instance an actual parameter which is just a real variable is translated into a parameter operation with its dynamic address. At the procedure call this causes the corresponding formal parameter accumulator to be set up with the evaluated dynamic address together with an identifying bit pattern. The evaluation of the dynamic address is done before any adjustments to *DISPLAY*.

Of more interest is an expression as actual parameter corresponding to a formal parameter called by name. An implicit subroutine of object program operations is generated, with a parameter operation giving the address of this subroutine. At a procedure call this parameter operation causes the formal parameter accumulator to be set up with the address of the subroutine, and the *PP* ruling at the time of the procedure call.

A call on this parameter causes the subroutine to be entered in much the same way as a procedure is entered, stacking vital information such as *PP*, *AP*, etc., during operation of the subroutine. Before completing entry to the subroutine, the value of *PP* in the formal parameter accumulator is used to set up *DISPLAY* in the state it had at the procedure call—this enables correct evaluation of the expression, as it is written in terms of declarations valid at procedure call. After the subroutine has completed the evaluation of the expression the normal mechanism for leaving a procedure resets conditions to those pertaining before entering the subroutine, but with the result of the expression in the top accumulator, just as if it had been placed there by a 'Take Result' operation.

### 4. Arrays

The organization of arrays in the Whetstone translator is fairly conventional. A word is set aside in working storage for each array, to contain the base address of the array, the starting address of the array, and the address of the storage mapping function of the relevant array segment. After entry to a block, operations are obeyed for each array segment, to set up the mapping function (the coefficients of a polynomial for evaluating the address of a subscripted variable), the array words, and space for the arrays, and to increase the working space, as indicated by the stacked working space pointer, to include the mapping function and the arrays.

Arrays as formal parameters are dealt with by handing on the address of the relevant array word. In the case of an array called by value the array is copied into the stack, after the current working space, and a suitably adjusted copy of the array word set up in the formal parameter accumulator.

### 5. *Labels and Switches*

Labels are allocated space in the working storage of their block. This space is set up with the appropriate value of the object program counter, and the current value of *PP*. These labels can then be manipulated in designational expressions, and handed on, perhaps repeatedly, as formal parameters, the value of *PP* being used if necessary to adjust *DISPLAY* when the label is actually used.

A switch can be thought of as a 'label procedure', which delivers the result of one of a set of designational expressions. Entry to a switch is like entry to a procedure, and thus can go recursive in a similar fashion. The end product is a label in the top accumulator, ready for the operation generated from the go to statement.

### 6. *For Statements*

A for statement is organized by a portion of the control routine (the for routine) which uses sections of the object program, for evaluating the various arithmetic and Boolean expressions, and the address of the controlled variable, as subroutines. This is done by stacking a User Code link to be found by a special object program operation at the end of each subroutine, which then returns to the appropriate point in the for routine. The system of making the expressions and controlled variable into subroutines allows each one to be translated once, in the order in which they appear, even for the step-until element, which has to simulate an expanded ALGOL version with repeated reference to these quantities.

A for statement is automatically made into a block, and thus sets up the normal stack positions for link data, etc. Then at any point where an interruption of the work of the for routine can occur, all relevant information is kept in the stack. Such an interruption will occur when the controlled statement involves a for statement (explicitly, or within some procedure call) or when evaluation of an expression in a for list element, or of the address of the controlled variable, calls on a function designator which involves a for statement.

### 4. The Translation Routine

The translation routine operates on the ALGOL program as it is read in, generating the object program in the core storage. The re-ordering of operations is performed using a translator stack and a system of priorities. This handles precedence of arithmetic operators, etc., and is used also for the bracket structure of ALGOL. A name list is used to contain details of identifiers encountered in the current and all the surrounding blocks. As there is no opportunity to scan the ALGOL program a set of state variables is used to differentiate between different uses of the same delimiter. The basic system is to read the ALGOL program until a delimiter is found, noting if an identifier or a constant has been read in. Each delimiter has its own routine, which has at its disposal a set of general subroutines for performing the various tasks common to two or more delimiters.

The need for strict one-pass translation necessitates being able to proceed with the generation of object program when lacking declarations of identifiers, and in fact never being able to use any non-local declarations until the end of a block is reached.

The arbitrary order of declarations can cause difficulties. For example, declarations for non-local variables to a procedure can appear after the procedure declaration. The context in which an identifier is used is not always helpful — in particular the case of use as an actual parameter to a procedure. The name list is used to contain declaration information, if available, or the sum total of information garnered from the various uses of an identifier.

Being able to proceed with object program generation is facilitated by designing the object program so that the operations generated from a given use of an identifier take a similar form no matter what kind of declaration is subsequently found. For instance, what appears to be a subscripted variable in an actual parameter list may in fact turn out to be a switch designator.

## 1. The Translator Stack

By assigning priorities to certain of the ALGOL delimiters the translator stack can deal very simply with questions of arithmetic precedence, bracket structure, conditional statements, etc. Essentially the stack is used as a holding store, and is used to re-order the ALGOL into Reverse Polish, which is the form of the object program, as described in Section 3.

The basic system can be illustrated on a simple arithmetic expression

$$A + B \times (C - D/(E + F \times G)) \uparrow H$$

This input string is read from left to right, and symbols can be transferred to the output string, or can go into the stack (used simply as a last in — first out store). Each operator has a priority; this is compared with the priority of the operator at the top of the stack, and determines the action to be taken. 1. Operands are transmitted straight to the output. 2. Left parenthesis is stacked with a priority zero. 3. Right parenthesis causes operators to move from stack to output until a left parenthesis is uncovered. This is then removed. 4. The remaining operators each have a priority. As each operator is met, its priority is checked against the priority at the top of the stack, and operators are moved from the stack to the output until an operator with a priority less than the priority of this current operator is encountered. The input operator is then itself placed in the stack.

The priorities are
$$+, \quad - \quad 2$$
$$\times, \quad / \quad 3$$
$$\uparrow \quad 4$$

(Unary '+' and '−' are not dealt with in this simple system.)

Right parenthesis is essentially controlling unloading of the stack with a priority of one, and hence must uncover its matching left parenthesis.

By this means the above expression would be re-ordered into

$$A, B, C, D, E, F, G, \times, +, /, -, H, \uparrow, \times, +$$

However, the system can be greatly extended by using a double priority system, to deal with conditional expressions and statements, statement brackets, etc. The double priority is necessary because certain delimiters perform what is essentially a double function. For example **then** can be used to terminate a Boolean expression and to precede a statement. In general each delimiter is given a 'stack priority' and a 'compare priority'. As their names suggest, the stack priority accompanies a delimiter when placed in the stack, and the compare priority is used to control unloading of the stack.

Thus **then** must unstack through a Boolean expression, which could be conditional, to its corresponding **if**, and **until** must unstack through an arithmetic expression to the delimiter **step**, etc.

Some delimiters, such as opening parentheses, **begin**, etc., go straight into the stack without doing any unstacking. Where necessary the translator stack is used to store away certain of the state variables with the current delimiter.

*Example*

The re-ordering performed using a stack and a double priority system can be illustrated on the following ALGOL statement.

**if** $b$ **then** $W$ [**if** $A = B$ **then** $C + A \times B$ **else** $D$] := $A + B > C$
  **else go to** $L$;

is re-ordered into

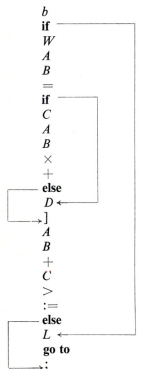

Here **else** indicates an unconditional jump,

**if** indicates a jump conditional on the top

accumulator being **false**, and ']' an indexing

operation, which forms the address of a

subscripted variable.

for resetting later. This avoids using explicitly recursive subroutines for dealing with, for instance, arithmetic expressions in a subscript in an arithmetic expression.

Syllable counters are stored with some delimiters, to permit later completion of the object program. For example at **then**, an incomplete implicit jump is generated, and the syllable number of its position stacked with the **then**. When the corresponding **else** finds this in the stack the implicit jump around the expression or statement following the **then** can be completed.

It is necessary to differentiate between the **then** and **else** used in conditional expressions and in conditional statements, and this is done by using the state variables. Similarly the various uses of comma, for instance, in subscript lists, for clauses, switch lists, etc., must be differentiated.

## 2. The Name List

The name list is used to contain information about each identifier in the current block, and in all surrounding blocks. Thus the name list, like the translator stack, can fluctuate in size.

An entry is made in the name list at the declaration of an identifier or at the use of an identifier which does not appear in the part of the list pertaining to the current block. Thus entries consist of the actual identifier, a bit pattern specifying type or expected type, number of dimensions or subscripts if applicable, some markers concerned mainly with checking, and either the dynamic address which has been assigned to the identifier or chaining information. Chaining is used to link together incomplete object program operations which are generated for calls on an undeclared identifier. Because of parallel declarations and the system of chaining it is only ever necessary to search through the section of the name list pertaining to the current block, rather than through the complete list whenever an identifier is encountered.

## 3. The System of Chaining

All object program operations concerned with calls on identifiers consist of a one-syllable operation code and a two-syllable address. Only when an identifier appears as a 'declared' entry in the name list for the current block can a use of the identifier be translated fully. If a set of incomplete operations have to be chained together the two syllables left for the address are used to contain a link of the chain, and the single syllable for an indication of the type of use being made of the identifier. When the relevant declaration is found the chain is scanned, replacing the single syllable by the appropriate operation code, and the link by the address of the identifier. Each use of an identifier is checked against information gained from previous uses, which is kept in the name list. By the time the declaration is reached the name list will contain the 'logical sum' of all the information known about the identifier, and this is checked against the declaration information.

The chaining system is basically as follows.

### i. At use of an identifier

The name list for the current block is searched. If it contains a 'declared' entry for this identifier then this is used, and no chaining is necessary.

If there is no entry a 'used' entry is added to the name list accompanied by two syllable counters, both set to indicate the position of the space left in the object program for the address of the identifier. These syllable counters, called $CS$ and $CF$, indicate the start and finish of the chain for this identifier.

If there is already a 'used entry' the value of $CS$ contained in it is placed in the object program in the space left for the address of this identifier, and then $CS$ is replaced by the syllable counter of this address space.

### ii.  At declaration of an identifier

The name list for the current block is searched, and if there is no entry a normal 'declared' entry is added. If there is already a 'declared' entry, a failure indication is given.

If there is a 'used' entry the chain must be followed through to finish the various incomplete object program operations. This is done by starting at the position in the object program given by $CS$. Each address space contains the syllable counter of its successor, the end of the chain being marked by a blank address space. Finally the 'used' entry is replaced by a 'declared' entry.

### iii.  At the end of a block

At the end of a block the section of the name list for this block is collapsed by deleting any 'declared' entries, combining any 'used' entries with corresponding entries in the containing block, or adding 'used' entries on to the list of the containing block.

Combining entries will either cause a chain to be followed through, as described above, when the containing block contains a 'declared' entry, or will cause two chains of 'used' entries to be joined. This is done by putting the $CS$ of the entry in the containing block in the address space indicated by the $CF$ of the entry in the inner block, and replacing this $CS$ by the $CS$ from the inner block entry. The inner block entry for this identifier is then deleted.

This basic system is slightly complicated by the need to check that expressions in the bound pair list of array declarations contain no local identifiers.

### 4.  State Variables

As has been mentioned above, state variables are used where necessary, to differentiate between the various possible uses of a delimiter and as counters, etc.

For instance the variable $V$ is set to zero at **begin**, to one at declarations, and to two at statements. This is used to differentiate between blocks and compound statements, and also to check out the occurrence of declarations amongst statements.

A counter $L$ is used for the number of declared identifiers assigned a working space position in the current block, and $NL$ is set to indicate the start of the current section of name list.

At the beginning of a block, a procedure block, or a for statement block, $V$, $L$ and $NL$ are stacked with the **begin**. Then a new $L$ can be started, $NL$ can be set up for use inside the new block, and $V$ zeroed, with the knowledge that translation can resume correctly for the outer block by unstacking the

**begin** and restoring the $V$, $L$ and $NL$, when the end of the new block is reached.

Other important state variables are $E$, which is set to $0$ for expressions, $1$ for statements, and $TE$ which is a bit pattern used in expressions to indicate the type of identifiers expected. $E$ and $TE$ are stacked with **if**, for example, allowing $E$ to be zeroed and $TE$ to be set to 'algebraic' (incorporates real, integer and Boolean) for the Boolean expression that must follow. On reaching the corresponding **then**, the stacked value of $E$ indicates whether it is to be taken as **then**$S$ or **then**$E$ (conditional statement or conditional expression, respectively), and for **then**$E$, $TE$ indicates the type of expression in which the **if** occurred. Since types are determined, and checked, dynamically at run time, the translator does not perform a full check on compatibility of types. Similarly checks on the compatibility of actual parameters with the specifications of their corresponding formal parameters are performed at run time.

Other state variables are used to mark progress through a for clause, to mark the fact of being within an actual parameter list, etc.

One important exception to the system of separate routines for delimiters is the translation of the heading of a procedure declaration. This uses no recursive definitions, and hence can be translated by its own special routine, which sets up parameter lists, information about value and specification parts, etc. Thus there need be no confusion between **real**, **array**, etc., used in declarations and as specifiers.

## 5. *Use of Core Storage by the Translation Routine*

During translation, space is required in the core storage for the translation routine itself, the object program being generated, the translator stack and name list, and a small fixed amount for the constants, state variables, etc.

Ignoring the fixed amount of storage required, space is thus needed for an object program which grows steadily in size, and for the name list and stack whose size varies continually, but ends up as zero. The system evolved is for the object program to start immediately after the translation routine, and for the name list to start at the other end of the storage, 'pulsating' towards the object program. The translator stack is placed in the centre of the store, to pulsate towards the name list. If the object program reaches the start of the stack or if the name list and stack reach each other the stack is moved, say 32 places, in the appropriate direction. If this would cause yet another clash translation is not possible and a failure will be indicated. This system allows maximum use of core storage, whether being used up by virtue of the size or of the complexity of the ALGOL program, and is illustrated in Fig. 1.

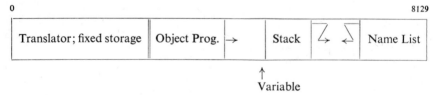

Fig. 1. Layout of storage during translation.

## 5. Code Procedures

A scheme for including procedures whose bodies are in User Code in an ALGOL program has been devised, and is to be implemented on both translators for the KDF9. Briefly this allows a normal procedure heading, with only the specifiers **procedure**, ⟨type⟩ **procedure** and **switch** being excluded, and then a procedure body in User Code bracketed by the symbols **KDF9** and **ALGOL**. Within the User Code of the procedure body access is allowed to the parameters by permitting pseudo-instructions calling on the formal parameters. All other communication with the surrounding ALGOL program is expressly disallowed. The rules for the inclusion of User Code procedures are in fact the required expansion of section 4.7.8 of the ALGOL Report (Ref. 6).

The scheme is quite powerful, allowing for instance, calls by name on arithmetic expressions, the use of Jensen's device (Dijkstra, 1961b), etc. The main reasons for designing such a scheme are to ensure compatibility between the two translators even for programs including code procedures, and to minimize duplication of effort between the two translator projects in providing input/output procedures, etc. Naturally casual use of this facility would impair ease of communication of programs and will be discouraged.

The implementation of procedures in User Code on the Whetstone translator has produced some interesting problems. In particular the method of communication at run time between an interpreted object program and a User Code procedure is of some interest but will not be discussed here, as being outside the scope of this paper.

## 6. Communication between ALGOL Program and Programmer

An important feature of the Whetstone ALGOL translator is the stress placed on ease of communication between ALGOL program and programmer. Thus it should be possible to check-out and test an ALGOL program with no knowledge of the generated object program.

The first problem is that of indicating to a programmer the point at which an error in his ALGOL program has become apparent to the translator. This is done by printing out the next 100 characters, or two lines, of the ALGOL (counting only non-trivial information). The line number, and the last label and last procedure identifier declared will also aid identification of the offending ALGOL. This information will be accompanied by a message describing the error (or rather, inconsistency).

It will be possible to continue, and search for further errors, only on the basis of making some reasonable estimate as to the cause of the inconsistency.

Error print-outs at run time will arise from two causes. Firstly, further checks on the validity of the ALGOL which are not easily checked at translation time are performed at run time (for example compatibility of formal and actual parameters). Secondly, actual errors in the program can result in numbers becoming invalid, subscript bounds being exceeded, etc. Error print-outs are formed using a 'failure tape' which has been set up at translation time. As any section of the name list is collapsed (see Section 4) a copy of the section is made on magnetic tape. This will include details of the block being collapsed (type of block, level number, line number at start of block, etc.) and information about every identifier in the block. The failure tape also includes, for each block, a table giving details of line number against object program counter. Thus using this failure tape, error print-outs can be made giving a description of the failure, the position where it occurred, and details of the current block. This tape could also be used for trace routines, post-mortems, etc.

## 7. Acknowledgements

A large measure of any credit for the Whetstone ALGOL Translator must go to Mr L. J. Russell, who with the author, is jointly responsible for the design and implementation of the translator, and who has assisted in the preparation of this paper.

The author's indebtedness to Dr E. W. Dijkstra, and also Professor A. van Wijngaarden, and Mr J. A. Zonneveld, will be obvious to anyone familiar with the ALGOL Translator for the X1 computer at the Mathematical Centre, Amsterdam.

The author also wishes to thank The English Electric Company Limited for permission to publish this paper.

REFERENCES

1. G. M. DAVIS (1960). The English Electric KDF9 Computer System. *Computer Bull.* **4**, 119–120.
2. E. W. DIJKSTRA (1960). Recursive Programming. *Numerische Mathematik* **2**, 312–318.
3. E. W. DIJKSTRA (1961a). An ALGOL 60 Translator for the X1. *ALGOL Bull. Suppl.* **10** (Translated by M. Woodger from the German in MTW **2**, 54–56 and MTW **3**, 115–119).
4. E. W. DIJKSTRA (1961b). Defense of ALGOL 60. *Comm. A.C.M.* **4**, 502–503.
5. English Electric (Data Processing and Control Systems Division) publication. KDF9 Programming Manual.
6. P. NAUR (1960). Report on the Algorithmic Language ALGOL 60. *Comm. A.C.M.* **3**, 299–314, and *Numerische Mathematik* **2**, 106–136.
7. B. RANDELL and L. J. RUSSELL (1962). Discussions on ALGOL Translation at Mathematisch Centrum. English Electric Report W/AT 841.

# 9. ON WRITING AN OPTIMIZING TRANSLATOR FOR ALGOL 60

D. H. R. HUXTABLE

*The English Electric Company Ltd., Stoke-on-Trent, England*

## Introduction

ALGOL 60, introduced in Chapter 4, is a powerful algorithmic language for describing numerical processes. At the same time it is an ideal language, because of its rigorous definition, for communicating problems, in numerical work, to a digital computer. This use of the language is only possible if there exists, for the computer it is desired to use, a program for converting ALGOL 60 into a form which the machine can understand. The readiness with which the machine can understand this 'intermediate language' is the prime factor in determining the running time taken to solve the problem specified.

Randall, in Chapter 8, gives a description of a program for translating ALGOL 60 into an intermediate language whose principal property is that it makes the translation process as fast as possible. It pays the obvious penalties in running speed. An optimizing translator, of the kind to be discussed, has as its principal object a fast running program. It translates into an intermediate language which the machine can readily and quickly understand; that is, machine code with a minimum backing of subroutines for performing functions not expressible in a single machine order.

The adoption of machine-code as an intermediate language does not automatically achieve the production of efficient programs. The usual yardstick for efficiency is direct comparison, both in time and storage, with a program written (to do the same job) by an average or skilled programmer. In order to achieve a reasonable comparison the program produced must satisfy the following requirements. (a) It must make all possible use of those built-in features of the machine which a programmer uses to write efficient programs. (b) It must not spend too much time making decisions which the translator could have made during translation. (c) It must not spend too much time in doing the organization or housekeeping necessary to the language, that is in maintaining the environment within which the program operates.

Within the context of ALGOL 60 and KDF 9 (KDF 9 Programming Manual; Davis, 1960) it can be readily seen that an optimizing translator should contain algorithms for achieving the following. (i) An efficient use of $Q$-store index registers, in evaluating suffix expressions when such expressions have successive values expressible by means of a recurrence relation. (ii) Efficient use of the KDF 9 nesting accumulator during the evaluation of arithmetic expressions. (iii) The detection of situations in which such optimizing algorithms can be used, and of situations in which generalized housekeeping techniques can be short-cut — for example, block entry mechanisms.

(iv) Definition of the run-time environment (object program organization during execution) in such a way that, while the recursive properties of ALGOL 60 can be implemented, the immediate access properties of the core store are preserved as far as possible.

The implementation of these algorithms depends on the accumulation and correlation of information available in a given ALGOL program. Some of this information is readily available, some not. Sometimes the amount of information required to describe a particular aspect of the program is more than can be readily stored. The writing of an optimizing translator is therefore a matter of compromise between time for translation and storage requirements during translation.

## Run-Time Environment

The term "Run-Time Environment" refers to those aspects of a programming system concerned with the organization of translated object programs during execution of the programs.

The design of the run-time environment, and the short cuts which are possible within that environment, is the greatest single factor in the design of an optimizing translator. In its turn the run-time environment hinges on the technique adopted for storage allocation.

## Storage Allocation

The present section is concerned with the basic stack storage allocation mechanism for procedure declarations and for blocks within procedure declarations or within the main program level.

Randell has already described (Chapter 8) the basic stack storage mechanism. This is the fundamental structure of all full ALGOL 60 translators; it is however capable of considerable improvement.

The basic stack-mechanism assumes that recursive re-entry is possible to any block of the program, this is not necessarily true. Recursive re-entry is only required for those blocks which define a procedure body. Inner blocks of such bodies cannot be recursively re-entered without passing through the outermost block. Therefore the unit of program which defines a block of storage for the stack is a procedure. Such a unit of program will be termed "program level".

For a given program level the fixed storage requirements (Parameters, Simple Variables, Array Words) are assessed for all the blocks comprising that level. Naturally when variables have disjunct scopes they may occupy the same store location. This assessment yields the maximum number of fixed stores required. This is used on entry to revalue the *ARROW*\*; the old *ARROW* value forms the new base modifier value. This has four immediate advantages.

---

\* The term *ARROW* has been used (6) to refer to the pointer to the next free stock storage location. It is equivalent to the accumulator pointer (AP) mentioned in chapter 8. For a given program level, the base modifier points to the beginning of the block of storage for that program level, and the *ARROW* points to the end of the block of storage. These two define the location and length of the storage block.

1. Only variables which are non-local to a procedure body have to be used via a non-local storage mechanism. 2. Variables local to the main program level are immediately accessible, since the main program can never be entered recursively its Base Modifier can be fixed and is fixed at zero. 3. The rather cumbersome stack manipulation involved in generating a new stack level is only used on entry to and exit from a procedure. 4. Internal block entry and exit is a very much simpler process and applies to all the blocks of the main program.

TABLE 1. Storage Allocation for a Programme Level

CORE STORE

| Arrow Value At Label / Base Address | 0 | 1 | 2 | 3 | 4 | 5 | 6 | 7 | 8 | 9 | 10 | 11 | 12 | 13 | 14 | 15 | 16 | 17 | 18 | (address |
|---|---|---|---|---|---|---|---|---|---|---|---|---|---|---|---|---|---|---|---|---|
| 16 L1 | — | 16 | — | A | P | Q | — | — | — | Dva | A[1] | A[2] | A[3] | A[4] | | | | | | relative |
| 21 L2 | — | 16 | 21 | A | P | Q | S | T | B | DVa | A[1] | A[2] | A[3] | A[4] | DVb | B[1] | B[2] | B[3] | B[4] | to the |
| 16 L3 | — | 16 | — | A | P | Q | — | — | — | DVa | A[1] | A[2] | A[3] | A[4] | | | | | | Base |
| 16 L4 | — | 16 | 16 | A | P | Q | X | Y | Z | DVa | A[1] | A[2] | A[3] | A[4] | | | | | | address) |
| 16 L5 | — | 16 | — | A | P | Q | — | — | — | DVa | A[1] | A[2] | A[3] | A[4] | | | | | | |

(address relative to the Base address)

As an example consider the storage layout of the following procedure:

> **procedure** *P*;
>     **begin**
>         **real array** *A[1:4]*
>          **integer** *P,Q*;
>     *L1*:
>             ⋮
>          **begin integer** *S,T*;
>              **array** *B[1:4]*;
>           *L2*:
>               ⋮
>         **end**
>       *L3*: ...
>          **begin** *integer X,Y,Z*;
>         *L4*:
>           ⋮
>         **end**
>      *L5*:
>        ⋮
>   **end** *procedure*;

On entry to *P* a new program level is set up, with the following storage layout (relative to the base address):

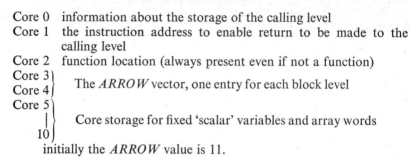

Core 0    information about the storage of the calling level

Core 1    the instruction address to enable return to be made to the calling level

Core 2    function location (always present even if not a function)

Core 3 ⎫
Core 4 ⎬ The *ARROW* vector, one entry for each block level

Core 5 ⎫
  | ⎬ Core storage for fixed 'scalar' variables and array words
10 ⎭

initially the *ARROW* value is 11.

After the first array declaration cores 11–15 are occupied by the array *A* and its associated Dope Vector (see Section on subscript optimization). This is the position at *L1*. It will be seen from Table 1 that *AV1* holds the value of the arrow for this block. At *L2* the array *B* is now declared and a new block has been entered, cores 16–20 are used for *B* and *AV2* given the new *ARROW* value which is 21 for this block. When *L3* is reached array *B* and integer *S,T*, are no longer required therefore *AV1* is used to revalue the *ARROW* and so exclude the array elements. At *L4* the locations for *X,Y,Z* overwrite those previously used for *S,T,B*. and the value of *AV2* is the same as *AV1* (no arrays). At *L5* the position is the same as at *L1*.

Program levels exist dynamically inside one another or themselves. The storage for each program level is therefore relative to a Base modifier (which is in fact the core location of core 0 of the level). This Base modifier can therefore change for successive calls of the Program Level.

Core 0, 1 of a level contain the information about the previous core (see Maintenance of the Stack Storage System). The program level mechanism stores the value of the Base modifier and *ARROW* for the previous level and uses the value of the *ARROW* to generate a new Base modifier to which is added an increment to give a new *ARROW*. This increment is the amount of storage required to cover the simple variables and Array words for the level (in the example it is 11).

The *ARROW* is incremented at each **begin** within a program level. Obviously the value of the *ARROW* must be decreased by the same amount when the corresponding **end** is found. Since it is possible to leave a block before the corresponding **end** is found, and jump to some lower block level, this decrement is achieved by a table look-up of the value corresponding to the block level to which control is being transferred. Space is therefore reserved in the fixed-space for an *ARROW VECTOR (AV)**. The size of this vector is equal to the maximum block depth reached in a given program level. However, jumps to labels which are in the same block do not have to refer to *AV* since the *ARROW* does not have to move — this is an example of a short-cut.

Jumps to labels local to another program level as well as exit from a level to the enclosing level require a different approach. To return to a level from

---

* A vector of successive values of the *ARROW*, there is one entry for each level of block in the program level. The arrow vector is analogous to the Display of Chapter 8, but is used only for references within a program level.

an internal level requires (i) the base modifier of the level; (ii) the *ARROW* for the level; (iii) the instruction address (in subroutine nomenclature a *LINK*). To jump to a label in an external level requires; (iv) the name of the level.

This latter is to identify the level so that when required a search can be made for the required level.

These four quantities are in effect *LINKS* to a subroutine, and are stored in the called level (in the first two locations of the level) in a manner exactly analogous to that of a subroutine entry. Similarly access to non-local variables (except those local to the main program) involves obtaining the base modifier for the relevant level.

There are two ways of doing this. Firstly, to keep an immediately accessible vector of base modifiers, and secondly to search for the last use of that level by examination of the *LINKS*.

The snag with the first scheme is the problem of keeping it up to date especially when jumps across levels are being made. That with the second scheme is the time factor. Scheme one is therefore adopted for those levels which are not recursive (a fact which immediately removes the updating problem), and scheme two for the levels which are recursive.

### Parameter Planting

This section is concerned with the way that actual parameters are planted within a procedure declaration when a procedure call occurs. Parameter locations for all levels are in a standard position, namely the next $n$ locations after the *LINKS*. Real, Integer and Boolean formals called by value are merely given the value of the expression during execution of the procedure call.

Real, Integer and Boolean formals called by name are given two values: (a) the address of a sequence of instructions for evaluating the actual parameter together with the base modifier for the level which plants the parameter, i.e. the level within which the parameter is to be evaluated; (b) the address of a sequence of instructions for yielding the address together with the base modifier. In cases where the parameter is an expression the value (b) becomes a sequence of instructions for dealing with the semantic failure resulting from an assignment to an expression.

Strings are given the address of the opening string quote. Procedures are given the address of the sequence of instructions defining the procedure. Arrays by name are given the array word. Arrays by value are given a modified array word and the elements are copied into the data space of the procedure. Labels by name are given the address of a sequence of instructions for yielding a label value. Labels by value are given a label value which is in three parts. (a) The label address. (b) Base modifier for the level containing the label. (c) The arrow vector address for extracting the *ARROW* value for the relevant block from the *ARROW* Vector.

### For Statements and Subscripted Variables

This section considers optimization techniques for **for** statements and subscripted variables. This is a particularly rich field of operation for an optimizing translator. Simple algorithms can produce quite large savings in time.

Firstly and most important is a brief description of the method adopted for storing arrays. Each array is stored compactly by columns and associated with each array is a vector of information, the "Dope Vector", which enables the address of any particular element to be calculated.

The dope vector consists of a series of increments $\Delta_i$ for the various suffix positions. Let $u_j$ and $l_j$ be the upper and lower subscript bounds for the $j$th Bound Pair list element of the array declaration for an array with $n$ subscripts.

Then
$$\Delta_1 = 1$$
$$\Delta_j = (u_{j-1} - l_{j-1} + 1) \times \Delta_{j-1} \quad 2 \leq j \leq n+1$$

where $\Delta_{n+1}$ is the total storage space required for the array,

Now the address of $A[i_1 \ldots i_n]$ (denoted by $L(A[i_1 \ldots i_n])$) is given by

$$L(A[i_1 \ldots i_n]) = L(A[l_1 \ldots l_n]) + \sum_{j=1}^{n} (i_j - l_j) \times \Delta$$

$$= L(A[l_1 \ldots l_n]) - \sum_{j=1}^{n} l_j \times \Delta_j + \sum_{j=1}^{n} i_j \times \Delta_j$$

$$= L(A[0, \ldots \ldots 0]) + \sum_{j=1}^{n} i_j \times \Delta_j$$

$L(A[0 \ldots 0])$ is a function of the declaration and storage position only and is entered as part of the array word.

(The array word also points to the dope vector and $L(A[l_1 \ldots l_n])$; the latter is principally for organization purposes.)

$L(A[i_1 \ldots i_n]$ has been defined as the location or address of $A[i_1 \ldots i_n]$.

$I(A[i_1 \ldots i_n])$ is now defined as an increment and has the value $i_1 \times \Delta_1 + \ldots i_n \times \Delta_n$. The use of increments for efficient implementation of **for** statements is illustrated in the following example, which shows the initialization and counting process in a double **for** loop performing square matrix transposition. In this example modification registers $M14$, $M15$, and incrementation registers $I14$, $I15$ are used. In KDF 9 machine language (KDF 9 Programming Manual; Davis, 1960) incrementation of an $M$ store by its corresponding $I$ store can be accomplished automatically during a transfer. This removes the necessity for the separate incrementation used in the example.

```
begin integer i, j, n; real X; .....
   Y: for i: = 1 step 1 until n do
   Z: for j: = i + 1 step 1 until n do
      begin
         X: = A[j,i];
      A[j,i]: = A[i,j];
      A[i,j]: = X   end  end
```

The above ALGOL program is implemented by the following sequence of machine operations (written in an ALGOL-like notation). It will be seen that most of the address computation has been removed from the inner loops, and **is** executed once only on entry.

**comment** initialization of address;

*Y:* $I14: = I(A[1,0])$; (this is $\Delta_1$ of the Dope Vector)
   $I15: = I(A[0,1])$; (this is $\Delta_2$ of the Dope Vector)
      $R1: = L(A[2,1])$; (starting address for $A[j,i]$)
      $R2: = \Delta_1 + \Delta_2$; (diagonal increment)
      $R3: = L(A[1,2])$; (starting address for $A[i,j]$).
      $R4: = \Delta_1 + \Delta_2$; (diagonal increment)
         **comment** outer loop;
         **for** $i: = 1$ **step** $1$ **until** $n$ **do**
**begin**
         *Z:* $M14: = R1$ ;
            $M15: = R3$ ;
         **comment** inner loop;
         **for** $j: = i + 1$ **step** $1$ **until** $n$ **do**
         **begin**
            $x: =$ 'address $M14$' ;
         'address $M14$' $: =$ 'address $M15$';
         'address $M15$' $: = x$ ;
         $M14: = M14 + I14$;  $M15: = M15 + I15$
         **end** inner loop;
         $R1: = R1 + R2$;
         $R3: = R3 + R4$
         **end** outer loop;

By 'address $M14$' is meant the content of the location whose address is in $M14$.

Further economies associated with $R1$ $R2$ $R3$ $R4$ are possible, quite apart from economies in counting, but this would obscure the fundamental treatment of subscripted variables.

In order to achieve this kind of optimization it is essential to work 'inside-out'. If, in an obvious notation, the **for** statement structure is

$$( \quad ( \quad ( \quad ) \quad ( \quad ( \quad ) \quad ) \quad ) \quad )$$
$$h \quad i \quad j \quad j \quad k \quad l \quad l \quad k \quad i \quad h$$

the order of treatment is $j$, $l$, $k$, $i$, $h$, i.e. the text between two parentheses is processed as soon as the terminating parenthesis is encountered. This order of processing corresponds to a Reverse Polish treatment of the bracket structure. See Ershov (1958) for further discussions on this topic.

At each stage in the processing of a **for** statement, the intermediate registers ($R1$, $R2$, $R3$, $R4$ in the above example) and the quantities assigned to them are not explicitly entered in the ALGOL text. They are contained in a Register List. This Register List is organized on a nested principle with "lockout" points determined by the placing of tags. That is whilst processing $k$, information about $l$ is relevant but information about $j$ must be locked out, and whilst processing $i$, information about $j$ and $k$ is relevant.* The size of the

---

* This "lockingout" reflects the disjunct dynamic properties of nested **for** statements, i.e. the dynamic effects of $j$ have no effect on the running of $k$.

register list requires that limitations be placed on the number and complexity of subscript expressions which can be optimized. These restrictions are as follows:

1. Less than four subscript elements.
2. Contains no identifier which is not a simple integer or constant.
3. Contains no more than three identifiers.
4. Contains no more than three operators, two adding and one multiplication.
5. No quadratics in any variable.

*Examples*

*Types considered*

$A[i]$, $A[l \times i + m, - n \times j - p]$

*Types not considered*

$A[1,2,3,4]$, $A[B[i]]$
$A[\text{if } b \text{ then } 5 \text{ else } 4]$, $A[1 \div m]$, $A[\sin (x \uparrow 2 \times PI)]$

Due to the inside-out method of working, the contents of a Register are placed as ALGOL assignment statements whenever the contents of the register, i.e. the arithmetic expression defining it, become loop dependent. This automatically ensures that register values are computed a minimum number of times; in the example the registers are set up only once.

There are two other types of optimization applicable to subscripted variables. (i) Economies due to the fact that $\Delta_1 = 1$ for all arrays, and that the $\Delta_i$ are calculable at translation time for fixed bound arrays. (ii) Equivalence of registers in the register list.

An example of the first is that $A[i + 7, j + 9]$, with an array declaration **array** $A[1:30,1:30]$, can be addressed from core 277 instead of core 0 and considered as a subscripted variable $A[i,j]$. This economy is performed before all others. Since $\Delta_1 = 1$ we can reduce $A[i+7, j+9]$ to $A[i,j+9]$, regardless of the declaration, by referring to it from core 7. To facilitate this economy lists are compiled of information concerning fixed bound arrays. If this list is filled all subsequent fixed bound arrays are regarded as dynamic.

An example of the second arises in the example, $R2 = R4$ and consequently $R4$ can be totally replaced by references to $R2$.

## Detection of Optimization Inhibition

This section is concerned with the detection of conditions in the **for** statement which preclude optimization along the lines outlined above.

Evidently the achievement of the above types of optimization is dependent on the contents of the **for** body. In general an ALGOL programme can interfere with the successive values of the control variable from within the **for** body. Such interference can arise through three things.

1. A statement exists statically or dynamically in the **for** body which (a) makes an assignment to the control variable; (b) which makes an assignment to a variable which occurs either statically or dynamically in the arith-

metic expression of a subscripted variable, or the $B$ or $C$ element of $A$ **step** $B$ **until** $C$, or the $E$ or $F$ element of $E$ **while** $F$.

2. A statement (static or dynamic) which causes exit from the **for** statement before the list is exhausted.

3. The control variable is not a simple integer, or the primaries in the $B$ or $C$ elements are not simple integers or simple integer variables.

The existence of any of these conditions will inhibit optimization to a greater or lesser extent. For example 1(a) precludes any attempt at optimization; 1(b) assignment to a $B$ element precludes any attempt at calculating increments. Assignment to a $C$ element precludes any attempt at counting the loop.

The problem is to evolve algorithms for detecting when these situations occur. Detection of condition 3 is obvious. Conditions in 1 can occur either through a direct assignment within the **for** body or through entry to a procedure; condition 2 can be detected by looking for switches and comparing labels on the left and right, it can also occur through entry to a procedure.

Since any procedure used within a **for** statement body is potentially capable of making an assignment to the control variable, but in fact very few do, the procedures are classified into the following three classes.

1. Normal

   (a) No **own** variables
   (b) No abnormal exits or use of any switch
   (c) No non-local assignments
   (d) Internal procedure calls limited to normal procedures
   (e) Parameters exclude label and switch
   (f) There is no explicit assignment to parameters called by name.

2. Conditional Sneaks

   Identical to normals excluding condition (f).

3. Unconditional Sneaks

   All other procedures.

(Sneak is a term used when a procedure effects variables outside its own procedure body.)

It will be seen that the definition of a normal procedure is recursive, the technique for dealing with this, and other aspects of the classification algorithms will be dealt with later.

The occurrence of a normal procedure in a **for**-body, cannot by definition, alter any of the variables in the **for** clause arithmetic expressions.

A conditional sneak procedure may (due to its assignment to an integer called by name) alter such variables if they are mentioned in the parameter list, i.e. its sneak property is conditional on its context.

An unconditional sneak is regarded as being just that. A procedure could of course be examined for the particular property or properties which place it in this class. The reasons for not doing this involve both time, space and the logical complexity of the problem. It is felt that the normal and conditional

classifications should cover all of the more normal procedures used in an
ALGOL program.

The occurrence of a procedure in a **for** body does mean that the controlled
variable must be preserved explicitly since it may be required as data for the
procedure.

Detection of explicit assignment to the control variable and elements of
the **for** list is achieved by holding a list of integers in an integer assignment
list. This list also covers assignment to integers by conditional sneak procedures, by including an examination of the parameter lists of such procedure
statements.

### Procedure Classification

This section discusses the techniques for classifying procedures into normal
procedures, conditional sneaks and unconditional sneaks.

Some of the gains to be expected from some form of procedure classification have already been indicated. One further and very important gain is that
it produces as a by-product the information necessary to optimize the
preservation and restoration of $Q$-stores.

The classification process involves discovering the total of all possible
run-time procedure call structures of the program. Some of these structures
may not occur dynamically, due possibly to data. A secondary problem is
to describe this procedure structure in a form suitable for processing.

Methods by which procedures can call other procedures are numerous but
can be broadly classified thus: (a) by formal parameters specified as procedures; (b) by formal parameter specified **real**, **integer**, **Boolean** or **label** by
name; (c) by use of formal parameters in the procedure body which are local
to a statically enclosing procedure; (d) the use of formal parameters in
actual parameters of class (a) or (b); (e) the use of parameters of class (a)
or (b) in statements of formal procedures, i.e. procedure statements where
the procedure identifier is a formal parameter identifier specified as procedure;
(f) procedures declared within the body of the procedure.

The technique adopted for discovering the procedure structure can be
described as taking place in several distinct phases. (1) Detection and description of explicit procedure statements within procedure declarations. (2) Detection and addition to the description of the use of procedure identifiers as
parameters. (3) Detection and addition to the description of the use of function designators with respect to their evaluation level* in expressions in procedure statements. (4) Detection and addition to the description of the
effect of the use of formal parameters in actual parameter expressions.
(5) Detection and addition to the description of the effect of explicit use of
formal parameters which are local to the statically enclosing procedures.
(During this detection and description phase formal procedure statements
are treated in exactly the same manner as actual procedure statements.)

This description is then processed to yield the second and further order
call sequences, i.e. if $A$ calls $B$ and $B$ calls $C$, the second order call implied

---

* The level which is currently in control when evaluation of the function takes place.

is that $A$ calls $C$. The description as set up only describes first order sequences.

In order to include the effect of actual-formal procedure correspondences a description is set up describing such correspondences and processed in a manner identical to that used on the description of the call sequences. This is because a formal procedure identifier may only correspond to an actual procedure identifier through several other formal procedure identifiers.

Since a call of a formal procedure is ultimately a call by a corresponding actual procedure and a call by a formal procedure is a call by a corresponding actual procedure, the call description is mapped, by means of the formal-actual description, on to itself, i.e. the column denoting the calls of a formal procedure are mapped onto the column denoting the calls of the corresponding actual procedure. Similarly, the rows denoting the calls by a formal procedure are mapped onto the rows denoting the calls by the corresponding actual procedure. This then includes the effect of formal-actual correspondences on the explicit calls, by the actual procedure bodies or statements.

### The Description

This is a Boolean matrix the rows of which correspond to the calling procedure and the columns of which correspond to the called procedure, i.e. if $A$ calls $B$ then there is a digit in row $A$ column $B$. This matrix is divided into four regions for the convenience of the mapping operation described above.

|          | Actual | Formal |
|----------|--------|--------|
| Actual   | $A$    | $B$    |
| Formal   | $C$    | $D$    |

Region $A$ corresponds to calls of actuals by actual procedures. Regions B, C, D, have similar meanings. The importance of this is in the mapping of this description onto itself. This matrix is called the call matrix.

The actual-formal correspondence description is a similar Boolean matrix, i.e.,

|       |        | Formal |
|-------|--------|--------|
|       |        | Actual |
| Value |        | Formal |

The rows correspond to the value and the columns to the formal, i.e. if the formal procedure $F$ has a value $P$ then there is a digit in row $P$ column $F$ ($P$ may be an actual procedure or another formal procedure). This matrix is called the correspondence matrix.

### The Description Processor

This process is a Boolean procedure operating on a matrix $B$ and producing a matrix $B^n$ where $B^n = B^{n+1}$. This resulting matrix describes the $n$th order paths of the original description. For a fuller discussion of the processor and connection matrix theory see Marimont (1959).

The processor algorithm is:

Let the matrix be Boolean array $B[1:n, 1:n]$;

```
begin integer i,j,k;
        for    j:=1 step 1 until n do
        for    i:=1 step 1 until n do
            begin
            if B[i,j] then begin for k: = 1 step 1 until n do
                         B[i,k]:= B[i,k] ∨ B[j,k] end
        end
end
```

This Algorithm is due to Warshall (1962).

### The Mapping Process

This maps rows and columns of the Call matrix onto rows and columns of itself. This is controlled by means of the correspondence matrix. A digit in row $i$ column $j$ of this matrix maps row $j$ onto row $i$ and column $j$ onto column $i$ of the call matrix.

This then yields the completed matrix describing the procedure structure of the program.

The recursive definition of normal procedures is achieved by Boolean post-multiplication of the call matrix by a vector denoting those procedures which are basically not normal. This yields a vector giving the procedures which are by implication not normal, i.e. an apparently normal procedure may, by virtue of the procedures which it itself calls, become not normal. The same technique applies in classifying the conditional sneak procedures.

### An Example of the Process

An example covering nearly all the aspects of the problem is given below

```
begin real s, u,m,g,PRINT,l;
    real procedure AA(t) real procedure t;
        begin real procedure A(tt); real procedure tt;
            begin real procedure X(v,K) real v; real procedure K;
                begin
                X := K(m,Q)+v
                end;
            A := tt(l,X,B)+8;
            end;
            real procedure L (a,b); real procedure a,b;
                begin
                    L :=a(b)+7;
                end;
        AA := L(A,t)+6;
            end;
```

**real procedure B**$(x,y)$; **value** $x$; **real** $x$; **real procedure** $y$;
 **begin**
   $B := y(s,u) \times z + x$;
 **end**;
 **real procedure** $C(d,e,f)$; **value** $d$; **real** $d$; **real procedure** $e,f$;
 **begin**
   $C := e(d,B) + f(g,Q)$;
 **end**;
 **real procedure** $Q(r,p)$; **value** $r,p$; **real** $r,p$;
 **begin**
   $Q := r \times p$;
 **end**;
$s := 1$; $u := 2$; $m := 3$; $g := 4$; $l := 7$;
$PRINT := AA(C)$
**end**

This calculates and assigns to *PRINT* the value of the following expression

$$s \times u + m + l + s \times u + g + 8 + 7 + 6$$

The above program declares the four procedures *AA, B, C, Q,* and, after assigning values to the variables, $s$, $u$, $m, g, l$, calls in the procedure *AA* with an actual parameter *C*. This leads to evaluation of the statement

$$AA := L(A,C) + 6;$$

where $L$ and $A$ are procedures declared within the procedure *AA*. The evaluation of $L(A,C)$ results in entry to the procedure *L*, and evaluation of the statement

$$L := A(C) + 7$$

Evaluation of $A(C)$ leads to evaluation of the statement

$$A := C(l,X,B) + 8$$

and $C(l,X,B)$ leads to evaluation of the statement

$$C := X(l,B) + B(y,Q)$$

$B(y,Q)$ results in

$$B := Q(s,u) + g$$
$$B := s \times u + g$$

and $X(l,B)$ results in

$$X := B(m,Q) + l$$
$$X := Q(s,u) + m + l$$
$$X := s \times u + m + l$$

Hence the statement

$$PRINT := AA(C)$$

results in assignment to *PRINT of*

$$s \times u + m + l + s \times u + g + 8 + 7 + 6 = 39.$$

| | Main Prog. | AA | A | X | L | B | C | Q | t | tt | k | a | b | y | e | f |
|---|---|---|---|---|---|---|---|---|---|---|---|---|---|---|---|---|
| **Main Prog.** | | | | | | | | | | | | | | | | |
| AA | | | | | 1 | 1 | | | | | | | | | | |
| A | | | | | | | | | | 1 | | | | | | |
| X | | | | | | | | | | | 1 | | | | | |
| L | | | 1 | | | | | | 1 | | 1 | | | | | |
| B | | | | | | | | | | | | | 1 | | | |
| C | | | | | | | | | | | | | | | 1 | 1 |
| Q | | | | | | | | | | | | | | | | |
| t | | | | | | | | | | | | | | | | |
| tt | | | | | 1 | 1 | | | | | | | | | | |
| k | | | | | | | 1 | | | | | | | | | |
| a | | | | | | | | | | | 1 | | | | | |
| b | | | | | | | | | | | | | | | | |
| y | | | | | | | | | | | | | | | | |
| e | | | | | 1 | | | | | | | | | | | |
| f | | | | | | | 1 | | | | | | | | | |

Call Matrix as initially set up.

| | t | tt | k | a | b | y | e | f |
|---|---|---|---|---|---|---|---|---|
| **Main Prog.** | | | | | | | | |
| AA | | | | | | | | |
| A | | | | 1 | | | | |
| X | | | | | | | | |
| L | | | | | | | | |
| B | | | | | | | | |
| C | 1 | | | 1 | | | | |
| Q | | | | | | | | |
| t | | | | | 1 | | | |
| tt | | | | | | | | |
| k | | | | | | | | |
| a | | | | | | | | |
| b | | | | | | | | |
| y | | | | | | | | |
| e | | | | | | | | |
| f | | | | | | | | |

Correspondence Matrix as initially set up.

|            | t | tt | k | a | b | y | e | f |
|------------|---|----|---|---|---|---|---|---|
| Main Prog. |   |    |   |   |   |   |   |   |
| AA         |   |    |   |   |   |   |   |   |
| A          |   |    |   | 1 |   |   |   |   |
| X          |   |    |   |   |   |   | 1 |   |
| L          |   |    |   |   |   |   |   |   |
| B          |   |    | 1 |   |   |   |   | 1 |
| C          | 1 | 1  |   |   | 1 |   |   |   |
| Q          |   |    |   |   |   | 1 |   |   |
| t          |   | 1  |   |   | 1 |   |   |   |
| tt         |   |    |   |   |   |   |   |   |
| k          |   |    |   |   |   |   |   |   |
| a          |   |    |   |   |   |   |   |   |
| b          |   | 1  |   |   |   |   |   |   |
| y          |   |    |   |   |   |   |   |   |
| e          |   |    |   |   |   |   |   |   |
| f          |   |    |   |   |   |   |   |   |

Correspondence Matrix as completed.

|            | AA | A | X | L | B | C | Q | t | tt | k | a | b | y | e | f |
|------------|----|---|---|---|---|---|---|---|----|---|---|---|---|---|---|
| Main Prog. |    |   |   |   |   |   |   |   |    |   |   |   |   |   |   |
| AA         |    |   | 1 |   |   | 1 |   |   |    |   |   |   |   |   |   |
| A          |    |   |   |   |   | 1 |   | 1 | 1  |   | 1 |   |   |   |   |
| X          |    |   |   | 1 |   |   |   |   | 1  |   |   |   |   |   |   |
| L          |    | 1 |   |   |   | 1 |   | 1 |    | 1 |   |   |   |   |   |
| B          |    |   |   |   |   |   | 1 |   |    |   |   | 1 |   |   |   |
| C          |    |   | 1 | 1 |   |   |   |   |    |   |   |   |   | 1 | 1 |
| Q          |    |   |   |   |   |   |   |   |    |   |   |   |   |   |   |
| t          |    |   | 1 | 1 |   |   |   |   |    |   |   |   |   |   |   |
| tt         |    |   | 1 | 1 |   |   |   |   |    |   |   |   |   |   |   |
| k          |    |   |   |   |   |   | 1 |   |    |   |   |   |   |   |   |
| a          |    |   |   |   |   | 1 |   | 1 | 1  |   | 1 |   |   |   |   |
| b          |    |   |   |   |   |   |   |   |    |   |   |   |   |   |   |
| y          |    |   |   |   |   |   |   |   |    |   |   |   |   |   |   |
| e          |    |   |   | 1 |   |   |   |   |    |   |   |   |   |   |   |
| f          |    |   |   |   |   |   | 1 |   |    |   |   |   |   |   |   |

Call Matrix after 'mapping' under control of the
Correspondence Matrix.

| Main Prog. | AA | A | X | L | B | C | Q | t | tt | k | a | b | y | e | f |
|---|---|---|---|---|---|---|---|---|---|---|---|---|---|---|---|
| **Main Prog.** | | | | | | | | | | | | | | | |
| AA | 1 | 1 | 1 | 1 | 1 | 1 | | 1 | 1 | 1 | 1 | 1 | 1 | 1 | 1 |
| A | | 1 | | 1 | 1 | 1 | | 1 | 1 | 1 | | 1 | 1 | 1 | 1 |
| X | | | | 1 | | 1 | | | | 1 | | 1 | | | |
| L | 1 | 1 | | 1 | 1 | 1 | | 1 | 1 | 1 | 1 | 1 | 1 | 1 | 1 |
| B | | | | | | 1 | | | | | | 1 | | | |
| C | | 1 | | 1 | | 1 | | | | 1 | | 1 | 1 | 1 | |
| Q | | | | | | | | | | | | | | | |
| t | | 1 | | 1 | | 1 | | | | 1 | | 1 | | | |
| tt | | 1 | | 1 | | 1 | | | | 1 | | 1 | | | |
| k | | | | | | 1 | | | | | | | | | |
| a | | 1 | | 1 | 1 | 1 | | 1 | 1 | 1 | | 1 | 1 | 1 | 1 |
| b | | | | | | | | | | | | | | | |
| y | | | | | | | | | | | | | | | |
| e | | | | 1 | | 1 | | | | | | 1 | | | |
| f | | | | | | 1 | | | | | | | | | |

The completed Call Matrix (B$^n$);

## Utilization of Machine Features
### Core Storage

This has already been covered in the discussion on environment.

### Q-Stores

These registers, which perform automatic indexing and incrementation, are used when fetching or storing subscripted variables. They are allocated quite simply on an inside-out basis, i.e. inner loop receives absolute preference. There are eleven such stores available and when these are all used one further register is shared by all the other subscripts. Each Program Level is allocated independently from other levels; which may call it or be called by it. On entry to each Level or procedure some or all of the Q-stores used must be preserved and an equivalent number restored on exit. The number $\phi$ to be stored on entry to level $q$ is given by:

$$\phi = Min\,(\max\,(n(pi)),\, n\,(q))$$

where $n\,(q)$ is No. of Q-stores used by the level $q$

$pi$ is one of the set of procedures which call $q$.

The preservation and restoration of $\phi$ Q-stores is part of the entry and exit mechanism of the procedure.

Max $(n\,(pi))$ is readily derived from the call matrix, the set of which $pi$ is an element is described by the column of the call matrix corresponding to procedure $q$.

### Nesting Accumulator

The use of this accumulator is intimately involved with the translation of arithmetic expressions. In general the reverse Polish form of an ALGOL expression requires a large nesting-store especially if it is required to enter a function within the expression; since this function will involve further expressions. Further a programmer using KDF 9 to calculate an expression will use the nesting store to store, when necessary, various partial results. Such partial results can arise from avoiding fetching the same variable twice or calculating the same subexpression twice.

Techniques for translating arithmetic expressions making full use of the nesting accumulator of KDF 9 to avoid redundant operations are naturally extremely KDF 9 oriented. The techniques for an optimizing translation of arithmetic expressions lead in general to using the nesting store for (a) avoiding redundant data fetching as in $(a+b)/a$; (b) avoiding calculation of common expressions as in $(a+b)/c-(a+b)$.

It uses the nesting store to hold such partial results and copies of them from the point of generation until they are required.

Due to the limited access to the nesting store and its finite length; provision must be made to store such partial results in the core-store, and to re-fetch them when they are required for use.

The necessity for such storage can arise due to the following reasons. (1) When a partial result is required for use it is inaccessible (on KDF 9 this means it is not in one of the top four cells). (2) Storage of this partial result in the nesting store causes the nesting store capacity to be exceeded. (3) Entry to a function will in general require an empty nesting store since its evaluation will involve completely new arithmetic expressions. (4) Evaluation of a **real integer** or **Boolean** variable by name will similarly require an empty nesting store since its evaluation may invoke a complete 'program' under the guise of a function.

Before examining techniques required to deal with these four groups it is worthwhile investigating to see if any can be avoided.

Reasons (1) and (2) are a function of the techniques used in planning the use of the nesting accumulator during the translation of a particular arithmetic expression as described by Hawkins and Huxtable (1962). Reason 4 is unavoidable since the effect of such a variable is quite indeterminable.

Reason 3, which is the most common ALGOL situation, can however be avoided in most of the common cases. Avoidance depends on the definition of a special function. This definition must satisfy the following conditions (1) Function Designator. (2) There are no **own** variables or local array declarations. (3) There are no abnormal exits. (4) Parameters are limited to **real integer** or **Boolean** by **value**. (5) No use is made of switches. (6) No internal procedure calls. (7) No use is made of or assignment made to, non-local variables.

The number of nesting stores used by such a function is determinable uniquely. Consequently it may be entered with a partially full nesting store. Conditions 3 and 5 ensure that no final interruption is made in the evaluation of the expression. An important property connected with the optimization of an expression is the inability of the special functions to alter any of the ALGOL variables, i.e. they have no side-effects. They do not use $Q$-stores and their variables and parameters can be located relative to the *ARROW* as it exists on entry. They do not require a completely new stack allocation with a new base modifier.

## Partial Result Stores

Since, due to the optimizing processes involved, partial results are not necessarily required in the reverse order in which they were stored, the partial result stores are in the fixed space of the program level. It will have been noted that the storage technique used is apt to leave spaces unused for short periods of time; where possible such spaces are used for the partial results.

When a partial result is stored due to reasons (1) or (2) the generating process must return to the point at which that result was generated and store it. The generation process then recontinues from that point. One further optimization point is that if the partial result which it is required to store is the result of a simple fetch instruction then there is no need to store it again. Such results are termed pseudo partial results.

Partial result storage due to reasons (3) or (4) do not generally involve a restart. Such partial results are merely stored away until the nesting store is sufficiently empty. There are no pseudo partial results unless the reason is for (3) and the function is a special function.

Partial and pseudo partial result lists are kept, indicating the partial result number and its location.

Although partial result storage due to reasons 3 and 4 does not initiate a restart, any later restart which involves going back to a point preceding such a storage, takes note that such storage is required and stores as the partial results are generated.

Detection of situations in which partial result storage is required is achieved by keeping a record of the nesting store state during translation of the expression.

## Conclusion

In a chapter of this length it is obviously impossible to write a full description of such a complex and interrelated program. It is hoped, however, that it has given some idea of the philosophy of writing an optimizing translator. It is also hoped that the rather brief description of some of the techniques used will show that such a translator is feasible.

## Acknowledgements

The author would like to acknowledge the work done on this scheme by E. N. Hawkins, L. Hodges and A. G. Price. The former being responsible for that part of the scheme dealing with subscripted variables. He is also indebted to F. G. Duncan for many hours of discussion on ALGOL and the techniques described in this paper.

This paper is published by permission of The Manager, Data Processing and Control Systems Division, The English Electric Company Limited, Kidsgrove.

### REFERENCES

1. G. M. DAVIS (1960). The English Electric KDF 9 Computer System. *Computer Bull.*
2. English Electric. KDF 9 Programming Manual. An English Electric Data Processing and Control Systems Division publication.
3. A. P. ERSHOV (1958). "A Programming Program for a High Speed Electronic Computer." Academy of Sciences of the U.S.S.R. (English translation: Pergammon Press.)
4. E. N. HAWKINS and D. H. R. HUXTABLE (1962). A Multi-Pass Translation Scheme for ALGOL 60. *Annu. Rev. Autom. Progr.* **3**.
5. R. B. MARIMONT (1959). Checking the Consistency of Precedence Matrices. *J.A.C.M.* **6**, No. 2.
6. S. WARSHALL (1962). A Theorem on Boolean Matrices. *J.A.C.M.* **9**, No. 1.

*Further discussion on* ALGOL *implementation topics may be found in:*

7. E. W. DIJKSTRA (1960). Recursive Programming. *Numerische Mathematik* **2**, 312–318.
8. J. JENSEN and P. NAUR (1961). An Implementation of ALGOL 60 Procedures. *BIT* **1**, 38.
9. J. JENSEN, P. MANDRUP and P. NAUR (1961). A Storage Allocation Scheme for ALGOL 60. *BIT* **2**, 89–102
10. K. SAMELSON and F. L. BAUER (1960). Sequential Formula Translation. *Comm. A.C.M.* **3**, No. 2, 76–83.

# 10. THE ELLIOTT ALGOL PROGRAMMING SYSTEM

C. A. R. HOARE

*Elliott Brothers (London) Ltd., London, England*

## Introduction

The System which is described in this paper has been designed for the National-Elliott 803 and the Elliott 503 high-speed computers. These two machines share the same instruction code, so that it has been possible to write a single translation program for both of them. This program has been written and thoroughly tested on the 803, and is now available to all users of an 803 with automatic floating point unit.

The aim of the Elliott ALGOL System is to combine in a single translating program the benefits of reasonably fast translation with reasonably efficient object program coding, without relying on the use of magnetic tapes or other forms of backing storage. From the start, it did not seem possible to achieve all these aims without making some compromises; we have therefore felt free to introduce a few minor restrictions on the more out-of-the-way facilities of ALGOL.

The guiding principles in the design of the system are as follows.

1. Normal straightforward ALGOL programs and procedures shall produce normal straightforward object coding, such as might be produced by a human coder.

2. More advanced features, such as recursion, shall be implemented by short book-keeping subroutines, which may be far from straightforward or efficient.

3. Features of ALGOL which are difficult to implement by methods 1 or 2 shall be removed from the language. These features are remarkably few, and are unlikely to be missed in practical programming.

## Error Detection

One of the most important features which must be provided by all programming systems is the checking of clerical and programming errors. In this respect we have observed the following principles:

1. The translator shall detect errors which make the continuation of translation impossible. The translator shall not waste time on making every possible check of the source program.

2. Every effort shall be made to detect errors arising during the running of the program (e.g. subscripts exceeding bounds).

3. In a few cases where neither 1 nor 2 is possible, the translation must be made in such a way that under no circumstances is it possible for a program to 'jump out of control'. This consideration is so important that it has in one case overridden considerations of efficiency.

## Optimization

Another feature which is considered desirable in a programming system is automatic optimization of the object program. By this is meant such activities as search for common subexpressions in an arithmetic expression. This is not generally allowed by ALGOL, and is in any case very time-consuming for the translator. Furthermore, it is an activity at present far better suited to human beings than computers. We have therefore decided not to attempt optimization in cases where the programmer is perfectly capable of providing it himself.

There are cases, however, where the programmer cannot specify an optimum program directly in ALGOL; for example, when the values of the subscripts of a variable are controlled exclusively by a for clause. The solution we have adopted is to provide additional standard functions which will enable the programmer to achieve optimization even without the use of machine code, and without violating the syntax of ALGOL. Optimum programs using these standard functions are not as easy to write as unoptimized programs; but when a program is to be run frequently, the extra effort may be considered worthwhile. It would be very wasteful for an ALGOL translator to apply optimizing techniques to all programs translated.

It must be remembered that the straightforward methods used in the majority of programs will be translated in a straightforward manner, to produce machine code of reasonable efficiency. Therefore the need for optimization is far less than it would be if a different approach to the task of translation had been adopted.

## Variables

Integer variables are stored in the computer as 39-digit words. One of these digits represents the sign, so that the absolute values of integers must be less than about 250 thousand million. If an integer exceeds this range, the error will be detected.

Real variables are represented by 39-digit floating point numbers, of which 9 digits store the exponent, and 30 the mantissa. This gives an accuracy of about two parts in $10^9$ and a range $\pm 10^{77}$ approx.

Boolean variables are also represented by 39-digit words, of which only the first digit (the sign digit) has significance (1 for **true,** 0 for **false**).

## Arithmetic and Logical Operations

The 803 and 503 have machine code instructions for addition, subtracton, multiplication, and division of floating point numbers; also addition and subtraction of integers. Multiplication of integers can be achieved by two machine instructions, but the division of integers has to be performed by subroutine, since the machine-code division instruction does not accord with the ALGOL definition. Exponentiation and conversion from real to integer is always performed by subroutine.

In order to perform arithmetic operations on numbers of different types, the integer is converted to floating point form by means of the appropriate machine instruction. This instruction is inserted by the translator wherever necessary; consequently the ALGOL specification of integer exponentiation cannot be observed exactly. In ALGOL 60 the type of the result of raising an integer to an integral power can only be determined during the running of the program, since only then is it known whether the exponent is negative. In Elliott ALGOL the result of exponentiation is always taken to be real.

The Boolean operations of conjunction, disjunction and equivalence are achieved by various combinations of collating, negating, and testing for overflow. No attempt is made to optimize Boolean expressions by omitting evaluation of the second limb of a conjunction or disjunction when the first limb has turned out **false** or **true** respectively. It is therefore the responsibility of the programmer who desires optimization to use the appropriate conditional Boolean expressions to achieve this effect.

The simple variables of an ALGOL program are assigned addresses by the translator in the same way as would be done by an elementary symbolic assembly program. Consequently reference to simple variables is made without use of address modification. This results in a considerable saving of time and object program length. It has the disadvantage that special methods have to be used to achieve recursion.

## Arrays

Arrays in ALGOL cannot be allocated addresses by the translator, since their size is, in general, not known until the program is being run. Therefore allocation is performed by a subroutine which is entered from the running program. This subroutine administers a dynamic stack, so that maximum economy is ensured in the sharing of array workspace between successive blocks. The use of a dynamic stack in this case results in very little loss of efficiency, since all references to subscripted variables have to be made by address modification anyway.

The parameters of the array allocation routine specify the lower and upper bounds of the subscripts, the number of arrays in the segment, and the address of the first of the block of 'representative locations' of the arrays of the segment. The representative location of an array is allocated an address by the translator in the same way as the simple variables of a block.

The array allocation routine first stores in the stack a 'dope vector' specifying the lower bound and range of each subscript, and then computes the size of the array. For each array in the segment, it then allocates a block of locations, and places in the representative location for that array the address of the first element of the block. The address of the dope vector is planted in the location immediately preceding each of the blocks. Thus the final picture is as follows: each representative location points to the first element of its array, which is immediately preceded by the address of its relevant dope vector. (Fig. 1.)

Reference to multidimensional subscripted variables is made by address calculation. Each subscript is first reduced by the value of its lower bound, and then multiplied by the product of the ranges of all subsequent subscripts; the results for each subscript are finally added together. This produces a

*representative locations*

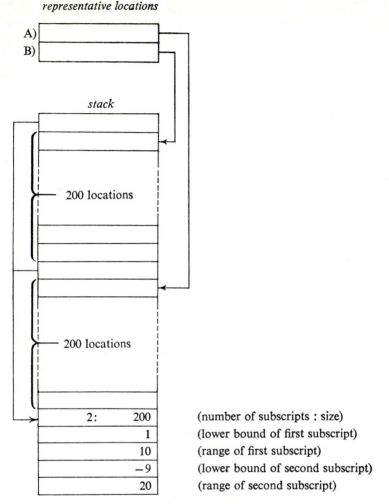

Fig. 1. Representation of: *away* A,B[1 : 10,—9 : 20] ;

single subscript value, which may be treated in the same way as the value of the subscript of a single-dimensional array.

During the calculation of the address of a subscripted variable, a test is made on each subscript, to detect whether its value has fallen outside the declared range. If it has, an error message is given, and the program stops. This check prevents accidental overwriting of the program itself, which would produce errors which are very difficult to trace to their source. Furthermore, the ALGOL translator will normally be held in the store of the computer throughout the execution of a batch of small programs. It would be very inconvenient to have the translator overwritten without warning during a batch run of ALGOL programs. Of course, if a program requires a lot of extra space, the translator will be overwritten anyway, but in this case the operator is given the appropriate warning.

The checks and multiplications involved in address calculations are very time-consuming. Where a subscript is the counting variable of a loop, the checks could have been made once for all, and the multiplications could have been replaced by additions. However, it is impossible for the translator to make a reasonably quick test of the validity of this optimization. The programmer is therefore given the facility of programming his own address calculation. Standard functions have been provided to make available the machine address of any array, and this address may be used to access the value of the variable stored at that address, or even to assign a new value to the variable. This may be done validly in ALGOL notation, and there is no need to be familiar with the machine code of the computer.

For example, the following block will compute the sum of the values of a vector $V$, storing the result in 'sum'

```
begin integer i, h;
    sum: = 0;
    i    : = address (V);
    h    : = size (V) + i − 1;
    for  i  , : = i step 1 until h do
         sum: = sum + location [i]
end
```

Since the programming of loops by address is rather more difficult than the use of subscripted variables, a number of the more commonly used matrix operations have been made available in the form of optimized ALGOL procedures.

## Expressions

The translation of an arithmetic, Boolean, or designational expression in ALGOL is a sequence of machine code instructions which places in the accumulator of the computer the value of the expression. The translation routine for expressions is written as a procedure, which enters itself recursively whenever called upon to translate a non-simple primary constituent of the expression which it is engaged on translating. On exit from the recursive activation, it is known that machine code has been produced which will place the result of evaluating the primary constituent in the accumulator.

For example, the expression $(A + B) \times C$ will be translated as follows:

On encountering the initial open bracket, a (recursive) entry is made to the routine 'compile arithmetic expressions' this will translate '$A + B$' and output code:

$$TAKE \quad A$$
$$ADD \quad B$$

and advance the input tape so that ')' is in the input buffer. On exit from this routine, a check is made the character in the buffer is a close bracket.

Then translation proceeds on the assumption that the result of evaluating the bracketed expression will be in the accumulator; the rest of the expression is therefore simply translated:

*MULTIPLY   C.*

Conditional expressions present no difficulty when recursion is used. After the **if,** the procedure which compiles Boolean expressions will produce machine code to place in the accumulator the value **true** or the value **false.** Since **false** is represented by a zero word, **then** may be translated as a jump on condition zero, with a destination to be determined later. Then the expression between **then** and **else** is compiled, and **else** is translated as 'jump to address to be determined later' immediately followed by the message 'this is the destination of the jump previously left undefined'. Finally, at the end of the expression immediately following **else,** the destination of the **else** jump may be defined.

The actual addresses of the jump instructions are filled in during a second internal scan of the object program. This scan starts at the end of the program and works back to the beginning. Whenever a 'destination' message is encountered, the machine address of the instruction just scanned is placed in a push-down list. Whenever an undefined jump is encountered, the destination address is removed from the top of the pushdown list, and planted in the jump instruction. This method allows simple processing of conditional expressions occurring inside one another to any depth, since the rules of ALGOL ensure that the **thens** and **elses** shall be properly nested in the same way as brackets—that is, **then** acts as an open bracket, **else** acts as a simultaneous close and open bracket, and the end of the expression after the **else** acts as a final close bracket. For this reason, the translation of **then** is called a 'nested jump', the translation of the end of the expression is called 'answer nested jump', and the translation of **else** is called a 'twisted answer'. (Fig. 2.)

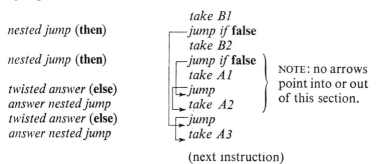

NOTE: no arrows point into or out of this section.

(next instruction)

Fig. 2. Translation of: *if* B1 *then* (*if* B2 *then* A1 *else* A2) *else* A3

## Blocks

One of the chief purposes of the block structure of ALGOL is to indicate the scope of arrays, so that the space used to hold arrays which are not currently in use may be reallocated for other purposes. The easiest way of 'deleting' the space used by a block is to record how much space was in use before entry,

C. A. R. HOARE

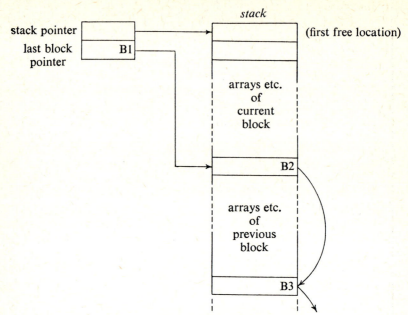

Fig. 3a. During execution of block B1.

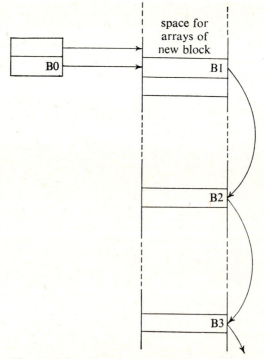

Fig. 3b. After entry from block B1 to block B0.

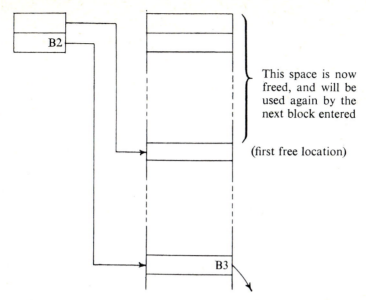

This space is now freed, and will be used again by the next block entered

(first free location)

B2

B3

Fig. 3c. After exit from block B1, back into block B2.

since this is exactly the amount of space that is still required on exit from the block. All the space in use at any time is on one side of the 'stack pointer' which always points to the first of the free (unused) locations. On entry to a block we record the address of this location (in fact, by pushing it down on the stack). Inside the block additional space will be used, so that the address of the first free location will be altered. On exit from the block, all this space again becomes free, so that all that has to be done is to reset the stack pointer to what it was before entry to the block. This is done by copying the value from the place where it has been pushed down. (Fig. 3.)

The ALGOL rules for exiting blocks by go to statements involves the compiling of the requisite number of block exit instructions before compiling the jump to a destination outside the block. To make this possible, it is necessary to know of each label the block to which it belongs. This is achieved by a rule in Elliott ALGOL that all labels prefixed to a statement of a block must appear in the switch list of a switch declaration in the head of the block. This achieves the same effect as declaration for all other identifiers of a block, that is, to introduce the identifiers which are to be treated as local to the block.

A further consequence of this method of treating blocks and jumps out of a block is the rule that a go to statement inside a procedure may not have a destination outside the procedure. A procedure may be called at several different block levels, and therefore it can only be discovered at run time how many block exits are necessary before the jump corresponding to such a go to statement can be made. In the system described above, this is not possible.

## Procedures

Undoubtedly the procedure structure of ALGOL is its most characteristic feature, and the one which presents the most difficulty in implementation. In order to secure reasonable efficiency in the vast majority of cases, Elliott ALGOL has had to introduce a few restrictions on the general structure; the reason for these restrictions will become clear as the methods are explained.

The translation of the procedure body presents little difficulty. Each parameter of the procedure is allocated an address in the same way as the local workspace of the procedure, and it is assumed that these locations will have been filled with the appropriate values before entry to the procedure. In the case of a parameter called by value the contents of the location will be the appropriate logical value or number (converted to the type specified). In the case of an array called by name, it will be a straight copy of the representative location for the array. In the case of a type parameter called by name it will be a word which contains a link address in its second half and a jump to a closed subroutine in its first half. This closed subroutine (or *thunk*) is the very portion of object program produced by translating the actual parameter. If the actual parameter is a variable, the thunk will place its address in the accumulator, or if it is an expression its value will be put in a fixed location whose address is placed in the accumulator.

On the assumption that the parameters have been planted before entry, each reference in the procedure body to a value parameter or a parameter specified as an array may be translated in exactly the same way as if it were part of the procedure workspace. Each reference to a parameter called by name (other than an array) is translated as a subroutine jump, followed by a *B*-lined reference to the desired value, or a *B*-lined storing instruction (in the case of assignment).

In order that the requisite parameter planting instructions may be compiled during compilation of the procedure entry (i.e. procedure statement or function designator), the procedure heading has to be known beforehand. This entails two restrictions, firstly that entry can only be made to previously declared procedures, and secondly that procedures cannot feature as parameters of other procedures; for it would not be possible to compile an entry to a procedure which is itself a parameter, especially if different corresponding actual procedure parameters had different value and specification parts.

## Recursion

Since variables and parameters are allocated fixed addresses at time of translation, special measures have to be taken when recursive entry is made to a procedure. In fact, the contents of all the workspace of a procedure being entered recursively are 'pushed down' onto the same dynamic stack as is used for the storage of arrays. When an exit is made from a recursive activation of a procedure, the contents of all the workspace locations are copied back from the top of the dynamic stack to their original fixed locations. The nested structure of ALGOL ensures that the information to be copied back will be at the top of the stack at the time when it is necessary to copy it back; so there is little difficulty in keeping records of what has to be copied and where to.

In the case of a procedure which contains a recursive activation of itself in its own body, the translator can detect this fact and compile the necessary pushing down and restoring instructions. It may be, however, that the recursive entry occurs during the evaluation of a parameter called by name, and this case is very difficult to detect during translation.

For this reason every procedure with one or more parameters called by name (other than arrays) is assigned a marker, which is set whenever the procedure is being currently activated, and cleared when the procedure is dormant. Before entry to the procedure, the marker is examined; if it is set, the workspace of the procedure is pushed down, a note is made to this effect, and on exit the workspace is restored to its original position; if the marker is clear, it is simply set, and no pushing down takes place. Again, the nested structure of ALGOL ensures that everything which has to be copied from the dynamic stack is at the top of the stack at the time when the copying is to take place.

This method of implementing recursive procedures necessitates a further restriction: that recursive procedures may not have any parameters called by name, other than labels and arrays. The reason for this is that during the execution of a name parameter thunk, the workspace referred to will not be in its proper place, since it will have been pushed down onto the stack to make way for the workspace of the current activation.

## Conclusion

During the construction of the ALGOL system, we noticed that many of the features of ALGOL which we had not intended to implement would be quite easy to re-introduce without altering the basis of the translating system. Some of these features were in fact incorporated, but those which would have involved much extra complication in the translating program have been postponed in the interests of achieving an early completion date.

## Acknowledgement

This paper is published by kind permission of Elliott Brothers (London) Ltd.

# 11. I.C.T. COBOL RAPIDWRITE

## E. HUMBY

*International Computers and Tabulators Ltd., London, England*

### Classes of Problems

There are two classes of computer problem. Without attempting a definition let us call them commercial and scientific. I am not saying that these are two clear categories into which everything falls, but that of all the programs there are certain problems which can be described as commercial and others which can be described as scientific. In reality, the distinction is that in scientific problems the variables alter according to divine rules, in commercial problems they alter according to human ones; that is, they vary according to the laws made by governments, the dictates of ministries, agreements with trade unions and special contracts for special customers. In the field of science, as we head towards the eternal truth, we can use subroutines of greater and greater generality. In the commercial field, as we add to the chaos of business activity we shall be requiring languages and routines which are heading more and more towards complexity. As each program becomes more and more particular, rather than more and more general, we shall need languages that reflect this movement.

In this book, which so far has only dealt with languages needed for scientific problems, nothing has been said about a completely common language. Here I shall try to make some distinctions. First of all, the mathematical side of programs are based largely on descriptions which are close to algebraic formulae. However, in commercial work formulae play an insignificant part. The arithmetic is trivial and decision-making is probably much more important than the resolution of long formulae. In commercial problems, because of their particular and special nature, very little use can be made of large libraries of sub-routines. Floating point calculation is of no use to the accountant. He often needs to specify results which are, for example, to three decimal places of pence or more. Data handling facilities are much more important in commercial work. Some languages do not cater very well for this. An accountant could be forgiven if, having read through the ALGOL 60 report, he failed to see any indication how he was to get anything on his printed invoices, how he could suppress zeroes on some of the quantities, or how he could replace the zeroes by asterisks or get a pounds sign to float up and down on them. He could be forgiven for having read from cover to cover and actually missed the precise statement which told him how to put data into the machine and get it out again. These differences in the type of problem are sufficient justification for separate languages, and the reason why, because there is a need for them, ugly languages like COBOL can compete favourably with ALGOL.

## History

The principal reason why the greatest progress has been made in the scientific field is because engineers, physicists and aero-dynamicists are generally used to using some commonly understood algebraic notation when discussing their problems. In the commercial field there is no such generally accepted language. Secondly, many of the problems in the scientific field were problems for which only one run was required; a specific answer was sought for a specific problem. At worst the program had to run spasmodically. In the commercial field, however, the general tendency of programs is that they are written to do a job which has to be performed day in and day out, and the efficiency of the object program is of prime importance. Generally, the scientific program can accept an interpretative rather than a compilational approach, and there has been a tendency with scientific languages to design them so that they are reasonably easy to compile. Thirdly, a feature of scientific problems is that the process is the important thing: just how the information has to be fed into the program and exactly in what form the results have to be output is often unimportant. On the other hand, in commercial problems the form is essential: the proper placing of the date on the invoice may be extremely critical.

Nevertheless, commercial users were anxious to establish some sort of common approach. They did require languages in which programs could be written for different computers. There were several manufacturers in the United States who sought to invent languages which could be used on several different types of the same machine. One of the first was designed by Dr Grace Hopper. There was difficulty in seeing what was common about commercial problems that people could use as a basis for inventing a commercial language. There was certainly no commercial algebra. It seemed to Dr Hopper that English formed a common language in which people discussed their problems, so Flowmatic was based upon an English format. Now, I think this was a dangerous decision to have made. But it was very acceptable. There were a number of people who misguidedly thought that, because they could read what a program was about, they would therefore be in a position to write programs easily. Secondly, there were difficulties with documentation. This always presents a problem when writing a program because the programmer is so anxious to get a machine-coded program working on the machine that he finds it very tedious to pause during or at the end of the program to record precisely what he is doing. These English-type languages gave the impression that no documentation was necessary, that the statement of the problem in a language like Flowmatic was sufficient documentation for the program. Really we are not providing documentation automatically with a language like Flowmatic. All that has happened is that a discipline has been imposed on the programmer. He produces the documentation as he goes along, but the onus of doing this manual clerical labour still falls upon him.

There were, however, a number of people who were pleased that programmers were being disciplined to produce documentation and so this idea spread and, as a consequence, we can see in the development of commercial languages generally the tendency to base them on a full English notation. This was so in the cases of COMTRAN and FACT.

In May 1959, just as this idea had become popular, the American Department of Defence held a symposium (the first meeting of *CODASYL*) to discuss common commercial languages. It was not surprising, therefore, that the language specified by the short range committee set up by this group should be based on free-flowing English.

## COBOL

By April 1960, the short range committee published their first report. This contained the specifications for COBOL 60. At the same time *CODASYL* set us a maintenance group whose job it was to keep track of the use being made of COBOL, to receive suggestions for its improvement and continually to modify the language in order to keep it up to date. This maintenance was carried out by a team of manufacturers and users. By September 1960, however, they decided that it was impracticable to keep continually modifying the language. Especially it annoyed the people who were trying to implement it and who were trying to write compilers. It was decided, therefore, that there would be an annual freezing of COBOL. Amendments and modifications would be collected and the language modified once a year only. A start was made with COBOL 61, which was published in' June 1961. *CODASYL* have now said that they have no intention of bringing out a COBOL for 1962. At the moment most users are implementing a form of COBOL 61.

Now a particular feature of COBOL 61 is that it separates the facilities into two categories. One category is called the 'Required' COBOL which *CODASYL* say must be used by each implementer before he can claim to be using COBOL. The other category is the 'Elective' COBOL, from which each implementer can choose the facilities he is going to add—at the expense, of course, of compatibility.

Perhaps I have over-emphasized the weakness of all these languages in having an English-type base. I shall, however, discuss this question later. In the meantime let us consider those aspects of COBOL which, in relation to the commercial problems for which they were intended, are most useful.

## COBOL Structure

The special value of COBOL seems to stem from its specific structure, for it is its divisional aspect that is particularly helpful in data handling. The designers of COBOL saw that in a machine-coded program for a commercial problem, instructions could be divided into three categories. 1. Instructions which were actually getting on with the job—adding numbers together and writing them out. 2. Instructions in the program which give, for example, the necessary scaling for the decimal point, editing features for printed output, instructions for getting the data in a form on which the real procedure can work. 3. Instructions related to the particular computer on which the program is running.

Next the designers of COBOL categorized this information and formulated the following three divisions. 1. Data division, in which the data is clearly described once and once only. It was then possible to handle names like *RATE* and *QUANTITY* and *AMOUNT* without any reference to editing, decimal point position, and so on. 2. Environment division, which is entirely concerned with describing the computer on which the object program will run; this will be all the information the compiler will require to build in the necessary instructions which deal with the limitations of the machine. 3. Procedure division, which is a pure procedure describing nothing but the process which operates upon the data and which can be read fairly easily by the computer manager or the systems man.

### Example

A complete COBOL program is shown in Fig. 1. Let us study the use made of a few facilities. For example, line 12 in the Procedure division reads *READ ISSUES RECORD AT END GO TO PRINTING*. It will be seen that in the data division there are three lines, 1, 9 and 14, which begin *FD*. Each *FD* line is a file description line and gives a name to the total stream of information which is going into or coming out of one piece of hardware. The first one of these is *FD ISSUES*, we have just given the instruction as 12 *READ ISSUES*, which means make available the elements in the next record from the file known as *ISSUES*. From that point on we can operate on any of the things in the *ISSUE-ITEM* record in the *ISSUE* file, and it contains the fields *STORES-NUMBER, CUSTOMER-NO, QUANTITY, GROSS-VALUE* and *DISCOUNT*. The '*AT END GO TO PRINTING*' means that there will come a time when you try to obey this *READ* and you will find that you will have exhausted the file completely. At that point in time computer control passes to the piece of program which has the paragraph heading *PRINTING*, and *PRINTING* is number 25 in the procedure.

If you look back at line 6 you will see that COBOL can cope with formulae. Here is a statement:

$$COMPUTE\ NET\text{-}VALUE\ EQUALS\ NET\text{-}VALUE + (GROSS\text{-}VALUE -$$
$$GROSS\text{-}VALUE * DISCOUNT/100).$$

The rules for priorities of exponentiation over multiply or divide, of multiply and divide over plus and minus are as in the normal algebraic rules one learns at school. Brackets are used in the same way to interrupt these priorities but all the operands are data-names each of which has been carefully defined in the data division.

There is a little subroutine, procedure step 35, called *TOTAL LINE-PRINT*. This shows an example of a conditional statement. In the actual problem we build up a table. There are two items on each line of the table and there is a possibility of 999 pairs in the table. The first item is called *STORED-QUANTITY*, the second item is called the *STORED-GROSS*, and the function of the whole sentence which begins at 36 is to arrange to have printed out the contents of each pair of stored items of this table, but only on condition that there is something to print in either of these two on each line. If on any particular line there should be two zeroes, then no printing

is intended to take place. That is the nature of this sentence, which says that
if the stored quantity, suffixed by a current count or if the store gross again
suffixed is not equal to zero (that is provided there's something worth
printing), then set up in print-out format the actual number that is dealt
with at the moment, the stored quantity and the stored gross. We then
compute the total gross as total gross plus stored gross; this is updating an
accumulator called *TOTAL-GROSS* which will be output separately at the
very end. We then *WRITE TOTAL-LINE*, which means print out now what
we have stored out ready for print. Now this little group called total line
print at 35 was a subroutine and it was called into operation by instruction
number 29 which said *PERFORM TOTAL-LINE-PRINT VARYING NO
FROM 1 BY 1 UNTIL NO EQUALS 999*. This perform statement tells
programmers that total line print is actually a subroutine and the count
number is to be modified from a starting value of one by increments of one
up to a total value of 999 and this statement sets the mechanism for the loop
operation.

### Readability and Rapidwrite

What I hoped you spotted in these examples was that these are pretty wordy
instructions. It would be tedious writing down this forty instruction program.
It would get very tedious indeed with a program of any useful size and the
file name *COMMODITY-TOTALS*, the programmer rapidly abbreviates to
something shorter when he has repeated it for the tenth time. This all arises
from this misconception that commercial users must have a source program
which is in English. This is not true. There are advantages in being able to
read a program, but these advantages of readability should not be foisted onto
the poor man who has to write the program down.

Rapidwrite was not a new language. I.C.T. accepted COBOL with all its
advantages. We considered that we should (*a*) make it much simpler to
present to customers, (*b*) make it much easier for programmers to write. We
would, nevertheless, provide all the advantages of readability at the time we
did the translation. We would get the computer to provide readability, not
ask the programmer to do it. Now the mechanism by which we did this was
merely to provide the programmer with a very rigid format in which he was
to tell the compiler the information required in the environment, data and
procedure divisions.

Look, first of all, at the sheet illustrated in Fig. 2. This is called the
Environment Division Sheet. Now look again at the COBOL programme on
its first page. Four items down it reads *ENVIRONMENT DIVISION*.
The Environment Division of the COBOL sheet takes up ten lines and thirty-
six words. The essential piece of information is the IAS size of 400 words,
the drum size of 12,000 words and the naming of the three files which are
attached to the reader, punch, and printer. So why should the programmer
have to write anything other than this essential information as none of it is
of value to the compiler. On the Rapidwrite form you can see, in manuscript,
the only information that is required, and it does not need much instruction
to tell you exactly where to write the 400 for the IAS size and the 12,000 for

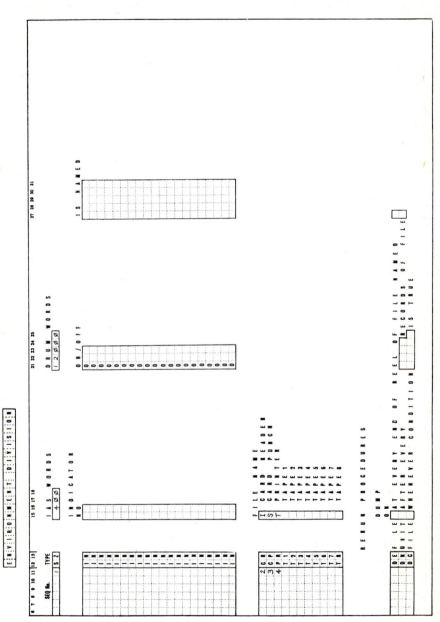

Fig. 2

the drum size; it does need me to tell you that when you invent names for file names they should only be one letter long and then you can see that it is fairly easy to write these file name letters against the card reader, the card punch or the card printer as indicated.

The other sheet (Fig. 3) shows the data division. There is a restriction on the data names which you see on the data sheet of five characters, made up from the COBOL set, letters, numbers and hyphen. Now all the description of each piece of data is a graphic description rather than a long English one. This lends itself to a much easier view of what the print output is going to look like or what the fields along a punched card are going to look like. Detailed rules for drafting the data division are given in a Rapidwrite manual.

With regard to procedure we still wanted to continue this idea of a pre-printed format because this meant that we could do half the writing by having the remainder already printed, we wanted to make it easy for the programmer to write so that the format led him to its completion very simply and the way to do this in the procedure statement was to supply him with eleven card types from which the whole of his program would be made. These contained the essential types *READ, WRITE, GO, STOP, MOVE, COMPUTE, PERFORM, IF, SUBSCRIPT, INCLUDE, PARAGRAPH.* All the fixed wording of the sentence was printed on the card and the programmer was simply left boxes into which he wrote his data-name, his paragraph-name or his literal. Three samples are shown in Fig. 4a-c. One advantage of having one sentence per card is that it is fairly easy to make insertions and deletions from a program. There need be no rubbing out of two lines and inserting six or scrapping a whole sheet because one had missed out an essential piece of program. The ordering of programming is simplified, one can even lay the cards out as though they were a prefabricated diagram as in the method which is shown on the large sheet inside the pocket of the manual.

Now, we had promised that in making these restrictions we would not destroy the value of having a readable version of the program. What we did was, in the compiling process, to supply all the words which the programmer was not required to write and the punch operator was not required to punch; these are supplied automatically at compilation time, so that we print out a full and valid COBOL version of the Rapidwrite programme which goes in.

In producing Rapidwrite we not only produced a simplified format but we made a reduction of the facilities as well, there were some facilities which we said were of marginal use; things like the *EXAMINE* verb. There is a redundancy in that COBOL not only has *COMPUTE* followed by formula but it has *ADD, SUBTRACT, MULTIPLY* and *DIVIDE.* The last four verbs are redundant and we left them out and we made reductions of this kind. One of the restrictions of this sort that we applied was not to have Rapidwrite deal with a case where there were several files on one input/output unit. Now if there is only one file per piece of hardware, then we can supply *OPEN* for all files at the beginning of a program and *CLOSE* for all files at the end of a program and, in fact, on the COBOL print-out you will see these opens and closes appear at beginning and end.

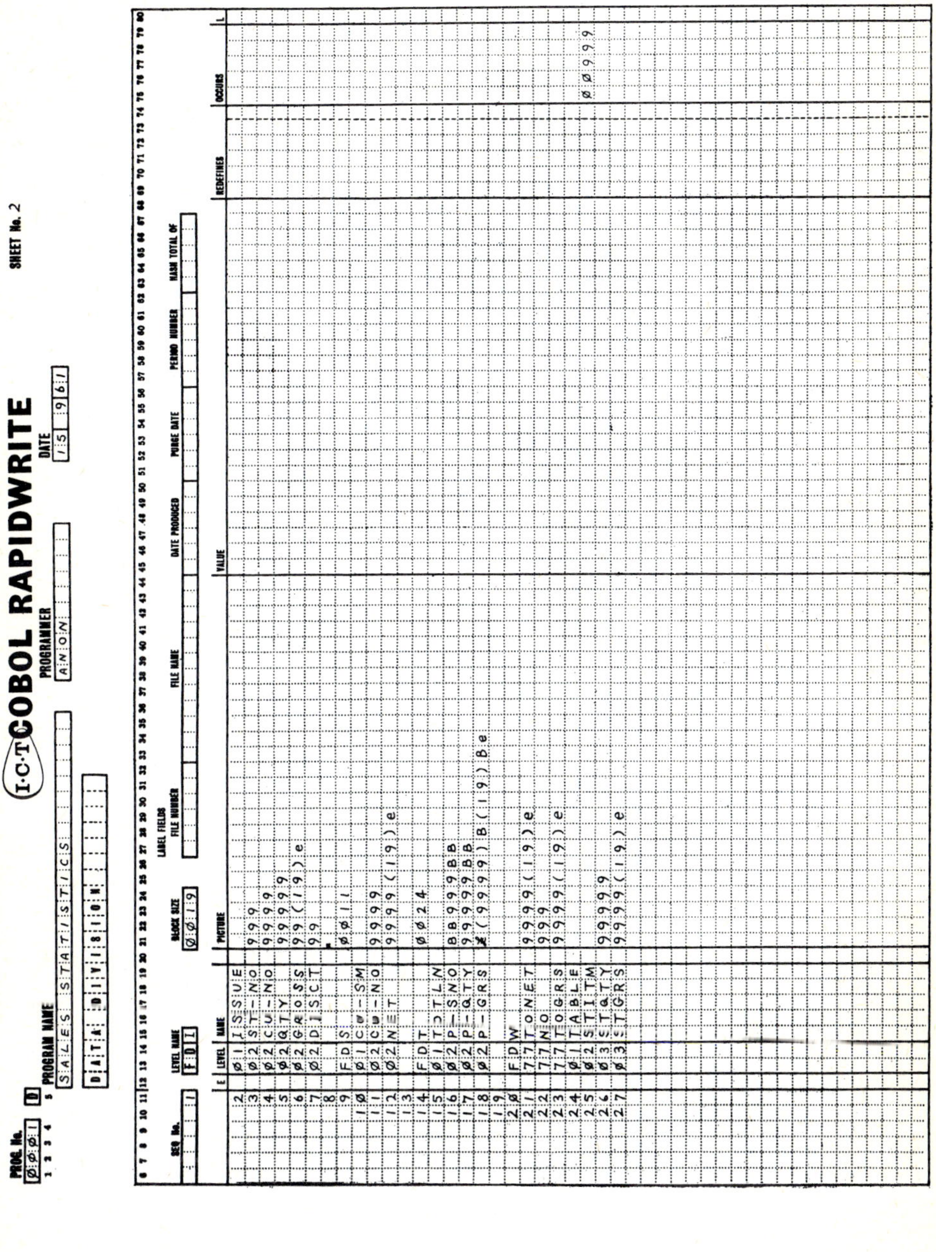

PROG. No. ØØØ1 D — PROGRAM NAME: SALES STATISTICS — PROGRAMMER: ANON — DATE: 15 961 — SHEET No. 2

I.C.T. COBOL RAPIDWRITE

DATA DIVISION

SEQ No.: 1 — LEVEL NAME: FDI — BLOCK SIZE: ØØ19 — LABEL FIELDS: FILE NUMBER, FILE NAME, DATE PRODUCED, PURGE DATE, PERIOD NUMBER, HASH TOTAL OF

| SEQ No. | E | LEVEL | NAME | PICTURE | VALUE | REDEFINES | OCCURS |
|---|---|---|---|---|---|---|---|
| 2 | | Ø1 | ISSUE | | | | |
| 3 | | Ø2 | ST-NO | 999 | | | |
| 4 | | Ø2 | CU-NO | 9999 | | | |
| 5 | | Ø2 | QTY | 99999 | | | |
| 6 | | Ø2 | GROSS | 99(19)e | | | |
| 7 | | Ø2 | DISCT | 99 | | | |
| 8 | | | | | | | |
| 9 | | FD | S | ØØ11 | | | |
| 1Ø | | Ø1 | CU-SM | | | | |
| 11 | | Ø2 | CU-NO | 9999 | | | |
| 12 | | Ø2 | NET | 9999(19)e | | | |
| 13 | | | | | | | |
| 14 | | FD | T | ØØ24 | | | |
| 15 | | Ø1 | TOTLN | | | | |
| 16 | | Ø2 | P-SNO | BB999BB | | | |
| 17 | | Ø2 | P-QTY | 99999BB | | | |
| 18 | | Ø2 | P-GRS | Z(9999)B(19)Be | | | |
| 19 | | | | | | | |
| 2Ø | | FD | W | | | | |
| 21 | | 77 | TONET | 9999(19)e | | | |
| 22 | | 77 | NO | 999 | | | |
| 23 | | 77 | TOGRS | 9999(19)e | | | |
| 24 | | Ø1 | TABLE | | | | |
| 25 | | Ø2 | STITM | | | | ØØ999 |
| 26 | | Ø3 | STQTY | 99999 | | | |
| 27 | | Ø3 | STGRS | 9999(19)e | | | |

Fig. 3

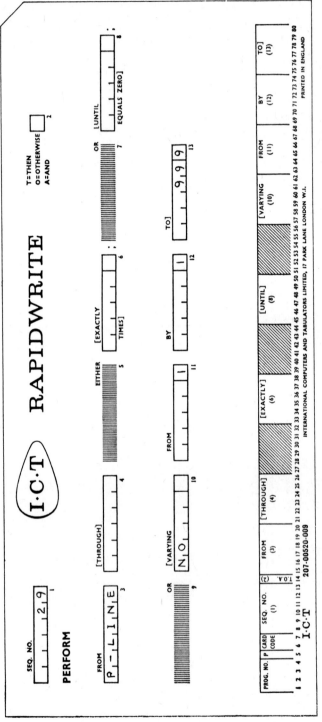

Fig. 4a

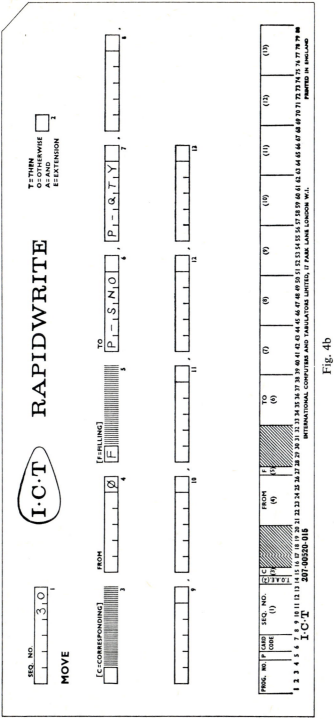

Fig. 4b

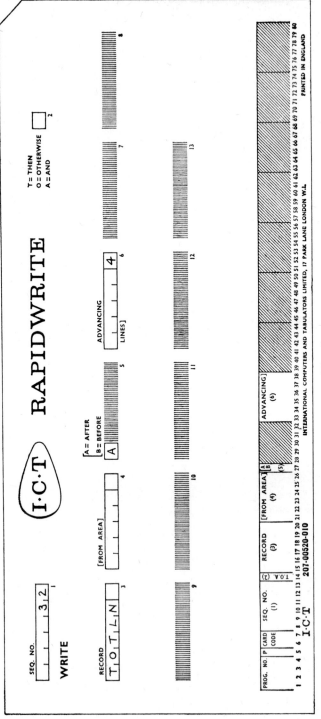

Fig. 4c

## Automatic Readability

The main job of the Rapidwrite scanner is to do an expansion of Rapidwrite statements up to COBOL statements. In order to do this it will have to do two things; it will have to fit in all the noise words that were missing from what the programmer wrote (the noise words which were pre-printed on the card), and for this we will need a 'format dictionary' which has words for the *WRITE* statement like *WRITE* and *AFTER ADVANCING* and *LINES*. These words will appear in this format dictionary, to be wrapped around the Rapidwrite string of data names which are going in it. Secondly, the programmer was happy to put up with one letter for files and five letters for the names of data names. Now the man who reads the program might not be content with this. Instead of the letter *C* for one file, he might want the whole word 'Customer-detail', so the program is prepared to accept a synonym table in which the programmer states once that he wants *C* to be printed out as *CUSTOMER-DETAIL*. This means that wherever the input said *C*, this printed output will enlarge it up to *CUSTOMER-DETAIL*, so any of the abbreviations can be expanded to something which is acceptable to the manager. Now then, this has been useful in quite another way. It gives us some flexibility in outputting in some other natural language. We said one of the disadvantages of COBOL was that it was international only so long as one spoke English. To be truly international one would have to be able to output in other languages. Now then, supposing an Italian were writing a Rapidwrite program, he would presumably write as data names, words which were meaningful to him in Italian. Now I.C.T. could supply him with an Italian Format dictionary which would wrap around these Italian names Italian noise words so as to produce complete Italian COBOL sentences and the Italian manager could read what his Italian programmer was doing. Supposing that a group in France wanted to use a program that had been written by this Italian group. All they would have to do would be to write to I.C.T. for a French Format dictionary, and get one man who knew both French and Italian to translate their Italian names into long French names in the form of a synonym table. The same pack of source program cards punched in Italian and fed into the Rapidwrite scanner would output a French version of this Italian program.

# 12. PROGRAMMING IN HONEYWELL FACT

## J. C. HARWELL

*Honeywell Controls Ltd., London, England*

FACT is a business language with all the facilities with which we are familiar in COBOL together with several others which make it a more powerful tool for data processing. Like COBOL the formal structure of the data on which operations are to be performed is described separately from the procedure statements representing those operations. There is a File outline form on which to describe the data and a Source Language form on which to write the sentences of the procedure.

The input of data on punched cards and the output of data in the form of printed reports or punched cards are given special treatment in FACT. A generated routine called the input-editor is provided to enable punched cards to be input, checked, edited and stored without the need to write procedural instructions for each card. A form is provided in FACT on which to describe the identification punches and the fields on each type of card to be read. In much the same way a form is used to describe the structure and content of reports to be made on the line printer or to be punched into cards.

The forms on which a FACT program is written serve also as punching documents. Each has 80 columns across and represents, if fully used, 20 punched cards. The program cards are called descriptors so that no confusion may arise with cards containing data for input to the FACT program.

## FACT Files

FACT files laid out on magnetic tape represent in serial form the contents and two-dimensional layout of a book-keeping ledger. Statements available in the source language make it possible to scan, as it were, across or down the columns of the ledger with a single programmed loop, and to copy entries, pages or the whole ledger with a single source program statement.

The source program statements refer to the name of a group of items (fields) of information on the file. Such groups, called 'secondary' may occur on the file any number of times; a secondary group may contain within it a lower level secondary group which also may occur any number of times. This feature of FACT whereby a secondary group may 'include' other secondary groups enables complex relationships to be expressed without redundancy of information on the file; higher level groups are not restated for each appearance of their included groups but only when they themselves change in value. The lowest level or terminating group contains no secondary group.

Here are some examples of procedure statements which might be used to obtain information from a file with the structure shown in Fig. 1. For example, Fig. 1 is a file outline form for a *STOCK-TRANSFER* file with any

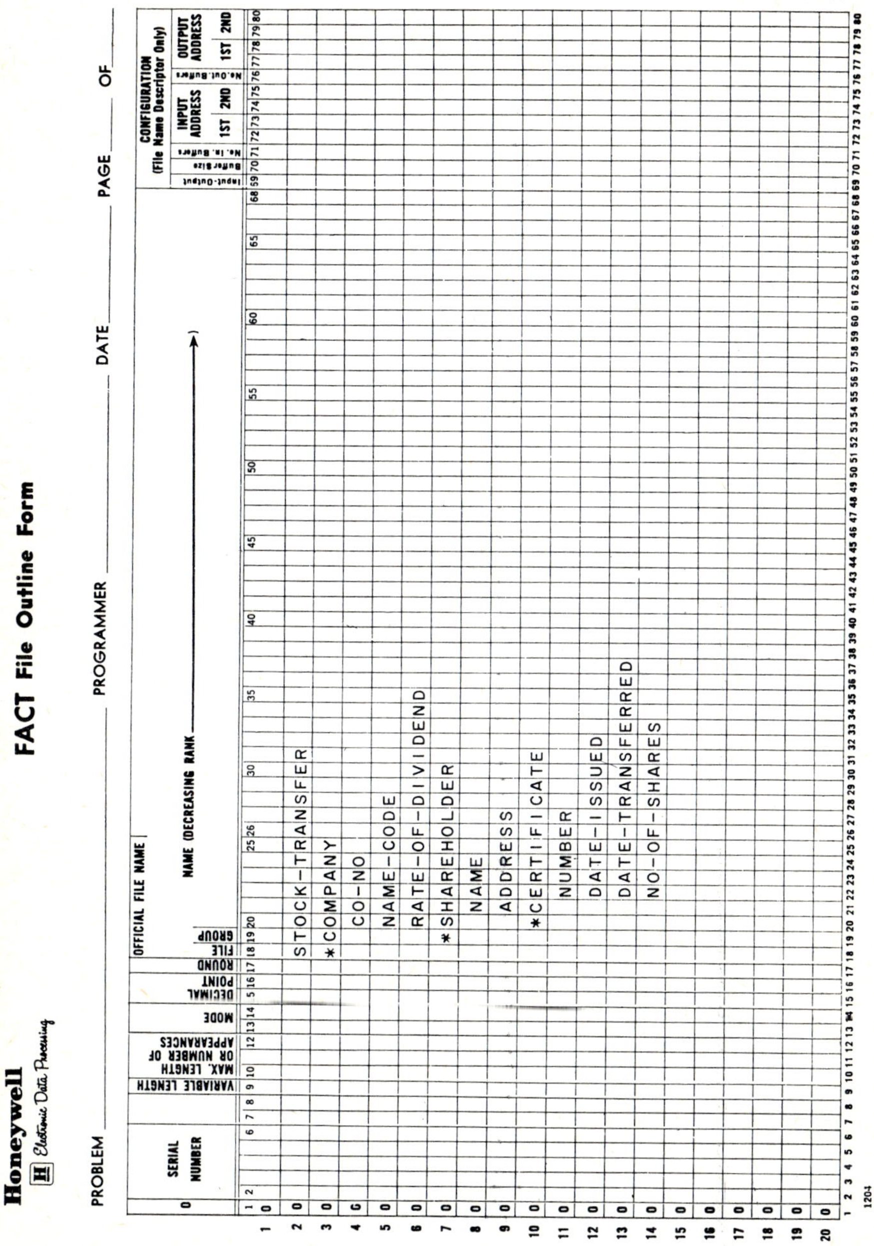

**Honeywell** — *Electronic Data Processing*

## FACT File Outline Form

PROBLEM _____  PROGRAMMER _____  DATE _____  PAGE ____ OF ____

NAME (DECREASING RANK)

| | NAME |
|---|---|
| 1 | STOCK-TRANSFER |
| 2 | *COMPANY |
| 3 | CO-NO |
| 4 | NAME-CODE |
| 5 | RATE-OF-DIVIDEND |
| 6 | *SHAREHOLDER |
| 7 | NAME |
| 8 | ADDRESS |
| 9 | *CERTIFICATE |
| 10 | NUMBER |
| 11 | DATE-ISSUED |
| 12 | DATE-TRANSFERRED |
| 13 | NO-OF-SHARES |

Column headings: SERIAL NUMBER · VARIABLE LENGTH · MAX. LENGTH OR NUMBER OF APPEARANCES · MODE · DECIMAL POINT · ROUND · FILE GROUP · OFFICIAL FILE NAME

CONFIGURATION (File Name Descriptor Only): Input-Output · Buffer Size · No. In. Buffers · INPUT ADDRESS 1ST 2ND · No. Out. Buffers · OUTPUT ADDRESS 1ST 2ND

1204

Fig. 1

number of companies, with information (*NAME-CODE*, *RATE-OF-DIVIDEND*, etc.) relating to each. For each company there may be any number of *SHAREHOLDERS* for each of whom *NAME* and *ADDRESS* will be recorded. Finally for each *SHAREHOLDER* one or more *CERTIFICATES* will be recorded, each with its *NUMBER*, *DATE-ISSUED*, and so on.

The source language statements available in FACT enable the programmer to obtain groups of information from the file, to by-pass groups in which he is not immediately interested, and to ascertain when he has reached the end of the group or file.

*Example*   *GET CERTIFICATE, IF NONE GO TO ABC.*

This will cause transfer of control to the paragraph named *ABC* when the last *CERTIFICATE* of the current *SHAREHOLDER* has been obtained.

*Example*   *OPEN NEXT SHAREHOLDER, IF NONE GO TO ABC*

The word *NEXT* ensures that any fresh *COMPANY* information that is encountered does not cause the transfer to *ABC*. The transfer of control will occur only when the end of the *STOCK-TRANSFER* file is reached. The word *OPEN* causes all groups below the *SHAREHOLDER* level, i.e. *CERTIFICATE* groups, to be ignored.

*Example*   *GET NEXT CERTIFICATE, IF END OF CURRENT SHAREHOLDER GO TO ABC, IF NONE GO TO BCD.*

Successive *CERTIFICATE* groups can be obtained. When the last *CERTIFICATE* information for each *SHAREHOLDER* is reached control goes to *ABC*. At the end of the file control goes to *BCD*.

*Example*   *GET NEXT GROUP OF STOCK-TRANSFER, IF NONE GO TO ABC*

The lowest level group is called regardless of its name. If there had been, for example, a *SHAREHOLDER-SUMMARY* group at the same level as *CERTIFICATE* then it would have been necessary to include in the source program sentence a statement to test the group-name viz: '*IF CERTIFICATE GO TO XYZ*' or '*UNLESS SHAREHOLDER-SUMMARY GO TO XYZ*'.

*Example*   *CLOSE SHAREHOLDER.*

This statement would cause all the *CERTIFICATE* groups contained within the current *SHAREHOLDER* to be by-passed. The statement would be useful if the file structure had several groups at the same level as *SHAREHOLDER* and if it were desired to by-pass the rest of the current *SHAREHOLDER* and obtain any one of those others.

### Primary Groups

Primary groups are fixed length lists, access to whose members is by subscripting. Three levels of subscripting are allowable. It is possible to refer, for example, to information on temperature and humidity for the '$(P + Q)TH$ *HOUR OF* $(M)TH$ *MONTH*'. The file outline would show *TEMPERATURE* and *HUMIDITY* as fields within the primary group named *HOUR*, itself within the primary group named *MONTH*.

*The File Outline Form and Facilities*

Data names are declared on the file outline form. Files are given an official file name, abbreviations for it, tape drives to be used, and whether the file is reversible. Secondary groups are named, marked with an asterisk and indented relative to contained fields and to other secondary groups.

Field names are indented (and lined up) within the secondary group or the primary group to which they belong. The field length in characters and whether that is variable, the position of the decimal point and whether intromissions to the field are to be rounded or truncated are declared; so is the mode of the field which may be one of over a dozen codes—e.g. decimal, alphabetic, alphanumeric, Hollerith, etc. The mode and the field length enable the compiler to pack the field with others in the group and to check the nature of operations upon it.

Alongside the field name may be written a literal value, or a series of conditional adjectives together with those values of the field which connote true conditions for the adjectives. Of primary groups the number of occurrences of the group is to be indicated. A fixed amount of memory space is allocated and the members of the list are addressed in source language by means of an ordinal number used as a subscript——*1ST, 2ND, (N)TH,* $(N + 1)TH$.

## Source Program

The source program is written as a sequence of sentences in a form of English. A sentence is made up of lexicon words, data names, ordinal and cardinal numbers and literals. Sentences are organized into paragraphs which may be named. Paragraphs are organized into named procedures. Semantic considerations govern the composition of paragraphs, considerations of memory space the size of procedures. Of the various types of English sentences, *FACT* makes use only of imperative and indicative ones. Imperative sentences become imperative *FACT* statements, and indicative sentences become *FACT* definitions.

*Example*  Imperative arithmetic statements in FACT.
1. *ADD 5 TIMES BONUS PLUS PAY TO GROSS.*
2. *DIVIDE A BY B MINUS C.*
3. *IF FIRST DIGIT OF NUMBER IS 5 SET TOTAL TO ZERO.*
4. *PUT A TIMES (B PLUS C) INTO D AND E.*
5. *IF VALID SET Q TO M + N / P − 2 * R * R.*

*Example*  A definition in FACT.
　　　*ALPHA. STATUS IN RECORD-FILE IS GREATER THAN RANK IN WEEKLY-FILE, AND IS LESS THAN 7.*

The name of the paragraph may be used as a boolean variable in a number of places: (a) in a sentence, e.g. *IF ALPHA, DO PARAGRAPH XYZ;* (b) as an acceptance condition on the value of a field on an input card; (c) as a print condition able to suppress a line of print; (d) as a logical multiplier in an arithmetic statement, for example

*SET WAGES TO BASIC-WAGE PLUS*
*ALPHA TIMES BONUS.*

A paragraph may comprise several imperative statements or it may consist of a single definition. It may be referred to by its name elsewhere in the source program with the result that it is obeyed at that point. This feature is used in the *INPUT-EDITOR* to allow special processing and acceptance conditions to be applied to each incoming field, in *REPORTS* to allow pre-print procedures, print conditions and tabulation conditions to be applied as lines are about to be printed. It is also used in the *SORT, UPDATE* and other statements to enable special contingencies to be met by the *FACT* programmer.

A non-significant paragraph is named *NOTE* and is merely reproduced in the program listing without effect on the coding.

A paragraph may include other paragraphs which are considered part of it; they form a hierarchy of which the structure is declared by the degree of relative indentation on the descriptors. Thus, one can '*GO TO*' a subsidiary paragraph (within one being performed) without losing the return control link if the main paragraph is subject to a '*PERFORM*' statement.

Procedures may be ranked in a similar way.

### Moving Data Within Core Memory

Groups of fields may be moved from an area in one file to an area in another file by use of the statement

*PUT XX group-name INTO YY group-name.*

Fields within the groups named will be matched by name and checked for likeness of mode and length.

Single fields may be moved by a *PUT, SET* or *REPLACE* statement. Validity checking is provided if the sentence includes or if the paragraph ends with, or is referred to in, a validity statement—'*IF VALID. . . .*', '*IF NO UNCHECKED VALIDITY ERROR. . . . .*'.

A field move is valid if the receiving field is long enough to contain all significant information in the originating field after any necessary scaling is effected.

The effectiveness of a statement may be extended by the use of *AND* as: '*PUT ABC INTO DEF AND GHI AND JKL INTO MNO AND PQR*'. The use of *AND* enables several fields to be juxtaposed to create a new field. For example, given a field *NAME* of length say, 16 hollerith characters and containing the characters *J. SMITH*, the statement '*PUT . . MR . . AND NAME INTO NAME*' would result in *NAME* containing '*MR J. SMITH.*'

7

**Honeywell**
Electronic Data Processing

# FACT File Outline Form

PROBLEM ______ PROGRAMMER ______ DATE ______ PAGE ______ OF ______

| Line | 0 | Serial Number | Variable Length | Max Length or Number of Appearances | Mode | Decimal Point | Round | Official File Name — File / Group / Name (Decreasing Rank →) | Input-Output | Buffer Size | No. In. Buffers | Input Address 1st | Input Address 2nd | No. Out. Buffers | Output Address 1st | Output Address 2nd |
|---|---|---|---|---|---|---|---|---|---|---|---|---|---|---|---|---|
| 1 | 0 | | | | | | | | | | | | | | | |
| 2 | 0 | 1 | | | NR | | | INPUT-SALARIES (INSAL) | OM | | | | | 2 | AB | AC |
| 3 | 0 | 2 | | | | | | *EMPLOYEE | | | | | | | | |
| 4 | G | 3 | | 5 | UD | | | NUMBER | | | | | | | | |
| 5 | 0 | 4 | | 10 | D | | | SALARY-TO-DATE | | | | | | | | |
| 6 | 0 | | | | | | | | | | | | | | | |
| 7 | 0 | | | | | | | | | | | | | | | |
| 8 | 0 | 5 | | | I | | | WORK-SPACE | | | | | | | | |
| 9 | 0 | 6 | | 6 | D | | | POUNDS (L) | | | | | | | | |
| 10 | 0 | 7 | | 2 | D | | | SHILLINGS (S) | | | | | | | | |
| 11 | 0 | 8 | | 2 | D | | | PENCE (D) | | | | | | | | |
| 12 | 0 | | | | | | | | | | | | | | | |
| 13 | 0 | | | | | | | | | | | | | | | |
| 14 | 0 | | | | | | | | | | | | | | | |
| 15 | 0 | | | | | | | | | | | | | | | |
| 16 | 0 | | | | | | | | | | | | | | | |
| 17 | 0 | | | | | | | | | | | | | | | |
| 18 | 0 | | | | | | | | | | | | | | | |
| 19 | 0 | | | | | | | | | | | | | | | |
| 20 | 0 | | | | | | | | | | | | | | | |

1204

Fig. 2

Also a field name may be replaced by an arithmetic formula as: '*SET ALPHA TO BETA* \* (*GAMMA* − *DELTA*) + *EPSILON*'.

The arithmetic operators + − \* / may be replaced by the words *PLUS, MINUS, TIMES, OVER*. Validity checks apply to intermediate as well as to final arithmetic results.

## Data Input

The pack of punched cards to be input will begin with one containing some sort of file name; it must end with a standard end card. Everything between those two will be processed to produce a *FACT* file on magnetic tape according to the correspondence between the card description form and the file outline form. The point in the main theme of the source program at which this input takes place is indicated by a single statement. There are provisions for the rejection of cards on which the information fails the exhaustive tests provided for. Each card is read and identified. For this any combination of columns may be used. Once the card is identified, the information in the columns is construed according to the card description and fields are placed in their groups in the file hierarchy for posting to magnetic tape. The existence of or any change in the value of a recurrent field may be used to govern the posting of groups of fields. The file destination of each field is implied in qualifying adjectives to the field name. When the end card is read the next statement in the source program is obeyed.

## Card Description Form and Facilities

For each field, or part of a field, these facilities and requirements are specified on the card description form: the address of the first and last columns occupied; the rows of those columns to be taken into account; the position and nature of any sign punched; the implied position of any decimal point; the mode of the information (alphabetic, alphanumeric, decimal, single punch, etc.); a code selecting action to be taken if the information does not accord with that mode; a similar code to select action if a blank column is found; a variable length field option; a code to declare whether the existence of or any change in the value of the field is to cause posting to file, i.e. to effect the grouping of fields; the name of a paragraph in the source program to be performed each time the field is handled; the name of a definition in the source program of which the truth is to be used as a condition of acceptance of the field and of the card. See example given in Figs. 2, 3 and 4.

In this example the file to be created is called *INPUT-SALARIES* (for short, *INSAL*); it is an output file using two medium size buffers, and the first reel is to be produced on tape drive *AB*, the second on *AC*, the third on *AB* and so on, alternating. That is declared in columns 69 to 80 of Fig. 2.

It contains groups called *EMPLOYEE* each of 2 fields.

There is an internal file called *WORK-SPACE* to allow working space for the arithmetic of converting pounds, shillings and pence on the punched cards into a sum of pence to be held on file.

The data cards are to be preceded by one punched *SALARY DATA* in the first 11 columns. There is only one type of card to be read and that has

**Honeywell**
*Electronic Data Processing*

# FACT Source Program Statement Form

PROBLEM _____   PROGRAMMER _____   DATE _____   PAGE _____ OF _____

PROGRAM STATEMENTS

| SERIAL NUMBER | Statement |
|---|---|
| 0 | PROGRAM SALARIES, SORT |
| 1 | SEE INPUT-EDITOR.    CLOSE NEW INPUT-SALARIES.    RELEASE PROGRAM. |
| 2 | TEST-SHILLINGS.   S   IS LESS THAN TWENTY |
| 3 | |
| 4 | TEST-PENCE.   D   IS LESS THAN 12. |
| 5 | |
| 6 | |
| 7 | TO-PENCE   SET INSAL SALARY-TO-DATE TO 240 TIMES L PLUS 20 * S PLUS D. |

1205

Fig. 3

# Honeywell
## Electronic Data Processing

# FACT Card Descriptor Form

PROBLEM _____ PROGRAMMER _____ DATE _____ PAGE _____ OF _____

| C | SERIAL NUMBER | FIELD NAME | LOCATION | | KEY | ROW SELECTOR | | MODE | MODE ERROR | SIGN | | | LOCATION | DECIMAL POINT | VARIABLE LENGTH | MAXIMUM LENGTH | JUSTIFICATION | ACTION CODE | REPORT OR PROCEDURE NAME | | ACCEPTANCE CONDITION | | | | | | |
|---|---|---|---|---|---|---|---|---|---|---|---|---|---|---|---|---|---|---|---|---|---|---|---|---|---|---|---|
| | | | | | | | | | | | | | | | | | | | | | | | CONFIGURATION | | | | | |
| | | | | | | | | | | | BLANKS | PLUS | MINUS | | | | | | | | | SOURCE | | Read Type | Check | ERROR | | |
| | | | FROM | TO | | FROM | TO | | | | | | | | | | | | | | | | TYPE | UNIT | | Check | Action | R'm'ks | UNIT |
| 1 | C | | 6 7 | 22 23 24 25 26 | 27 28 29 30 31 32 | 33 34 35 | 36 37 38 39 40 | 41 42 43 44 | 45 46 | 48 49 50 51 | | | | | | | | | | | 65 66 | | 70 71 72 73 74 75 76 77 78 79 80 | | | | | | |
| 2 | C | 1 | SALARY DATA | 1 1 1 | | C F | | | | | | | | | | | | | | | | | CRGANYWYFB | | | | | |
| 3 | C | 2 9 | | | 4̄ | I D | | | | | | | | | | | | | | | | | | | | | |
| 4 | C | 3 | ABC | 7 8 8 0 | | I D | | | | | | | | | | | | | | | | | | | | | |
| 5 | C | 4 | INSAL NUMBER | 6 1 0 | | U D | | | | | E | | | | | | | | | | | | | | | | |
| 6 | C | 5 | POUNDS | 1 1 1 5 | | D | | | | | | | | | | | | | | | | | | | | | |
| 7 | C | 6 | SHILLINGS | 1 6 1 7 | | D | | | | | | | | | | | | | | | TEST-SHILLINGS | | | | | | |
| 8 | C | 7 | PENCE | 1 8 1 9 | | D | | | | | | | | | | | | | | TO-PENCE | TEST-PENCE | | | | | | |
| 9 | C | | | | | | | | | | | | | | | | | | | | | | | | | | |
| 10 | C | | | | | | | | | | | | | | | | | | | | | | | | | | |
| 11 | C | | | | | | | | | | | | | | | | | | | | | | | | | | |
| 12 | C | | | | | | | | | | | | | | | | | | | | | | | | | | |
| 13 | C | | | | | | | | | | | | | | | | | | | | | | | | | | |
| 14 | C | | | | | | | | | | | | | | | | | | | | | | | | | | |
| 15 | C | | | | | | | | | | | | | | | | | | | | | | | | | | |
| 16 | C | | | | | | | | | | | | | | | | | | | | | | | | | | |
| 17 | C | | | | | | | | | | | | | | | | | | | | | | | | | | |
| 18 | C | | | | | | | | | | | | | | | | | | | | | | | | | | |
| 19 | C | | | | | | | | | | | | | | | | | | | | | | | | | | |
| 20 | C | | | | | | | | | | | | | | | | | | | | | | | | | | |

1 2 3 4 5 6 7 8 9 10 11 12 13 14 15 16 17 18 19 20 21 22 23 24 25 26 27 28 29 30 31 32 33 34 35 36 37 38 39 40 41 42 43 44 45 46 47 48 49 50 51 52 53 54 55 56 57 58 59 60 61 62 63 64 65 66 67 68 69 70 71 72 73 74 75 76 77 78 79 80

1203

Fig. 4

either the numeral 9 punched in column 4 or the letters *ABC* punched in the last 3 columns of the card. As the cards are read the fields in columns 11 to 15, 16 to 17, 18 to 19, are to be construed as decimal numbers and placed in the internal file as fields *POUNDS*, *SHILLINGS* and *PENCE* respectively. There is an acceptance condition on the *SHILLINGS* field that it shall not exceed 19 and on the *PENCE* 11.

The paragraph named *TO-PENCE* will be obeyed as the *PENCE* field is being processed and will perform the conversion to pence leaving the result in the file. As the next card is read the group *EMPLOYEE* will be posted to the file *INSAL*.

## Printed Output

Each report to be printed is described by the programmer on the report description form. There are 3 kinds of descriptors; one for the name of the report, one for each type of line, and one for each field of each line. The order in which the descriptors are presented, or numbered, determines which fields belong to which lines, and which lines to which reports.

The types of line which exist are (a) the title line which occurs only at the beginning of the report; (b) the heading line which is printed at the head of every page; (c) the footing line which is printed at the foot of every page; (d) the detail line containing the information produced by the program; (e) the total lines containing accumulations of fields in the detail line; (f) the final total line produced when the report is closed.

Title, heading and footing lines are printed automatically according to the effective movement of the paper through the printer; total lines when the value of a controlling field changes; only the content of the detail line need be prepared by source program as other lines are derived from that or from the line count. The source statement is the verb *WRITE* and the report name.

FACT allows up to 26 levels of totals.

A logical line may be 'folded' to comprise a number of physical lines of print.

The fields contained in a line may be program variables or they may be literals written as a field image, or a combination of these.

## Report Description Form and Facilities

The report description form provides, for the report *name* descriptor, the name and the number of lines per page.

For the *line* descriptor it provides the name, the type (title, heading, footing, detail, total) the level of total, the number of lines of pre-print page skip and of post-print skip, the sub-line number (if part of a folded line) and space for three other entries; one is for the name of a paragraph in the source program which is to be executed whenever the line is about to be printed; one is for the name of a definition of which the truth will permit, the falsity inhibit, printing; and one is for the name of a control field, any change in the value of which is to cause total-line printing, and the tabulation associated with total lines, to take place.

**Honeywell**
Electronic Data Processing

## FACT Source Program Statement Form

PROBLEM ______ PROGRAMMER ______ DATE ______ PAGE ______ OF ______

| P | SERIAL NUMBER | PROGRAM STATEMENTS |
|---|---|---|
| P | 0 | PROGRAM LIST-SURTAX-SALARIES |
| P | | |
| P | 1 | ABC. GET NEXT OUTSAL EMPLOYEE. IF NONE CLOSE PAYROLL |
| P | 2 | REPORT AND RELEASE PROGRAM. |
| P | 3 | WRITE PAYROLL REPORT AND GO TO ABC. |
| P | | |
| P | 4 | SURTAX. POUNDS IN OUTSAL IS NOT LESS THAN |
| P | 5 | FIVE THOUSAND. |

1205

Fig. 5

The *field* descriptor contains the field name, qualified if necessary to indicate the file hierarchy from which it is to come, an option to have the field tabulated through to the total lines, an option to suppress the field in the present line, a cross-footing facility to enable simple addition and subtraction to be performed on fields within a line and the result included in the same line, a zero suppression option, an option to suppress repetitions from line to line of the same field value, a sign code selecting one of several sign conventions, an increment to be added to the field every time it is printed (for page numbering and other counts) a shift provision to alter the scale of a decimal number from that at which the number is held in memory, a character to be floated (for example, a £ sign) down to the first non zero digit of a number, the maximum number of characters in a variable length field, left and right margin positions of the field on the line of print, and a field image containing literal characters.

### Report Layout Form

Where a line consists largely of literal characters the Report Layout form, which permits 120 characters in each line, may be used with advantage. The line image can be laid out as it is to appear in print. The layout of the whole of each line can be seen at a glance and relative position of literal information among several line-types can be easily checked.

*Example*   Program List-Surtax-Salaries. Figs. 5, 6, 7.

This example shows a program to print a report of all salaries in the file which equal or exceed £5,000.

The file contains, for each of several Departments, the number and salary of each employee.

The report has a title

* * PAYROLL * *

on a page by itself. Only those employees are tabulated whose salary-to-date meets the *SURTAX* tabulation condition. Totals are printed by Departments and a final total is printed. For five employees in two Departments the report printed would look like this:

| Dept | Employee | Salary to Date | Page No 1 |
|------|----------|----------------|-----------|
| 1 | 5176 | 5,250 | |
| 1 | 5921 | 5,560 | |
| | Department total | 10,810 | |
| 2 | 3915 | 6,100 | |
| 2 | 7810 | 5,050 | |
| 2 | 8126 | 5,100 | |
| | Department total | 16,250 | |
| | Final total | £27,060 | |

**Honeywell**
Electronic Data Processing

# FACT File Outline Form

PROBLEM ________ PROGRAMMER ________ DATE ________ PAGE ____ OF ____

| | 0 | Serial Number | Variable Length | Max. Length or Number of Appearances | Mode | Decimal Point | Round | Official File Name: File Group / Name (Decreasing Rank →) | Configuration (File Name Descriptor Only): Input-Output, Buffer Size, No. In. Buffers, Input Address 1st/2nd, No. Out. Buffers, Output Address 1st/2nd |
|---|---|---|---|---|---|---|---|---|---|
| 1 | 0 | | | | | | | | |
| 2 | 0 | 1 | | | NR | | | OUTPUT-SALARIES (OUTSAL) | IM2ADAE |
| 3 | 0 | 2 | | | | | | *DEPARTMENT (DEP) | |
| 4 | G | 3 | | 4 | UD | | | CODE | |
| 5 | 0 | 4 | | | | | | *EMPLOYEE | |
| 6 | 0 | 5 | | 5 | UD | | | NUMBER | |
| 7 | 0 | 6 | | I | | | | SALARY-TO-DATE | |
| 8 | 0 | 7 | | 6 | D | | | POUNDS | |
| 9 | 0 | 8 | | 2 | D | | | SHILLINGS | |
| 10 | 0 | 9 | | 2 | D | | | PENCE | |
| 11 | 0 | | | | | | | | |
| 12 | 0 | | | | | | | | |
| 13 | 0 | | | | | | | | |
| 14 | 0 | | | | | | | | |
| 15 | 0 | | | | | | | | |
| 16 | 0 | | | | | | | | |
| 17 | 0 | | | | | | | | |
| 18 | 0 | | | | | | | | |
| 19 | 0 | | | | | | | | |
| 20 | 0 | | | | | | | | |

1204

Fig. 6

**Honeywell**
*Electronic Data Processing*

## FACT Report Description Form

PROBLEM _____  PROGRAMMER _____  DATE _____  PAGE _____ OF _____

| R | SER. NO. | REPORT NAME / LINE NAME / FIELD NAME | Type or Level | Pre-Print Skip / Post-Print Skip / Field Supp / Tab Action | CROSS FOOT | Sign / Check Indicator | INCRE-MENT | SHIFT (Type / Float Char / Extent) | MAX. NO. OF CHAR. | LEFT MARGIN | RIGHT MARGIN | FIELD IMAGE / PRE-PRINT PROCEDURE | PRINT CONDITION |
|---|---|---|---|---|---|---|---|---|---|---|---|---|---|
| R | 1 | 22 PAYROLL | | | | | | | | | | | |
| A | 2 | TITLE-LINE | | TTEJEJ | | | | | | | | ** PAYROLL ** | |
| F | 3 | | | HD | 02 | | | | | 80 | | | |
| A | 4 | PAGE-HEAD-LINE | | | | | | | | | | 5 DEPT | |
| F | 5 | | | | | | | | | 15 | | 15 EMPLOYEE | |
| F | 6 | | | | | | | | | 30 | | 30 SALARY TO DATE | |
| F | 7 | | | | | | | | | | | | |
| F | 8 | PG-NO | | | | | 001 | | | 40 | | 40 PAGE NO | |
| A | 9 | DETAIL-LINE | | 00 | 01 | | SURTAX | | | | | | |
| F | 10 | DEP CODE | | | | | DEP CODE | | | 5 | | | |
| F | 11 | NUMBER | | | | | | | | 15 | | | |
| F | 12 | POUNDS | | T | | | | | | 30, | | | |
| A | 13 | DEPT-TOTAL-LINE | | 010102 | | | DEP CODE | | | | | | |
| F | 14 | POUNDS | | T | | | | | | 30 | | 30 DEPARTMENT TOTAL | |
| A | 15 | FINAL-TOTAL-LINE | | FTOIEJ | | | | | | | | 30 FINAL TOTAL | |
| F | 16 | POUNDS | | T | | | | | | | | | |

1207

Fig. 7

## The Sort Statement

Sorting is done by a statement of the form: *SORT file-name-a TO file-name-b, CONTROL ON Key-1, . . . . Key-n*. Other source program procedures may be performed on information in the file during the preliminary and final phases of the Sort by including appropriate procedure names in this extension to the Sort statement—*WITH PRE-SORT PROCEDURE ALPHA AND POST-SORT PROCEDURE BETA*.

The file is sorted into ascending order according to the value of the indicated control fields which are stated in major to minor sequence.

To sort into descending order the words '*REVERSE SORT*' may be used.

Before entering a *SORT* statement the FACT programmer positions his tapes so that the correct file is presented for sorting. Where there are several files on a single reel of magnetic tape the statement '*FIND BEGINNING OF file-name*' will position the tape. Otherwise '*REWIND file-name*' is satisfactory. In any event the sorting will only proceed at object time if the correct file name is found on the tape.

In the case of multi-reel files each reel is sorted separately. The input may be taken from 2 tape units alternately, thus allowing the operating staff to change tapes without delaying the program; output may be similarly alternated. When all reels of the file have been sorted a plan of collation is computed in relation to the number of reels and the number of tape units available. The plan is displayed on the computer console so that the operators can prepare to load, remove and label tapes correctly. The result of the collation is a sorted version of the original multi-reel file.

The sorting technique used is the polyphase sort which can employ any number of tape units from 3 upwards.

*Example*   To sort a file of playing cards. Figs. 8, 9, 10.

This example sorts a file containing, in this case, known information into order for printing.

The mode *WT* in columns 13 and 14 of the File Outline form (Fig. 8) indicates that work-tapes are being named. The input file is not used as a work-tape, the output file tape is. Each pass of the file, whose library name is *PLAYING-CARDS*, is separately named for program reference.

The statement (on descriptor P4 of Fig. 9) to release the sorting procedure enables the core memory used by that procedure to be overlaid, if necessary, by another program segment, in this case the *LISTING PROCEDURE*.

The report printed by the listing procedure consists very simply of a page-heading and successive values read from the file. The page heading consists of 2 lines of print. A source program statement is here used, instead of a control break in the report, to print each *SUIT* on a fresh page.

**Honeywell**
H Electronic Data Processing

# FACT File Outline Form

PROBLEM _____  PROGRAMMER _____  DATE _____  PAGE _____ OF _____

| SERIAL NUMBER | MODE | OFFICIAL FILE NAME / NAME (DECREASING RANK) | CONFIGURATION (File Name Descriptor Only) |
|---|---|---|---|
| 1 | NR | PLAYING-CARDS (P-C-RANDOM) (PCR) | IM 2 AB |
| 2 | WT | AC, AD, AE | |
| 3 | NR | PLAYING-CARDS (P-C-SORTED) (PCS) | OM / 2 AE |
| 4 | NR | PLAYING-CARDS (P-C-FOR-LISTING) (PCL) | IM 2 AE |
| 5 | | *SUIT | |
| 6 | A | CODE | |
| 7 | | *VALUE | |
| 8 | 2UD | NUMBER | |

Column headers (configuration section): Input-Output | Buffer Size | No. In. Buffers | INPUT ADDRESS 1ST 2ND | No. Out. Buffers | OUTPUT ADDRESS 1ST 2ND

1204

Fig. 8

**Honeywell**
Electronic Data Processing

# FACT Source Program Statement Form

PROBLEM ______ PROGRAMMER ______ DATE ______ PAGE ______ OF ______

| | P | SERIAL NUMBER | PROGRAM STATEMENTS |
|---|---|---|---|
| 1 | P | | |
| 2 | P | 1 | SORTING PROCEDURE. |
| 3 | P | 2 | REWIND PCR, PCS. |
| 4 | P | 3 | SORT PCR TO PCS, CONTROL ON CODE AND NUMBER. REWIND PCS. |
| 5 | P | 4 | RELEASE SORTING PROCEDURE AND GO TO LISTING. END |
| 6 | P | 5 | OF SORTING PROCEDURE. |
| 7 | P | | |
| 8 | P | | |
| 9 | P | 6 | LISTING PROCEDURE. |
| 10 | P | 7 | LIST-START. GET NEXT PCL VALUE, IF NONE CLOSE P-CARDS |
| 11 | P | 8 | REPORT, REWIND PCL AND RELEASE PROGRAM. WRITE |
| 12 | P | 9 | P-CARDS REPORT. IF END OF CURRENT PCL SUIT |
| 13 | P | 10 | CLOSE PAGE OF P-CARDS REPORT. |
| 14 | P | 11 | GO TO LIST-START. END OF LISTING PROCEDURE. |
| 15 | P | | |
| 16 | P | | |
| 17 | P | | |
| 18 | P | | |
| 19 | P | | |
| 20 | P | | |

EDP 34 (430)

Fig. 9

**Honeywell**
H Electronic Data Processing

# FACT Report Description Form

PROBLEM ______ PROGRAMMER ______ DATE ______ PAGE ______ OF ______

| | R / A / F | SER. NO. (2–6) | REPORT NAME / LINE NAME / FIELD NAME (7–24) | Type or Level / Tab Action, Field Supp. (25–26) | Pre-Print Skip / Cross Foot (27–28) | Post-Print Skip / Z/G (29–30) | Sb Ln No / Sign (31) | Check Decimal (32) | Increment (33–35) | Shift Type (36) | Shift Extent (37–38) | Float Char. (39) | Max. No. of Char. (40–42) | Left Margin (43–45) | Right Margin (46–48) | Pre-Print Procedure / Field Image (49–64) | Print Condition (65–80) |
|---|---|---|---|---|---|---|---|---|---|---|---|---|---|---|---|---|---|
| 1 | R | 1 | P-CARDS | | | | | | | | | | | | | | |
| 2 | | | | | | | | | | | | | | | | | |
| 3 | A | 2 | PAGE-HEADING | HD | | 01 | 1 | | | | | | | | | | |
| 4 | F | 3 | | | | | | | | | | | | | 60 | PLAYING CARDS STATEMENT^ | |
| 5 | F | 4 | TODAY | | | | | | | | | | | | 120 | DATE ^ | |
| 6 | A | 5 | PAGE-HEADING | HD | | 02 | 2 | | | | | | | | | | |
| 7 | F | 6 | | | | | | | | | | | | | 20 | SUIT^ | |
| 8 | F | 7 | | | | | | | | | | | | | 30 | VALUE^ | |
| 9 | F | 8 | PAGE-NUMBER | | | | | | 001 | | | | | | 120 | PAGE NUMBER ^ | |
| 10 | | | | | | | | | | | | | | | | | |
| 11 | A | 9 | INFCRMATION-LINE | 00 | | 01 | | | | | | | | | | | |
| 12 | F | 10 | PCL CODE | | | G | | | | | | | | | 18 | ^ | |
| 13 | F | 11 | PCL VALUE NUMBER | | | | | | | | | | | | 27 | ^ | |
| 14 | | | | | | | | | | | | | | | | | |
| 15 | | | | | | | | | | | | | | | | | |
| 16 | | | | | | | | | | | | | | | | | |
| 17 | | | | | | | | | | | | | | | | | |
| 18 | | | | | | | | | | | | | | | | | |
| 19 | | | | | | | | | | | | | | | | | |
| 20 | | | | | | | | | | | | | | | | | |

1207

Fig. 10

The general aspect of the report:

| | PLAYING CARDS STATEMENT | | DATE 631231 |
|---|---|---|---|
| SUIT | VALUE | | PAGE NUMBER 1 |
| C | 1 | | |
| | 2 | | |
| | 3 | | |
| | . | | |
| | . | | |
| | . | | |
| | 10 | | |
| | 11 | | |
| | 12 | | |

| | PLAYING CARDS STATEMENT | | DATE 631231 |
|---|---|---|---|
| SUIT | VALUE | | PAGE NUMBER 2 |
| D | 1 | | |
| | 2 | | |
| | 3 | | |
| | etc. | | |

## File Maintenance—The Update Statement

A common data processing job is the updating of large standing files with a relatively small number of amendments. FACT has a statement to generate a single routine to do that. The actual alterations to the information are made by paragraphs in source program whose names are incorporated in the update statement. Such a paragraph is performed when that updating condition occurs with which its name is associated. The statement is

*UPDATE FILE-A BY FILE-X TO FILE-B, CONTROL ON P, Q, AND R, WITH MATCHED-MASTER (ALPHA), UNMATCHED-MASTER (BETA), UPDATED-MASTER (GAMMA), NEW-MASTER (DELTA), . . .*
and so on. Other conditions that might occur in the course of an update are *UPDATED-NEW-MASTER, UNORDERED-MASTER, UNORDERED-DETAIL, IRRELEVANT-MASTER, MATCHED-NEW-MASTER.*

The control fields here named $P$, $Q$ and $R$ in the main file and the detail file are compared by the object program in order to determine which updating condition has occurred.

## Abbreviation of Data Names

Here is a brief summary of the uses of abbreviations or synonyms in FACT.

Any data name on the file outline form may be followed by one or more synonyms in brackets. This saves writing in the source program while leaving it possible to have a full descriptive name for a piece of information. The short form of a file or group name is advantageous when the name is qualifying another as an adjective. In the case of files the synonym uniquely indicates the instance of the file intended in the source program whereas the given name is usually the same for all instances of that file because of tape file library requirements.

In the source program a long and much qualified name may be given a single short synonym which may be used thereafter.

In the source program dynamic abbreviations may be used to relate formal variables to names of fields required as parameters by a source language subroutine.

## Semi-automatic Segmentation

In order to allow a large program to run in a small memory, FACT programs are segmented. The programmer has some control over the size of the segments, and the course which the program follows at object time determines which segments are required in memory. The programmer may *RELEASE* segments which he knows to be no longer required.

Segments are major source program procedures, file hierarchies, the input-editor, reports, and the like. They each represent a body of coding required to be available at run time as a unit. They communicate with each other by way of entries in a table of references (from) and definitions (in) at the head of each one; when a segment is brought into memory on call at run time the segmenter routine makes adjustments to the reference tables in other segments and completes the references in the present segment. It also keeps a record of all segments in memory, whether released or not, and of their starting address and length in words.

The scheduling operation which selects the programs to be included in the production run (the Honeywell 800 is a multi-program machine and programs may be running in parallel) places limits on the memory space available for any given FACT program; the segmenter relocates segments only within that space.

The segmenter computes the space available and compares that with the known length of the newly called segment. If necessary it will relocate existing active segments by moving them within the memory to make space. It then brings in the new segments. Inter-segment reference tables of addresses and memory maps are amended as necessary.

It is worth note that a segment which the source program has released is only overlaid if the space it occupies is required; if space is not required a later source program reference to the segment will involve only a small alteration to the control tables, not a re-call of the segment coding from secondary storage.

## Operating Context

The chief output of the FACT compiler is a magnetic tape of punched-card images. Those are available for input to the *ARGUS* assembly process along with hand-coded programs and the output of other compilers. Assembled programs are held on magnetic tape in both machine relocatable and symbolic form. They may be selected for input to the Program Test System or to a production scheduling run which sets up programs for later inter-dependent and parallel running.

It is possible, under the program test system, for the programmer to request the insertion of automatic derails in his program so that memory dumps, tape dumps and conditional snap-shots of memory can be taken while it is being run under test.

A secondary output of the FACT compiler is a listing of the original source program as written, together with diagnostic comments on any clerical errors found in it. In practice a special short version of the compiler is used to obtain the diagnostic listing; full compilation is seldom required unless the source program is free from all errors which the compiler can identify.

# 13. AN INTRODUCTION TO COMMERCIAL COMPILERS

## A. d'AGAPEYEFF

*Computer Analysts and Programmers Ltd., London, England*

## 1. Introduction

It is desirable to begin by defining what we mean by a compiler. In the broadest terms this might be described as a Programming System, running on some computer, which enables other programs to be written in some artificial source language. This result is obtained by the simulation of the artificial machine represented by the source language, and the conversion of such programs into a form in which they can be executed on one or more existing computers.

This definition, however inadequate, at least avoids any artificial distinction between 'Interpreters' and 'Compilers' or 'Translators'. For although these terms are still in widespread use it now appears that the distinction between them is only valid for particular facets of any modern programming language, and even then only as a rather inadequate indication of the moment in time that certain criteria are evaluated.

On the more positive side the definition does bring out a number of points which are sometimes forgotten.

### 1. The Compiler as a Program

A compiler is a program of a rather specialized nature. As such it takes a considerable time and effort to write and, more particularly, to get debugged. In addition it often takes a surprising amount of time to run.

Nevertheless compilers are concerned with the generalized aspects of programming and have in consequence been the source of several important techniques. These could be applied to a wider field if a sufficient number of programmers would take an interest in such developments.

### 2. The Three Computers

There are three possible computers involved—the one on which the compiler will run, the artificial computer, and the one which will execute the program (although the first and last are not necessarily distinct).

In general the more that the facilities in the computers involved diverge the harder is the task of the compiler. On the other hand the use of a large computer to compile programs for smaller computers can avoid storage problems during compilation, and any consequent restrictions in the language, and make the process more flexible and efficient. This can be readily appreciated from the fact that some COBOL compilers running on small computers take more than forty passes! But the full benefit of large computers used at a distance for this purpose is dependent on cheap and reliable data links, since at the moment they introduce delays in compilation and the reporting of errors.

### 3. Presentation to the User

Any user of the system must, to be effective, learn how to write programs in the artificial source language which will fit the capabilities of both the artificial and the actual object machine. This requirement has become obscured by the current myths of the so-called 'Natural' or 'English' languages, and the widespread claims that 'anyone can now write programs' are highly misleading. Indeed existing source languages are rather difficult to learn and show no particular indication that they are well adapted toward the task for which they are intended.

A more serious drawback of the 'Natural' language approach is that it hinders or prevents the new facilities being presented in terms of a machine. This is unfortunate because to do so would probably give a better mental image of the realities involved and a better understanding of the rules and restrictions of the language, which tend to be confusing until it is appreciated that they are compiler-, or computer-, oriented.

## 2. The Main Requirements of a Commercial Compiler

A major problem in commercial compilers is the diversity of the tasks which they are required to achieve, some of which often appear to have been specified without regard to the complexity they introduce into the compiler compared to the benefit they confer on users. This ambitiousness may be contrasted with that of the authors of ALGOL (Backus *et al.*, 1960) who concentrated on the matters which were considered important and capable of standardization (e.g. general procedures), and largely ignored those considered of lesser importance (e.g. input/output). There is no doubt that this concentration is the chief reason why ALGOL compilers normally work on or about the date intended whilst commercial compilers normally do not. The main tasks which are commonly required are discussed here.

### 1. Training and Protecting the User

The System must enable intending users who have no previous experience of computers to obtain that experience. This means that the language must include both a 'child's guide to programming' and the facilities which the user will require when he actually comes to writing real and complex programs.

In addition the compiler is expected to protect the user, as much as possible, from the results of his own folly. This implies extensive checking of both the source and object program and the production of suitable error reports. But the main difficulty is to provide error protection which is not unduly inefficient in terms of time or restrictive on the capabilities of the user.

### 2. Data Declarations

The declaration of the properties of the users' data should be separable from the procedures which constitute a particular program, because the data may have an independent existence that is quite distinct from the action of any one program. Thus for example a Customer Accounts File of a distributing company may be originally set up by one program and regularly updated by a number of others. In terms of the 'global' and 'local' concepts of ALGOL this introduces a 'universal' declaration which is valid for all, or a number, of programs.

This requirement means that the compiler should keep a master file of declarations which is accessible to all programs, and at the same time provides the means of extending, amending and reporting on the contents of this file.

### 3. Input/Output Data

The input and output data must have a wide range of formats and representations because it is normally intended to allow users to continue with the same media, and the same codes and conventions, which they employ at present. And there is of course no assurance that these conventions were designed, or are particularly suitable, for a computer!

This is the kind of requirement which is very hard on the compiler writer. If the specification of format and any other information is to be made in the data description it must be done in a way that is understandable and not too complicated for the users, which means the compiler may not find it simple to pick up the relevant parameters. The actual process of implementation is a choice of one of the following.

(a) A very generalized routine is built to cover all possibilities. This is safe but inefficient in the average case.

(b) A fairly general routine is built to cover the anticipated range. This is less safe but only slightly more efficient.

(c) Individual routines are constructed for each particular variation. This is very efficient but also very expensive in terms of compiler effort.

(d) A combination is provided of both (a) and (c) which is economical only if a correct guess has been made of the most commonly occurring cases.

But this is of course the type of quandary which arises in several different areas of a compiler.

### 4. Properties and Manipulation of Data

It must be possible to form data structures during the running of the object program and to be able to manipulate data in a reasonably general way. The latter has been deliberately left indefinite because there is considerable disparity between the different commercial languages as to both the properties and the manipulation of data. The points of distinction are:

(a) Whether the most common unit of data (normally referred to as a Field) should be allowed to vary dynamically in length. The argument in favour of this property centres on such items as postal addresses—these usually vary between twenty to 100 or more characters with an average of forty or less.

This property has a very marked effect on the compiler. Not only must the address determination of such fields be handled in a particular way but other fields may have to be moved round dynamically to accommodate their changes in length.

(b) Whether two or more Lists of fields (i.e. vectors) should be allowed in the unit of data handled sequentially on input and output (normally referred to as a Record). Some types of Record kept by conventional methods are claimed to have this property but it is very difficult for a compiler to handle more than one list economically. The problem is simply one of addressing when the lists grow unevenly.

(c) Whether characters within fields should be individually addressable. This is the kind of facility which is very important when master files are being loaded on to magnetic tape for the first time. Such loading often constitutes the largest single task of an installation and may be very complex because of the variety of media in which parts of these files were previously held. The addressing of characters even on fixed word machines turns out to be quite simple using a variation of the normal representation of subscripts.

## 5. *Efficiency*

There is a greater emphasis on the efficiency of object programs in Commercial as opposed to Scientific Languages due to the higher frequency of use expected of such programs. Unfortunately this emphasis usually takes the form of rather superficial comparisons in terms of time, whereas on most computers actually available in Europe space is the dominant factor. The distinction between the two is however as valid for a compiled program as any other, the production of open subroutines will take least time and most space whilst closed subroutines, particularly if the calls and parameters are evaluated at object time, will take most time and least space.

## 6. *Operating Characteristics*

Little attention is normally given to the operating characteristics of either the Compiler or the Object Program until some user is actually running both. Yet both are important in practice. In regard to the former this involves *inter alia* the details of loading the compiler and source programs, the options available in the media of the Object Program and the production of reports thereon, and the actions to be taken on the detection of errors. They are all quite trivial tasks for the compiler and usually depend on the time available to add the necessary frills to make the compiler more convenient to the user.

The operating characteristics of the Object Program are much more serious and largely dominated by the question of debugging and the action on errors detected through checks inserted by the compiler. There is no doubt that the proper solution to both lies in making all communication between the user and the machine in terms of the source language alone. At the same time the difficulty is obvious because there is no other reason why such terms should be present in the Object Program. In addition the dynamic tracing of the execution of the program in source language is hindered both by any optimization phase included in the compiler, and by the practice of compiling into some kind of Assembly Code.

No existing Commercial Compiler has succeeded in solving this problem.

Instead it is customary to print out a full report of the Object Program which is related to the source language statements (e.g. by printing them side by side). Error messages will then refer to that report and special facilities may be provided to enable test data to be run on the program with similar messages as to the results obtained. It will be apparent that this is not very difficult for the compiler, since it is normally possible to discover what routine gave rise to an error jump, but more knowledge is required by the user in terms of the real machine than is otherwise necessary.

The other items which can be considered as part of the Operating Characteristics are greatly assisted by the hardware facilities available and include: (a) checks that the correct peripherals have been assigned, and the correct media loaded, for the relevant program; (b) changes in the assignments of input/output channels due to machine faults, and options in peripherals for the same reason; (c) returns to previous dump points particularly in regard to the positioning of input/output media.

### 3. Some Influences on the Methods of Implementation

Few of the details which cause most controversy in source languages exert much influence on the methods of implementation. Thus for example the introduction of an 'English' version of ALGOL, which might induce commercial programmers to find it acceptable, would have very little effect on existing ALGOL translators.

There are however a number of points which are awkward in particular areas of the compiler.

#### 1. Details of the Languages

The influences which stem from the representation of the source program include:

*1. Character Codes.* The specification of character codes is a major problem for anyone designing generalized programming systems due to the lack of standardization and the limited range available on output devices. The only real solution is to make the user declare the details of his own set. In a compiler this may be achieved as follows.

(i) The characters or particular range of characters which form some entity in the syntax (e.g. letters, digits and each symbol, or combination of symbols, which have a specific meaning such as :=, >, + etc.) are formed into a standard named, or numbered, set.

(ii) The user declares what codes, or range of codes, he will use for each of these entities. It is desirable that he be allowed to declare that more than one of his characters will be used for an entity which is a single symbol in the standard set (e.g. he will use *GT* to represent >).

(iii) On the initial input of the source program the compiler compares each character with the list of declarations in order to determine its meaning.

The above caters for variations in the program set and would allow most languages to be punched on anything from a Flexowriter to the simplest punch. The data set cannot usually be handled in this way due to the resulting inefficiency, but something similar must be provided if the input differs from the output range.

*2. Context Dependent Syntax.* It is obvious that context dependent syntax introduces complications but it can seldom be avoided due to a lack of symbols and a preference in 'English' to use the same word in different circumstances. Thus 'and' may appear as an optional separator outside conditionals but be a key item within them.

One approach is to scan the input backwards (i.e. from right to left) because the variable unit of syntax generally follows the key item. But in the first scan this usually means keeping a varying amount of the source program in hand at one time.

Another method is always to take one possibility, normally the simplest, and to change this on discovering it was wrong.

Thus, for example, given

| | |
|---|---|
| *GO TO* | Label name |
| and | |
| *GO TO* | label name — 1, label name — 2, |
| | label name — 3, ............... |
| *DEPENDING ON* | *field name* |

it is clear that when present *DEPENDING ON* is an operator which could cause the original *GO TO* to be deleted.

However this kind of re-arrangement can be less trivial than it might at first sight appear. Consider for example

| | | | |
|---|---|---|---|
| *SUBTRACT* | *field name 1* | *FROM* | *field name 2,* |
| and | | | |
| *SUBTRACT* | *field name 1* | *FROM* | *field name 2* |
| *GIVING* | *field name 3,* | | |

where the last named field is always the destination and the field names can be subscripted by an arbitrary expression which can include calls to functions, etc.

If general formulae facilities are available in the language one is tempted to compile the last of the above by re-arranging it as follows:

$$\textit{field name 3} := \textit{field name 2} - \textit{field name 1}.$$

This involves the shuffling of arbitrary units of length (because of the subscripts) but is also incorrect because the subscripts are not being evaluated in the order in which they are written. Thus to do this simple operation properly requires a separate routine.

*3. Field or Data Names.* The association of procedural references to fields and other units of data with their properties as given by the Data Declarations is the cause of much delay and difficulties in many compilers. This occurs chiefly because the total number of data names is normally unrestricted and it is not therefore possible to keep all such names, and their properties, in working store during the scan of procedures.

The problem is increased in many languages, such as COBOL (Report, 1961), by the absence of any reference in the data name to the record in which it is contained, and in addition records are not specifically associated with any particular segment or other section of the program. However, these languages do require the data declarations to be read in with each program.

There are two methods which are known to be used in tackling this problem. The first is to list all data names found in the procedures and the data declarations, sort both into alphabetical order, match one against the other and finally sort the procedural references back into their original order. The second is merely a variation of the first. The names are similarly listed but each such reference within a procedure is replaced by an identifying field number. The properties of the items listed are extracted from the data declaration and entered into tables under field numbers. On the next scan of the procedures a simple table look-up will obtain the required property.

Both these methods are slow, largely due to the way the languages have been specified.

## 2. Data Properties

The available properties of data do exert a considerable influence on the whole of the compiler because not only do they largely determine the storage allocation and addressing processes but they also specify the amount of parameter information which has to be passed to most routines.

The chief effect of this influence is reflected in the maps of storage which have to be constructed for major units and the level of addressing and specification of length for minor units.

*1. Files.* The main properties of files are to associate the file name with some input/output channel or peripheral device and to establish its physical relationship with the relevant media. The former merely gives an address and perhaps some control information, but the latter may indicate that a map must be constructed of the files that will be written on some reel of tape. In addition parameters will be accumulated for the file recognition routines (e.g. re tape labels).

*2. Records.* The main properties of records are to determine the area in working store in which they will be processed (and read into and written out from) and the mapping or other controls that will be required for the individual fields.

If records are in fact input and output in batches it will probably be necessary to construct a map for each batch specifying the starting address of each record. A 'current record' pointer is also required to indicate the record-in-hand. Most compiler writers using this technique rather draw a veil over what happens to the batching sequence when records are dynamically created or deleted, particularly where the records vary in length.

*3. Fields.* Fields which do not vary dynamically in length, and are not members of a list or a batched record, can in general have their absolute address assigned by the compiler. Their parameter information is simply their length and address.

The addressing of variable length fields is normally done by assigning a location to hold either the length and address of each, or the address from which this information may be obtained. Such a location may itself be stored within the record, or outside as part of the unpacking process performed on the input of each record. Fields within lists will use a similar location as a base address from which, with the value of the subscript, the starting address of the required list element will be obtained. If the list only contains fixed length fields then each field address will be relative to the beginning of the element, in other cases a further level of indirectness is required (e.g. by carrying a map of the variable fields within each list element).

### 3. Procedural Facilities

Few of the individual verbs and operators of a language pose in themselves much of a problem in a compiler. Possible exceptions are *MOVE*, due to the various type and editing conversions which are often associated with it, and certain aspects of the arithmetic particularly on binary machines.

Most of the real difficulties stem from the properties of the structures in which the verbs and operators may appear.

*1. Conditional and Arithmetic Expressions.* In their more general form these expressions are mostly simply handled by the methods described by Mr Randell. Such processes however inevitably rely on the evaluation of more criteria during the execution of the program than is required, or sometimes felt tolerable, elsewhere in commercial compilers.

As a result, and perhaps because they were specified before the stack techniques became widely known, most of the existing commercial languages are very restrictive on both the formation and use of expressions. There is at least one obvious reason why this is unfortunate. By a trivial alteration to the stack processes any expression can be an assignment statement, and so provide a simple way of writing loops which largely obviates the need for the cumbersome *PERFORM — VARYING* facility of COBOL or the *FOR* clause of ALGOL. Consider the following simple example:

$$Loop \quad ADD \ k \ [x := x + 1] \quad AND \quad y \ [x]$$
$$GIVING \ z$$
$$IF \quad x \quad IS \ GREATER \ THAN \ ?$$
$$THEN \ GO \ TO \ ? \ ELSE \ GO \ TO \ Loop$$

which sums two fields of a list.

*2. Blocks and Functions.* The use of Blocks and Functions can be just as advantageous in commercial as in scientific languages. Between them they allow (a) sections of programs to be written without regard to the possibility of duplicating names (e.g. such as labels) used elsewhere. This is achieved by keeping the list of local declarations under blocks and starting the search from the innermost block. (b) Economy of effort due to the generalized use of functions with replaceable parameters. If complete generality is to be allowed in the formation of the actual parameters then it is necessary to treat each in turn as a function without parameters.

It is also desirable to be able to jump out of functions other than at the normal exit point in order to execute error actions. The simplest method of achieving this is to insist that such jumps must be to labels in the outermost block of the program which allows all current entries in the stack to be deleted.

## 4. The General Operations of a Compiler

The various operations that a compiler must perform can be considered as a series of phases, although these will not necessarily correspond to the individual 'passes' of any particular compiler. A multi-pass system has, however, been assumed throughout.

### 1. Accumulation of Data Declarations

The data declarations which are made separately from the procedures will normally be compiled first. This compilation will consist of accumulating the different data properties under each unit of data, and similarly for any group or conditional names. The accumulations will then be ordered in accordance with the method used to extract data references from procedures.

### 2. Recognition

The first task is to recognize each of the syntactical entities of the program. This will be done from its physical structure (e.g. is this a word in capitals?) and the next action will depend on the type of entity. For example (i) Normal keywords may be replaced by a unique identifying code number (for this purpose most symbols, including even a comma, act as keywords). (ii) Declarations, which include left-hand labels and perhaps the description of functions, groups and local variables, will be entered into dynamic lists with details of their scopes. Since in general these items may be referenced before they are declared a simple numbering system is desirable for references on the first pass, the result of the declarations being picked up subsequently. (iii) Invented names may be listed, as mentioned previously, and replaced by an identifying number. It may be desirable to form separate lists for the different major levels of data (e.g. field, groups and records) since most, if not all, verbs will apply to a specific level.

### 3. Applying Declarations

Having recognized the different entities it is necessary to associate their properties with them. In this respect keywords may be considered to have system properties. The process of association may consist of performing a table look-up as and when required or, due to storage troubles, a separate pass may be performed to replace each identifying number by the relevant set of properties.

In the latter case a considerable amount of re-arranging of the program may be carried out including (i) the repetition of clauses stemming from the use of group names; (ii) breaking down macro verbs into the micro routines available in the compiler; (iii) insertion of the jumps and calls implied by conditional statements, function references and segment changes; (iv) the listing of literals, function and subroutine bodies, and parameters required in the object program, particularly in regard to input and output (e.g. a READ may require a parameter for each field in the input record).

In addition, if a stack technique is employed in the Object Program all necessary procedures may be put into reverse Polish notation by the process described by Dr Dijkstra (1961).

## 4. Selection of Verbs and Operators

The specific meaning of a verb or operator is determined by a combination of its context, the properties of its operands and the effect of any subsidiary verb. When this information has been assembled it is possible to compile the 'package' represented by the verb or operator. This may consist of clothing some skeleton routine or generating a call to a closed subroutine.

Whatever its form the details of the package, in regard to length and references to other packages, must be listed as parameters to the loader.

## 5. Storage Assignment and Loading

The first parts of the storage assignment process can begin at an early stage in some languages, particularly in respect of the increments of relatively addressed fields. If, however, the working store is effectively two levels the assignment of addresses to base locations and fixed length fields will be performed during the loading of the procedural packages.

During the process of loading an instruction counter will be kept and all cross-references will be updated. This will include loading all necessary literals, closed subroutines and parameter information and keeping tables of the items, and their addresses, which have been loaded. The details of the process are of course simplified if the output of the phase is in some kind of assembly code.

Various optimization processes may also be performed here. This may be done by simulating the conditions that will exist in the Object Program to lessen unnecessary store accesses, particularly in respect of backing store, preservations of index registers and accumulators, and the wastage of processing time following autonomous operations. Full optimization can only be achieved by a complete analysis of the flow of the program but some gain will be obtained by considering separately each section between branch points.

## 6. Checking the Source Program

It is, of course, desirable that the source program be checked as early as possible in the compiler in order to avoid wasting compilation time. Unfortunately in the convenient sequence of operations for compilation some errors do not become apparent until the later phases (e.g. the program is too large). And in most compilers each phase performs the checking appropriate to its function.

If the effort is available there is much to be said for having two versions of the compiler, the first being a 'checker' and the second the compiler proper. In practice existing compilers perform more often as the former than the latter.

## 7. Print-Outs

In the absence of trace facilities in source language it is normally necessary to provide a complete print-out of the Object Program and to relate this to

the original Source Program. This is done by keeping a record of the transformations performed on the latter during each phase or pass of the compiler.
It is then a simple matter to print out the following information. (i) A side
by side listing of the source statements and the resultant compiled code.
(ii) Details of the subroutines, constants etc., which have been loaded
together with their addresses. (iii) The addresses which have been assigned to
records. (iv) Input/output channel numbers which have been assigned to files
and other operating information.

Certain other details are also welcomed by some users, such as label points,
in order to facilitate the patching of the object code. It would seem an open
question whether this practice should be encouraged.

## 5. Some Characteristics of Compilers for Large Machines

### 1. Flowmatic

The first genuine commercial compiler was that of *FLOWMATIC*, designed
for *UNIVAC I* and *II*, and it has been described in detail by Dr Hopper (4).
This compiler has had a considerable influence on all subsequent commercial
languages and in many cases on their methods of implementation.

The *FLOWMATIC* compiler consists essentially of three main phases—
Translation, Selection and Conversion which operate as follows.

(i) Translation—this examines each of the sentences in the source program
and performs the operations described in 4.2 and 4.3 above. Its output is a
'file entry' which consists of a code word for the verb, the properties of the
operands and details of any implied jumps.

(ii) Selection—this uses the code word in the file entry to call a 'generator'
which produces the assembly code for the sentence. It also lists the storage
requirements of the code produced, and any constants and cross references.

(iii) Conversion—this uses the lists produced in (ii) to allocate storage
economically and then acts as an Assembler to the output code. It also
produces a print out on the lines described on p. 209.

The method used in this compiler had two great drawbacks. First each
sentence, which consisted of the scope of a verb, had to be treated as an
independent entity which prevented any form of expression being allowed.
Second the generators tended to produce open subroutines which made the
Object Program very long.

### 2. Closed Sub-Routines

The next step was the development of a system of linkages which allowed
the object code to consist of jumps and parameters to closed subroutines.
Input/output, sorting and file handling came to be handled by very large
routines which were included more or less automatically in the Object
Program, whilst others were loaded as required.

Formulae were still very restricted and handled in most cases by open
subroutines. Procedures or subroutines in the Source Program were also
restricted because there was no mechanism whereby the inner subroutines
of the system could be called recursively.

## 3. Other Techniques

There are currently a large number of compiler writing teams in existence, all of whom are no doubt evolving new techniques. Very little has, however, appeared in print. Nevertheless it has become apparent that in America the recent emphasis is toward increasing the object time efficiency rather than adding to the facilities of the languages. These techniques have included the following.

*1. Separation of Input from Processing.* On fast machines with scatter read/write facilities it has become possible to have a number of records, on serial files, going through a process of input, unpacking, processing, packing and output. The system is arranged to be ahead of the user, in the sense that it is dealing with records he has not yet referred to, and by a suitable system of swing buffering delays on input/output are minimized.

Inevitably the technique uses a great deal of space (but see *3* below) but where this is available it can also be used to spread out consecutive variable length items to reduce the time spent allocating space when they expand.

One of the biggest difficulties here is to prevent the system being inflexible (e.g. unpacking records which will be skipped by the user) and knowing the state of the machine when errors are signalled subsequently (e.g. a parity error on an output tape).

*2. Packing of Words.* Large machines which do not employ character addressing tend to have large machine words and fast shift facilities. These circumstances are often felt to imply that data should be packed into and across words. However, this adds enormously to the addressing problem and any dynamic re-assignments of space.

There are in essence two methods which are used. The first causes the fields to be unpacked as part of *1* above. This is slow and will lead to redundant operations but does allow the mask to be stored with the data. The record unpacks the item when it is needed, which is slower in loops and requires the mask to be stored with the program.

Although this kind of technique can prove very advantageous there are grounds for believing that they have been the cause of considerable delays and debugging troubles in a number of compilers.

*3. Dynamic Assignment of Program Storage.* On parallel programming computers it is desirable that programs should be able to take advantage of the varying amounts of storage that may be available. This has lead to techniques such as the segmentation features in FACT.

Here the user's program is divided into segments which are assigned storage when required by the program sequence. This tends to make the program use the store efficiently and allows room for flexibility in the handling of data.

## 6. Some Characteristics of Compilers for Small Machines

There are two schools of thought as to how commercial languages should be applied to small machines. The first is to take the kind of language, such as COBOL, which is more suitable for large machines and to restrict it as necessary. This is being done quite widely in America, and to some extent in England, using the kind of techniques described above (5.1 and 2). The second stems from a belief that the results of the above methods are not worth their cost and that greater advantages can be obtained from similar techniques to those employed in ALGOL implementations.

The course of the latter view is that it is now quite simple to provide very general procedural facilities (e.g. such as functions) on quite small machines. A language can be tailored around this fact which does not incorporate the large number of special purpose routines that so often stem from facilities included in the data declarations, but allows these to be catered for by functions as and when required.

It appears that this can lead to commercial languages with more powerful capabilities than that proposed hitherto, at a cost of leaving rather more for the programmer to do. But even this drawback should be materially reduced as the library of functions is built up.

In the long run of course users will decide between the two schools based on the convenience and efficiency of the results produced. In the meantime the main elements of the latter are:

## 1. Data Mapping

Fields will tend to be ordered within the record so that a simple control map will suffice. This allows records to be held on magnetic tape in a way which is not too different from conventional methods and so the interchangeability of tapes is retained. At the same time the user is able to construct more complex structures within a record through an ability to address any characters and most of the control fields.

A simplified example of such a record taken from *TALK* (English Electric, 1963) is given in Fig. 1. From this it is possible to see how a system of mapping the maps could be build up to allow the batching of records.

## 2. Changes in the Stack Technique

A stack is a convenient if not always an efficient way to communicate parameters for all routines that are required by a commercial compiler. In addition its use for return instructions allows housekeeping and other such routines to go recursive quite freely. It is nevertheless helpful in these circumstances to make a number of changes to the methods originally proposed by Dr Dijkstra. These include—(i) Since items of different lengths must be handled place their address, rather than their contents, into the 'call' stack. (ii) For the same reason introduce a second stack, the 'work' stack to hold anonymous intermediate results. The pointers of this stack must be placed in the call stack on the activation of each Block or Function. (iii) Hold data references (i.e. parameters) in interpretable units which indicate the distinction between absolute, relative and indirect addresses. (iv) It may also be convenient to retain parameter locations in order to avoid individual routines manipulating the stack pointers. This means that the parameters in such cases must be moved from the stack to the locations prior to the call to the routine.

*SIMPLIFIED EXAMPLE OF A MAPPED RECORD*

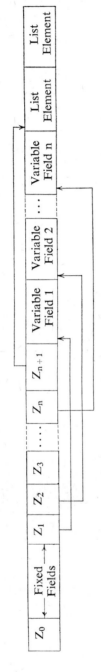

Notation:  $Z_0$ = Length of Record
           $Z_1$ = Length & Address of 1st Variable Field
           $Z_n$ = Length & Address of nth Variable Field
           $Z_{n+1}$ = Address of 1st List Element

*GENERALIZED EXAMPLE OF BATCHED RECORDS*

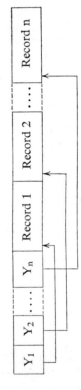

Notation:  $Y_1$ = Address of 1st Field ($Z_0$) of the 1st Record.

Fig. 1

The above gives a basic structure whose efficiency can be improved in many ways. It is for example possible to avoid calling many routines via the stack, and in addition where appropriate open subroutines can still be generated. In this connection advantage could be taken of the techniques described by Mr Huxtable.

## 7. Conclusion

The only conclusion that appears possible after a consideration of compilers is that the dominating requirement is to begin with the right kind of language. At the same time it is apparent that we are only slowly learning how to specify source languages in a way which is reasonably optimum for the user and the machine. Improvements in logic design may remove the difficulties of the latter but those of the former will remain. In the meantime the suggestion that any language is yet fit to act as 'the standard' in any field is foolish in the extreme.

## 8. Acknowledgements

I am glad to acknowledge the assistance of my colleagues, Mr H. D. Baecker and Mr B. S. Gibbens in the preparation of this paper.

### REFERENCES

1. J. W. BACKUS et al. (1960). Report on the Algorithmic Language ALGOL 60 (Ed. P. Naur). Regnecentralen, Copenhagen.
2. D. J. DIJKSTRA (1961). Making a Translator for ALGOL 60. *A.P.I.C. Bull.* No. 7, Brighton.
3. English Electric Company (1963). Talk Reference Manual.
4. GRACE HOPPER (1959). "Automatic Programming: present status and future trends". Mechanization of Thought Processes, Vol. 1. HMSO, London.
5. Report (1961) to the CODASYL Committee (COBOL 1961). Department of Defense, Washington D.C.

# 14. INTRODUCTION TO TIME-SHARING

## S. GILL

*International Computers and Tabulators Ltd., London, England*

### 1. Parallel Activities

The sort of program that we are most familiar with consists of a series of statements, each of which specifies in some form or other an operation to be performed by the computer. These operations must be done in a prescribed sequence laid down by, and depending only on, the program, and the data fed to the computer. Thus at any stage in the execution of the program, by examining the contents of the machine (i.e. the store contents and any special registers, accumulators, etc.) we can deduce exactly what will happen next. Each operation triggers off the next one, so that we get a simple chain of causation (see Fig. 1a). (This sequence obviously need not be the sequence in which we write the instructions, but nevertheless it can be deduced strictly from the program and the data on which it is operating.) No two of these operations can happen at the same time or in the wrong order.

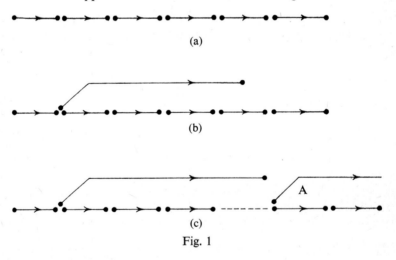

(a)

(b)

(c)

Fig. 1

At least that is the principle of the thing—a nice orderly convention to use in interpreting these programs; and certainly the effect of what the machine does is as if the programs were carried out in this way. But there have in fact always been a number of minor exceptions in what actually happens in the machine. For example, the first machines had punched tape readers and punches on them, and we soon discovered that these were rather slow compared with the individual internal operations in the machine, and that they could be operated independently of the ordinary arithmetic. Thus one could link the machine with a little buffer holding some information, maybe only one character, to go to a tape punch, and one could arrange that when a character was to be punched out it was loaded into the buffer. A transfer from the buffer to the punch was then initiated while the machine was being used for further instructions. Thus we had a branching of the sequence, in which at some point we triggered off another rather longer operation which carried on in parallel with the succeeding instructions in the program (see Fig. 1b). (There were other instances of this kind of thing. They usually involved input and output, but occasionally other things. For example, on the Pilot Ace, multiplication could be done by some special equipment which was independent of the execution of further instructions, and it was therefore allowed to continue in parallel.)

This, of course, requires an interlock, to make sure that, in the case of buffered input-output, the machine does not attempt to execute a further instruction in the program which loads another character into the buffer before the punching of the first one is finished. That is, there must be some kind of check to make sure that if, for example, instruction A in Fig. 1c involves punching, then the execution of the sequence is delayed until the punching of the first character is finished. The interlock in this case is probably a piece of hardware which is arranged so as to preserve this fiction of purely serial programs.

A much bigger instance of this kind of thing happens in the case of magnetic tape units, which transfer dozens or hundreds of words, usually autonomously, under the control of special circuits associated with the tape equipment. This can be done simply by having a much bigger buffer, linked to the magnetic tape deck, and loading the entire block of information into the buffer first. In this case the situation is very similar to the punched tape one. Usually, however, it is not done this way, because the transfer of an entire block of information from one store to another essentially similar store is rather a waste of time. Instead, the magnetic tape transfers usually go directly to or from some area of the main store. An area of store is allocated to this job, and carries out its transfer to or from the magnetic tape, while the rest of the store is available for the central processing unit which carries on with further instructions (see Fig. 2a). So we have parallel operations going on, involving two parts of a temporarily divided main store. During this process these store areas are logically separate.

You can in fact, in a situation like this, allow an area to be common to both processes if they are purely reading from it; that is to say if the magnetic tape equipment is writing on to the tape from the store (i.e. reading from the store to the tape), and the central processing unit is only using the area for reading. Often one doesn't bother with this, although it is done in some cases. In the Orion Computer for example, which has hardware that will protect a store area from activities that are not supposed to be concerned with it, the central processing unit is nevertheless allowed to read from an area that is involved in a writing transfer to magnetic tape.

In fact several computers have hardware to keep these areas fenced off from one another. This forms a positive check, to guard against references to an area by an activity which is not supposed to be concerned with that area.

This can be looked on simply as a hardware check against errors (usually program errors) which might otherwise be extremely difficult to track down, since the sequence of events is now dependent upon the relative speeds at which the central processing unit and the peripheral unit get on with their jobs. When we have activities occurring in parallel it is possible for precisely the same program, with precisely the same data, to result in different sequences of operations in real time. This is because on different occasions the magnetic tape for example, although it is behaving strictly according to its specification, may run at a slightly different speed so that the relative rate at which it proceeds with its job, compared with the central processing unit, is different. In a case like this if there is an error in the program so that the *CPU* starts referring to a store area that is supposed to be hidden from it for the time being, the effect of such an error will depend on the precise timing of the tape transfer which may vary from one run to another, so that one can be faced with an extremely difficult diagnostic problem. This is the main reason why some systems at least do have a positive check, usually in the form of hardware, against incorrect references to a store area.

This is not quite the same thing as the interlock that I mentioned in the simple case, which prevents one activity from going on beyond the point at which it would begin to interfere with the other. But in fact if you do have this positive check on the use of the store, it does provide you (or can provide you if it is arranged properly) with just the kind of interlock that you want. This is because the point at which you need to hold up, for example, the *CPU* to wait for the tape activity to finish, is simply the point at which the *CPU* begins to want to make use of the store area that is being used by the tape unit. So having some form of hardware that checks the store addresses being used can provide you quite simply with the necessary interlock. It is not necessary to get the interlock in this way: it is sufficient, if you can trust the program, merely to provide it with a test instruction to enable it to find out whether the magnetic tape equipment is still proceeding with its transfer or not.

## 2. Time Sharing

This chapter is supposed to be about time sharing and I must now introduce that idea. The areas of store in Fig. 2a are quite distinct, and in fact while this process is going on we could think of these as two separate machines, except for the fact that the store may be a magnetic core store which is in one

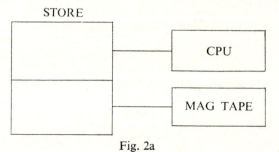

Fig. 2a

engineering unit and therefore has common access and selection circuits. We would then have the sort of situation shown in Fig. 2b where the little bit in the middle is the core store selection circuit, which is used by both activities. This bit of equipment is therefore time-sharing, because it is occasionally doing a job for the *CPU* and occasionally for the tape unit. We are not time-sharing individual parts of the core store, because each individual word is only associated with one activity, at least so long as the tape transfer lasts,

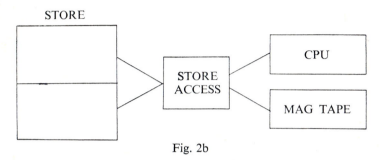

STORE

Fig. 2b

but we are time-sharing the common access channel to the core store. This is a typical time sharing situation; there are two activities going on involving partly (in fact largely) separate equipment, but some common equipment. The reason for doing this is that, owing to the speed features of the equipment involved, it pays to do so. We find in fact that the central processing unit or the tape unit alone would not be sufficiently fast to keep the selection circuits busy. This is usually the reason why time-sharing is adopted. (There may possibly be logical reasons why it is desirable or convenient to do a job this way and I will come to them later on.)

You must of course have a priority rule to decide which of the activities is going to have use of the common equipment next. For example, in the case of the magnetic tape situation, the rule is usually that the tape equipment has top priority; as soon as the core store has finished a reading or writing cycle, if the tape unit wants the use of the core store, then it gets it and the *CPU* has to wait. To be quite specific we must say that we do not interrupt a core store cycle; once it has started we let it finish. If the tape unit suddenly calls for a word when the core store is in the middle of a cycle for the *CPU*, we let that finish and then hold up the *CPU* while the tape unit has a cycle. Thus we have some kind of priority rule saying which equipment or activity has priority over the other, and at what moments it is allowed to interrupt.

In the case of a magnetic tape transfer, usually the whole of its activity, together with the observation of priorities, is controlled by a special built-in device. The transfer is initiated by the *CPU*, and then hardware entirely controls the progress of the tape transfer until it is finished. It might not be done entirely this way, for example, in some *IBM* machines a tape transfer can involve not merely one area of store but a number of different batches of words in different places in the store, and so these must be specified in some form for the tape unit to accept. This is done by what is effectively a little program of tape commands in the store, the program being executed by a kind of control unit, the magnetic tape control unit, and this has some of the features of a general purpose computer in that it does follow through a series of instructions of a kind. These instructions are in a language that relates solely to words to be transferred to or from a tape deck. They do not allow all the features of an ordinary program; they do not, for example, provide for conditional jumps. However, we do as a result have two or more activities going on, both of which are controlled in some sort of way by a program.

This situation gets very much more pronounced in the Gamma 60, where we have a number of control units each following programs in their own language and doing various jobs, many of them associated with input or output equipment. You might conceivably have two identical control units,

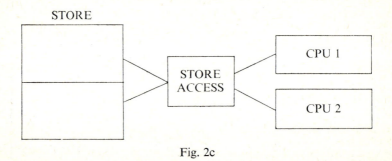

Fig. 2c

each obeying programs in the same code (I don't know whether this has ever been done, though it was certainly projected for the *LARC*). So you could have the situation shown in Fig. 2c, in which there are two processing units, each of them obeying its own program, and sharing the core store.

### 3. Time Sharing by Programs

In fact you might go further than that and, instead of having two separate processing units, have a single processing unit which is shared along with the core store access, so that there are now two activities involving two different parts of the store but time-sharing the *CPU* and the access to the store. This sort of thing is fairly easy to follow and works out nicely if all the working variables for each of these activities, including the accumulator and control counter, are harboured in the store area for that activity (see Fig. 2d). Then the entire status of that activity is represented by its store area, and all that the *CPU* does is merely to act as a logical organ which carries out a transformation on the store area concerned and progresses it from one state to the next. It has no memory of its own. In that case we simply picture the *CPU* as deciding, on some priority basis or other, which of these activities to work on; taking the necessary information about it; doing whatever it has to do in order to carry out the transformation entailed in obeying one instruction from the program; and advancing the control counter. It has then finished dealing with that program for the time being and it can perhaps change its mind and decide to progress the other activity next. There may, of course, as I mentioned earlier, be a common area which you allow to be used for both of these activities provided that they only read from it and don't write to it, and this may perhaps contain a common section of program.

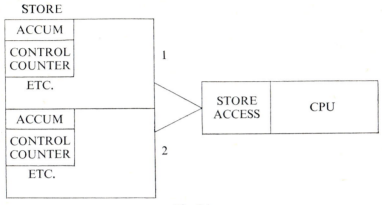

Fig. 2d

You still need a priority rule, of course, some basis on which to decide which of these activities to proceed with next. The Honeywell 800, for example, has a certain amount of built-in hardware which will arrange for the *CPU* to deal with up to eight programs simultaneously, and the priority rule is simply that these programs are dealt with in rotation. There is a counter which repeatedly counts up to eight, and as it goes through each position the computer carries out one instruction from the corresponding program (unless that program is absent or waiting for some external condition to be satisfied, in which case the computer skips on to the next one).

I said that the special registers—control counter, accumulator, and so on —are kept in the store area relating to that activity. Of course in actual physical fact they probably would not be in the ordinary core store; you would probably have fast registers for them, provided that you were prepared to duplicate these and to allocate one set to each activity. However, if you are going to have several parallel programs going on at once, you would need a lot of high speed registers for this. In practice it is not usually necessary to switch very rapidly from one program to another. It is usually quite appropriate to obey a dozen, a thousand or even a million instructions of one program before switching to another. Depending on the frequency with which you need to switch programs, it may be quite satisfactory simply to use one set of the special registers associated directly with the central processing unit, and to arrange that they are copied or 'dumped' into the core area concerned (or into some particular area reserved for that activity) when the computer switches to another activity. Most of the time the computer will be working with the common set of high speed registers. Low speed registers would suffice for the ultimate 'dump' of these quantities because dumping would occur comparatively rarely.

In fact it may even be possible to arrange that the computer does not always have to dump the entire contents of these special registers. You may be able to restrict the points in the program at which you allow the system to switch from one activity to another. For example, supposing you have a single-address machine with an accumulator, you may be able to arrange the system so that switching from one program to another is only allowed when the contents of the accumulator are immaterial; that is to say, when they have just been cleared or they are just about to be cleared. In that case there is no need to dump the accumulator. In practice this is not often done; usually these systems are arranged so that they can interrupt between any pair of instructions, and one just accepts the need to dump the registers concerned.

I think it is worth noting that one doesn't relax this restriction any further than that: one doesn't usually allow an interruption *within* one instruction, because during the execution of an instruction there are, of course, several other intermediate quantities existing inside the control and arithmetic unit, and if you broke off the instruction in the middle of its execution then you might be faced with a very difficult problem in picking up where you left off. Usually, therefore, interruptions are only allowed to occur *between* instructions.

Another possibility, instead of actually restricting the points at which you allow interruptions of a program, is merely to arrange that on returning to that program again the computer goes back to some suitable restart point. It might for example be able to interrupt a program in the middle of the execution of an instruction, but be able to go back to it simply at the beginning of that instruction again. This happens in Atlas, which may interrupt the execution of a program because it has got half way through obeying an instruction and finds that it needs a word which is not in the core store. The word has to be fetched from the drum, and this is rather a protracted business, involving the execution of part of the supervisor program; hence it is necessary to interrupt the main program in the middle of an instruction. The instruction code is such that it is always sufficient to go back and begin that instruction again.

So you may be able to establish restart points, which is a rather looser restriction than restricting the points at which you allow interruptions at all. This is carried further in the case of the Atlas supervisor which Dr Howarth is going to talk about later, and which consists of quite a large number of procedures which may go on logically in parallel but in fact time-sharing. There he allows interruptions of the various branches of this program at any point—at least between any two instructions—but he doesn't attempt to pick up every part of the program again at exactly the point where it left off. He has various key points which are usually starting points of routines, and it is sufficient, if a routine has been interrupted, simply to go back to the beginning of that routine again.

So in practice we don't have to have separate registers for all the variables concerned in each activity; we may be able to time-share common registers for this purpose, provided we can cope somehow with the problem of dumping, or of restricting the points at which we allow interruptions, or of establishing restart points. Whether this is worth doing depends on how frequently we are going to want the system to switch from one activity to another. In practice of course we strike a compromise on this, and the question is *how many* common registers there are. There may be some activities which jump in very frequently, and these would have several high-speed registers of their own, but programs which are only switched to and from comparatively rarely would have their high-speed registers taken care of by dumping.

## 4. Entering and Leaving Parallel Programs

Well, how do we get the system into this situation? If we want to launch it off obeying two activities like this, then we need to define an area for each activity, and we have to set any initial contents where necessary. We certainly have to set the control counters saying which instruction the unit is supposed to obey first for each activity, and we may have to set the accumulators, depending on whether the initial state is assumed by the program or not. Then we just give them a push and let them carry on, taking turns according to some priority rule.

We must, of course, have some superior system which takes care of all this: it may be done almost entirely by hardware as in the case of the Honeywell 800, or largely by the software system, as for example the Atlas Supervisor. (In Atlas there is some hardware which provides a few simple facilities, but almost all of the logic concerned with taking care of parallel programs is provided by the Supervisor Program.) The priority problem is usually dealt with by reassessing the situation whenever the status of the peripheral equipment changes. Usually the reason for doing time-sharing is that one of the activities involves some peripheral equipment (this is liable to be rather slow compared with the operation of the *CPU* so that if the machine obeyed that activity alone the *CPU* would be held up for long periods), so the usual arrangement is to let the *CPU* proceed with the same activity until the status of the peripheral equipment changes. This means either that the program requires some peripheral transfer to be completed, in which case the system looks around to see whether there is some other activity that could be proceeding with the use of *CPU* and which is not held up by a peripheral transfer at the moment; or that an activity which has higher priority than the one which is now proceeding becomes free to proceed because a peripheral transfer associated with it has now finished, so that the higher priority activity can now make use of the *CPU*.

Now this is all right for programs which are logically independent of one another and which remain so throughout their life. Many people think of time-sharing in computers purely in this light—as a situation where you want to be able to do two or more quite independent programs at once, these programs being within themselves purely serial and conventional programs. For this, it is simply necessary to have some supervisory system, provided by hardware or software or a mixture of the two, which will allow you to load up new programs at any time provided that there is a store area for them, and to let them run in parallel with whatever else is there.

But what about a program which starts off serially and then splits itself into two or more parallel branches? This is quite possible, and in fact it is the sort of thing which happens in a classical type of machine when it initiates a buffered peripheral transfer, controlled by autonomous equipment. This is, if you look at it in detail, an example of a program splitting itself into two parallel activities. (I tried to define what I meant by an 'activity' for this lecture, but I found it so difficult that I gave it up. The idea of an activity is something that we probably grasp instinctively well enough: it is simply a chain of causation, a series of events each of which triggers off the following one; but to give a rigid definition of it is very difficult.) We can also conceive of a program which splits itself into two or more parallel branches each of which involves following an ordinary bit of program obeyed by the central processing unit; in fact there are already some cases where this turns out to be desirable. For example, in Atlas we run into a situation similar to the one which is solved in the IBM7090 by having a separate set of tape commands. Atlas will deal with this not by having separate tape commands, but simply by having tape commands that can be obeyed by the control unit as part of the ordinary program. We then arrange to have a string of these executed in parallel with a string of instructions in the main program by allowing programs to split themselves into parallel branches. No doubt many other machines have a similar facility.

The best way that I can illustrate this is to describe the facilities that are provided in the Atlas code. Atlas allows several branches to be set up by a program, and to be numbered. There is an instruction that will tell the machine to initiate a new branch, with a particular number, starting at a particular address in the store. There is also an instruction that will tell the machine to 'kill' (i.e. to abandon) a branch; for this it is merely necessary to give the number of the branch. This, of course, allows a branch to abolish itself, as well as other branches. And finally there is an instruction which will allow one branch to test whether another branch is alive.

The various possible uses which one can make of these instructions are not yet quite clear; at least they're not clear to me. No doubt we shall be gaining a lot of experience in their use over the next few years. I mentioned that we can see quite clearly their use in controlling a series of tape transfers which proceed in parallel with calculation; but obviously there are a lot of other tricks you can play with them too. We haven't made any attempt to allow store areas to be reserved for the use of particular branches. It is assumed that these branches all belong to a program written essentially by one man, who will take care of the danger of one branch wrongly referring to information which is still being used by another branch, and that any necessary interlocks of that kind will all be taken care of by using the instruction which allows a branch to test whether another branch is still alive.

### Discussion

QUESTIONER: Do you think that this will impose a very heavy burden on the programmer?

DR. GILL: Only on the kind of programmer who wants to write this sort of program. As I said, the main reason why we put this in was to allow people to set up a series of magnetic tape instructions, and this is simple enough. Obviously if anybody does want to use these instructions in a very sophisticated way, then he will have to think very carefully about it. It may well be in the future that some kind of autocodes will be developed which will allow us to write programs that make use of these instructions in a way that makes it difficult to make a mistake. But that's for the future.

Of course, the Atlas supervisor itself consists of several parallel branches: we'll be hearing more about these later on. The logic of the interlocks between them is very complicated. The facilities which I described for parallel branches in Atlas are provided below the supervisor level; it is in fact the supervisor which provides the branch facilities for use in ordinary programs. The interlocks within the supervisor itself are dealt with by more *ad hoc* programming methods, and a rather elaborate series of conventions has had to be laid down for the writing of the supervisor.

## 5. The Structure of Parallel Programs

You can get into some involved situations in an apparently simple case. Suppose for example that you have two activities going on, involving two separate areas of the store. One of these is perhaps a program which is generating a whole string of items; these items are just dumped in a suitable place in the store, and then later on used for output. The output itself may involve some further recoding of the items in order to get the sort of printed notation that you want, and so you may have two activities going on, one of which generates these items and the other of which pushes them out as fast as it can. If you're generating them at a fairly constant speed, then it's probably quite sufficient to use simply one ordinary serial program which alternately generates an item and puts it out. But if the items are being generated at a rather irregular rate, then it might be worth while to queue them up, so that you have a common area in between the two activities which contains a

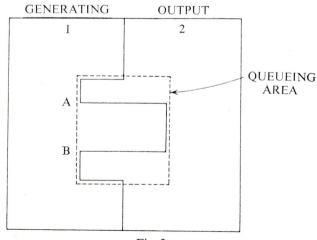

Fig. 3

queue. You probably let this area be used cyclically, so that the loading takes place from top to bottom and then starts at the top again. Thus at any one moment some of these items would have been freshly planted by the generating activity, and some of them would already have been dealt with by the output activity. So strictly speaking the boundary between the areas belonging to the two activities is as shown in Fig. 3. $A$ is the point at which the generating activity can plant its next item, and $B$ is the point from which the output activity should take its next item for output. The interlocking of the routines gets very elaborate. Before an item is used, the output routine must check that it is already there; and before inserting an item in the queue, the generator must check that it is not going to put it on top of an item which has not yet been accepted by the output routine (i.e. that the queue is not already full up). If either of these things happens, then the corresponding activity must be held up for a while. This therefore means that after using an item the output routine must also check to see whether, before it did this, the generating routine had been in a held-up state, and can therefore now be released to generate another item; similarly after placing a new item in the queue, the generator must check to see whether the output routine was previously held up because it hadn't got an item, and can therefore now be allowed to proceed. Many such interlocks have to be taken care of inside the Atlas supervisor. Usually the reason for creating this kind of situation is that the timing of events is uneven or irregular, and that you want to even out the use of the equipment, but even in what appears to be a fairly simple situation you may be led into a number of ramifications of the program.

I mentioned earlier that there may also be a purely logical reason for wanting to describe the activity of the computer as consisting of several activities proceeding in parallel. An example of this is a case where you may be searching for the solution of a problem by a heuristic technique, where you just try several possible approaches to see whether any of them will lead to a solution. You don't know which approach is most likely to be successful —you just proceed with all these approaches until one of them comes up with an answer; and you want to proceed with them all at roughly the same rate so that whichever one is going to give the answer quickest will produce it before you waste too much time on the others. Then logically the program can be written as one that splits into several branches each following up one possible approach, and all proceeding in parallel. (Whether you have parallel equipment or time-shared equipment is beside the point here.) In this example, you want to describe the program in terms of parallel branches for the purely logical reason that this is the way in which the problem arises.

## 6. Effect on Programming Languages

In fact this seems to be a general trend in the way that we write programs: we are tending to do away with explicit sequencing of operations. We cannot say how a computer will set about evaluating an involved expression written in FORTRAN or ALGOL: there's no one 'correct' sequence in which the various operations are to be done, and various compilers come up with various sequences for evaluating the sub-expressions. Furthermore, programs tend to contain more and more declarations: type declarations, data descriptions and so on, which are statements forming part of the program but which have no particular time relevance.

The extreme in this direction seems to be the function language, in which what you write down is a series of definitions of things to be computed, without implying that they are to be computed in a particular sequence. It is up to the system to find an appropriate sequence in which to evaluate them. Certainly the idea that I illustrated with reference to Atlas, of adding a few instructions to an otherwise serial order code to allow one to create and destroy and to test various parallel branches, seems to be a rather clumsy way of introducing time-sharing. I think that we've got to look to changes in programming language structure to provide us with the real solution to this problem.

Before I finish I should mention a technique which has been used with some of the bigger computers like Stretch and Atlas, for increasing the computing speed. In order to make the processing unit as fast as possible, the engineers have put in more and more hardware. As a result, the processor contains several major parts such as the floating-point arithmetic unit, the unit for address arithmetic, the instruction decoder, and so on, all rather massive and specialized in various ways. In order to make the best use of all of these they have to do operations in parallel; the computer must begin to decode one instruction while it is doing the arithmetic on the previous one, and while it is storing the results of the one before that, and so on. Now this is in fact an attempt, by means of hardware, to convert into parallel operations something which is described by a purely serial program. The engineers have found that if a serial program is to be written without this requirement in mind, then the system required to convert it into a set of parallel activities without coming unstuck is fiendishly complicated. This is because there are many special cases which could arise in an ordinary serial program and which must all be taken account of in a special way by hardware when it tries to do things in parallel.

All this shows, I think, that the future will probably see a swing to programming notations which are less specifically serial, or perhaps I should say more specifically parallel. The sequence in which a computer carries out operations is often very largely arbitrary. If you think of the arithmetic that you are trying to get a machine to do in the case of a big calculation, and imagine that you are presented with all the data required for the job, then there are probably a thousand and one different things that you could tell the machine to do first. But if you're writing a serial program you must make an arbitrary decision about the sequence in which you are going to get these things done, and you base this decision perhaps on considerations of the speed of the equipment, or perhaps on the sheer logical simplicity of describing the program. I think that the development of the trend towards non-serialism is going to depend very largely on designing suitable languages and getting used to them. However, it does seem to me to be the main reason why the sort of programming languages we are using today will eventually become obsolete.

## Discussion

QUESTIONER: Can it be taken for granted that human beings will be able to think in terms of non-serial languages as easily as in terms of serial ones?

DR GILL: I think that it will probably be a little more difficult to grasp, but I don't see why it should be impossibly complicated. There are already a lot of problems in the planning of computing activities which have to be done in parallel in a business office for example, where you very often have an office of some hundreds of clerks who are working in parallel, and somebody has to tell them what they are to do and make sure that they are doing it right. The same sort of thing has happened in scientific calculations too in the past; in the aircraft industry for example, before they had electronic computers, they often had to employ teams of dozens of desk calculator operators to get the job done in time. So people have had to face this problem in the past and have solved it somehow or other.

# 15. THE ATLAS SUPERVISOR PROGRAM

D. HOWARTH

*International Computers and Tabulators Ltd., London, England*

Atlas is the name given to a large, comprehensive computing system developed jointly by Manchester University and Ferranti Limited, originating in the team led by Professor T. Kilburn at Manchester University Computing Machine Laboratory. All activities of Atlas are controlled by a program stored in the computer known as the Supervisor Program (Kilburn *et al.*, 1961a); the computing system is fully time-shared in that the functioning of the peripheral equipments overlaps that of the central computing unit, the central computer sharing its time between object programs and the control of peripheral equipments. Logically, the only program in control of Atlas is the Supervisor program, and all activities of the system constitute branches of this program. Since, however, the central computer is only used by the Supervisor for a small proportion of the available time, a more realistic picture is obtained by regarding the Supervisor as a dormant program which is called into action whenever any part of the computing system cannot proceed further with its built-in operations and requires attention. For example, if a paper tape reader is constructed to read one character to a buffer register, the Supervisor will be called in to transfer this register to store. It is convenient in this context to consider an object program as a branch of the computing system which uses the central computer for long spells and which calls the Supervisor into action whenever it requests an action, such as a tape or peripheral transfer, which is subject to control by the Supervisor.

Although the Supervisor program constitutes a piece of 'software', the detailed objectives and methods of implementation are intimately related to the 'hardware' of the computing system, and it is thus advantageous to outline those features of the hardware which determine the nature of the Supervisor program. The system comprises a single central computing unit, which includes one double-length floating point accumulator and 128 index registers, or $B$ registers. Instructions are of the one-address type, specifying two index registers; accumulator functions use an operand modified by both index registers, whilst most functions operating on index registers use a singly modified operand and also specify the index register to be operated upon. Special use is made of eight of the $B$ registers, $B120$ to $B127$. For example, one of these ($B124$) holds the exponent of the accumulator, and three ($B125$ to $B127$) are used as three control counters, Main, Extracode, and Interrupt control. Although at any one time only one of these can be in effective control, the presence of three distinct counters allows three distinct types of use of the central computer to proceed in series without the need for preserving and restoring control counters. Main control is used by object programs; interrupt control is used by parts of the system demanding immediate attention, such as peripheral equipments whose buffers must be filled or emptied by the computer before being used again by the equipments; extracode control is used both by subroutines initiated by an object program and by the Supervisor program.

The computing system includes several types of storage. Immediate access storage comprises the core store for general use, the fixed store (which is a fast access read-only store holding subroutines and many routines of the Supervisor) and a separate core store known as the subsidiary or working store which is used as working space by the Supervisor. Backing store is provided by magnetic drums, and magnetic tape units, and a large quantity and variety of input and output peripherals can be attached. In order to control these equipments and to supply small buffer stores for peripheral transfers a collection of flip-flops is provided which is collectively known as the $V$ store. Although the $V$ store is not a store in the conventional sense, it is addressed as a store by the central computer, and hence no special basic instructions need be provided for peripheral, tape or drum control. The main core store is divided into blocks or pages of 512 forty-eight bit words, and with each of these pages there is associated a page address register, holding the most significant address digits of the block of information occupying the page at any time. An additional digit in each page address register is known as the lockout digit, which provides a means of protecting any pages in the core store.

Basic protection of store is supplied by hardware, and the rules of protection depend upon the control register in use. Under main control, access to the subsidiary store, to the $V$ store, and to pages of core store for which the lockout digit is set is forbidden and an attempt at any such access causes interruption of the object program. Access to the fixed store is allowed but is harmless since information stored there cannot be overwritten. Under interrupt control, access is permitted to all stores, including pages of core store for which the lockout digit is set. Hardware protection thus allows mutual protection of object programs and routines of the Supervisor using interrupt control, since separate control registers are used and interrupt routines can use store which is locked out from object programs. Under extracode control, the subsidiary store and $V$ store are accessible; access to locked out pages of core-store can be obtained by setting a flip-flop which is itself addressable as a digit of the $V$ store. By this means, extracode control can be used both in subroutines for the object program, known as 'Extracode Functions', and in the Supervisor program.

The mechanism by which the Supervisor program is called into action depends upon the type of activity requiring attention. The most frequent activation is by peripheral equipments which require the Supervisor to empty or fill the buffer attached to the equipment; when they require attention, these equipments set a digit in the $V$ store known as a 'look at me' digit. A separate digit is set for each cause of interruption, and if any one is set, control switches to Interrupt Control, and a program in the fixed store is entered to determine the cause of interruption. Further interruptions are inhibited whilst interrupt control is in use, but the 'look at me' digits remain set, and will cause another interruption as soon as the first sequence under interrupt control is completed. Special hardware attached to one of the *B* registers, *B123*, enables the highest priority cause of interruption to be distinguished by obeying two to five instructions; the priority is conditioned by the critical time of the various equipments, i.e. the time within which the buffer must be emptied or filled or the control digits set. The short interrupt routines run under interrupt control are protected from object programs by hardware protection of store, and since they use only certain *B* registers (*B111–118*), which are not used by object programs, no additional programmed protection is required on entry to an interrupt routine.

Since interruptions can occur at random times, many interruptions can be called for simultaneously. The relevant interrupt routines are obeyed in sequence, and an upper limit is placed on the time taken by any one interrupt routine which ensures that attention is given to each equipment within its critical time. When an interrupt routine calls for a longer sequence of instructions to be obeyed (such as when a paper tape reader interrupt routine requires to transfer a block of main store between core and drum stores), the routine switches to extracode control to enter a long interrupt routine, or a Supervisor Extracode Routine. Supervisor extracode routines (*S.E.R.*s) form the principal branches of the Supervisor program. Short interruptions are permitted whilst an *S.E.R.* is in progress and thus no time limit is observed by each *S.E.R.*, although by their nature, most use the central computer for only a small proportion of the total time. Since interruptions can occur at random intervals, the interrupt routines can call for *S.E.R.*s at random intervals. If whilst the central computer is in use by one *S.E.R.*, others are activated, they are placed in queues to await entry when the current *S.E.R.* is completed or halts itself; an *S.E.R.* is interrupted only by short interrupt routines, using interrupt control, and is never interrupted by another *S.E.R.*

Object programs call the supervisor into action either by causing an interruption and initiating a short interrupt routine, or by initiating an *S.E.R.* Interruptions occur whenever certain errors are detected, such as an attempt to refer to the working store or *V* store, an attempt to obey an undefined instruction code, an overflow of the accumulator exponent or an attempt to divide the accumulator by zero. These interruptions cause entry to a short interrupt routine and thence to an *S.E.R.* to cause the program to be monitored. An object program may also initiate an *S.E.R.* directly in order to organize an operation which is under control of the supervisor; for example, since access to the *V* store by an object program is not permitted, all peripheral, tape, and drum transfers must be organized by calling the Supervisor into action (drum transfers are subject to special organization, described later, and in fact can be initiated by means of an interruption as well as by direct entrance to an *S.E.R.*). An object program enters the supervisor via one of a possible maximum of 512 instructions known as Extracode Instructions, which have the effect of switching control to extracode control and entering the fixed store programs at one of 512 possible points. This is the only means by which an object program can use extracode control, and the finite number of entry points to the supervisor enable complete protection to be enforced by the Supervisor program. All references to peripheral equipment, and to blocks of main store, by an object program use logical numbers within the program to define the equipment or block, and these are related by the Supervisor program to the actual equipment or store block. In this way, complete protection of the Supervisor and object programs is achieved, and by use of logical numbers to define features of the computer, an object program may be written in a form largely independent of the environment in which the program runs.

The Supervisor is also activated by means of interruptions in the event of certain computer failures such as parity errors in core or drum store. It is also entered at intervals of 0.1 sec by a clock interruption; although in many ways the clock resembles a peripheral equipment in that it causes a regular interruption, it also fulfils a special function in that it can always prevent the Supervisor being rendered inoperable. The S.E.R. entered from the clock interrupt routine enables the Supervisor to investigate whether any part of the computing system has ceased to function as expected, and to take appropriate action.

As has been already explained, S.E.R.s are arranged to be run in series and no S.E.R. is interrupted by another one. The routine organizing this is itself an S.E.R. known as the co-ordinator, which is stored in fixed store; it is the program equivalent of the hardware facility whereby interrupts are inhibited and requests 'queued' whilst a routine is being obeyed under interrupt control. Extracode routines awaiting entry are held in four queues in the working store, and whenever one routine is completed or halts itself, the first routine in the highest priority queue is entered. The number of entries in each queue is limited to the number of possible causes of interruptions, namely, one or two per peripheral equipment together with one for each object program being obeyed; logically the Supervisor constitutes a program of many branches, the number of branches being the number of activities of the computing system which are being controlled at any one time. Each branch may consist of a sequence of S.E.R.s each of which use the central computer for only a small proportion of the total time. For the remainder of the time, the S.E.R.s may either be dormant, awaiting activation by an interrupt routine, or may be halted, awaiting completion of a transfer between core and drum stores, for example. In this latter case, when an S.E.R. is halted awaiting completion of another S.E.R., the routine is recorded in the queues in the working store, and some of its working registers are preserved for subsequent resumption. Since S.E.R.s are only halted by virtue of their own request for information, halts can be foreseen, and it is not necessary to preserve the entire working registers of an S.E.R. This is in contrast to object programs, which can be halted at any time to permit a higher priority program to be obeyed, and whose working registers are therefore preserved in toto. Since S.E.R.s are not entered as frequently as are short interrupt routines, program protection of certain working registers, such as Extracode control, which are also used by object programs, is permissible without serious loss in efficiency. However, to reduce the switchover time as far as possible, Supervisor routines generally use only certain B registers (B100–110), which are not available to object programs; if further working registers are required, such as the accumulator, the routines themselves arrange to preserve and restore the original contents. By such means, the time to switch the central computer from an object program to an *S.E.R.* and back again is generally around 40 instructions.

The Supervisor program is designed to maintain the fullest possible activity in all the branches of the computing system which are required to be in action, or in other words to minimize periods during which a branch is idle through awaiting information from another branch. It is the function of the Operating System to arrange the overall organization to achieve this end; before describing this system, however, it is advantageous to consider in more detail how the Supervisor controls transfers between the core store and drums, magnetic tapes, and peripheral equipment. The organization of these transfers can materially influence the choice of operating system, although it in no way forces the acceptance of one particular system; the routines concerned with this organization are stored in the fixed store, since they are activated frequently, but are used within the context of the operating system which occupies main store, and which can thus be modified in the light of experience, or to suit particular demands.

The drum store is divided, like core store, into blocks of 512 words, known as sectors, and transfers between drum and core store always take place in these units, between a sector of the drum and a page of the core store. The addresses used in instructions refer to blocks of information in the combined core and drum store and one of the activities of the Supervisor is to arrange that blocks are transferred to the core store when required for use. Associated with each page of core store is the page address register, which holds the most significant address digits, or the block label, of the block occupying the page. When access to the main core store is required, the hardware scans the page address registers and if equivalence is found, the required word in that page is selected. Should no equivalence be found between the requested block label and any of the page address registers, an interruption occurs, and the Supervisor is entered through an interrupt routine. The Supervisor maintains in the working store a list of all blocks in use associated with each program, together with the page or sector currently occupied by the block, and hence should a block be occupying a sector of the drum when reference is made to it in an instruction, it can be transferred to a page of the core store. The page address registers are themselves addressable as digits in the $V$ store, and hence can be set by the Supervisor to hold the correct block label. When the required block has been read into core store, the instruction which caused the interruption is repeated; equivalence is now found between the required block address and a page address register, and the program is free to proceed. In order to read a block from the drum to core store, it is first necessary to create a space in the core store to accommodate the block (unless an empty page exists already). In fact, in order to establish the block in core store with as little delay as possible, the Supervisor always maintains an 'empty' page in the core store, to which a block can be read immediately; during the transfer from the drum, a new page is selected to be made empty, and the block occupying this page is then written to an empty sector on the drum. The routine responsible for selecting a suitable page to write to the drum is known as the 'learning program'; it analyses past use of the blocks in core store to determine the page holding the block least likely to be required in core store, and which is therefore the most suitable page to be made 'empty'. Each time a transfer is made to or from core store, the block directory in the working store is altered to record the new position of the block of store. This system of using the combined core and drum store gives rise to the 'one level store' concept, whereby the two level nature of the store is concealed from the user; the system is used by all programs using the main core store, including object programs and the Supervisor program itself. Many of the routines of the Supervisor which are not frequently used are stored in the core and drum store; they will normally occupy sectors on the drum, but are brought into core store when needed, with no disruption to any object programs using core store at the time (apart, of course, from a possible increase in the number of drum transfers required, since temporarily the amount of core store available to the object programs is reduced). The ease with which individual blocks may be moved in the combined core and drum store is of incalculable worth in the functioning and implementation of an efficient operating system.

In addition to the 'automatic' drum transfers carried out by the Supervisor, it is possible for an object program to use the drum store in a conventional way by use of extracode functions, causing information to be transferred in blocks between drum and core store and for blocks to be copied from the drum to the core store and the copies subsequently lost after use. These instructions are implemented throughout by using the one-level store concept; the Supervisor program at all times maintains control of the pages of core store and may at any time transfer blocks to the drum should space be required for other purposes. However, in order to avoid halting an object program or $S.E.R.$s which can usefully organize transfers in advance, a queue of requests for drum transfers is held in the working store so that drum transfers can proceed at maximum efficiency whilst object programs can continue until being halted when immediate access is requested to a block not available in core store.

Transfers between core store and magnetic tapes are arranged in a similar manner, except that no attempt is made to include magnetic tapes in the 'one level store'. Information is recorded on the tapes in blocks of 512 words; the blocks are numbered sequentially on tape, and tapes are tested and preaddressed on the computer before use. Extracode instructions are provided to enable object programs to position the tapes and to transfer blocks to and from tapes; certain extracodes also enable object programs to transfer information in units other than 512-word blocks, the Supervisor using blocks of core and drum store as buffer areas. Programs are not halted when a tape transfer instruction is given; the orders are stored in a queue in the working store, and only if direct reference is made to a block still involved in a tape transfer is a program halted. A single queue accommodates tape instructions for all eight channels which may be transferring simultaneously, and for all decks connected to these channels.

Both drums and tapes transfer words directly into the core store, and only call the Supervisor program into action when a complete block has been transferred. Other peripheral equipments, however, have a sufficiently low transfer rate to activate the Supervisor to transfer characters or groups of characters between their buffer registers and the core store. In contrast with drums and magnetic tapes, there are no naturally defined units, such as blocks, in which transfers can be made, and the overall unit of transfer is a property defined by the operating system. Whatever the operating system, however, information relating to different peripheral equipments must be separated in store and on magnetic tapes, and the natural unit of storage for this purpose is one 512-word block. However, core storage must be available to hold information currently involved in transfers and the 'lock down' of one complete block of core store for each peripheral equipment would result in gross inefficiency in the use of core store when several peripheral equipments are functioning simultaneously. The Supervisor program in the fixed store is therefore designed to read from all the input peripherals to a single block in core store, and to supply all the output peripherals from another single block. When the 'part page' allocated to any equipment is filled or emptied by the short interrupt routine controlling that equipment, an *S.E.R.* is entered to replenish the part page from a block of store held on the drum. In this way, many input and output equipments can function simultaneously, their information being held in separate blocks on the drum, and only two blocks need be maintained permanently in the core store.

The aim of the Operating System is to so organize the transfer of information between the various branches of the computing system that periods of idleness in any branch whilst it awaits completion of activities of another branch are reduced to a minimum. The operating system on Atlas comprises a series of Supervisor Extracode Routines in the main and fixed store, operating within the framework of the co-ordinator routine and using the fixed store routines to control drums, tapes and peripheral equipments; the system effectively controls the passage of jobs through the computer, organizes peripheral transfers accordingly, and communicates with the human operator when operator decisions or actions are required. The central problem confronting the operating system is that of achieving an efficient balance between parts of the system which handle information at widely differing rates. The central computer can accept or produce information at peak rates in excess of $10^6$ characters per second; magnetic tapes can transfer at rates of around $10^5$ characters per second; other peripheral equipments achieve rates of $10^3$ characters per second or less; the actions of human operators are, by comparison, very slow indeed. It should be observed that if the jobs available are all such that the central computer demands or supplies information at a rate faster than it can be accommodated by the peripheral equipments, then the central computer will remain idle awaiting peripheral transfers, no matter how efficiently the Supervisor arranges the overlap of computing with transfers. The function of the Supervisor is to achieve the maximum overlap possible consistent with the demands of the available jobs.

The most common jobs involve use of the central computer and the input and output peripheral equipments. There are three principal ways by which activity of the central computer and the peripheral equipments could be maintained. The first is by 'off-line working', in which information is supplied to and accepted from the central computer by magnetic tapes; information is transferred between tapes and peripherals as an essentially separate activity. The maximum transfer rate of information to and from the central computer is increased by this use of tapes, but is still not sufficient to meet the peak demands of the central computer. In addition, the maximum transfer rate is only achieved if information is recorded on tape in the order in which it is required by the central computer, in order to avoid loss of time in scanning the tape; efficient ordering on a magnetic tape poses a severe problem, especially if it is desired to increase effective peripheral speeds by operating several equipments in parallel. For this reason, the off-line system of operation is not standard on Atlas, although, as will be seen later, it can be accommodated by the operating system as a means of supplementing transfers through the peripherals.

The second method of operation is to reduce the peak demands of the central computer by frequent switching of control between several object programs. Assuming that the average rate of transfer through the peripherals is sufficient to meet the average demand of the central computer, then switching of control amongst the correct mix of programs should smooth out the peak transfer rates. It is, however, unlikely that the ideal mix of programs will be met; and even if a correct balance could be obtained by skilled operating methods and sophisticated computer scheduling, the operative parts of all such programs must occupy immediate access core store, in order that control should be switched frequently without incurring extra drum transfers. Inefficient use of core store is an immediate consequence of this method of operation, which was the method envisaged in early papers on 'time-sharing', and for this reason it has been rejected as a standard operating system. It is worthy of note that switching of controls between object programs inevitably implies greater use of the central computer than does switching between an object program and the Supervisor program, since object programs use common working registers, which must be preserved and restored when controls are switched. Since it is not proposed to rely upon frequent switching of controls to implement the operating system, no serious attempt has been made to reduce the object program change time by, for example, allowing only restricted use of the working registers by each program.

If the peak demand of the central computer is not to be reduced by switching of control between several object programs, the demand can only be met by passing information between the central computer and the main store, rather than directly between the central computer and peripheral equipments or magnetic tapes. This can be achieved by using parts of the core and drum store as buffers which can be emptied and filled by the central computer at computer speeds and by the peripheral equipments at peripheral speeds. These 'wells' in core and drum store should be of sufficient size to 'smooth out' the varying demands of the central computer, and the transfer rate of the peripherals which will vary due to operator intervention to reload the devices. For the sake of the present discussion, it is sufficient to assume that effectively infinite wells can be provided in main store for both input and output; a more detailed consideration of the size of these wells and their extension onto magnetic tapes will be presented later.

If it is assumed that the input and output wells are of sufficient size to accommodate the entire input and output material of a job, then during execution of the job, the central computer will not be held up. Therefore, even though the use made by one job of input and output equipment may exceed the use made of the central computer, the job will still be computer limited whilst it is using the central computer. If all jobs are of this nature, of of course, on balance, the provision of input and output wells of a sufficient size enables the jobs to be run in series, and whilst one job uses the central computer, information relating to other jobs is occupying the input and output equipment. Since peripheral equipments typically take several seconds to fill or empty one 512-word block of store, it is obvious that a reasonable size of well is sufficient to act as a buffer for peripheral equipments. The same obviously does not apply to magnetic tapes, which can transfer sixteen blocks per second on each channel. Therefore direct use of tapes by object programs is permitted and in order to maintain activity in the central computer when one job is held up awaiting tape transfers, control is switched between this job and one which is computer limited.

It would thus appear that jobs could be passed through the computer in two streams, comprising tape limited jobs and others, and within each stream the jobs could be processed in series. Input and output information can be held in the drum store thus allowing all but a small section of the core store to be available for the execution of one job from each of the two streams. This method of operation requires some modification, however, in order to accommodate long jobs using the central computer for a long period. The presence of such a job would prevent information relating to short jobs being extracted from the input well or passed to the output well, resulting in a cessation of peripheral activity through lack of space in the input well and lack of material in the output well. In addition to impairing the efficiency of the computing system, such a situation would be intolerable for the user, as it would prevent a rapid 'turn over' of short jobs. There is need therefore for a third 'stream' of jobs, namely jobs using the central computer for a long period; these jobs are not expected to share time in the conventional sense with short jobs (which are effectively computer limited) but can be interrupted to execute a sequence of short jobs in order to maintain satisfactory levels of input and output wells.

In order that the scheduling routines which comprise part of the Supervisor program should be able to assign jobs to one of these three categories, it is necessary that some information should be supplied to the computer with each job to define the job and indicate the expected behaviour. This information is supplied as input material to the computer as part of each job, and the precise form of this Job Description has been published elsewhere (Howarth et al., 1961). It includes the titles of all separate input documents required to run a job; a job may comprise several separate input documents which may be supplied to the input well through any of the peripheral devices in any order, and since each document is required to bear a title, the Supervisor is able to assemble complete jobs in the input well prior to execution. The Job Description also lists all output documents to be created, relating the logical numbers used to refer to these documents in the program to the type of equipment for which the output is intended. Similarly, the logical numbers used to refer to magnetic tapes are related in the Job Description to the titles of the tapes, which are recorded in the first block of each tape. The Supervisor program is therefore able to relate logical numbers of peripheral documents and tape reels to particular mechanisms, thus implementing indirect addressing of peripherals which is an essential feature of a time-sharing computer controlled by supervisory programs. Lastly the Job Description includes estimates of the combined core and drum store requirements, computing time, time including magnetic tape transfers, and quantity of output which are used by the Supervisor program both to assign the job to its appropriate stream and to protect the program from the effect of errors such as failure to emerge from an iterative computing loop.

The availability of the job description reduces the need for human intervention in the computing system to a minimum. Furthermore, the presence of the input and output wells enables the effect of reloading the peripheral equipment to be 'smoothed out', so that to a large measure the actions of human operators are overlapped with the functioning of the remainder of the computing system. Operator handling of magnetic tapes cannot be entirely overlapped in this manner, but the effect of delays is reduced by the Supervisor program instructing the operator to mount tapes which are listed in a Job Description before execution of the job is begun, as soon as tape mechanisms become available. Should a job require additional tapes to be mounted during its course of execution (such as a job processing a file of tape reels), the job may be held up whilst the required tape is mounted, and may be 'dumped' onto magnetic tape if main store space is required for other programs. The operating system can handle such a situation, but has been designed to reduce such interruptions to a minimum; the space occupied by a program during the execution will generally exceed the space occupied by the input material, and hence there is strong incentive to retain a job in the input well rather than to begin execution and then halt the program for an extensive period.

In the foregoing discussion, it has been assumed that main store can be set aside to provide input and output wells of a sufficient size to 'smooth out' the peak demands of the central computer. The amount of store required for this purpose will vary continually according to the available jobs, and indirect addressing of the 'one-level' store, implemented in core store by the page address registers, enable the supervisor to vary the allocation of main store continuously. Reallocation of store implies only a relabelling of blocks in the block directory rather than modifying or copying the material stored in the blocks. In spite of the ease with which store allocation can be altered, however, a finite limit is obviously set on the input and output wells by the size of core and drum store and the store required for execution of problems. The wells in core and drum store are therefore supplemented by use of system magnetic tapes, the organization of which has been described elsewhere (Kilburn *et al.*, 1961b). One tape is used to expand the input well and another to expand the output well, whilst a third, the system dump tape, acts as a general overflow for problems which are halted during execution or for material which cannot be accommodated on the system input and output tapes. The system input and output tapes are used in a systematic manner to record all input and output material and to read this material back into the main store should the space available in main store be insufficient to accommodate the entire input and output material. A single tape can be used for both reading and writing. The average supply of information to and from the wells is governed by the transfer rate of the peripheral equipments, and since the transfer rate of a magnetic tape is typically a factor of one hundred faster, time is available to search over a region of magnetic tape without impeding the transfer of information through the peripherals. There is thus a scannable area on each system tape which progresses along the tape as information is recorded on the tape, and which can be used to expand the input and output wells without excessive use of core and drum store. Typically, an input well of around eight blocks of main store will permit a scannable area of over one hundred blocks on the system input tape, and similar figures apply to the output well in main store and on the output tape. The scannable areas of the system input and output tapes are used effectively as extensions of the random-access main store; the fact that the storage is not in fact of random access is taken into account by the assembly routines of the supervisor which order transfers to and from the tapes in advance to nullify the effect of search time. If material is held up so long in the wells that it is outside the scannable region on the system tapes, either this region is increased by increasing the size of the wells in core and drum store or the excess information is recorded on the system dump magnetic tape until it can be passed through the wells.

The method of use of the system input and output tapes permits of extreme flexibility in the operating system. Information can be recovered subsequently from the system tapes, for a permanent record is retained of all input and output information. Thus, for example, repeated input of long documents through the peripherals can be avoided by recovery of the documents from magnetic tape. If desired, off-line operation can be simulated by copying all information to a magnetic tape, and subsequently reading this information from tape to the central computer or to the output equipments. Alternatively, the operating system is of sufficient flexibility to permit use of the system magnetic tapes to be dispensed with should the tape mechanisms be required for use by a problem during its execution; the system will function as described in the absence of system tapes, although, of course, efficiency may be reduced by the reduction in the effective size of the input and output wells.

The flexibility of the Supervisor program is extended by permitting requests from the human operator to change the normal course of events. As an example of such a request, the operator can afford priority to any job, ensuring the rapid passage of this job through the system even if this results in a temporary loss of efficiency. Provision is also made for control by the operator of the use made of peripheral equipments and magnetic tapes, and in particular 'remote' operating stations can be established such that jobs input through one device are output on one particular output device. The final limit of flexibility is provided by permitting, through an operator request, modification to the Supervisor program in main store. Those parts of the program called into action most frequently are held in the fixed store, but these fulfill a passive role and are controlled by routines in the main core and drum store. Changes in these routines and their associated parameters can hence alter the entire method of operation of the computing system. As an example of this flexibility, it has been possible to produce an Intermediate Supervisor for use during commissioning of the system which can occupy core store rather than fixed store and which can be used when only a minimum of core store is available. This Intermediate Supervisor comprises routines of the complete Supervisor program with the addition of only two or three hundred extra instructions. The structure of the Supervisor program thus permits of simple modification to deal with this special situation, and is obviously capable of similar modifications in the future in the light of operating experience or to meet the needs of any particular situation.

### References

1. D. J. HOWARTH, R. B. PAYNE and F. H. SUMNER (1961). The Manchester University Atlas Operating System, Part II: User's Description. *Computer J.* **4**, 226.
2. T. KILBURN, R. B. PAYNE and D. J. HOWARTH (1961a). The Atlas Supervisor. *Proc. E.J.C.C.*
3. T. KILBURN, D. J. HOWARTH, R. B. PAYNE and F. H. SUMNER (1961b). The Manchester University Atlas Operating System Part I: Internal Organisation. *Computer J.* **4**, 222.

# 16. TIME-SHARING ASPECTS OF THE STRETCH COMPUTER

## J. A. NASH

*I.B.M. United Kingdom Ltd., London, England*

### Introduction

Stretch has only one Central Processing Unit (*CPU*), and only one Instruction Counter (*IC*). In the strict sense of the words, it cannot therefore execute more than one program at once. Machines exist on which this can be done. Since there is only one Instruction Counter, a program must capture control of it in order to get anything done. Possession of the *IC* may be surrendered spontaneously by some other program, or it may be necessary to snatch control away forcibly by means of an interrupt, which is a mechanism for breaking into a program in order to perform some other urgent task. Time-sharing on Stretch is therefore some sort of battle between two or more routines, not necessarily related, for possession of the Instruction Counter. A brief description of the hardware is necessary in order to appreciate the programming aspects.

### Hardware

*1. General Layout (Fig. 1)*

The Memory Bus Control Unit (*MBCU*) is the communication centre of the whole system. The *CPU*, Core Storage, and the two input-output Exchanges are all hung on the *MBCU*. Each of these major units is autonomous and

### GENERAL LAYOUT

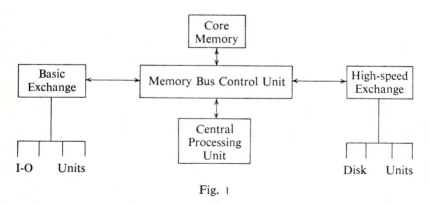

Fig. 1

proceeds independently with any task it is required to perform. Even sub-units within core storage and the *CPU* operate asynchronously. The Basic Exchange services autonomous input-output channels serving magnetic tape units, card readers, card punches, line printers, and operating consoles. The High-Speed Exchange serves autonomous Disk channels. STRETCH is thus essentially an asynchronous system. A great deal of local overlapping is built into the hardware, so that, in a sense, many circuits are 'time-shared' automatically, without any effort on the part of the programmer.

## 2. Core Storage (*Fig. 2*)

Each 16K storage box is autonomous, and has a cycle-time of 2.18 $\mu$s. Words have 64 data bits, and eight check bits, which allow automatic correction of single bit errors, and detection of double bit errors. The *MBCU* can

### CORE STORAGE

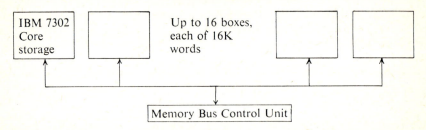

Word length: 64 data bits + 8 check bits.
Cycle time: 2.18 $\mu$s.

Fig. 2

address any box even though other boxes may be executing access cycles due to previous requests. The effective information-rate is therefore much faster than one word every 2.18 $\mu$s, and in practice storage access time is not a limitation on the speed of the system.

### CENTRAL PROCESSING UNIT

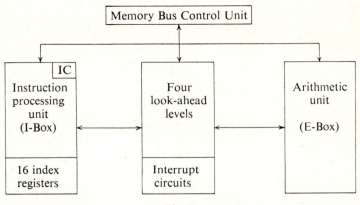

Fig. 3

### 3. Central Processing Unit (Fig. 3)

The instruction processing unit (I-box) fetches instructions from storage under control of the *IC*, and processes them ready for execution. Instructions which can be executed entirely by the I-box, e.g. index arithmetic and some branch instructions, are then completed, provided this will not upset the logic of the program. Other instructions, which require execution by the arithmetic unit (E-box), e.g. floating-point arithmetic, are passed into one of 4 levels of Look Ahead, and fetch request is sent to the *MBCU* for the data, if any. Look Ahead holds decoded instructions, together with their data, until the E-box is ready to process them, in correct logical sequence. Each of the units is autonomous, and up to 11 instructions may be in the *CPU* at any time. The interrupt circuits can break into a sequence of instructions when signals are received from various sources.

### 4. The Basic Exchange (Fig. 4)

All channels, and the Basic Exchange itself, are autonomous, and can operate simultaneously. On a tape channel, only one tape unit can be operating at any instant, but other units may be rewinding. Operators' Consoles are not intimately associated with the *CPU*, as in most computers, but are just input-output units. It is programming function to respond appropriately to signals and messages given by the operator. I/O operations are initiated by the *CPU*, and on completion of the operation, or on discovery

**BASIC EXCHANGE**

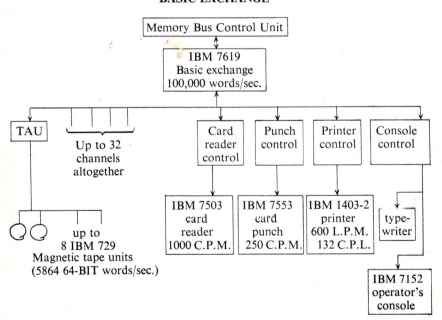

Fig. 4

of errors, signals are sent back to the *CPU* to activate the interruption mechanism. Signals can also be injected manually at each channel by the operator, to cause an interrupt.

### 5. *The High-Speed Exchange (Fig. 5)*

Only one disk unit can be operating at any instant, but others may be in the process of locating access arms to the desired track on the disk. Each disk file has two sets of access arms, one addressing odd-numbered tracks and the other even-numbered tracks. When a Locate instruction is given by the *CPU*, the appropriate arms move to the specified track, and the other arms move

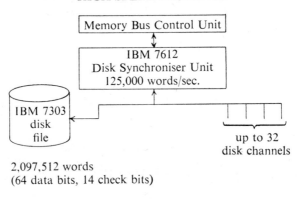

**HIGH SPEED EXCHANGE**

2,097,512 words
(64 data bits, 14 check bits)

Fig. 5

to the next sequential track. When operating, one set of arms is transmitting information while the other is automatically moving to the next track, to provide continuous operation. Programming for disk operations is rather similar to programming magnetic tape units, except for the relatively quick access to any part of the disk area. For this reason we loosely refer to the disk as an *I/O* unit, although it is really backing storage.

### 6. *The Interruption System (Fig. 6)*

The successful implementation of time-sharing depends largely on the interruption system, and it may be worth spending time on a fairly detailed description.

The *CPU* can be in one of two states—'enabled' or 'disabled'. When enabled, interruptions can occur as soon as signals are received from the source of interruption. When disabled, interruptions are inhibited, and are stacked in the *CPU* to be released in order of priority when the system is re-enabled. The instructions for enabling or disabling are Branch Enabled (*BE*) and Branch Disabled (*BD*).

Within the *CPU* there are some special registers and circuitry associated with the interrupt system. The indicator Register has 64 bits, each of which

## INTERRUPTION MECHANISM

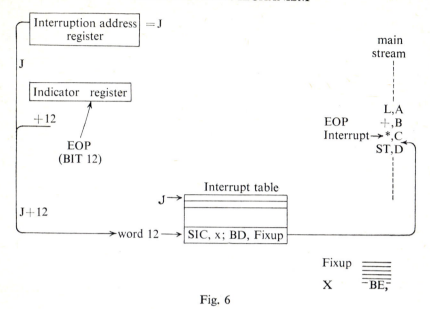

Fig. 6

reflects the state of the machine in some particular respect. The main types of indicator, in order of priority, are as follows.

1.   Machine Malfunction           l
2.   Time Signals                  l
3.   *I/O* Reject                   l
4.   *I/O* Status                   l
5.   Memory protection             l
6.   Program exception conditions  m
7.   Data Flagging                 m
8.   Arithmetic & Index Result     o

Types 3 and 4 are of particular interest for time-sharing. The *I/O* reject indicators are set on if the *CPU* sends an instruction to the exchange which cannot be accepted. This is usually the result of programming errors. The *I/O* status indicators are set on when a channel completes an *I/O* operation, to indicate to the program how that operation turned out. The most important are the Unit check indicator, which is put on when data errors or unit malfunction has occurred, End-Exception, which is put on when the unit runs out of material during the operation (Tape-mark in the case of magnetic tape); the End-of-Operation indicator is set on when the operation is completed; the Channel Signal indicator can be turned on by pressing the channel signal key at the channel concerned. The identification of the channel is entered automatically in another register at the time the *I/O* status indicators are set up.

Another special register is the 64-bit *MASK*. This register specifies whether the corresponding indicator shall be able to cause an interrupt. The bits corresponding to categories 1-5 are always masked on. Types 6 and 7 can be set by the program. Type 8 is always masked off, and can never cause an interrupt.

When an indicator is turned on, e.g. *EOP* by a tape channel successfully completing an operation, provided the system is enabled and the corresponding mask bit is set to one (for *EOP* it always will be), an interrupt occurs.

The Interrupt Address Register can be set by the program to contain the base address of a so-called 'interrupt table'. When an interrupt occurs, the instruction currently being executed is normally completed, and then the serial number of the indicator causing the interrupt is automatically added to the address contained in the Interrupt Address Register. The instruction at the resulting address is sandwiched into the program at that point. That instruction may or may not change the contents of the instruction counter.

The memory protection feature is also of interest in the context of time-sharing. The Memory Boundary Register is another special register in the *CPU*, and can be set by programming to specify the storage limits within which a given program is expected to operate. Any attempt to address storage outside that area while the system is enabled, will cause one of the memory protection indicators to be turned on. A supervisory routine can then gain control and throw the offending program off the machine.

## Software

It is quite possible to use STRETCH without any supervisory routine. However, to do so for anything but the most trivial programs involves the programmer in a massive task of housekeeping and special routines. Apart from this, between-job delays would be quite intolerable from an operational point of view. For these reasons a supervisory program is a 'must' for a system as large and complex as STRETCH.

The supervisory program provided by *IBM* for use on STRETCH is called the Master Control Program, *MCP*, which was devised and written by *IBM* in consultation with prospective users. Also part of the STRETCH Programming System are three language processors—the STRETCH Assembly Program, *STRAP*, which is a one-for-one assembler; the STRETCH Macro Processor, *SMAC*, and the *FORTRAN IV* Compiler. The processors are under the control of *MCP*. The main functions of *MCP* are (1) automatic operator; (2) job control and system supervisor; (3) system input; (4) system output; (5) operating messages; (6) simultaneous on-line utility programs; (7) input-output for the problem program (*PP*); (8) error control.

As an automatic operator, *MCP* accepts commands from the human operator, to alter its mode of operation or to perform various functions as required, e.g. to terminate the current output tape and begin a new one. In conjunction with Job Control it automatically loads jobs in sequence and types instructions and comments for the operator. As a System Supervisor, *MCP* provides the necessary system programs for each job (processors, loaders subroutines), and monitors jobs during execution, when it throws off any jobs which don't obey the rules. The System Input Program inspects the stream of information entering the system up to 20 jobs ahead, in its so-called *SCAN* phase, and passes operational requirements to the automatic operator for advance instructions to be typed. The number of jobs to scan ahead is actually a parameter within *MCP*, and can be varied to meet varying operational requirements. It also buffers the input data in the execution phase, to provide rapid core-to-core response to requests for data from user programs. The System Output Program buffers system printer and punch output on to magnetic tape, for later processing by a separate utility program. The Commentator program types messages for the operator at the request of any other part of the system or the *PP*. *MCP* allows simultaneous utility programs to be run quite separately from the rest of the system, though using *MCP* facilities. Routines for actuating *I/O* units are part of *MCP* and other programs can invoke their use by executing suitable calling sequences. The Error Control package handles all error conditions, both machine and program, and takes appropriate action. Above all, *MCP* at all times retains control of the interrupt table. When an interrupt occurs, it is *MCP*'s job to investigate it, decide who it belongs to, and transfer control appropriately.

Most of *MCP* operates asynchronously, and therefore *MCP* itself can be regarded as a number of separate, though intercommunicating routines, all time-sharing the machine. For example, the Output Program, when asked to put out some data, gathers the data into its buffers, and if a buffer becomes full, it initiates a tape write operation, using one of the actuator routines. Once this is initiated control is returned to the requesting program, which continues its operations (it might be a problem program (*PP*), or some other part of *MCP*, e.g. the logging routine). When the tape channel signals completion of the write operation by turning on the *EOP* indicator, the routine then in control is interrupted and an *MCP* program called the Receptor takes over. The Receptor receives all interrupts from *I/O* units, decides to whom they belong and the address at which that routine requires control when that particular interrupt occurs. In the present case, control would be given to a specified point in the Output program, which could then carry on with further work. When it no longer has any work to do, it gives

**ONLINE MODE**

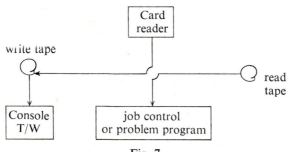

Fig. 7

control to a Return routine, also in *MCP*, which returns control to the interrupted routine.

At the *PP* level, time-sharing may be going on between *PP I/O* and computing. Simultaneous utility routines may also be time-sharing the machine for their appointed tasks.

*MCP* has three operating modes, called *ONLINE*, *OFFLINE* and *BYPASS*. In the *ONLINE* mode (Fig. 7), a card reader is the system input source. Cards are ready by the Input Program and blocked on to a magnetic tape called the *WRITE* tape. During this process, control cards at the head of each job are interpreted, and advance tape-mounting instructions are typed for the operator. All *I/O* units required by a *PP* are specified symbolically by these control cards, and the actual physical units to be allocated are decided by *MCP* depending on the availability of units and the requirements of previous jobs in the queue. Magnetic tape reels are labelled, and *MCP* checks to see the right reel is mounted. At the same time, the *READ* tape, which was earlier a *WRITE* tape, is being buffered into storage by the Input Program, and Job Control is loading jobs and giving them control in turn. There is a queue of some 10 to 20 jobs in the system at any time, waiting for execution.

The *OFFLINE* mode is similar to *ONLINE*, except that the input has been written on to tape as a separate operation by an off-line utility program, e.g. on an *IBM* 1401 (Fig. 8).

**OFFLINE MODE**

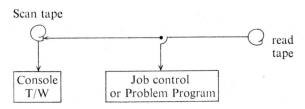

Fig. 8

In the *BYPASS* mode a card reader is the system input source. There is no overlapped scanning of the input, and cards are buffered directly into core storage. This mode is intended for use by priority programs, and effectively enables jobs entered in the *BYPASS* mode to overtake any jobs already queuing in the system in one of the overlapped modes. There is no pre-assignment of *I/O* units for *PP*'s and this mode is therefore very inefficient operationally.

Now consider what time-sharing is going on in a typical situation in the *ONLINE* mode (Fig. 9). The Input Program is time-sharing the card-to-*WRITE* tape and the *READ* tape-to-*PP* operations. The Commentator is time-sharing the typing of operator messages. The Output Program is time-sharing the writing of the output tape. The simultaneous print and punch routine is processing an output tape, previously written by the Output Program, as a totally independent, time-shared function. The *PP* is time-sharing its computation with its *I/O*, to magnetic tapes and disk.

## ONLINE OPERATIONS

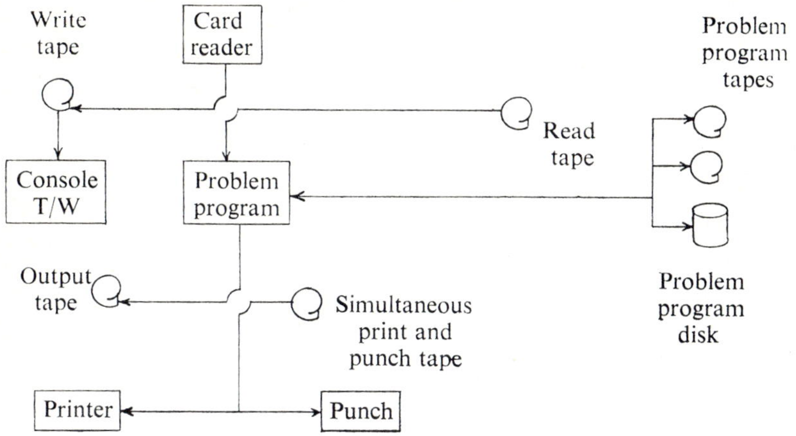

Fig. 9

It should be noted that at its present stage of development, *MCP* cannot handle comprehensive multiprogramming. Only one *PP*, or user program, can be in the execution phase at any time. Except in the limited sense of preprocessing control cards, and processing output tapes on a simultaneous basis, there is no provision in *MCP* for time-sharing between users. This does not prevent programmers from dressing up a number of logically separate programs to look like one job, to time-share their activity between them. But there is no automatic mechanism to provide user time-sharing.

Perhaps three main lessons have so far been learnt through experience with *MCP*. In its present form it may seem to some of you a rather modest and unambitious supervisory program. Nevertheless, the complexities that can arise are such that the implementation of *MCP* proved a major undertaking, although rather less than was originally estimated for the project. This indicates that the sophisticated programming systems of the future will have to be very carefully planned in order to keep cost and effort down to reasonable proportions.

Again due to the variety of interrupt situations that can occur, *MCP* spends a non-trivial percentage of *CPU* time over its housekeeping activities, saving and restoring index registers through a number of buffers, table-management, and so on. This has been done to relieve the problem programmer of the burden of doing this housekeeping himself. Such generality is bound to result in needless work being done for quite a lot of the time. With the prospect of multi-level programming, these complications will be even more acute, and it will be necessary to consider very carefully how much should be done for the user, and how much left to the user's discretion.

The third lesson we have learnt concerns the incidence of unrecoverable machine errors. In a system the size of STRETCH it can be shown on statistical grounds that at any time there is a certain number of components that have

9

failed. For example, a given small number of transistors in a STRETCH system is probably unserviceable at any particular moment. Awareness of this problem led to the inclusion of extensive error checking and correction circuits in the STRETCH system, to reduce the number of unrecoverable errors and to eliminate, as far as possible, the occurrence of undiscovered errors. When operating under *MCP*, an unrecoverable error normally means that the system has to be re-initialized when the error has been investigated and corrected. It would be extremely risky to do otherwise, since parts of the machine may have been contaminated as a result of the error. In an over-lapped mode, the operator then has quite a headache to sort out which jobs had been run and which were still waiting on the input tapes when the error occurred. This would normally take at least five minutes, and often more, to which must be added the time lost by the last job to be run, the time to initialize the system, perhaps a minute, and the time required to re-scan the jobs that had already been scanned. It is more than likely that all the tape assignments will now be different, and operators will have a jolly few minutes unloading and reloading tape reels. The total time penalty may be as much as 15 minutes of *CPU* time. To keep wastage down to acceptable limits, say 5%, this requires a mean error-free period of about 4-5 hours. This is a very stiff target to meet, from an engineering point of view, although STRETCH systems are achieving it after the initial settling-down period following installation. With more elaborate supervisors in future, it will be necessary to design them so that a minimum of time is required to sort out the debris after a machine failure, and restart the system.

REFERENCE

1. W. BUCHHOLZ (Ed.) (1962). "Planning a Computer System". McGraw-Hill, New York.

# 17. THE USE OF SYNTACTIC ANALYSIS IN COMPILERS

## D. MORRIS

*Electrical Engineering Laboratories, The University, Manchester, England*

## Introduction

Most readers will be familiar with the meta-linguistic variables and formulae used to describe syntax in the ALGOL 60 report (Backus *et al.*, 1960). The purpose of this paper is to discuss how formulae of this kind are used in compilers. Of the several compiling systems (Brooker *et al.*, 1962a, b; Irons, 1961; Gibbons, 1961; Glennie, 1960), which use the notion of meta-linguistic variables and formulae as a means of identifying the various kinds of statements (instructions or commands) which may occur in the programs to be compiled, we shall be mainly concerned with the Atlas Compiler Compiler System (Brooker *et al.*, 1962a). The meta-linguistic formulae in question describe the language implicitly by means of a set of substitutions which generate all the legal statements of the language. They are used by compilers in order to discover the sequence of substitutions which leads to each statement, and this reveals its meaning. The process is referred to as syntactic analysis.

Usually compilers based on this principle can be applied to several different languages by substituting the appropriate sets of meta-linguistic formulae. In the Atlas Compiler Compiler system these formulae are legal statements of the compiler writing language, but in some of the other systems they have to be hand coded.

## Meta-Linguistic* Formulae

The meta-linguistic formulae we are concerned with are simply a means of assigning names to semantically similar strings (i.e. concatenations) of symbols. For example, the name '*INTEGER*' might be assigned to the class of integer constants. The names are regarded as meta-variables and may appear in other strings to indicate that any of the strings with which they are associated is a permissible substitution at that point. It is therefore necessary to distinguish symbol strings representing meta-variables from symbol strings in which each symbol represents itself. The obvious solution is to enclose the meta-variable in some form of parentheses, but this implies that the opening bracket is a meta-symbol which marks the start of a meta-variable, and it cannot then be used to represent itself. In Brooker *et al.* (1962a) meta-variables are written thus [*name*] and opening brackets not used in this context are represented by the reserved name [[]. Again in this system commas are used to separate the alternative strings in a definition and [,] is reserved to represent a comma not used in this meta-sense. Following this notation we

---

\* In what follows 'meta-linguistic' will be abbreviated to 'meta'.

may now consider the definition of the class of integer constants (to which we assign the name [*INTEGER*]).

It is convenient first to define a meta-variable representing the class of decimal digits, thus:

[*DECIMAL*] = 0, 1, 2, 3, 4, 5, 6, 7, 8, 9
[*INTEGER*] = [*DECIMAL*] [*INTEGER*] , [*DECIMAL*]

This recursive definition states that an integer is either a decimal digit followed by a further integer or just a decimal digit. Thus 107 is the decimal digit 1 followed by the integer 07 which is the decimal digit 0 followed by the integer 7, which is the second kind of integer. For further examples the reader is referred to Backus *et al.* (1960) and Brooker *et al.* (1962a), but before continuing to consider how these formulae are used in syntactic analysis it is appropriate to mention two rules which they must obey if they are to be used by algorithms such as the one described below.

It will be seen that the definitions are scanned in a left to right direction and the first alternative string which is found to match the string of symbols at the head of the input stream is accepted. Hence if one alternative is a stem of another it must appear after the other. Secondly in recursive definitions some non-recursive meta-variables or symbols must appear to the left of the recursive element otherwise an endless loop would result. The following therefore are not acceptable.

[*INTEGER*] = [*DECIMAL*] , [*DECIMAL*] [*INTEGER*]
[*INTEGER*] = [*INTEGER*] [*DECIMAL*] , [*DECIMAL*]

The formulae used by Backus *et al.* (1960) do not obey these rules, but they are formulae for synthesis and not analysis.

## Implementation of Syntactic Analysis

Some schemes, for example Glennie (1960) do not employ meta-formulae directly. Instead each meta-variable is defined by means of a routine, which is coded to search for each of the symbol strings associated with that meta-variable in turn. Where the strings involve symbols the routines make the relevant comparisons with the symbols at the head of the input stream, but where they involve meta-variables the corresponding routines are called as sub-routines. Obviously the routines must have a potential for recursive use. If they are successful in the search which they carry out they will advance the pointer in the input stream and report the success to the calling routine. If they are unsuccessful this also will be reported and the calling routine will then explore the next possibility or report failure itself if the last possible string is being explored.

In contrast, other schemes (Brooker *et al.*, 1962a; Irons, 1961; Gibbons, 1961) store the meta-formulae and a single routine is used to carry out the syntactic analysis. This routine references the formulae in order to identify the symbol strings associated with the meta-variables which they define. The input parameters to this routine are effectively, the address of the formula defining the meta-variable which it is to attempt to recognize, and a pointer marking the current position in the input stream. Its output parameter is a binary variable which states whether or not the routine has recognized a string corresponding to the given meta-variable, and if it has the pointer in the input stream will have been advanced. The routines used by Brooker *et al.*, Irons and Gibbons appear to be logically similar, and only one used by Brooker *et al.* (1962a) will be described.

First we must consider how the meta-formulae are recorded in this scheme. Internally, both symbols and meta-variables are represented by integers (24 bit words on Atlas). The integers representing symbols are the actual symbol code plus a 'shift' digit and are less than 128. Meta-variables are represented by integers greater than 128, and these integers are the addresses of registers in an index which in turn contain the addresses of the corresponding definitions. Thus the definition of a meta-variable consists of one or more strings of integers which are either the values of symbols or indirectly the addresses of the definitions of other meta-variables. For reasons which will become apparent below, the strings are enumerated in natural order and this 'category number' is appended to each string. Further, if adjacent strings in a definition have a common stem the stem will only be recorded once. Thus, denoting the integer representing [INTEGER] by I and [DECIMAL] by D, and writing the category numbers explicitly, the definition given earlier for [INTEGER] would become

In order to record such definitions in a consecutive sequence of store registers a special kind of integer is used to mark branch points. It is distinguished by using as a 'flag' a digit not otherwise required. The value of such integers is the address of the last word in the branch which follows them, and the next branch follows immediately after this. In order that we may know where the last string in a definition ends, an extra branch word is placed in front of each definition 'pointing' to the last word in the definition. Denoting branch words by & and indicating the word whose address they contain by arrows, the above definition is coded as:

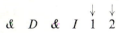

Returning to the syntactic analysis routine, this routine is entered with two parameters, namely the integer representing the meta-variable for which it is to search, and the address of the next character in the input stream. First it looks up the address of the definition of the meta-variable and sets a pointer on the first word. It also sets up a local push down list to be used when & words are encountered. Now the main loop commences. The current integer in the definition is examined and if it is an & word it goes into the push down list along with the current value of the pointer in the input stream. The pointer in the definition is then advanced and the process is repeated. If the integer is not an & word the routine next tests if it is the last word (i.e. category word) of the string. This is done by comparing its address to the last & word entered in the push down list. If these agree then the current integer is the category word and the routine ends by returning control to the place from which it was last called and reporting its success. However, if the current integer is not the last in a string, a comparison has to be made. If it represents a symbol (i.e. is <128) the comparison is made directly with the symbol at the head of the input stream. If they correspond both the pointer in the definition and the pointer in the input stream are advanced and the loop is repeated. Otherwise both pointers are reset from the last entry in the push down list and the loop is then repeated to test for the next alternative. When the push down list is empty (or contains only the first &) there are no further possibilities to explore, therefore the routine ends and reports failure. The comparison process in the case where the current integer is a meta-variable is effected by the routine calling itself recursively. In due course control will return and the routine then continues exactly as it does after the comparison of symbols.

For the purpose of extracting the meaning from a statement it is necessary to have some output from the syntactic analysis routine. It is at this point where the various schemes referred to begin to show a marked difference.

## Synthesis of Target Program

It is not within the scope of this paper to discuss fully the problem of transforming source programs into machine coding, but it is interesting to compare briefly the schemes previously referred to. Glennie (1960) and Irons (1961) appear to have produced somewhat similar solutions although the latter is interpretive. In these schemes the analysis and synthesis phases merge into one, and an output stream representing the target program is generated as the input stream is being digested.

Each meta-variable has a 'meaning' which is to be copied into the output stream each time the meta-variable occurs in the input stream. Its meaning may be expressed as a sequence of output language symbols, as a function of the recognized input symbols, or as a transformation to be carried out on symbols already in output stream.

In Brooker et al. (1962a)—Gibbons (1961) is similar—the output from the analysis phase is a 'tree' record of the statement showing which alternative form of each meta-variable in the statement on hand has occurred (i.e. its category number). Each node in this tree corresponds to a meta-variable and it contains the category number of the recognized alternative form of this meta-variable followed by the addresses of the nodes defining the meta-variables which appear on this alternative. When an alternative consists entirely of basic symbols, the category number only is recorded and this is an end node. Thus the tree record for the integer 107 analysed with respect to [INTEGER] is

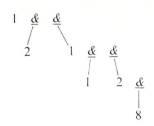

Its one dimensional layout would be

but the details of this need not concern us here, and the mechanics are described in more detail in Brooker *et al.* (1962b).

For each kind of statement in the language the user has to provide a routine for the purpose of converting the tree record for the statement into target language.

The overall structure of these routines is very similar to that of routines in other languages, e.g. FORTRAN, in so far as they consist of a sequence of instructions with a labelling system for effecting transfers of control. Whereas in 'conventional' routines, however, the types of quantity being processed are usually integers and floating point numbers, in our case the two principal types are integers and *expressions*, the latter being represented internally by trees. Integer variables are either local to the routine in which they appear and denoted by $a_1$ $a_2$ $a_3$ ..., or they are global and are denoted by $\beta_1$ $\beta_2$ $\beta_3$.... The local ones occupy space in an area of store which is used as a stack and are thus protected during recursive use of the routines. The global ones represent the index registers of Atlas, of which only the first 40 are generally available. Both kinds of integer are used for much the same purposes as integers in other languages, e.g. counting, remembering addresses, and so on; and the usual arithmetic and logical operations are available for manipulating them, or the integers in the store registers whose addresses they contain. There are, however, no formal arrays and for systematic working space (e.g. lists of labels and associated control numbers, type declarations, array dimensions) we use chained lists. In these each item occupies two consecutive store registers; the item itself being in the first word and the address of the next item being in the second word. The addresses of these lists are recorded as $a$'s or $\beta$'s, and examples of the instructions for manipulating lists are:

$$\text{add } a_4 + 10 \text{ to list } \beta_7$$
$$\text{list } a_5 = \text{list } a_{10} + \text{list } a_{11}$$

If the lists become too numerous to keep track of in the $a$ and $\beta$ registers their addresses may be stored in further lists, and in this way complicated list structures are built up.

The *expressions* with which routines are concerned are the constituent parts of the statement being translated. They are represented in the store by the tree record produced by the syntactic analysis routine, and these tree records are referred to by using the meta-variables as identifiers. The operations to be performed on expressions consist of: resolving them into their constituent sub-expressions, testing for a given alternative form of an expression, or perhaps constructing new expressions using the existing expressions as sub-expressions. Examples of the kinds of instruction available whose meanings are fairly obvious are:

$$\rightarrow 1 \; UNLESS \; [INTEGER] \equiv [DECIMAL] \; [INTEGER]$$
$$a_1 = CATEGORY \; OF \; [DECIMAL]$$
$$1)\; LET \; [INTEGER] \equiv [DECIMAL]$$

Internally the operations of this kind amount to matching trees in a topological sense, locating the top nodes of particular sub-trees, and linking incomplete tree structures to particular sub-trees.

To give a clearer picture of how this system works in practice we must consider briefly the form in which the user presents his compiler. It will consist mainly of three kinds of statements called *PHRASE*, *FORMAT* and *ROUTINE* statements. For every legal statement of the source language a *FORMAT* statement must be supplied to define its syntax (this definition is simply a string of symbols and meta-variables), and a *ROUTINE* statement must be supplied to transform its tree record into target language. The Compiler Compiler collects together all the *FORMAT* statements and assembles them as the alternative strings in the definition of a meta-variable representing the class of source statements (denoted by [SS]). The category number assigned to each alternative in this definition is the index number (i.e. indirect address) of the associated *ROUTINE*. When the Compiler Compiler is translating source program the 'master' routine calls in the syntactic analysis routine to analyse the input stream with respect to [SS]. When this routine has identified the source statement at the head of the input stream control will return to the master routine. This routine then examines the top node of the tree record to discover the category number of the recognized statement, and from this locates the routine which is to be used to translate the statement. The master routine now calls in this routine supplying it with the tree record as a parameter and the statement is thus converted to target coding. When control is returned to the master routine the process is repeated.

### Conclusions

The principal virtue which the compiling systems mentioned above have in common is that they greatly simplify the detailed coding of a compiler. Also the structure of the resulting compiler is such that to modify it to accept new or extended statements is a less hazardous undertaking than with a conventional hand coded compiler. They do nothing, however, to assist in choosing strategies for mapping the target program and its working space into the available store, or for optimizing the target program.

## REFERENCES

1. J. W. BACKUS, F. L. BAUER, J. GREEN, C. KATZ, J. MCCARTHY, P. NAUER, A. J. PERLIS, M. RUTISHAUSER, K. SAMELSON, B. VAUQUIS, J. H. WEGSTEIN, A. van WIJNGAARDEN and M. WOODGER (1960). Report on the Algorithmic Language ALGOL 60. *Numerische Mathematik* **2.**
2. R. A. BROOKER, I. R. MacCALLUM, D. MORRIS and J. S. ROHL (1962a). The Compiler Compiler. *Annu. Rev. Autom. Progr.* **3.**
3. R. A. BROOKER, D. MORRIS and J. S. ROHL (1962b). Trees and Routines. *Computer J.* **5,** No. 1.
4. A. GIBBONS (1961). Running Pegasus Autocode Programs on Mercury. *Computer J.* **3,** No. 4.
5. A. E. GLENNIE (1960). On the Syntax Machine and the Construction of a Universal Compiler. *Technical Report No. 2, Computation Center, Carnegie Institute of Technology.*
6. E. T. IRONS (1961). A Syntax Directed Compiler for ALGOL 60. *Comm. A.C.M.* **4,** No. 1.

# 18. THE ROLE OF ADDRESSING IN PROGRAMMING SYSTEMS

J. K. ILIFFE

*International Computers and Tabulators Ltd., London, England*

## 1. Introduction

One of the most important aspects of computing activity is that of ensuring that the operands of a routine are correctly situated for its use at the time it requires them. Failure in this respect is, of course, one of the main sources of programming errors. Here, as in other aspects of programming, the correct procedure to adopt is to follow a well-defined set of rules designed to minimize such errors. The rules may form part of the programming system, or they may be built into the hardware of a machine. In either case, in what follows they will be termed *addressing rules*.

A simple addressing rule, for example, would be to assign a fixed location number $L(x)$ to each variable $x$ occurring in a routine. Whenever the value of $x$ was required as an operand, use of location number $L(x)$ would be sufficient to call it out of storage. Whilst this rule is satisfactory for elementary routines and simple operating systems, it is well known that it fails to meet present-day requirements for a number of reasons. Amongst these are the fact that a routine may be written to operate on blocks of data of varying size, in which case an efficient assignment of location numbers may become difficult; another problem is that most routines are written to be run in conjunction with a set of independently written routines, where a feasible assignment of location numbers for one routine may conflict with one or more of the others.

Independence of location number assignment in programming is achieved to a greater or lesser extent by the use of symbolic references to operands. In its simplest application, this is no more than a means of delaying the actual assignment of location numbers until the routine is read into the machine for execution. More generally, the assignment may be delayed even up to the point in time immediately prior to the use of the specific operand.

In discussing addressing, therefore, a problem of translation may be involved, and care must be taken to distinguish the form taken by a reference at various stages of the translation. We shall term a symbolic reference as used by the programmer a *name*; a reference as it appears in a routine held in store and awaiting execution will be called a *routine address*; the actual information sent to a memory bank to enable it to read out a particular operand is the *location number*.

The class of addressing rules we seek defines a translation from a name to an operand. In the following section on Symbolic Addressing, the desirable properties of names are discussed. In Section 3 a variety of devices for passing from a routine address to an operand is examined: these, of course, are generally understood to be part of the 'hardware' addressing facilities of a machine. Given the general requirements of naming systems, and a range of possible tools, we then proceed to discuss in Section 4 a variety of addressing rules which have been, or might be, exploited.

## 2. Symbolic Addressing

### 1. Program Structures

The use of a name for an operand has two distinct interpretations. It may denote a location number by immediate substitution, as in fact we might imply in our previous example by writing down the symbolic addresses '$L(x)$', '$L(y)$', etc., wherever reference to $x$ or $y$ was implied. In this context, it becomes meaningful to use a variant of the symbol, e.g. '$\#L(x)$', meaning the integer location number associated with $x$, and to use this in arithmetic operations, e.g. '$\#L(x) + 2$', to derive in effect further location numbers of data. More generally, however, immediate substitution is impossible since $\#L(x)$ may in fact vary without the knowledge of the programmer, and consequently only restricted forms of address arithmetic are possible. The second interpretation of a name is independent of the location number concept, and here it is used merely to denote an operand whose value is to be substituted for the name upon *execution* of the expression in which the name appears.

Unless stated otherwise, we shall consider names from the second point of view. This is obviously more satisfactory when the needs of problem-oriented languages are taken into account, since it avoids the introduction of a concept foreign to the problem. Only when the problem-oriented language falls short of the ideal is it necessary to introduce the idea of a location number.

In a program written in symbolic code, the obvious intent in using a name '$A$' is to denote the current value of the same operand $A$ upon executing various parts of the program. This apparently simple requirement has, however, been found to fail in only moderately complex programming situations. One common cause of failure, for example, is that a program may be written by several individual coders, who must be protected from using the same name for different operands. Another, less serious, difficulty is that different names may be used, on occasion, for the same operand. In fact, we are quite short of names, and want to use them as efficiently as possible.

It has therefore become necessary to look at the program as a whole, and give rules for determining the extent of text over which a name may be assumed to refer to the same operand: such text is called the 'scope' of the name of ALGOL terminology. Clearly the rules which are given must introduce as few arbitrary boundaries in the text as possible, and one looks to see what natural divisions of the text can be used for this purpose.

The most natural boundaries to choose are those of the routines which may be embedded in the program text: natural because they are usually very clearly marked, because they define logical units at least partly independent of the rest of the text, and because they depart from the sequential ordering of execution which is normally implicit in the text as written. The routine boundaries are indeed chosen as scope delimiters in most programming systems; in ALGOL a finer scope structure is chosen, down to the level of *blocks* within routines (procedures). The latter extension has few advantages, and will not be discussed further here since it has no new implications in the problem of addressing.

A peculiar property of many logical units of a program text, however, is that they themselves may contain instances of similar logical units, and so on *ad infinitum*. This is true of routines, which may contain subroutines, etc. Having decided on using routine boundaries as scope delimiters, the problem arises: should the scopes of names be nested one within another in the same way as routines, or should we accept only the highest level routines for the purpose of defining scope? For practical purposes, it should be remembered that we rarely want to go to a depth beyond one or two routines, so the choice is not of major importance. One would be tempted, therefore, to choose the ruling with the greater mathematical nicety, and this in fact is what has been done in ALGOL. In FORTRAN II, on the other hand, only a single depth of routines is allowed and hence scopes are not nested.

Obviously, it is not sensible to cut through all scopes at every routine boundary since the continuity in meaning of names is necessary to give coherence to the program as a whole. One must distinguish, therefore, at (say) the *entry* to a routine, just those names whose scopes are bounded at that point and, by implication, at the corresponding *exit* point of the routine: the remaining names have continuity of meaning through the routine boundary. Such distinctions may be made by implication in a particular programming system, often supplemented by declarations at the beginning of the routines. We shall not detail here any particular methods of giving this information: once aware that they exist, it is usually easy to spot them.

Again adopting ALGOL terminology, we shall say that if the scope of a name $A$ extends to the boundaries of routine $R$ but not beyond them, then $A$ is *local* to $R$. Within the text of $R$ there may be a subroutine $Q$: if $A$ occurs in $Q$ and the scope of $A$ extends from $R$ into $Q$, then $A$ is non-local to $Q$; on the other hand, $A$ may not occur in $Q$, or it may be defined as local to $Q$, and hence distinct in meaning from the name $A$ local to $R$.

Once the extent of text over which a name has a consistent meaning has been defined, there is usually no need to retain the program text in its original form. For further discussion it will be convenient to detach it into its separate routines, and consider the properties of a typical one of these, $R$. From what has been said already, it should be clear that any name appearing in the program text is local to one and only one routine.

Let $R$ contain the local names $R_1$, $R_2$, . . ., $R_n$. Any of these, say $Q$, may stand for a routine with local names, $Q_1$, $Q_2$, . . ., $Q_m$. Let us suppose, moreover, that the name of a routine is always local to the routine in which it is immediately enclosed. In this case, the name relationships in a program can be represented in the form of a tree (Fig. 1) in which each routine name represents a node from which grow branches corresponding to its local names. The value of this Figure is that it indicates exactly those operands which may be referred to in a given routine: namely those local to the routine, or accessible to it in the tree by downward and horizontal paths only, with the proviso that if any name is encountered two or more times in this process, then the first occurrence is always taken to define the name. In the Figure, reference in $Q$ may be made only to operands named in the following set:

$$\mathbf{Q_1, Q_2, \ldots, Q_m, R_1, R_2, \ldots R_n, T_1, T_2,} P \qquad (2.1)$$

e.g. not to $\mathbf{U_1}$ or $\mathbf{U_2}$. The set of names which have meaning within a routine will be termed its *context*.

Our discussion so far has been based on the 'static' program description. It is well known that certain local names in a routine are not used to denote the same operands at all times, but are destined to be given meaning each time the routine is *activated*: these are the *parameter names*. In general they are defined by the calling routine, which gives an expression to be evaluated each time the parameter value is required—some important subclasses of definition exist ('call by value', 'call by simple name'), but in the interest of generality we shall consider only parameters defined by expressions in the context of the calling routine. Other names denote not operands but *functions* which are to be used in obtaining the value of an operand. The representation of a function is a routine either in the same program or in an assumed 'library' of common routines. A function name may also be a parameter name.

The difficulties raised by parameters and functions are, of course, aspects of the same problem: the dynamic sequencing of program execution. Only rarely does the static program description bear any similarity to the hierarchy of routines which is built up during the process of applying a program.

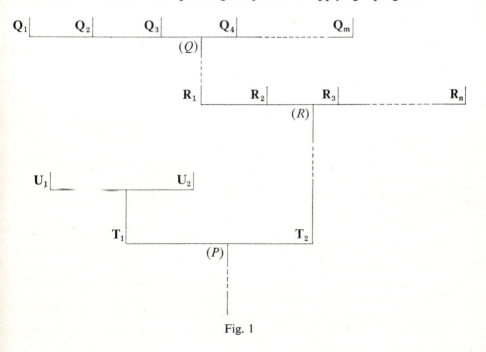

Fig. 1

Consider, for example, a situation in which $Q$ is active (Fig. 1). The context (2.1) is defined, and we may envisage a situation in which from within $Q$ the routine $T_1$ is activated, its parameters being defined by means of expressions in context (2.1), and control passes to to $T_1$. At this point, the context becomes:

$$\mathbf{U}_1, \mathbf{U}_2, \mathbf{T}_1, \mathbf{T}_2, P \tag{2.2}$$

Thus execution of $T_1$, whilst normally based on (2.2), may involve reference to (2.1) whenever a parameter is called for. Clearly, one of the $\mathbf{Q}_i$, $i = 0$, $1, \ldots, m$ may itself be a parameter of $Q$, so a further change of context may be required when evaluating a parameter expression, and so on.

The situation is still further complicated by the fact that $Q$ may directly or indirectly activate itself. In our example, $T_1$ may activate $T_2$, and thence $R$ and $Q$. One might ask, on entering $Q$ for the second time although the first activation of $Q$ is not completed: are the variables local to $Q$ to retain their values from the first activation, or should they be defined anew? A case may be made for either ruling, depending on the intentions of the programmer, and the greatest generality is achieved by partitioning the local variables into two groups: those whose identity is preserved through all activations of the routine (the **own** variables of ALGOL), and those which are redefined on each activation.

It remains to be said, when working in a given context, which activation of the routines defining the context should determine the variables referenced at a given time. When a routine $R$ is activated from a context C, it should be clear from our previous remarks that a new context $C^R$ is determined, comprising a subset $\mathbf{C}$ of C plus the local variables of $R$. The activations referred to in $\mathbf{C}$ are by definition the same as those referred to in the corresponding portion of C; this activation of $R$ creates a new set of non-own variables, which is destroyed when the corresponding termination of $R$ is encountered. With this information, and an initial context $C^0$ which is supplied by the programming system, it is possible to follow through a program and determine without ambiguity the correct context at any point in time.

## 2. *Data Structures*

A brief note should be made of the logical structure of data which is used in a programming system. Whereas the complexities of program structure generally derive from the requirements of scientific systems, complications in data structure derive from commercial demands or, quite often, from system programmers themselves.

Elementary operands are defined as numbers, words, character fields, etc. These may be grouped together to form *records*. Records may also include other records. Thus a name $A$ within a routine may denote a single elementary operand, or a set of elementary operands and records. Some operations may be performed on $A$ as a whole. Others require access to individual items within $A$; this may be achieved either by naming them and using an appropriate *compound name* in the routine ('*AGE OF EMPLOYEE*' etc.), or by using a suitable numerical index system ('A$_i$' etc.). The first method involves some elaboration of the idea of a context as developed above. Either can be considered as extensions of the tree referencing system (Fig. 1) allowing restricted paths to be taken *up* the branches as well as down.

Unlike routines, data structures may vary quite freely during the execution of a program. Records of various sizes may, for example, be read from a file on magnetic tape, and some means must be provided for detecting whether or not the last item in a record has been processed or not. This leads us to note, in passing, that actually naming an operand is not the only way of referring to it, for when the data possesses a certain structure one may obtain an operand by specifying its position in the structure relative to that of another item: indexing may be taken as an example of such referencing, and the various operations of list processing yield further examples. One must distinguish rather carefully, however, between referencing based on the logical data structure, and that based on the memory structure on which a program is realized. For obvious reasons, the first has a certain invariance, or is under control of the programmer, whilst the second is under control of the operating system and may vary arbitrarily during the course of a program.

Much of data processing is concerned with transmitting data from one medium to another, often with a change in structure. The programming system may require this to be done entirely by writing the appropriate routines, or by allowing the use of *data descriptions* which are used by the compiler and possibly by the operating system whilst a program is running. The latter possibility seems to be generally more satisfactory, since data structures are often the most fluctuating parts of the problem.

### 3. The Operating System

A complete problem description generally consists of a program, a set of data descriptions, and a set of data. The regime under which these three items are processed constitutes the operating system of a machine. Fig. 2a illustrates the flow of information we have in mind, when the operating system is conceived as one with the machine. This simple picture, however, is the source of many troublesome requirements of an addressing system.

For in most programming languages the degree of complication is such that an initial phase of program translation is necessary: certainly the names must be translated into routine addresses. The translation may or may not involve the data descriptions. This scheme is represented by Fig. 2b, in which 'translation' and 'execution' are two separate processes, probably on the same machine. Typically, program text is supplied to the translator, data is supplied to the executive machine, and data descriptions may be supplied to both. It now becomes an objective of system design to minimize the total time spent in the translation phase of any one program, including reruns due to program errors, changes in the problem requirements, and so on. The horns of this dilemma are quite well known: a fast compiler produces a slow-running object program, and vice versa. One way towards a more efficient operating system is to segment the translator into a number of separate stages which follow one another, such that those parts of the problem description most likely to be subject to variation are only taken into account at the later stages of translation. In this way, a minor change in the problem may involve only repeating part of the translation, or repeating the translation for only part of the problem.

This is the situation in the scheme based on a loading routine (Fig. 2c). Here the program is segmented into routines which are translated separately,

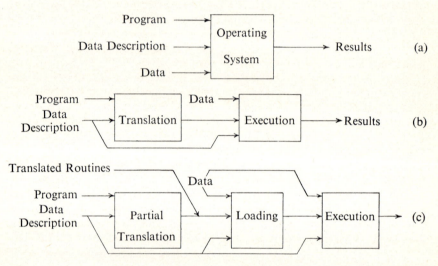

Fig. 2. Elementary operating systems.

but combined together by a loading routine immediately prior to execution. One of the main tasks of the loader is to establish the correct context, in the sense discussed above, for each routine as it is loaded. We shall return to this problem in Section 4.

To summarize our findings up to this point, we may say that the use of a name in a program text has been found to involve following certain rules which determine its scope. Conversely, within any routine of the program a certain set or context of meaningful names is defined. When a routine is obeyed, one must be sure to establish the correct context for each routine, which means, when recursive use of routines is involved, establishing reference to the correct variables in each activation of each routine. Use of a name may involve not only direct reference to an operand, but also reference through a data structure along a path chosen by one or more modifiers of the name (which may themselves be named); or reference to an expression (parameter) which is to be evaluated in another context, or again, reference to a procedure (function) whose evaluation will eventually lead to the value of the desired operand. Finally, any chosen realization of names must allow for the types of modification which are most frequently made in programs or data descriptions. Before examining possible solutions to these problems, we must examine the techniques at our disposal.

### 3. Routine Addresses

Some years ago, in order to refer to a certain item of data in memory it was considered sufficient to allow the programmer to place a location number in the instruction word of his program. In our sense, the routine address was identical with the location number. That these days are past is not so much due to the demands of symbolic addressing outlined in the last Section as to the observed patterns of access to storage in a large selection of programs during execution. A major question, which remains largely unanswered at present, is the extent to which patterns of access to storage have changed as the result of the growth of symbolic programming techniques, either because of the change in style of translated programs, or because of the demands of the translators themselves. In spite of changes in demand, however, the basic economics of storage which have dominated computer design in the past seem likely to do so in the future, so we shall continue to be faced with realizing a problem description on a hardware configuration which is at first sight ill-adapted for this purpose.

Let us list, first of all, some of the forms which a routine address may have.

*1. Implicit Address*

Certain functions of the machine involve registers which are not explicitly given in an instruction. For example, the Accumulator in a single address machine, or certain Indicator registers.

*2. Truncated Address*

The full range of location numbers may demand a field length of 15 or more bits to specify an operand. Part of the store can be addressed by a shorter field if an assumption is made concerning the value of the missing bits. Locations 0–31 of the store may be addressed through 5 bits, for example, if the remaining bits are always assumed to be zero.

*3. Relative Address*

A routine address may be added to a pre-assigned 'base address' in order to determine a location number. This technique is often combined with method 2.

*4. Modified Address*

This is similar to the relative address, except that the base address is contained in a modifier register (B-register, index register) selected by part of the routine address. A variant of this technique places the base address in the instruction and the relative part in the modifier register.

*5. Block Address*

This is similar to truncated addressing, but the high order bits of the location are obtained from a register selected by a block number, which is given as part of the routine address.

## 6. Detached or Indirect Address

A routine address may be used to indicate a register whose content is to be used as a routine address. A B-modifier used alone is a special instance of a detached address. The facility may be extended to any register in the machine.

## 7. Immediate Address

The routine address, or part of it, may be used 'immediately' as an operand.

## 8. Associative Address

This is the only instance in which the location selected depends on the value of its content. In an associative memory, input of a bit pattern and a mask results in the selection of one or more locations in which the stored information coincides with the given pattern in the positions determined by the mask. Such a memory is potentially very useful in certain applications, but it has not yet reached the point of large scale economic use. The Atlas page-address registers may be regarded as a very special form of associative memory, although in this case the output is a selected location number.

*          *          *          *

Thus the object of machine addressing, which is to determine an operand from a routine address, is pursued in a variety of combinations of *addition* and *substitution* operations; the sequence of operations may be fixed rigidly in the hardware of a computer, or it may be allowed to vary according to information found in routine addresses. In the latter case, this information must indicate whether the present routine address gives the operand, or the location number of the operand, or whether it is to be used to give a new routine address. As usual, the penalty of increased flexibility is the provision of selection bits in the routine address, but this is a cost which it has been found increasingly worthwhile to pay. On the other hand, machine addressing systems which require appreciably more time than a single main memory cycle to obtain an operand require careful justification.

We may distinguish trends in machine addressing systems towards four main objectives, to which we shall return in Section 4 when we examine overall system requirements. These trends are as follows.

1. To increase the 'information content' of an address, and hence the efficiency of instructions.

2. To increase the mobility of programs, so that storage allocation is simplified.

3. To allow efficient use to be made of the more expensive (i.e. high speed) parts of the store.

4. To permit flexible communication links to be set up between routines and data.

Problems of economy in storage have led to many further complications in machine addressing. We have already noted that a given range of location numbers may cover different levels of store of varying access speeds. There may in addition be different location numbering systems associated with different categories of storage (e.g. B-register number 3 and location number 3 may mean different registers in the same machine). One of the greatest problems is that part of the storage system may not be directly addressable, and the efficiency of a problem realization which exceeds the capacity of addressable store then depends critically on the way transfers of information to and from the 'backing store' are organized. Such transfers are generally restricted to blocks of words: the longer the block length the less time, per word, is spent in the mechanics of arranging for data transfers to take place, but the more difficult becomes the problem of efficient use of store.

In contemporary machines, the addressing system must also permit the addressable store to be shared by several activities (programs, backing store transfers, peripheral transfers, etc.) at once, and prevent one activity from interfering with another. This can be achieved either by 'locking in' each activity to its own region of store or 'locking out' each activity from all others —a combination of the two methods may be used. In practice, therefore, any location number obtained during machine addressing may be subject to one or more comparisons with boundary markers before it can be used, and a number of high-speed registers must be deployed to contain the location numbers limiting the regions into which the store is divided.

To summarize the present position in machine addressing, we have noted that a series of memory devices of increasing size but decreasing speed is likely to remain the most efficient basis for a computer store. In the past, order codes have been arranged so that the hand coder could take maximum advantage of the different levels of store. More recently some of the high speed registers have been used for specialized purposes such as lock-out registers, block or page-address registers, and so on. As computer programs increase in size and complexity more and more of the storage allocation problem will have to be handed over to the programming system. The problems which will have to be solved automatically relate to the use of high-speed registers, the presentation of a core store and one or more levels of backing store as an effective 'single level store', and the mutual protection of several activities using the store simultaneously.

### 4. Translation Processes

Let us formalize the system of names used in a program $P$ in the following way. Let $R$ be a routine in $P$. Denote by $\mathbf{R}$ its set of local names, i.e. $\mathbf{R}_1$, $\mathbf{R}_2$, . . ., $\mathbf{R}_n$, where $n$ is a number dependent on $R$. Let the first $l(0 \leqslant l \leqslant n)$ of these names stand for parameters, and let the next $m(0 \leqslant l + m \leqslant n)$ stand for non-own variables; the remainder (if any) stand for own variables.

Let $R$ be local to the routine $\lambda R$, i.e. $R$ is a name in the set $\lambda \mathbf{R}$; more strongly, assume that $R$ is an own variable name in $\lambda \mathbf{R}$. Further assume the name $\lambda R$ is local to $\lambda(\lambda R) = \lambda^2 R$, and so on. Then the context of names defined in $R$ consists of the union of sets:

$$\mathbf{R}, \lambda \mathbf{R}, \lambda^2 \mathbf{R}, \ldots, \lambda^k \mathbf{R} \tag{4.1}$$

where $\lambda^k R$ is the highest level routine in $P$.

In general, corresponding to each routine $R$ and set $\mathbf{R}$ of local names there will at any time be defined a series of sets of operands, each corresponding to one of the current activations of $R$. The number, $h$, of such sets depends not only on $R$ but also on the time at which this observation is made. These sets of operands will be denoted by $\omega^{(1)}\mathbf{R}, \omega^{(2)}\mathbf{R}, \ldots, \omega^{(h)}\mathbf{R}$. Each set has the same number of elements, and we know (by definition), that the operands corresponding to the subsets of own variables are identical between any two sets in the series. Since similarly defined sets exist corresponding to each activated routine, the actual operands corresponding to the context (4.1) of a particular activation of $R$ can be described as the union of the following sets:

$$\omega^{(j_0)}\mathbf{R}, \; \omega^{(j_1)}\lambda\mathbf{R}, \; \omega^{(j_2)}\lambda^2\mathbf{R}, \ldots, \; \omega^{(j_k)}\lambda^k\mathbf{R} \qquad (4.2)$$

where the index $j_i$ selects the particular set of operands corresponding to $\lambda^i\mathbf{R}$ at this time.

When $R$ calls a new routine, it must be a member of one of the sets in (4.1), say $T$ in $\lambda^i\mathbf{R}$, $0 \leqslant i \leqslant k$. When control is transferred to $T$ the new context of names will be

$$\mathbf{T}, \lambda^i\mathbf{R}, \lambda^{i+1}\mathbf{R}, \ldots, \lambda^k\mathbf{R} \qquad (4.3)$$

Corresponding to these are the operands

$$\omega^{(h')}\mathbf{T}, \; \omega^{(j_i)}\lambda^i\mathbf{R}, \; \omega^{(j_{i+1})} \lambda^{i+1}\mathbf{R}, \ldots, \; \omega^{(j_k)}\lambda^k\mathbf{R} \qquad (4.4)$$

i.e. a new set of operands $\omega^{(h')}\mathbf{T}$ is activated for $\mathbf{T}$, and the operands common to the contexts of $T$ and $R$ are retained.

When $T$ calls for parameters defined by $R$, reference is made to an expression using terms in the sets (4.2). When $T$ terminates, the context (4.1) of R is re-assumed, with the operands (4.2). It should be noted that although $T$ cannot change directly any operand named in the sets $\mathbf{R}, \lambda\mathbf{R}, \ldots, \lambda^{i-1}\mathbf{R}$, (since it has no name for them), it may change the values of operands named by $\lambda^i\mathbf{R}, \lambda^{i+1}\mathbf{R}, \ldots, \lambda^k\mathbf{R}$, an effect which may or may not be considered desirable ('side-effect' in ALGOL).

The discussion in Section 2 showed that each defined operand may be an 'elementary' item of data, or a structured piece of information with named sub-items or numerically indexed lists of sub-elements. With regard to the 'fine structure' of elementary operands, we remark that once a word has been read from memory, an item of data may be retrieved from this by further manipulation. Some machines include special functions in the order code for packing and unpacking data and addressing sub-elements of words. Analysis of such operations is beyond the scope of this discussion, which is primarily aimed at giving rules for deriving, from a name, single word units of information from storage. We have to take some account, however, of the extent to which data structures may vary during the course of a calculation.

The foregoing paragraphs set out the broad requirements of a naming system. We shall now discuss various aspects of its realization on the machine configurations of Section 3, and consider what modifications to our general requirements are necessary to attain efficient program execution.

## 1. Mapping onto Addressable Store

Consider the execution of routine $R$, with defined operands (4.2). Suppose that the addressable store is sufficient to contain representations of most, if not all, of the operands in the context of $R$. If the store is composed of several units of differing access times, the problem arises of how to dispose the operands of $R$ in the best possible way in the store. More exactly, we may state this requirement as that of minimizing the contribution to program running time in a certain time interval, arising from accesses to the store in the same interval. Efforts to solve this problem depend very much on the chosen time interval; it may be a fixed period in the activity of a machine, or the time devoted to executing $R$, or the total time of program execution for a given set of data, or the time accumulated in translating $R$ and running it for many sets of data with certain characteristics. The basic information necessary to formulate a solution is the sequence of access to operands over the chosen time interval.

In FORTRAN, for example, much effort might be spent in optimizing the use of B-registers over the execution time of a given program. The necessary basic information is derived in part from an analysis of the program and partly from extra statements which may be made by the programmer; assuming the accuracy of this information, effectively optimized programs may be generated. On enlarging the time interval of optimization to cover the compilation time as well, it has often been found that gains in execution time have been more than offset by the increased time of compilation.

Another device which has been used when a small number of fast registers is involved is to name these and include them as own variables local to the highest level routine in the program (Ref. 1). This technique applies only to single word operands. In this way the task of optimizing is left in the hands of the programmer, though he is still free to use problem-oriented input languages. The difficulty of introducing fast-register names local to any but the highest level routine is that the task of saving and restoring them when control is switched from one routine to another can easily annul any speed advantage gained from their use.

One is frequently asked: given a machine with a main core memory but with an additional memory of, say, $\frac{1}{10}$ the access time, how much fast memory should be at the disposal of a compiler? It is probably fair to say that without outside help the number of fast registers a compiler can use efficiently for named operands is quite small. Allocation within a short series of statements is comparatively easy and pays good returns with up to four or five words of fast store; allocation over loops and between different routines requires much more work and often involves placing undesirable restrictions on the source language. An average compiler would find six to ten fast registers all it could cope with. The fact remains that a good programmer can make effective use of many more fast registers in certain classes of problem, and if a machine has them he should not be prevented by the source language from using them. The technique of including them in the local names of the highest level routine is to be recommended.

One aspect of machine addressing systems that is not desirable from the point of view of translation is the possibility of two or more different ranges of location numbers. We have already noted three distinct classes of local variables: if each of these can be translated into several classes of storage, compilation quickly becomes intolerably complicated. The ideal addressable store is given by a single unbroken range of location numbers, a part of which, at least, may correspond to a series of fast access registers.

## 2. Mapping onto an 'Apparent' Single Level Store

If addressable store is insufficient for a complete problem representation use must be made of a suitably sized backing store of drums, discs, etc. As in the case of optimization of high speed store, there are three main lines of attack on the problem associated with a backing store.

(i) Structural, i.e. by building into the source language commands to be used by the programmer for transferring data to the addressable store.

(ii) Analytical, i.e. by allowing the translator to examine the flow of the program and make the decisions on where transfers should be made. As with other analytical methods, this demands for success either complete and accurate information on a problem or a series of lucky guesses, neither of which can be guaranteed to a programmer.

(iii) Dynamic, i.e. the assignment of transfers as they are required during the running of a program. This may hold up the program, but if another can be run until the transfer is completed the actual time wasted may be negligible.

Most first generation programming systems make structural provision for organizing transfers of information to and from backing stores. Present trends of large machine systems indicate that even if a programmer can confidently predict the storage demands of his own program, it will be executed in conjunction with others of which his knowledge is zero. Clearly, if efficient storage control is to be attained over a mixture of programs sharing a machine, the only possible source of control is the supervisor program. The philosophy of dynamic storage allocation has been adopted on many machines of the present generation, an example being the Ferranti Atlas, where the page-addressing system is specifically designed to allow flexible allocation of space over drum and core stores (Ref. 2).

There are two primary requirements of dynamic storage allocation schemes: (a) that from a routine address it should be quickly deducible whether an operand is in (say) core or drum store; (b) that the information representing a program should be partitioned into sections which can easily be relocated individually to any part of the store, without causing major re-addressing operations to take place. Requirement (b) finally removes the possibility of location numbers being used as routine addresses: at least one stage of addition or replacement is essential, and at the same time a check can be made in the presence of the operand in core store. If it is present, the program should proceed with no appreciable loss of time; if it is not, a transfer of the data from backing store must be arranged.

We noted earlier that the time taken by a backing store transfer can be reclaimed by switching control to another program or another part of the same program. The time taken to organize the transfer, i.e. finding vacant space in the core store, which may involve reorganizing data in the core or transferring data from core to drum, represents a positive loss in computation time which must be balanced against overall system efficiency. A division of the store into blocks of fixed length seems to offer the best possibility for organizing inter-level transfers efficiently.

An alternative division of the store, based on the natural lengths of blocks into which representations of routines and data fall, has been implemented (Ref. 4). The advantage of this technique is that it makes for efficient packing of core store, and it solves at the same time some of the problems associated with storage maps (see (*4.4*), below).

### 3. Reservation and Lock-out

It was noted above (*4.2*) that between a routine address and the corresponding location number at least one substitution or addition must take place if a routine is relativized, and at the same time a check may be made on the presence of the operand in addressable store. It is possible to make further tests at this point to ascertain that protected regions of store are not being violated.

Storage protection schemes fall into two main groups: 'block reservation' and 'limit register'. In a store organized for coping with dynamic storage allocation problems, the blocks into which the store is divided may be individually protected at the expense of one bit in the word through which the block is addressed, and sufficient hardware to detect its status. In the case of fixed length blocks, choice of a length which is some power of 2 automatically (in a binary address) avoids the possibility of exceeding the limits of the block. In the case of variable block sizes, having selected a block and checked that its use is permitted, a further check must be made to ensure that the element selected lies within the block: comparison of an index value with a given block length is implied.

In the absence of a given storage block structure, limit registers may be used to indicate which storage areas are within bounds. These are pieces of hardware which are liable to be expensive, and once again complete generality must be relaxed in order to get an economical system. Ideally, one would like to have *available* to a routine those parts of store occupied by its operands (e.g. corresponding to (4.2)), *less* those regions engaged at any time in other activities with higher priority, e.g. drum and peripheral transfers. In practice, a routine may only have a single reserved region available (into which (4.2) must be mapped), and a fixed number of limit registers which can be used to lock out subsidiary regions involved in other activities. If the latter are insufficient, either the routine must be held up, or the activity can proceed at the programmer's risk, or the supervisor may be able to allocate space to the activity outside the reserved region.

Obviously there are various *degrees* of protection which can be offered by the programming system. The minimal practical requirement is that a routine should not interfere with the supervisor itself. Beyond that, it should not be able to refer to **any operands** outside the program in which it is used. More strongly, it should not be able to refer outside the operands (4.2) defined by its context.

There is, however, an even stronger possible degree of protection. For within (4.1) we can list (at translation time) all operands which are *actually* referred to by $R$ (this is normally a proper subset of the context of $R$) and arrange that reference to any other operand is impossible. This strong form of protection is in some respects the easiest to effect, for one can guarantee *during translation* that certain routine addresses refer during execution to operands known to be present (i.e. guaranteed by the supervisor) in specific parts of the store. This is particularly true of simple operands and known elements in arrays of known structure (e.g. $A_{3,4}$ in a $10 \times 20$ matrix A): it is not possible when unknown data structures are involved, or when named subscripts are used (e.g. $A_{i,j}$). Similarly, the assembly of a routine generally ensures that control cannot pass accidentally outside the routine area and further hardware checks on the content of the control register are superfluous (except in the case of transfer through a 'switch vector'). This type of protection has long been an implicit benefit from symbolic assembly systems: its potential application in overall system design has perhaps been neglected when considering protection problems in time-sharing machines.

## 4. Storage Maps

We return to the problem of representing the operands of a routine $R$ in what appears, at least, to be a homogeneous, random access, store. Let $\Pi$ denote at a given time the totality of operands defined in a program. Of $\Pi$, the sets:

$$\alpha = \bigcup_{i=1}^{h} \omega^{(i)}\mathbf{R} \text{ where } h = h(R)$$

and

$$\beta = \bigcup_{i=0}^{k} \omega^{(i_i)} \lambda^i \mathbf{R},$$

constitute subsets. Here $\alpha$ denotes the union of local operands of each current activation of $R$, and $\beta$ denotes, as in (4.2), the context of operands defined in a given activation of $R$.

Our discussions have shown that when control passes from $R$ to a new routine $T$, a new set of operands local to $T$ is defined. Hence, from (4.4):

$$\Pi' = \Pi \cup \omega^{(h')}\mathbf{T} \tag{4.5}$$

When $T$ terminates, we have:

$$\Pi'' = \Pi \tag{4.6}$$

Clearly, therefore, $\Pi$ can be represented as an expanding and contracting list of operands in which items are only added and deleted from one end. Provided, once defined, operands do not vary in structure, it is then possible

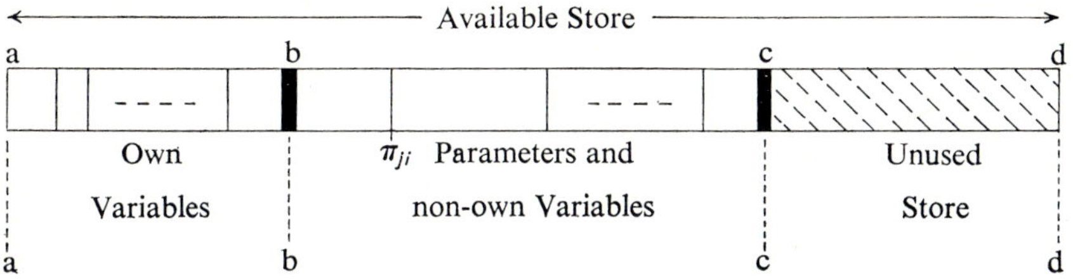

Fig. 3.  Stack organization.

to represent $\Pi$ in store by the familiar 'push-down' list or 'stack' (Fig. 3). We note that own variables local to R are common to all the sets $\omega^{(i)}R$, and hence may be stored more efficiently in a permanent section ($ab$) at the head of the list. In the same section $ab$, representations of the routines themselves can be stored. If the limit $c$ of used store exceeds the limit $d$ of available store, this storage mapping fails, but this happens sufficiently infrequently to allow the stack to have been applied successfully and elegantly by many designers (Ref. 3).

Several programs can share a store if it is divided appropriately into regions of the type $ad$. In terms of routine addresses, it is clear that own variables can be referenced relative to the base $a$ (or $b$); other variables must be addressed relative to an appropriate base in the region $bc$. For, let $\pi^{(l_i)}\lambda^i R$ denote the subset of $\omega^{(l_i)}\lambda^i R$ consisting of its parameters and non-own variables, which is therefore represented in a section of the region $bc$. Let $\pi_{ji}$ denote the starting location of this section. Then to refer to the $n$th word in this region the pair $(\pi_{ji}, n)$ must be given. But $\pi_{ji}$ is unknown to the translator, which must give the pair $(i, n)$, the actual value of $\pi_{ji}$ being derived at execution time by reference to a table (the 'display' if Dijkstra) which is maintained by the supervisor program. Evidently, a change of context $((4.2) - (4.4))$ can be achieved simply by changing this tabular information.

The stack concept is not incompatible with a two-level store organized on a page-addressing system: after the address corresponding to $(i, n)$ has been derived, the page-address comparisons can be made. There are, however, a number of defects to the 'pure' stack.

1. It is difficult to share two or more activities within the same program, since one may get out of phase with another and wish to overwrite a part of the list $\Pi$ which is still in use.

2. Data structures cannot easily vary in size, once defined.

3. Rather more information than is strictly necessary is kept in the addressable part of the store.

None of these difficulties makes use of a stack intolerable, but their removal is of more than academic interest in large machines.

Some progress is made by maintaining an 'index' with one entry for each distinct operand used in the program. At a given time, the index entry will give the location number (or its equivalent) of the current representation of each operand (Fig. 4). When a new routine is entered, new blocks are activated for its non-own variables, the previous representation being chained on to the new one; when a routine terminates, its last set of non-own variables is discarded, and the set before that (if any) becomes accessible through the index. The use of a push-down list can now be restricted to parameters, link data, and working stores, although it is sometimes also convenient to use this area to contain scalar non-own variables, which can then be referred to relative to a local pointer. All non-scalar items are referenced through the index region and are represented by independent blocks of storage; not only may they vary in size dynamically to suit the programmer, but they may vary in position to suit the requirements of the storage allocation system, provided the index is kept up-to-date.

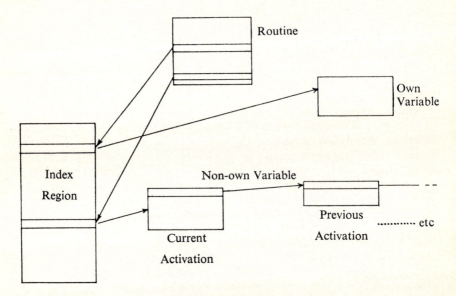

Fig. 4. Addressing through an index region.

It is not difficult to see the similarity between the index region proposed for storage mapping and the set of storage control registers required by a block-addressed reservation scheme. The combination of both functions can be performed by one set of registers in a storage system based on variable block lengths (Ref. 4).

Control of storage through an index removes most of the difficulties left by the stack. Storage areas can be handed over to peripherals for action without interrupting the program activity; data structures can be allowed to vary; and at any given time the only essential items in the addressable store are the current routine, the index region, and the stack. The above representation has to be elaborated slightly to deal with time-sharing branches of the same program, but it can in principle deal also with that situation.

## 5. *Communication*

One of the ideals of system design is to be able to add to, delete and modify parts of a program without taking undue time in retranslating the program. We have noted that this is assisted by segmenting the translation process into distinct phases. One of the last phases is concerned with establishing appropriate channels of communication between independently compiled routines and the data on which they operate. If information is relocated dynamically, this phase must link up to the system used in the supervisor.

The most flexible solution to this problem is provided by the index region of *(4.4)*. For to any named operand corresponds a unique item in the index, and a routine can be translated (and hence re-translated) independently provided the positions in the index corresponding to its context (4 1) are known. It is rather obvious that if $R$ is re-translated, then any routine local to $R$ must also be re-translated.

Quite often, the actual index positions cannot be supplied at translation time. In this case, a communication region may be set aside at the end of a routine, with an entry for each non-local name used in the routine. It is the function of the loading routine to insert correct references to the index in the communication regions of each routine in a program being set up for execution.

At first sight, FORTRAN possesses a flexibility in communication not given to ALGOL. In fact, independent translation is generally more difficult in ALGOL, but not impossible, and if restrictions are placed on the nesting of procedures at least as powerful and flexible a system can be derived. One can anticipate such restrictions being necessary should a large scale user build ALGOL into a programming system.

## 6. *Pointers*

The routine address, as we have described it, 'points' to an operand in a language which can be interpreted by a machine addressing system. It may point to another 'pointer' which is defined at the last stage of translation, or placed in a modifier register by the routine. A list structure, based on the use of pointers, is the ultimate in variability and indirectness. Since at each stage of an indirect addressing chain a location number has to be derived, it is tempting, having reached the end of the chain, to keep the last location number formed (that of the operand) and derive from it the location number of the next operand (e.g. by addition). Such action is dangerous unless the block which is being operated on is somehow 'locked down' into fixed locations by the supervisor program.

In general, therefore, a pointer held in an index register, or in a list element, should have the same form as a routine address; in particular, it must be independent of location numbers.

## 5. Summary and Conclusions

The conflicts of addressing arising in programming system design derive in the main from the following: (i) the name structure imposed by source languages; (ii) the requirement to use two or more levels of addressable store; (iii) the desirability of using automatically a backing store as an extension of the addressable store; (iv) the need to share the store amongst several activities; (v) the need to retain programs in a flexible form throughout most of their working lives.

Mere statement of the problems involved is incomplete without some assessment of their relative importance. This is perhaps most easily seen by considering the consequences of dispensing with some generality. In name structure, for example, little is lost by removing the possibility of recursion, and corresponding to the context (4.1) we then have the sets of operands:

$$\omega R, \ \omega \lambda R, \ \omega \lambda^2 R, \ \ldots, \ \omega \lambda^k R \tag{5.1}$$

More simplicity is gained by limiting the degree of nesting of scopes to two levels only. The variables of $R$ are then either local ($\omega R$) or non-local ($\omega \lambda R$): this, in effect, is all that is provided in FORTRAN.

We may also restrict array structures to be invariant during execution of a program, and limit parameter specifications to simple names or values, and once again the majority of source languages in regular use would be within our scope.

Hence the generalization we have attempted serves mainly to signpost land beyond the practically useful territory available to today's programmers, and to classify a few lone trails. Academic programmers may enjoy questioning some of the assumptions we have made: Should the partition of local variables into own/non-own/parameter classes be identical at each activation of a routine? Should the routine itself have the ability to 'generate' names dynamically? Is the 'tree' hierarchy of names adequate for all programming problems? How might it be generalized? The answers to some of these questions have been anticipated by list processing systems, but it should be obvious that in spite of advances in traditional programming methods, we still face list processing across a considerable gap in addressing technique. Ideally, one would like to buy the full flexibility of list processing only when it is essential; future translators should recognize the degree of generality called for in a particular situation. Far too often the steam hammer has to be used on every nut.

The most significant trend in machine addressing is to impose at least one stage of substitution or addition between a routine address and the corresponding location number. To maintain speed, this is done by placing the most frequently used substitutes or addenda in special fast access registers. Besides giving in effect location numbers, these registers may also be used to select a modifier, to indicate the presence or absence of an operand from the addressable store, and to provide reservation facilities. In a data oriented system, i.e. one in which the block sizes in store are chosen to correspond to individual pieces of data, substitution provides further power in the ability to monitor selected operands, and to provide for alternative modes of definition, which is important, for example, when general parameter specifications are considered. Control of storage through an index region seems to offer much of the graded flexibility that efficient programming demands.

## REFERENCES

1.  J. K. ILIFFE (1961). The Use of the Genie System in Numerical Calculation. *Annu. Rev. Automat. Progr.* **2,** 1.
2.  T. KILBURN *et al.* (1963). One Level Storage System. *I.R.E. Trans. Electronic Computers* **EC-11,** 223.
3.  E. W. DIJKSTRA (1961). An ALGOL Translator for the XI. *ALGOL Bull. Suppl.* **10.**
4.  J. K. ILIFFE and J. G. JODEIT (1962). A Dynamic Storage Allocation Scheme. *Computer J.* **5,** 200.

# 19. CONTINUOUS EVALUATION

## J. K. ILIFFE

*International Computers and Tabulators Ltd., London, England*

## 1. Introduction

In Chapter 18, the possibility of segmenting a program into individual *routines*, and separating the processing into several *phases* was noted. One objective of such partitioning is to match, as far as possible, the degree of generality in a program at a certain stage of processing to the amount of precise information which a programmer can supply. Greater generality would lead to inefficient programs, and less would make the programs inflexible.

Complete flexibility is gained by carrying out at execution time ('dynamically') processes which might otherwise be performed during translation, e.g. storage allocation, parameter evaluation. The present chapter is concerned with the reverse process, i.e. recognizing during translation situations in which action, otherwise delayed until the execution phase, might take place. In this way, both time and space may be saved in executing a program. For want of a better term, we shall call this intermixing of the translation and execution processes *continuous evaluation*.

Programming abounds with recognizable instances of continuous evaluation. An optimized compiler specifically seeks out situations where the object program may be simplified by preliminary calculation (see Chapter 9), and a list processing system (see Chapter 20) mixes the translator-like action of symbol manipulation with the interpretive activity of the '*APPLY*' operator. With such good precedents our attempt to formulate certain rules for evaluation which *automatically* recognize executable situations is justified, and a brief account follows of an investigation along these lines.

## 2. Evaluation Rules

A calculation proceeds by assigning *values* to certain *operands* or *variables*. Values are either given *a priori* in the form of initial data, or are derived from given values by the application of certain *operations*. We shall consider for the time being only the binary operations represented by '$+$' and '$\times$', applicable to values taken from the domain of integers. When the calculation stops, a subset of the values derived for the operands is termed the *result* of the calculation.

The calculation is usually represented as a series of consecutive steps, at each of which a value is assigned to a particular variable. The value derived at one step is typically determined by a *formula* involving the application of one or more operations, and the complete value assignment involved in one step may be represented by an *equation* obtained from the schema:

$$\mu = F \tag{2.1}$$

by substituting a variable name for $\mu$ and a formula for F, e.g.:

$$A = B + C \times D \times (2 + B) \tag{2.2}$$

The interpretation of equation (2.2), when it is executed, is that $A$ is to be assigned the value obtained by evaluating the right-hand side of the equation using the current values of $B$, $C$, $D$ (and '2').

It is fairly clear that in order to evaluate a formula F three sets of information must first be provided: (i) a full value assignment for each operand named in F; (ii) a set of precedence rules which determines the order in which the operations in F are to be evaluated, and the operands to which each is applied; (iii) a set of evaluation operators, one for each operation, which determines for given (pairs of) operand values, the result of applying each operation to these. We shall denote the evaluation operator for '+' by $\epsilon^+$ and represent its application to two integers $\mu$, $\nu$ with result $\rho$ by the schema:

$$\epsilon^+(\mu, \nu) \to \rho \tag{2.3}$$

Thus, a particular application of $\epsilon^+$ gives:

$$\epsilon^+ (3, 4) \to 7 \tag{2.4}$$

Similar remarks apply to the evaluation operator $\epsilon^\times$ corresponding to the '$\times$' operation.

It is of interest to note that the ability to evaluate F depends in turn on the ability to apply the $\epsilon$ operators, which may themselves be defined in terms of similar formulae. This circular mode of definition is stopped, however, by the particular form of $\epsilon$ operator exemplified by the multiplication and addition tables for the integers 0-9, on which the multiplication and addition of other integers is made to depend. Another set of $\epsilon$ operators on which an evaluation may ultimately rest is the function set of a particular computer, which is, of course, of immense practical importance in the present context.

For the principal task of a compiler is to reduce a calculation represented in a problem-oriented language to a sequence of single applications of machine functions, or of operators (e.g. subroutines) defined directly in terms of machine functions. It does this for a particular formula with reference to the precedence rules (ii) of the formula, and the list of available machine functions and subroutines corresponding to the set $\epsilon$; normally, no reference is made to any value assignments (i) which may hold at the time of compilation. When a calculation is obeyed by a machine, it is normally followed on the *assumption a*: that all value assignments required for the evaluation of each formula have been made. The role of continuous evaluation may perhaps be clarified with reference to the statement $a$. In 'normal' compilation, a converse of $a$ is assumed; in evaluation, we have noted that $a$ is assumed to be true; under a regime of continuous evaluation, however, the truth or falsity of $a$ must strictly be determined at each attempt to apply an operator $\epsilon$.

In practice, the necessary control information is supplied by associating with each variable in the context of a calculation one or more bits which determine its 'state of definition', $\sigma$. Although in theory one bit is sufficient it is convenient to consider four possible definition states of a variable:

$\sigma = 1$. Undefined.

$\sigma = 2$. Defined as a function of one or more parameters and other variables.

$\sigma = 3$. Defined formally in terms of other variables.

$\sigma = 4$. 'Numerically' defined.

In each state, we assume that the domain in which the variable finds its values (e.g. integer, word, complex number etc.) is known, hence the definition state refers strictly to the representation of its value in that domain. In state 1, no information concerning the variable is known; in state 4, its full value is known, a condition we term *numerically* defined, although it may equally apply to a variable in the domain of character strings. States 2 and 3 correspond to intermediate degrees of knowledge in which the state of definition of the variable depends in turn on the definition states of others. For an arbitrary variable $v$, we shall denote its definition state by $\sigma(v)$.

Thus, in applying the operator $\epsilon^+$ to two variables $\mu$, $v$ sixteen possibilities have to be accounted for. If $\sigma(\mu) = \sigma(v) = 4$, then $\epsilon^+$ can be applied normally, as in (2.3). If $\sigma(\mu) = 1$ or $\sigma(v) = 1$ then $\epsilon^+$ cannot be applied. In each of the other eight cases, applicability of $\epsilon^+$ depends on the resolution of the state of $\mu$ or $v$. Specifically, in case $\sigma(\mu) = 3$, a numerical value of $\mu$ can be obtained only if all variables appearing in the formal definition of $\mu$ are themselves numerically defined. Also, if $\sigma(\mu) = 2$, then a numerical value of $\mu$ can be obtained only if all parameters required by $\mu$ and all variables required by its functional definition are numerically defined.

In devising a continuous evaluation system, therefore, it is important to be able to scan as rapidly as possible the additional information required in case $\sigma = 2$ or $\sigma = 3$. We must describe the action of the machine when confronted with any one of the above situations, or give reasons to believe that certain situations could not arise in practice. Before doing so, however, we must develop a simple method of describing a calculation which enables continuous evaluation techniques to be more fully exploited.

### 3. Definition Sets

Most current programming languages rest heavily on the traditional *sequential* mode of procedure description derived from the earliest concepts of stored program machines. In this, although permitting the use of formulae has introduced the idea of implicit rather than explicit sequencing, the essentially temporary character of the value assignment made by a single calculation step remains unaltered. It is now recognized that the dynamic value assignment characterized by (2.2) and its interpretation must be supplemented by static assignments which are not part of the sequential description of a procedure. Most obvious candidates for this group are definitions of pre-set parameters, macro-operations, and subroutines.

Accordingly, we shall decompose a description of a calculation initially into a finite set of definitions. Each definition in our simplified system will have either the form of an equation (2.1) or a function obtained from the schema:

$$\phi(\pi) = F \qquad (3.1)$$

by substituting distinct variable names for $\phi$ and $\pi$, and a formula containing the name $\pi$ for F, e.g.

$$f(x) = x + x \times y \times z \qquad (3.2)$$

We shall permit formulae to contain function names (e.g. '$f$' in (3.2)) with actual parameters in the usual way. We shall also extend formulae to include predicates defined by the elementary arithmetic relations and Boolean operations '*and*', '*or*', and '*not*', used in conditional equations, thus:

$$y = x - 1 \text{ if } A, x \text{ if } x < 0, 1 - x \qquad (3.3)$$

Finally, we shall permit function definitions obtained from the following schema, which we shall call a 'routine':

$$\phi\,(\pi) = \{G_1; G_2 \ldots ; G_n\} \qquad (3.4)$$

by substituting distinct variable names for $\phi$ and $\pi$, and an equation for $G_j, j = 1, 2, \ldots, n$, where at least one equation has a formula involving $\pi$ in the right-hand side, and at least one equation has the name $\phi$ on the left-hand side. The form (3.4) is obviously an elementary species of problem-oriented program. From another point of view, the right hand side of (3.4) is a formula with rather involved precedence rules which are used to determine the order in which the equations are applied, for we assume that the application of an equation $G_j$ determines also the index $j'$ of the next equation to be applied, or else stops the calculation. The function (3.2) can be represented as a program in the following way:

$$f(x) = \{\underline{u} = x \times y; \underline{v} = \underline{u} \times z; f = x + \underline{v}; STOP\} \qquad (3.5)$$

The use of programs in definitions introduces complications in naming which in practice are extremely complex. Here we shall distinguish names local to a program (and hence meaningless outside that definition) from other names in the definition set by underlining, as in (3.5). We shall disallow side effects: i.e. the left hand side of any $G_j, j = 1, 2, \ldots, n$, must either be the function name ($\phi$) or an internal name of the definition. A sufficient condition for the applicability of a program is that its parameter and all non-internal names which occur in it should be numerically defined.

We are now in a position to consider the reduction of an elementary definition set by hand. Given *a priori* the integers, denoted by '1', '2', ... etc. and the truth values '*TRUE*', '*FALSE*', consider the following set $D$ of definitions:

1. $v(t) = 0 \text{ if } t \leq 0, t \times (u + u \times t)$           (3.6)
2.    $a = 15$
3.    $u = 50$
4.    $w = v(10) + 2 \times a$

For ease of reference, we have numbered the four definitions. The information available in this set is summarized in Table 1. Definitions 2 and 3 consist of value assignments to the variables $a$ and $u$ respectively. Definition 1 is of the function $v$, and $w$ is formally defined in 4. In the table we list numerical values

TABLE 1

| Def. | $v$ | $\sigma(v)$ | F | Dependent on: |
|------|-----|-------------|---|---------------|
| 1 | $v$ | 2 | 0 if $t \leqslant 0$, $t \times (u \div a \times t)$ | $t$(parameter), $u$, $a$ |
| 2 | $a$ | 4 | 15 | — |
| 3 | $u$ | 4 | 50 | — |
| 4 | $w$ | 3 | $v(10) + 2 \times a$ | $v$, $a$. |

where they are known, otherwise listing the defining formula F and the names appearing in each definition. Our intuitive evaluation of the definition set then proceeds as follows:

(i) $v$ depends only on $u$ and $a$ and is therefore a known function;

(ii) $w$, depending on $v$ and $a$, can therefore be evaluated to give the value 2030;

(iii) Since the function $v$ cannot be further reduced, this completes the reduction of the definition set.

Obviously this trivial example in a simplified language can do no more than illustrate a method of argument. It is a method, however, which can be carried over into much richer languages, with powerful results. What is particularly needed, apart from a larger set of elementary operations, is a type of operation leading to the cyclic or iterative behaviour observed in sequentially written programs. The mathematical expression of iterative calculation is contained in recurrence relations, and we may, for example, consider the following as a definition of the variable $r$, where $i$ is an integer greater than 1:

$$r_i = 2r_{-1} - r_{i-2}, r_o = 1, r_1 = 0$$

Evidently this is a special case of a function $r$ with parameter $i$, and the appearance of say '$r_{10}$' in a formula would receive essentially the same treatment as '$v(10)$' in (3.6) above. This and other extensions to the definition set, and their efficient encoding, are beyond the scope of the present discussion.

## 4. Definition Set Processing

A definition set is presented to a machine, or, for that matter, read by a human being, as a linear string of symbols. Consequently, if only part of the machine's computing capacity is absorbed by the reading process, some attention can be given to a parallel transformation of the definitions. In practice, as applied experimentally on the Rice University machine (Ref. 1), this transformation amounts to:

(i) Recognizing numerically defined operands, and where possible, applying operations between them.

(ii) Transforming all function definitions (including programs) into sequential machine code.

(iii) Forming a table, similar to Table 1, to assist subsequent processing.

Some of these effects are illustrated in the example given by the definition set in Table 2, containing a program $P$ written out with the usual line con-

TABLE 2

| | |
|---|---|
| 1. | $i = 1$ |
| 2. | $j = 2$ |
| 3. | $A = TRUE$ |
| 4. | $B = FALSE$. |
| 5. | $P(C) = \{$ |

$$x = i + j + k$$
$$\underline{y} = j \text{ if } A, i \text{ if } B, 0$$
$$\underline{z} = i \text{ if } B \text{ and } C, j \times k$$
$$\bar{P} = x + \underline{y} + \underline{z} \text{ if } B, \underline{x} \times \underline{y} \text{ if } A \text{ and } C, 0$$
$$STO\bar{P}\}$$

vention. As the set is read in, $P$ can be transformed to an internal representation of the program $P'$ given in Table 3. This form of processing is obviously

TABLE 3

| Def. | $v$ | $\sigma(v)$ | F | Dependent on: |
|---|---|---|---|---|
| 1 | $i$ | 4 | 1 | — |
| 2 | $j$ | 4 | 2 | — |
| 3 | $A$ | 4 | $TRUE$ | — |
| 4 | $B$ | 4 | $FALSE$ | — |
| 5 | $P$ | 2 | | $k, C$ (parameter) |
| | | | $\{x = 3 + k$ | |
| | | | $\underline{y} = 2$ | |
| | | | $\underline{z} = 2 \times k$ | |
| | | | $\bar{P} = x \times \underline{y} \text{ if } C, 0$ | |
| | | | $STO\bar{P}\}$ | |
| 6 | $k$ | 1 | — | — |

dependent on the sequence of definitions in the set, since if $P$ preceded the definitions of $i, j, A$ and $B$ a similar reduction would not be possible. Clearly the result of applying $P$ in either case would be the same, and what is achieved is merely a degree of optimization. The above example typifies a situation which arises frequently in the design of systems of programs where a very general program is written initially (e.g. $P$), leaving as variables parameters which are ultimately to be fixed. As the design proceeds $P$ becomes more refined, and by recompiling rather than rewriting (and introducing new errors) it is brought to its final form. A particular example is provided by optional print-outs which are inserted in a program for debugging purposes, finally to be eliminated.

The definition set constitutes a very satisfactory unit of information for an operating system to handle. Indeed, the set we have described bears a strong resemblance to the collection of *documents* needed to define a *job* in the Atlas operating system, and both, of course, rest on the fundamental idea of a calculation as a procedure supplemented by sufficient numerical definitions to make it applicable. Further developments of similar systems will undoubtedly be rewarding; methods of building up new sets from old; of cross-referencing between sets; and (for mathematicians) of nesting one set of definitions inside another must be established. We note that the data-oriented storage control systems mentioned in Chapter 18 are ideally suited to the control of data sets by extending the interpretation of lock-out bits to include an indication of the definition state of each variable: in fact, a data region which is locked out in the conventional sense is effectively undefined at that time ($\sigma = 1$), in the sense we have been discussing. Compare particularly the Index Region (Fig. 4, Chapter 18) with our tabular presentation of the definition set.

By analogy with the behaviour of a time-sharing machine, we can therefore envisage the reduction of a definition set proceeding in several definitions at once. When an undefined variable is encountered in one definition, control switches to another, and so on, until by a continuous scanning process the set is reduced to its simplest form. The application of several scanning and computing devices to the same set is theoretically possible.

## 5. Conclusion

In this very brief introduction to the idea of continuous evaluation, it was hoped to illustrate the advantage of basing a problem solution on a set of definitions rather than a sequential procedure description. This has already been recognized to some extent in the design of operating systems and of commercial compilers; it is believed to be equally advantageous for descriptions of mathematical procedures, which have become too closely enslaved to the early sequential forms of computer language. It is strongly felt that machines of the future will require to break away from sequential activity, and we must beware of having to face the task of automatically breaking up a sequential code into parallel activities: it seems easier to start from a 'parallel' code, and make it sequential when necessary.

The potentiality of definition sets remain to be fully realized. We have a great deal to learn about their properties and interpretation, but they appear to be capable of influencing appreciably both language and machine design in the future.

REFERENCE

1.  J. K. ILIFFE (1961). The Use of the Genie System in Numerical Calculation. *Annu. Rev. Automat. Progr.* **2**, 1.

# 20. LIST PROGRAMMING

## D. P. JENKINS

*Royal Radar Establishment, Malvern, England*

In addition to their well established use in carrying out arithmetical operations on numbers, digital computers are being applied more and more to non-numerical data processing. Work on pattern recognition, information retrieval, problem solving and decision making is still in an experimental stage, but such activities may well become of great importance in the future. A more immediate non-numerical use of computers is the compilation of machine instructions from programs written in problem oriented autocodes. While the familiar operations and conventions of arithmetic and algebra have influenced the specification of computers, the data they operate on, and the languages used to describe problems, there is no obvious comparable guide for non-numerical applications. Indeed it may well be asked if there is any hope of a unified approach to such a great diversity of problems. There has been a tendency to treat each non-numerical application in isolation, finding a computer representation which suits the particular data and defining ad hoc ways of operating with it. While this leads to efficiency for one problem on one machine, it may hinder communication and make it more difficult to appreciate any similarities between problems in different fields. A solution to these difficulties may arise from studies in list processing being carried out by Gelernter *et al.* (1960), McCarthy (1960), Newell and Tonge (1960) and Perlis and Thornton (1960). McCarthy's *LISP* system is typical of the programming languages being devised and it can conveniently be described in what follows as an extension of ALGOL. To keep to ALGOL syntax some minor changes must be made from the notation used by McCarthy who was hampered by a restricted character set.

Instead of the digits of numerical data processing, the basic items of information in *LISP* are called atoms. These atoms may be anything appropriate to the problem under consideration, algebraic symbols, points on a geometry diagram, playing cards, echoes on a radar display. To allow numerical and non-numerical information to be mixed, constants of various types, integers, floating point numbers, logical values, alphanumeric strings, should also be considered as being like atoms. Individually such atoms are of little interest, it is the way in which they are grouped together which matters. The group used in *LISP* is called a list and is written as a string of items separated by commas and enclosed in square brackets. An item may be a constant, an atom, or a list, each atom being represented by its print name, typically a sequence of upper case letters (though other characters may also be used) distinguished from an alphanumeric string by the absence of string quotes, ⟨ and ⟩. Examples of lists, including the special case of an isolated atom, are:

QUEEN OF SPADES
[A, B, C]
[CIRC, EQUALS, [3.1416, TIMES, DIAM]]
[[A, [✳ STRING ✳, OR, CONSTANT], B], C]

Following the fashion for syntactic definition

$$< list > :: = < atom > \mid < constant > \mid [< open\ list >]$$
$$< open\ list > :: = < list > \mid < list >, < open\ list >$$
$$< atom > :: = < u.c.\ letter > \mid < atom > < u.c.\ letter >$$

The atoms $A, B$ . . . . are self-sufficient entities, but it will be seen later that they can be thought of as the programmer's names for particular lists called by McCarthy the association lists of these atoms. An association list contains information which characterizes the properties of the atom. For example, the association list for the '$QUEEN\ OF\ SPADES$' in a card playing program might show that this card is in the Spade suit, ranks as a Queen, and is of special importance in games like Bezique.

Given data arranged in lists, the only processing possible is the breaking down, reordering and building up of lists. However, these processes are of a very general nature covering probably anything that need be done to the data. The four examples of list notation which follow illustrate respectively arithmetic, sorting, rearrangement from algebraic to reverse Polish notation, and transformation from string to branched list representation

[[ONE, SIX], PLUS, [THREE, TWO]] → [FOUR, EIGHT]
[T,H,I,S,I,S,A,S,O,R,T] → [A,H, [I,2], O,R, [S,3], [T,2]]
[A, TIMES, [B, PLUS, C]] → [A,B,C, PLUS, TIMES]
               or [[A, TIMES, B], PLUS, [A, TIMES, C]]
[OPEN, A, OPEN, B, C, CLOSE, CLOSE] → [A, [B,C]]

One common type of list operation is that required to control the push down lists which play an important part in the translation and running of ALGOL programs. Here items are only added at the front of a list and later removed, again from the front, in the reverse order. More general operations might copy lists, adding or removing items from the middle, or growing out sublists like the branches of a tree.

Before describing procedures which can be used to manipulate lists it may be helpful to describe one way of representing lists in the store of a computer. Such features of lists as their branched structure and variable length make normal sequential storage unsuitable. Instead a series of address pointers is stored, following a technique which has been used in computer programming for some time without explicitly referring to lists (for example, Wilkes et al., 1957). Every list has an internal name which is the address of the first of a series of words in the computer memory, not necessarily consecutive, forming the stored representation of the list. These words, conveniently called list words, each contain two addresses, an item address and a successor address.

In the first word representing a list, the item address is the internal name of the first item in the list, while the successor address points to a second list word holding the address naming the second item in the list, and so on. The address used to represent an atom is that of the first word of its association list. The word corresponding to the last item in a list clearly requires a special second address since there is no successor word to which it can point. McCarthy's solution is to make it the address naming a special atom *NIL*, giving it for convenience the value 0 which should, therefore, be the address of the start of the association list of this atom. Thus the list [*A,B*] would be stored in two list words as follows:

The first list word contains a pointer to the association list of the atom *A*, and a pointer to the list cell which is its successor, while the second list word contains pointers to the association lists of *B* and *NIL*.

Since any item in a list is represented by an address it may well be asked how it is possible to tell if the item is itself an atom or a list. The answer is that the first item in an association list is a special atom—say *ATOM*—which is not used in any other context in lists. To unify enquiries into the nature of any atom it is desirable to have a convention for the structure of association lists like that used by McCarthy. His association lists have items which are alternately atoms naming attributes and lists which are the values of those attributes for the atom in question. It is also essential to include the print name as an alphanumeric string, say as the first item following *ATOM*, since otherwise it would not be possible to print the list answers to a problem. Thus, the association list of the Queen of Spades mentioned before might start as follows:

[*ATOM*, ⦓*QUEEN OF SPADES*⦔, *SUIT*, *SPADES*,
            *DENOMINATION*, *QUEEN*,...]

The first entry '*ATOM*' is the special marker indicating that this is an association list, and the second entry ' ⦓*QUEEN OF SPADES*⦔ ', is the print name of this atom. Further information on suit ranking value and point count could be found in the association lists of *SPADES* and *QUEEN*.

Items which are constants may be shown by item addresses pointing to the words holding the constants—provided that such words are distinguishable from the two address list words. Alternatively, a constant may be represented by a list word whose item address is the name of the atom defining the type of constant word to which its successor address points; this seems more consistent with the structure of atom association lists. For example, the list

[*A*, [ [*B*, *3.14*], *A*, [*B*, *3.14*] ] ]

**might be stored as follows**

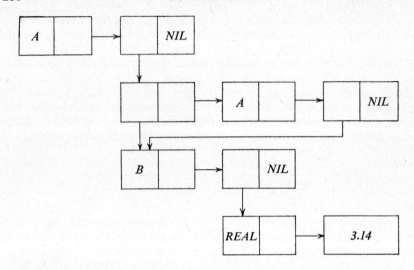

This list structure of nine words can be represented by the following list of nine labelled quantities, where *L1* is the name of the complete list, *L4* is the name of the sublist [*B*, *3.14*] and there is a one one correspondence between labels and words in the machine representation.

> *L1: A, L2*
> *L2: L3, NIL*
> *L3: L4, L8*
> *L4: B, L5*
> *L5: L6, NIL*
> *L6: REAL, L7*
> *L7: 3.14*
> *L8: A, L9*
> *L9: L4, NIL*

All of these words except the one labelled *L7* are list words holding two addresses here shown either as a label or, when the required address is the start of an atom association list, as the name of the atom. The word *L7* holds the normal computer representation of the number *3.14*. It will be seen that the sublist [*B*, *3.14*] is only stored once though, like the association lists, it is referred to from more than one place. This is an important feature of McCarthy's method of representing lists which, of course, is not the only one possible. The authors mentioned earlier use variations on this scheme, often making use of other digits in each computer word in addition to the two address parts, and further variations have been proposed by Collins (1960) and Weizenbaum (1962).

So far, ways of representing and referring to data in the form of lists on paper and in the store of a computer have been discussed. McCarthy calls this level of nomenclature *S*-language (Symbolic language) as opposed to the *M*-language (Meta language) in which procedures for manipulating lists are written. The *M*-language to be used here is ALGOL 60 with the addition of the declarator **list** as the 'type' of those variables and function designators whose values are list references. Lower case letters will be used for all the identifiers used in the ALGOL constructions to distinguish them from the upper case letters reserved for atom print names.

The procedures which McCarthy introduces as the primitive set required to operate with lists are all what ALGOL calls value procedures reflecting the fact that *LISP* is essentially a functional rather than a command language. That is, *LISP* programs are not a series of operations which assign new values to variables on the way to an answer which is the value of one of these variables. Rather the result is the value of a function designator arrived at by evaluating first its arguments which may themselves be the values of functions. The only intermediate working variables are any formal parameters which are 'called by value' and the only explicit assignment statements in the program are those defining the values of function designators. Lists appear in the actual parameters of these procedures as list expressions which are either list variables or list function designators; list constants and operators (other than the assignment operator :=) are avoided because they would require too many extensions to an existing ALGOL compiler.

The first two functions are Boolean procedures used for recognizing the values of list expressions. *Atom* (*l*), a function of one list expression, has the value **true** if the value of this expression refers to an atom (including *NIL*), and is otherwise **false**. The other Boolean procedure, *eq* (*l,m*) is strictly defined only if the values of both of the list expressions forming its parameters refer to atoms; the value of the function is then **true** if they refer to the same atom, **false** if to different atoms. In practice, it is convenient to extend the definition of *eq* so that its value is **true** if its parameters refer to identical list internal representations. In terms of the machine representation, the value of a list expression is an address in the list store, the function *atom* of this expression is **true** if the word addressed has the address *ATOM* in its item part, and *eq* of two expressions is **true** if the addresses to which they evaluate are the same and **false** if they differ.

Lists could in principle be built up as list expressions using the list operator comma in conjunction with list brackets. Thus it might seem reasonable to write

[*l,m*] and [*l*] paralleling the arithmetic expressions $(a - b)$ and $(- a)$.

However, new operators add new concepts to a language while new functions can be defined within the framework of ALGOL. A two parameter list procedure *cons* is therefore introduced as the primitive for making new lists. The value of *cons* is a reference to a list whose first item is the value of the first parameter, any list expression, while the remainder of the list is identical with the list referred to as the value of the second parameter. This prohibits a reference to any atom other than *NIL* by the second parameter, and since list constants are not allowed, *NIL* must be replaced by the list variable *nil* whose value is this list constant (compare with the possible use of a global identifier *pi* whose value is always *3.14159...*). The operator expressions above now become *cons(l, cons(m,nil))* and *cons(l,nil)*. Those familiar with McCarthy's paper will recognize that the untidiness of *cons* as described here is the result of avoiding the slightly more general dot notation used by McCarthy in his mathematical formulation, but not, apparently in his programming system. Clearly the machine representation of the value of *cons* is the address of a new list word whose item address is the value of the first parameter of the function and whose successor address is the value of the second parameter. Note that the representations of the lists referred to by the values of the actual parameters are not copied; the list referred to by *cons* shares them as sublists. To allow computed numerical and logical constants to be included in lists it must be possible to invoke 'transfer' functions between such constants and their list counterparts, possibly as part of the machine realization of *cons*.

The two remaining primitive list procedures *car* and *cdr* are used to isolate the individual items of a list. They both require as parameter a single list expression whose value should refer to a non-atomic list; the value of *car* refers to the first item in the list while that of *cdr* refers to the remainder of the list. Thus, allowing list operators for the moment,

the value of      *car* ([*k,l,m*]) is that of the list variable *k*
    and of       *cdr* ([*k,l,m*]) is that of the list expression [*l,m*]
    while        *cdr* ([*l*]) refers to the atom *NIL*.
Hence,       *car* (*cons* (*l,m*)) is *l*
and          *cdr* (*cons* (*l,m*)) is *m*

In the machine representation the values of *car* and *cdr* are the item and successor addresses respectively in the word whose address is the value of the actual parameter. In passing it may be noted that the convention adopted for association lists makes it possible to replace *atom* (*l*) by *eq*(*car* (*l*), *atom*) where the variable *atom* refers to the atom *ATOM*.

The identifiers *cons, car* and *cdr* are not very euphonious but will be used here for consistency with McCarthy (the names *join, head* and *tail* have been suggested as suitable alternatives). It is interesting that the procedures they name are precisely those required to control push down lists, but they also suffice to carry out any calculation based on lists. For this purpose the primitive functions are used in conditional expressions to define other functions usually recursively, the functional language equivalent of loops in command languages. In what follows it seems most consistent to use the ALGOL syntax for conditional expressions though McCarthy uses either a very neat abbreviation of ALGOL or a more clumsy functional form.

To illustrate, here are some of McCarthy's simple *LISP* functions defined as ALGOL procedure declarations. It will be noted that 'value calls' are used wherever possible, a general feature of *LISP* which ignores name calls except in a few rather special procedures which usually have an indefinite number of parameters.

**boolean procedure** *null* (*l*); **value** *l*; **list** *l*;
    *null* := **if** *atom* (*l*) **then** *eq* (*l,nil*) **else false**;

**integer procedure** *length* (*l*); **value** *l*; **list** *l*;
   *length* := **if** *atom* (*l*) **then** 0 **else** (*length* (*cdr* (*l*)) + 1);

**list procedure** *append* (*l,m*); **value** *l,m*; **list** *l,m*;
   *append* := **if** *null* (*l*) **then** *m* **else** *cons* (*car* (*l*), *append* (*cdr* (*l*), *m*))

*Null* frequently appears in other list processing procedures as the condition to be satisfied for exit from a recursive loop; the only comment it requires is a reminder that the global list variable *nil* is used instead of the list constant *NIL*. *Length* is a little more complicated—and what is here written as the final simple arithmetic expression is expressed by McCarthy as the function *sum*(*length*(*cdr*(*l*), 1). Its aim is to find the number of items (atoms or lists) at the highest level of the list *l*, and for the list [*A*, [*B*, *C*], *D*] the steps are

*length* ([*A*, [*B*, *C*], *D*]) = *length* ([[*B*, *C*], *D*]) + 1
*length* ([[*B*, *C*], *D*])   = *length* ([*D*]) + 1
*length* ([*D*])          = *length* (*NIL*) + 1
But *length* (*NIL*) is 0 hence eventually *length* ([*A*, [*B*, *C*], *D*]) is 3.

The purpose of *append*, which requires non-atomic parameters, is to make a new list which starts off as a copy of the top level of *l* referring to the same sublists, but then runs into *m* without copying it. For example

*append* ([*A*, [*B*, *C*]], [*D*, *E*]) = *cons* (*A*, *append* ([[*B*, *C*]], [*D*, *E*]))
*append* ([[*B*, *C*]], [*D*, *E*])   = *cons* ([*B*, *C*], *append* (*NIL*, [*D*, *E*]))
But *append* (*NIL*, [*D*, *E*]) is [*D*, *E*] after which back substitution gives
   [*A*, [*B*, *C*], *D*, *E*] as the final answer.

Of course, declaring a procedure in ALGOL does not cause that procedure to be obeyed. It is necessary to write in the same block a procedure statement or an expression containing a call of the procedure quoting the actual parameters for which the evaluation is to be made. Now it would not be difficult to implement an extension of ALGOL in which a complete procedure declaration could appear wherever a procedure identifier is permitted. Such a unification of declaration and call is particularly natural in a functional language where the whole program is wrapped up in a single, very complicated, function. The notations which McCarthy adapts from Church for this purpose are worth describing though they are a digression from the ALGOL approach used here. For example, the above declaration of *null* followed by the call *null* (*m*) can be replaced by

λ ((*l*), (**if** *atom* (*l*) **then** *eq* (*l*, *nil*) **else false**)) (*m*).

Two parts of a non-recursive function declaration, its formal parameter list and the expression defining its value, appear as the two parameters of a 'declarative procedure' λ. This complete unit then replaces a procedure identifier, being followed by an actual parameter list to make an expression. This λ notation shows to particular advantage when writing calls of procedures with parameters which would, in ALGOL, have to be the identifiers of previously declared procedures. A very useful *LISP* procedure of this type would be declared in ALGOL:

**list procedure** *maplist* (*f*, *l*); **value** *l*; **procedure** *f*; **list** *l*;
    *maplist* := **if** *null* (*l*) **then** *l* **else** *cons* (*f*(*l*), *maplist* (*f*, *cdr* (*l*)))

Some typical calls of maplist might be

*maplist* (*g*, [*A*, [*B*, *C*], *D*]) giving [*g* ([*A*, [*B*, *C*], *D*]), *g* ([[*B*, *C*], *D*]), *g* ([*D*])],

while *maplist* (*car*, *m*) is a list which differs from *m* only in the actual machine representation of its top level.

*Maplist* (λ ((*x*), *atom* (*car* (*x*) )), *m*) produces a 'one level' or string list parallel to the top level of *m* but with the boolean item **true** if the corresponding item of *m* is an atom, and **false** otherwise, so that [*A*, [*B*, *C*], *D*] gives [**true**, **false**, **true**].

However, suppose it was required to form a list of the lengths of the separate items in *l*, [0, 2, 0] from [*A*, [*B*, *C*], *D*] and [1, 2, 0] from

$$[[A], [B, [C, D]], E].$$

Clearly the expression used in the earlier declaration of *length* must appear in a λ declaration. But *length* is a recursive procedure and some way of defining the identifier *length* as the complete λ declaration is required. McCarthy introduces a second declarative procedure *label* to do this, and would write

*maplist* (*label* (*length*, λ ((*m*), (**if** *atom* (*m*) **then** 0 **else** (*length* (*cdr* (*m*)) + 1)))), *l*)

The two parameters of *label* are an identifier, and the expression represented by the identifier; indeed, *label* corresponds to the ALGOL declarator **procedure.** Like λ declarations, label declarations can be followed by actual parameter lists to form expressions. At such calls of label and λ declarations the procedure name and the formal parameters remain bound to the expression and the actual parameters respectively throughout the evaluation of the expression until the same identifier appears again following λ or label. This gives the functional language a block structure very like that of ALGOL, including 'holes' in the scope of an identifier. There is also the same possibility of reference to non-local quantities, the body of one procedure referring to formal parameters of another from which it is called. However, this also exposes a weakness of the technique since in a program which contained an expression like *f*(*g*(*l*), *g*(*l*)) either the label declaration of *g* would have to be repeated or else a synthetic enclosing function defined. McCarthy's system avoids this difficulty by introducing side effect procedures which are equivalent to the ALGOL declarations. Similar procedures are also used to allow the results of list computations to be printed—the inability to do this is a serious embarrassment to the purity of a functional language.

From the side effect procedure it is only a short distance to a command structure language and indeed McCarthy introduces a series of such procedures which parallel some of the operators of ALGOL. They make it possible to alter lists whereas the procedures described so far can only construct new lists and forget old ones. A sequence of calls of these procedures is tied together into the equivalent of a block by making each call a parameter in a multi-variable function called *program*. The notation is sufficiently explained by the following versions of the procedure *length*, one in ALGOL, the other in program feature *LISP*.

```
integer procedure length (l); value (l); list (l);
    begin list w; integer r;
        w := l;
        r := 0;
    L: if atom (w) then length := r else
        begin r := r + 1;
            w := cdr (w);
            go to L
        end
    end length
```

```
label (length, λ ((l),
    program ((w, r),
        setq (w, l),
        setq (r, 0),
    L, if atom (w) then exit (r),
        setq (r, sum (r, 1)),
        setq (w, cdr (w)),
        go to (L)
    )))
```

In the *LISP* version the 'declaration' of the local variables *w* and *r* and the placing of the label *L* are the only parameters of *program* which are not functions, and the value of the complete function is that of the parameter of *exit* when the latter is first met. Clearly the assignment function *setq* requires its first parameter to be called by name.

At risk of causing some confusion, it is interesting to indicate the way in which McCarthy implemented *LISP*. An essential feature of any list processing language is the ability to read and print lists. It is also necessary to be able to read in the program which operates on the lists, and since programs are very like lists there is a strong temptation to read programs into a machine by expressing them in the same format as data lists (as used to be done with machine language programs in the early days of computers). This is particularly easy to do with McCarthy's way of writing *LISP* providing the function *cond* is used to represent conditional expressions. It is only necessary to move each function name inside its parameter brackets to give a bracketed Polish structure, the transformation being completed by writing all identifiers in upper case letters as the print names of atoms. After reading the program in this list form it is obeyed interpretively, the meanings of any unfamiliar atoms representing procedure names being found by referring to their association lists. Indeed the program usually starts with some side effect procedures which add the data lists representing the 'bodies' of new procedures to the association lists of the atoms by which they are named. This method of operation is well suited to mixing compilation and execution, and also allows data lists to be used as actual parameters in the program.

However, from what has been said already there seems to be good reason for writing list programs in ALGOL and then compiling and running them like any other ALGOL program. This requires the ability to use ALGOL recursively, but the stack method of Dijkstra (1961) used non-interpretively allows this to be done with reasonable efficiency. For this purpose it is no hardship to discard McCarthy's λ and label declarations even though the

ALGOL substitutes of separate declaration and call are more clumsy. Possibly a more serious loss is the inability to modify program lists as if they were data though this is a facility that rarely seems to be used in *LISP*. It is also not practicable to allow list constants in the program since to read them the compiler would need much of the mechanism of the running list processor. Instead the constants must be read at run time and assigned then to the list variables which represent them in the written program. On the credit side, ALGOL allows great scope in the definition of new procedures and it is not difficult to provide side effect procedures which give dynamically the list tracing and building operations provided by Perlis and Thornton through a static 'thread'. Similarly, features of the more primitive *IPL V* language of Newell and Tonge could be included if desirable.

The only difficult addition to recursive ALGOL is a mechanism for finding space for the representations of lists. The list variables themselves follow the usual block structure of ALGOL and by keeping them in the run time stack they are automatically abolished on exit from their own blocks. However, the list representations to which the list variables point cannot be freed at the same time because they may share words with lists which are still active. A solution to the problem is to keep the list representation words in a part of store quite distinct from the stack, rather as own arrays are stored in Sattley's (1961) implementation of ALGOL. Initially, all of this list area is on a 'free list' from which the *cons* routine takes one word at each entry. When the free list is exhausted it does not mean that there is no more unoccupied space in the list area. Lists formed during procedures will cease to be required after exit but although the corresponding list variables vanish the list representations remain, with nothing pointing to them. Provided all the stack words storing list variables are linked together as a result of the declaration **list** it will be possible to trace all currently active words in the list area. It is then easy to form the unused words into a new free list and start again. This 'garbage collection' phase can be made more sophisticated, both in the list tracing (which involves a systematic tour through the very branched structures) and in making the new free list. For example, it has been found possible (Brown and Strachey) to rearrange the active list words so that they are close packed at one end of the list area leaving the remaining consecutive stores free.

It may now be appropriate to comment on the semantics of the list variables which have been introduced. At first sight it might seem more natural to make their values the representations of lists rather than references to lists. However, if this approach is adopted, value calls of procedure parameters would cause the complete list representations to be copied in the same way as ALGOL arrays called by value. This is particularly extravagent in space since the list procedures hardly ever alter lists, one of the reasons for value calls. On the other hand, name calls are very wasteful of time in a recursive language because the running program must constantly change level from the innermost procedure all the way down to the outermost block forming the main program in order to obtain each actual parameter. Both of these difficulties are solved by the suggested definition of list variables. Normally value calls will be most convenient, but there may be places where name calls are required and are not inefficient as long as they do not penetrate too deeply into a recursion.

To summarize, it appears that McCarthy's *LISP* system and similar schemes offer a convenient way of dealing with many of the situations which arise in non-numerical data processing. Since ALGOL seems to be a very suitable language for expressing *LISP* it is desirable to implement some list processing procedures in ALGOL. This can be done by extending the compiler to include the declarator **list** and all it implies. Alternatively, a user with a recursive ALGOL compiler could declare suitable code procedures to carry out the necessary red tape operations rather as Gelernter *et al.* used FORTRAN in their list processing language. Each list declaration would then be replaced by an integer declaration followed by a call of the appropriate red tape procedure. While the object programs resulting from this home made approach would not be as efficient as those generated by list ALGOL, the facilities provided would increase the power of the language considerably.

### REFERENCES

1. N. BROWN and C. STRACHEY, Private communication.
2. G. E. COLLINS (1960). *Com. Assoc. Comp. Mach.* **3**, 655.
3. E. W. DIJKSTRA (1961). "ALGOL 60 Translation", *ALGOL Bull. Suppl.* No. 10.
4. H. GELERNTER, J. R. HANSEN and C. L. GERBERICH (1960). *J. Assoc. Comp. Mach.* **7**, 87.
5. J. McCARTHY (1960). *Com. Assoc. Comp. Mach.* **3**, 184.
6. A. NEWELL and F. TONGE (1960). *Com. Assoc. Comp. Mach.* **3**, 205.
7. A. PERLIS and C. THORNTON (1960). *Com. Assoc. Comp. Mach.* **3**, 195.
8. K. SATTLEY (1961). *Com. Assoc. Comp. Mach.* **4**, 60.
9. J. WEIZENBAUM (1962). *Com. Assoc. Comp. Mach.* **5**, 161.
10. M. V. WILKES, D. J. WHEELER and S. GILL (1957). "The Preparation of Programs for an Electronic Digital Computer", 2nd ed., p. 132. Addison-Wesley, Reading, Mass., U.S.A.

# 21. INTERPRETATION, STACKS AND EVALUATION

## W. H. BURGE

*Univac Division of Sperry Rand Corp., New York, U.S.A.*

## 1. Introduction

This chapter starts with a brief description of the GIPSY (General Interpretive Programming System) system which has been implemented on *EMIDEC 2400*. GIPSY interprets programs consisting of lists of names of functions.

This is followed by an account of a method of describing the combining of operations called a 'construction process'. A tree diagram is used to describe this construction process and rules of evaluation of a construction process which use a stack are introduced. Operations which transform tree diagrams to produce equivalent tree diagrams are discussed. The evaluation of equivalent tree diagrams produce the same result but the time taken or storage required may differ.

The restrictions on operations which are allowed in the GIPSY system are relaxed. The generalization allows operations which are included in other operations to address the arguments of an outer operation.

## 2. Description of the GIPSY System

There are three basic functions built in to the GIPSY system called '*DEFINE 1*', '*DEFINE 2*' and '*INTERP*'. By using *DEFINE 1*, a piece of program or a subroutine can be written in machine code, given a descriptive name and added to the system. The program *INTERP* accepts a list of names as argument and interprets the names one at a time. Interpreting a name which corresponds to a machine code subroutine causes the associated subroutine to be executed. Control then returns to the interpreter to interpret the next name. The list of names is called GIPSY language. The function *DEFINE 2* is used to define new subroutines whose body is written in GIPSY language, e.g. '$AB + C - ACf +$'.

The specification of the subroutines and the names are left to the user. When a new subroutine is defined, the body of converted subroutine is placed at the end of an area of store called the 'function area'. The name and the address of the body of the subroutine are placed in a 'function table'.

The interpreter accepts a name and looks it up in the function table. If the name is found the interpreter passes control to the body of the subroutine. Each machine coded subroutine can be activated in two ways:

1. By a subroutine jump from machine coded programme.
2. By interpreting its name.

The function *DEFINE 2* is used to define new subroutines whose body is written in GIPSY language. The body is placed in the function area, its name and address are placed in the function table. The function table contains one bit with each name and address pair to tell the interpreter whether the body of the subroutine is in GIPSY language or in machine code.

When the interpreter interprets the name of a GIPSY language subroutine the interpretive control number is stored and changed to point to the beginning of the body of the subroutine. Each GIPSY language subroutine can be activated in two ways:

1. By interpreting its name.
2. From machine code of the form 'a special subroutine jump followed by the name'.

A register 'C' holds the address of the name which is currently being interpreted and is called the 'interpretive control number'.

So far a description of a basic GIPSY system has been given. A user can start at this stage if he wishes. However, a number of less basic but fairly general functions have been written and will now be described.

All names in GIPSY language are names of operations. The names are written in the same order as the operations are to be obeyed. Both the links between subroutines and the variables are stored in a stack. Each operation finds its arguments at the top of the stack and replaces them by its results. Two registers $A$ and $P$ are used as reference pointers to the stack.

The register $A$ contains the address of the top member of the stack and is called the 'accumulator pointer'; $P$ contains the address of the last link and is called the parameter pointer.

Both machine coded and GIPSY language subroutines are written in a standard way. The first instruction is an 'entry' subroutine. This entry instruction stores the control number or interpretive control number in the stack together with a bit which signifies whether the entry to the subroutine was from machine code or GIPSY language. The value of $P$ is also stored in the stack and $P$ is re-set to point to this new link. The last instruction of a subroutine is an exit order which overwrites the input variables by the output variables, restores the value of $P$ and makes a machine or interpretive jump to the return address.

The arguments of a subroutine are brought forward from behind the link to the head of the stack by the functions called $G1$, $G2$, $G3$ etc. There are also functions which transfer an argument back from the head of the stack to a parameter position called $T1$, $T2$, $T3$ etc.

Interpretive conditional and unconditional jumps are also standardized. The names 'TEST' 'BEGINS' 'ENDS' are used in that order to separate the list of names into two parts. The names between 'TEST' and 'BEGINS' are interpreted and those between 'BEGINS' and 'ENDS' are skipped if the stack holds the Boolean variable 'true'. If the stack has 'False' as its top member the names after 'BEGINS' are interpreted. When the function 'TEST' finds 'false' in the stack it searches forward to find the 'BEGINS' bracketed with it, any other bracketed 'TEST''s and 'BEGINS''s are ignored. When it finds 'true' in the stack, 'TEST' allows interpretation to carry on with the next name. When the function 'BEGINS' is interpreted it skips interpretive control until after its bracketed 'ENDS'.

Unconditional jumps are of the form 'JUMP' followed by a number. The position jumped to is made up of the name 'TAG' followed by the same number.

The process of interpretation described is very slow because the interpreter searches the function list for each name. Interpretation is speeded up if the interpreter does translation from the name to address and replaces the name by the address on the first interpretation. The first time the interpretive control passes through the names is slow but subsequent interpretations of the same program are faster. The basic input characters go through a slight translation before they are interpreted. Names are put into one machine word, numbers are converted to binary and character strings are fitted into an integral number of computer words.

There is a compiling process in the GIPSY system which compiles a subroutine in GIPSY language to a subroutine in machine code. It changes the body of a '*DEFINE 2*' item into the body of a '*DEFINE 1*' item.

### 3. Construction Processes

An operation of degree $n$ is a method of combining $n$ objects in a definite order to produce a new object. The $n$ objects are called the arguments of the operation and the new object produced is called the result of applying the operation to its arguments. I will introduce the operation of evaluation, which, when applied to an operation and its arguments will produce the resulting object. A stack (Dijkstra, 1960) will be used for storing objects. I will also introduce the operation of interpretation, which is applied to a set of names, or a string of basic symbols to give them meaning in the sense of evaluating the operations associated with the names.

A construction process (Curry and Feys, 1958) is a description of the way in which old operations are combined to produce a new operation. A tree diagram represents a construction process. Each old operation is represented by a node of the tree. If the operation is of degree $n$ it has $n$ branches pointing into it corresponding to its $n$ arguments taken from left to right. The one line pointing out of it represents the result. There is a unique root node on the tree and any node other than a root node is connected to one and only one node above it. Each node has the name of the associated operation attached to it. An example is given in Fig. 1. This tree could have been produced from

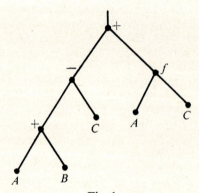

Fig. 1

the following string of characters '$A + B - C + f(A, C)$' which represents an arithmetic expression. It could equally well have been produced in another way from one of the strings '$+ (-(+(A, B) C), f(A, C))$', '$A\ B\ +\ C\ - ACf +$', '$+\ -\ +\ ABCfAC$', '$SOMEF\ (A,\ B,\ C,\ +, f)$'.

## 4. Evaluation

There are two types of operations. (i) Simple operations which are represented by a node of tree and have a name. (ii) Compound operations represented by a tree with more than one node. There are two rules for evaluating a compound operation which fix the order in which old operations are to be evaluated from the shape of the tree.

*Rule 1:* The arguments of an operation must have been evaluated before the operation is evaluated.

*Rule 2:* All arguments to the left of a given argument which can be evaluated by Rule 1 must have been evaluated before that argument.

The names of the operations of the example in Fig. 1, written in order of evaluation follow on the next line.

$$AB + C - ACf +$$

The evaluation of the construction process produces the same result as if the operations associated with the string of names '$AB + C - ACf +$' were evaluated in that sequence. For this to be so one name must always be associated with the same operation and the evaluation of the simple operation produces an object. The operation of scanning the string of names one by one and evaluating the associated operation will be called 'interpreting' the string of names.

Both computers and compilers scan strings of basic symbols in order to find out what to do. The simple language in which one basic symbol means one operation in terms of program or hardware is called reverse Polish or postfix language (Burks *et al.*, 1954). Interpretation of such a language requires a pointer or 'control number' which starts at the beginning of the string and moves through the string one symbol at a time evaluating the associated operations one by one.

## 5. Storage for Objects during Evaluation

Computers and compilers require storage for storing the objects of the system. Each object requires one 'cell' or position for storing the information which characterizes it. A stack of cells will be used for storing the objects of the system.

Each value of the control number implies a line which cuts the tree diagram. This line or cut does not pass through a node of the tree. The nodes below the line represent operations which have been evaluated, those above the line represent operations which have not.

This line cuts the branches of the tree in points which represent the cells of the stack. An object in such a stack position has been produced by evaluating the construction process represented by the subtree which hangs from the cut point. Each operation takes its arguments from the top $n$ positions of the stack and replaces them by its result. Fig. 2 shows a tree with all its cuts, each cut is numbered with the control number.

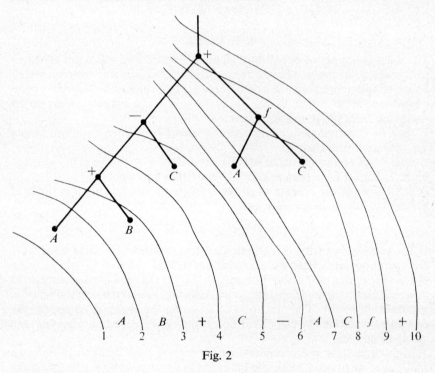

Fig. 2

Between two adjacent stack cuts lies one operation node. This operation transforms the stack from the state represented by the lower cut to the state represented by the upper cut. The end nodes, any subtree or the complete tree represent operations which leave one object in the stack.

A list of successive stack states corresponding to Fig. 2 follows. The notation used is that '$a$' stands for the object produced by the operation $A$ and '$a + b$' stands for the object produced by operating on the objects $a$ and $b$ with the operation $+$. Commas separate distinct objects.

1
2  $a$
3  $a, b$
4  $a + b$
5  $a + b, c$
6  $a + b - c$
7  $a + b - c, a$
8  $a + b - c, a, c$
9  $a + b - c, f(a, c)$
10  $a + b - c + f(a, c)$

## 6. Functional Abstraction

We have seen how it is possible to define a new operation without arguments in terms of old operations. This section is concerned with defining a new operation of a more general nature which may have arguments. In other words it is a method of defining the operations corresponding to the nodes of the construction process tree which are not end nodes, in terms of old operations.

A contour may be drawn around a set of connected points of the tree to represent a new operation. The new operation is a combination of old operations whose nodes lie inside the contour. This contour can be shrunk to a new node. The lines of the tree which point into the contour represent

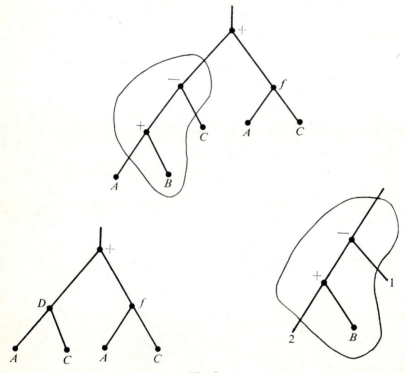

Fig. 3

the arguments of the new operation. The line pointing out of the contour represents the result. Fig. 3 shows the old construction process plus contour and the new construction process with the new operation named $D$.

The rules of evaluation must be extended so that evaluation of the old tree and evaluation of the new tree, in which evaluation of $D$ switches evaluation to the description of $D$, must produce the same result. To make this possible, new operations must be introduced within the contour at points where the contour cuts the branches of the tree.

The evaluation of the new tree is equivalent to interpreting the string '$A\ C\ D\ A\ Cf\ +$'. The evaluation of the operation $D$ is of interest. When passing through a contour the stack will have an additional item put into it called the 'link' (Dijkstra, 1960). This link stores the state of the 'machine' before crossing the contour. There is a register which stores the address of this link called the parameter pointer. This pointer is available so that reference may be made to the arguments of the new operation from within the contour.

The arguments of an operation are numbered from the top of the stack starting at 1. The new operations introduced are operations which address the arguments and move them forward in the stack. They will be called '$g\ (i,\ 1)$' (for get) where $i$ is the argument number and the $1$ indicates that only one contour is crossed to find the argument. The operation $g\ (i,\ 1)$ transfers the $i$th argument to the top of the stack and also leaves it in its position below the link.

Another new operation must be introduced at the point where the result line points out of the contour. This operation removes the arguments from the stack and replaces them by the result or results (i.e. any objects above the link). This operation will be called 'col $(n)$' (for collapse) if there are $n$ arguments. Finally an operation corresponding to going out of a contour is to remove the link from the stack and to restore the state of the machine. The operations of entering and leaving a contour will be called '$PLK$' and '$RES$' for 'plant link' and 'restore'.

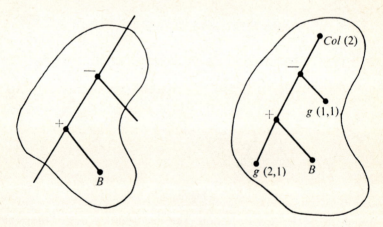

Fig. 4

The evaluation of the operation $D$ in the example is the same as interpreting the string '$PLK\ g\ (2,\ 1)\ B\ +\ g\ (1,\ 1)\ -\ \text{Col}\ (2)\ RES$'. Figure 4 shows the old and new trees for $D$ and Fig. 5 shows the new trees, stack cuts and corresponding postfix notation.

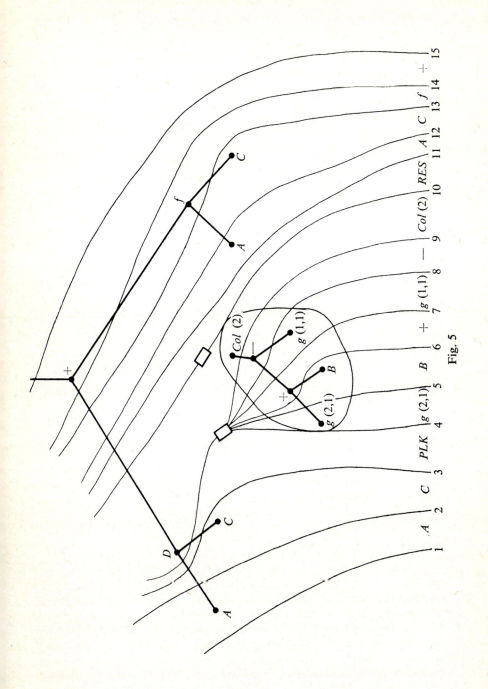

Fig. 5

The successive stack states for the example in Fig. 5, where $L$ represents the link, are:

$$
\begin{array}{ll}
1 & \\
2 & a \\
3 & a, c \\
4 & a, c, L \\
5 & a, c, L, a \\
6 & a, c, L, a, b \\
7 & a, c, L, a + b \\
8 & a, c, L, a + b, c \\
9 & a, c, L, (a + b) - c \\
10 & (a + b) - c, L \\
11 & (a + b) - c \\
12 & (a + b) - c, a \\
13 & (a + b) - c, a, c \\
14 & (a + b) - c, f(a, c) \\
15 & (a + b) - c + f(a, c)
\end{array}
$$

A notation is now required for writing a description of the new operation $D$ in terms of its constituent operations. The effect of the operation can be described by describing the state of the stack before the operation and after the operation. We would also like to interpret this description and produce a postfix language description containing control operations '$g$ $(i, j)$', 'col $(n)$', '$PLK$' and '$RES$' which tells us how the operation is evaluated.

The new operation is described by using the names of the old operations which are included in it together with names to represent the argument positions. The notation used is called $\lambda$-notation (2). The application of function to argument will be written by writing the name or description of the function followed by its argument in brackets. The new operation $D$ can be written

$$(\lambda\, X\, Y\, .\, -(+(X, B),\, Y))$$

The tree can be recovered from this notation by connecting the names of arguments to the name of the function which is applied to them.

$$\lambda\, X\, Y\, .\, -\, (\, +\, (\, X\, ,\, B\, )\, .\, Y\, )$$

The $X$ and $Y$ are called bound variables, $-(+(X, B),\, Y)$ is called the $\lambda$-body or the 'scope' of $X$ and $Y$. The names $X$ and $Y$ may be changed to any two different names not clashing with $-$, $+$, $B$ and the description will be a description of the same operation. The function $D(A,\, C)$ may be written

$$(\lambda\, X\, Y\, .\, -(\, +\, (\, X\, ,\, B\, ),\, Y\, ))(\, A\, ,\, C\, )$$

and the lines crossing the contour may be recovered by joining the arguments to their corresponding names in the $\lambda$ list by a line and joining the occurrences of the bound variables to the same name in the λ list. Finally the contour is drawn around the scope as shown.

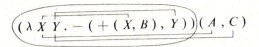

When the $X$ and $Y$ are removed from this structure, a tree representation of the function $D$ applied to actual arguments $A$, $C$ is obtained.

The simple scheme of drawing one contour can be extended. It is a special case of an operation which has nested scopes, i.e. contours within contours. A tree diagram which has one contour lying within another will describe the operation unambiguously. It may be possible, however, for the evaluation of the operation to be performed in several different ways. The different

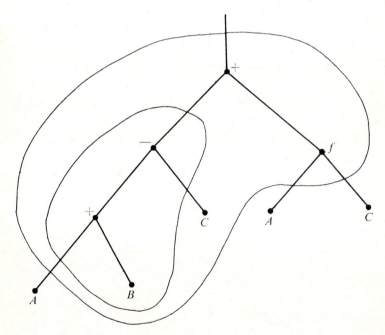

Fig. 6

methods of evaluation can be described using the λ-notation and the process of converting a description of an operation into an equivalent description is called 'conversion' in the λ-calculus. Figure 6 is an example of a construction process tree with two contours one inside the other.

The branch leading to the leftmost '$A$' in the diagram is cut by two contours. The outermost contour is an operation on 3 arguments ($A$, $A$, $C$) the inner

contour is either an operation with one argument $C$ or of two arguments.
The description of this construction process can be written in four ways:

(1) $(\lambda XYZ. +((\lambda UV. -(+(U, B), V)) (X, C), f(Y, Z))) (A, A, C)$
(2) $(\lambda XYZ. +((\lambda V. -(+(X, B), V)) (C), f(Y, Z))) (A, A, C)$
(3) $(\lambda D. (\lambda XYZ. +(D(X, C), f(Y, Z))) (\lambda UV. -(+(U, B), V))) (A, A, C)$
(4) $(\lambda D. (\lambda XYZ. +(D(X, C), f(Y, Z))) (A, A, C)) (\lambda UV. -(+(U, B), V))$

In the first case the object $a$ is carried forward to become an argument of
the inner operation. In the second case the argument of the outer operation
is used inside the inner operation.

To deal with the case of getting arguments of outer operations from within
inner operations the operation $g$ $(i, 1)$ must be extended. The operation
$g$ $(i, j)$ will get an argument. It will get the $i$th argument and will cross $j$
contour lines to get it. The numbers $i$ and $j$ can be obtained from the $\lambda$
notation description. The names in the list following the $\lambda$ are numbered
starting at one from the end to obtain $i$ and $j$-$1$ is the number of $\lambda$ scopes
between occurrences of the name in the $\lambda$ list and in the bound expression.

The diagram of Fig. 6 is described by expression 2 and the corresponding
postfix notation is:

$$A\,A\,C\,PLK\,C\,PLK\,g\,(3, 2)\,B + g\,(1, 1) - col\,(1)\,RES\,g\,(2, 1)\,g\,(1, 1), f + col\,(3)$$
$$RES$$

The tree diagram of Fig. 7 shows the tree corresponding to expression 1.

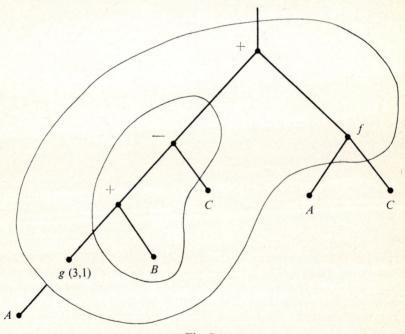

Fig. 7

In the case of expression 1 the inner contour is not dependent on its context and may be given a name and abstracted to get expressions 3 or 4. In the case of expression 2 the inner contour is dependent on its context and cannot be abstracted. The operations associated with these descriptions will be called 'context dependent' and 'context independent' operations. The evaluation of expression 2 is more efficient in the use of stack space than the evaluation of expression 1 but in expression 1 the inner operation may be abstracted and used in a wider context. The corresponding postfix notation is:

$$A \, A \, C \, PLK \, g \, (3, 1) \, C \, PLK \, g \, (2, 1) \, B + g \, (1, 1) - col \, (2) \, RES \, g \, (2, 1) \, g \, (1, 1)$$
$$f + col \, (3) \, RES$$

The stack mechanism required is similar to that described by Dijkstra (1960, 1961). The link contains two pointers. One is the value of the parameter pointer at the moment of call of the operation. The other is a pointer to the link corresponding to the contour which encloses the operation at the point of call. If the evaluation of the operation changes the control number then its value before the change must be stored in the link. There are two chains through the links of the stack. The first is a chain of activation and all the links are chained in order by this chain. The second chain is a chain of links corresponding to the contours and are used by the $g \, (i, j)$ operations to address objects. The second chain is the context in which operations are to be evaluated. Operations which address only their arguments are called context independent operations, their addressing is only relative to the last parameter pointer and they do not use the context chain.

### 7. Operations as Arguments

An operation called 'apply' will be introduced which has as arguments an operation and objects which are the arguments of the operation. The result of evaluating apply is the same result as applying the operation to its arguments. The construction process of the example can be changed to Fig. 8 using apply.

The names of the operations $+ -$ and $f$ must be interpreted in a different way. Evaluation of these new operations will put an object in the stack which stands for the operation. The effect of evaluating the apply operation is to take the object at the top of the stack and treat it as an operation to be applied to the members of the stack below it.

If the operation is context dependent then the context must be carried with the description of the operation, and the apply operation must store the old context, establish the new context, evaluate the operation and then restore the old context. A new notation is used in the tree diagram. A rectangular box enclosing a construction process will signify that evaluation of this box means put a description of the operation on to the stack. The representation of such an operation in the postfix string will be the word quote followed by a postfix description of the operation in brackets. Evaluation of the construction process of Fig. 8 is equivalent to interpreting the string '$A \, B$ quote $(+)$ apply $C$ quote $(-)$ apply $A \, C$ quote $(f)$ apply quote $(+)$ apply.'

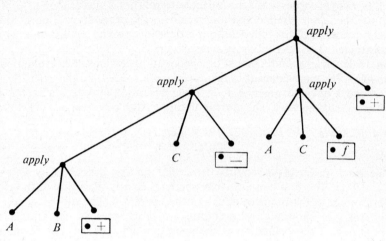

Fig. 8

Another version of the apply operation is one which has two arguments. One argument is an operation and the other an object. The result can be either an operation or an object. The example in Fig. 9 uses this operation which is called 'ap'.

The postfix notation is:

$B\,A$ quote $(+)$ ap ap $C$ quote $(-)$ ap ap $C\,A$ quote $(f)$ ap ap quote $(+)$ ap ap. Note that the operations $+\;-$ and $f$ differ from the previous operations.

The quote operation is used to delay evaluation of the construction process so that a description of the operation is passed to an operation instead of the

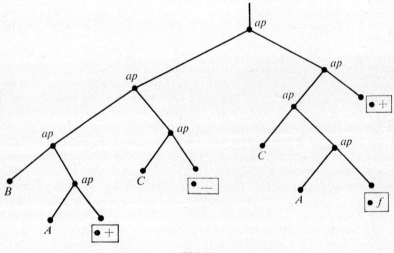

Fig. 9

result of evaluating this operation. This is similar to the call by name feature of ALGOL 60 (Naur *et al.*, 1960). An operation apply or ap must be applied to the description within the operation so that it is evaluated. However, other operations could be applied to the description.

In order to abstract any operation name from a construction process it is necessary to make it an end point of the tree by using the apply function and then to draw a contour which surrounds all the tree except the end node. The diagram of Fig. 10 shows the operation *f* abstracted from the construction process.

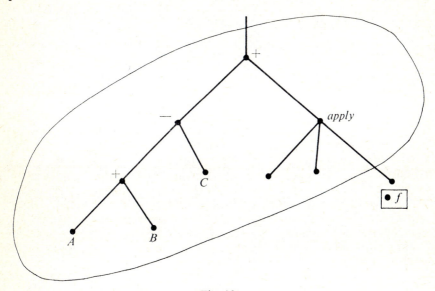

Fig. 10

## 8. Recursive Operations

An operation is recursive if a node representing it is the same operation as a contour which surrounds the node. The operation may or may not be context dependent and so cannot necessarily be abstracted from its context. We need a new concept or method of description of a recursive operation without giving the operation a name. This operation is called 'label' by McCarthy (1960a, b). The description 'label $(a, E)$' denotes an expression $E$ providing that occurrences of '$a$' within '$E$' be interpreted as referring to the expression as a whole. There is another way of thinking about this. The operation named '$a$' can be abstracted from the construction process $E$ by introducing an apply and drawing a contour. This produces a new operation which is $\lambda a.E(a)$. If the recursive operation is named $X$ then

$$X = \lambda a.E(a)\ X \qquad (3)$$

To describe the operation independently of $X$, the $Y$ combinator is used. The operator $Y$ is applied to an operation $F$ to produce an operation with the property $Y(F) = F(Y(F))$:

    factorial $(n) = E$ (factorial $(n - 1)$)

$\therefore$    the operation 'factorial' is described by '$\lambda n.\ E$ (factorial $(n - 1)$)'. We now abstract the name factorial and obtain

factorial $= (\lambda X.\ \lambda n.\ E(X\ (n - 1)))$ [factorial]
hence factorial $= Y(\lambda X.\ (\lambda n.\ E\ (X\ (n - 1))))$.

This expression is described in tree form as

$$\lambda x. \overline{(\lambda n.\ E\ (x(n - 1)))}$$

## 9. The Naming of Operations

The names of operations have been attached to nodes for the convenience of description. Any name can be considered to be a bound variable. If an operation is context independent it can be considered as an argument to the global or master operation being performed and treated as an object. The operation 'apply' is the only operation which needs to have arguments. The other operations put objects and descriptions of operations in the stack, or are the special control operations. The meaning of context independence is that the operations have the same context throughout the master operation.

The construction process tree example can be re-written in the form of Fig. 11.

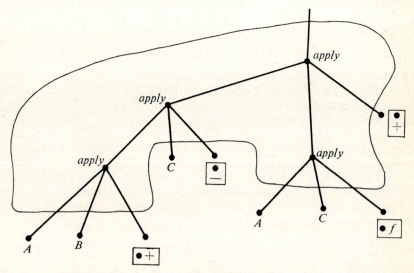

Fig. 11

It is described in λ notation by:

$$(\lambda RSTUVWXYZ \ . \ (Z(V(T(R, \ S), \ U), \ Y(W, \ X))))$$
$$(A, \ B, \ +, \ C, \ -, \ A, \ C, \ f, \ +)$$

or if certain arguments are identified:

$$(\lambda RSTUVY \ . \ T(V(T(R, \ S), \ U), \ Y(R, \ U))) \ (A, \ B, \ + \ C, \ -, \ f)$$

The evaluation of the complete program proceeds by putting the descriptions of the primitive operations and context independent operations and objects on to the stack and entering a master operation. Since the arguments to the outermost function must be fixed in position in the stack throughout the master operation this can be implemented in a simpler way. The sequence 'get description of basic operation, apply' can be simplified to a subroutine jump to a fixed position. The operation 'get description of basic operation' can be simplified to an operation which puts the address of the subroutine in the stack.

### 10. Examples of Methods of Improving the Efficiency of Operations

1. The *PLK* and *RES* operations plant and restore three items, the pointer to the context, the pointer to the last link and the control number. The pointer to the context need not be stored for context independent operations. The pointer to the last link need not be stored for basic operations which do not include other operations. The control number need not be stored if no change of control is made.

2. Context independent recursive operations need no description of context and also if the operation is not used as an argument the call can be implemented by a subroutine jump.

3. Extraction of common subexpressions. The arguments of an operation may be used more than once inside the operation. They need only be evaluated once and brought forward in the stack more than once by operation of the type $g \ (i, j)$.

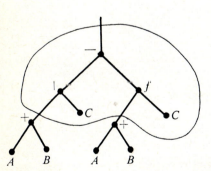
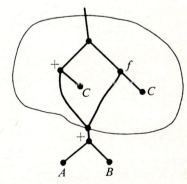

Fig. 12

For example the expression:

$$(A + B) + C - f(A + B, C) \text{ can be re-written}$$
$$\lambda X. (X + C - f(X, C)) (A + B)$$

A new operation is produced and applied to the argument $A + B$. Fig. 12 shows the tree diagram representation.

## 11. Shrinking of Operations

The examples of Fig. 6 and Fig. 7 show two ways of considering the same operation. The tree in Fig. 6 gives rise to more efficient evaluation because to get $A$ it does one operation instead of two. The process of shrinking produces context dependent operations. The same process can be applied to recursive operations.

For example:

$$\text{subst } (xyz) = E \text{ (subst}(x \ y \text{ car } z), \text{ subst } (x \ y \text{ cdr } z), x, y, z)$$
$$\text{subst } xy \quad = \lambda u . E \text{ (subst}(xy \text{ car } u), \text{subst}(xy \text{ cdr } u), x, y, u)$$
$$= \lambda V . (\lambda u, E \ (V \text{ car } u, V \text{ cdr } u, x, y, u)) \text{ [subst } x \ y]$$
$$= Y \ (\lambda V . (\lambda u . E \ (V \text{ car } u, V \text{ cdr } u \ x, y, u)))$$
$$\therefore \quad \text{subst} \quad = \lambda xyz . (Y(\lambda V . (\lambda u . E \ (V \text{ car } u, V \text{ cdr } u, x, y, u))) [z]$$

The evaluation of the resulting expression is more efficient because the recursive loop includes a carrying forward of only $z$ at each recursion rather than $x \ y$ and $z$.

## 12. Collapsing of Operations

If the sequence '$f$ col $(n)$ RES' occurs in the description of a context independent operation in postfix notation, where $f$ is an operation of the form

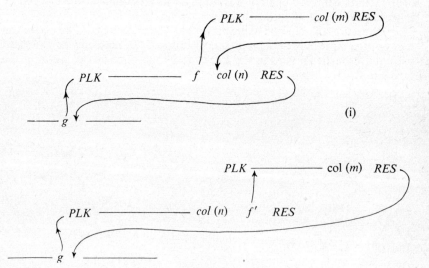

Fig. 13

*PLK* ... col (*m*) *RES*, than it can be replaced by a string of the form *col'* (*n*) *f' RES*. The operation *f'* means change control to the string *f* entering after the *PLK* operation. The link which remains in the stack is the link corresponding to the operation which called *f*. The *RES* at the end of *f* sets the arithmetic unit back to the state it was in before it entered the operation which called *f*. The two sequences of interpretation are shown in Fig. 13.

In particular if *f* and *g* are the same operation a recursive operation is being collapsed to produce an iterative one. In this case the col (*n*) operation can be simplified and combined with *g* (*i*, *j*) operations to make new operations which transfer objects back in the stack to overwrite the in put parameters.

1. Changing the shape of the construction process tree by using information about the properties of operations and combinations of operations to produce a new tree diagram which can be shrunk, collapsed or from which common subexpressions can be extracted.

2. Changing the construction process tree to fit the shape of the machine. For example one address, one accumulator machines are efficient for evaluating

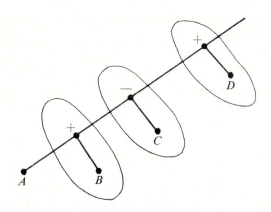

Fig. 14

trees in which each node is joined to an end point. These can be split into operations as indicated in Fig. 14 and in which each operation is a machine instruction.

3. If a contour encloses operations which make up a substring of the postfix string, i.e. the contour cuts the bottom branches in the same places as one of the stack cuts of the original postfix string, then the *PLK* and *RES* operations can be reduced to a simple change of control. Contours of this type correspond to substrings of the original string. The number of lines pointing into a contour is called the tail stratification of the string by Gorn (1962a, b). The number of lines pointing out of the contour is called the head stratification.

## REFERENCES

1. A. W. BURKS, D. W. WARREN and J. B. WRIGHT (1954). An Analysis of a Logical Machine Using Parenthesis Free Notation. *M.T.A.C.* **8**, No. 46, 53.
2. A. CHURCH (1941). The Calculi of Lambda-conversion. *Annu. Math. Studies* **6**.
3. H. B. CURRY and R. FEYS (1958). "Combinatory Logic". North Holland Publ. Co., Amsterdam.
4. E. W. DIJKSTRA (1960). Recursive Programming. *Numerische Mathematik* **2**, 5.
5. E. W. DIJKSTRA (1961). An ALGOL 60 Translator for the X1. *ALGOL Bull. Suppl.* 10.
6. S. GORN (1962a). "An Axiomatic Approach to Prefix Languages". Symp. on Symbolic Languages in Data Processing, Rome.
7. S. GORN (1962b). "The Treatment of Ambiguity and Paradox in Mechanical Languages". *Proc. Symp. Pure Maths*, Vol. V: Recursive Function Theory.
8. J. McCARTHY (1960a). Recursive Functions of Symbolic Expressions and their Computation by Machine, Pt. 1. *Comm. A.C.M.* **3**, 184.
9. J. McCARTHY (1960b). "The LISP Programmers' Manual". M.I.T. Computation Centre.
10. J. McCARTHY (1961). A Basis for a Mathematical Theory of Computation. Preliminary Report, p. 225. Proc. Western J.C.C., Los Angeles.
11. P. NAUR et al. (1960). Report on the Algorithmic Language ALGOL 60. *Comm. ACM* 3.
12. A. G. OETTINGER (1961). "Automatic Syntactic Analysis and the Pushdown Store". Proc. Symp. Structure of Language and its Mathematical Aspects. American Mathematical Society.

APPENDIX

# THE FUTURE OF COMPUTERS*

## D. GABOR

*Imperial College, London, England*

I want to discuss in turn the importance and potentialities of computers for science, for economics and for human life. I will start with science because this is the most satisfactory and the least controversial aspect of the whole complex problem.

I will divide the scientific applications of computers into three types of problems. Problems of the first type are of great importance by any traditional standard, which could not be solved without computers. The second type are problems which are also solvable by computers, which are, however, not of great interest by traditional standards, but whose solution is forced on us by the complexities of a growing civilization. The third type are those problems which are solvable by computers, whose solution is neither of scientific nor of economic interest, but which are tempting by the very fact that we now have computers to do the job, and computers, like any other sort of vested capital, must be used!

The most satisfactory and the least controversial are, of course, those great scientific problems which could never have been solved without computers. The field in which computers had their greatest scientific triumphs for the time being is that of molecular biology, the unravelling of highly complicated organic molecular structures. The great work of Bragg, Hodgkin, Perutz, Kendrew and Crick would have been quite impossible without fast electronic machines. Take, for example, the astonishing work of Kendrew; the complete resolution of the structure of the protein myoglobin. This is a molecule with a molecular weight of 18,000, with 1,200 atoms, not counting hydrogen, and every one of these atoms was put into its place by a computation which involved fitting 20,000 Fourier-coefficients in a million points by least squares. Even the material which had to be fed into the computer could not have been obtained without automatic machinery. Measuring out the thousands of photographic plates with a million X-ray spots in them would have taken a worker 250 years, if he had used old-fashioned methods.

The most satisfactory feature of this work, in my mind, was that it was a beautiful example of collaboration between man and machine. The scientists by their chemical knowledge and flair had to supply the guesses; without this even the fastest machine would have needed astronomical times for putting 1,200 atoms into their places. I am sorry to say though, that the part of genius is likely to diminish somewhat in the future. In the June 6 number of the *Proceedings of the Royal Society*, Dr. Judith Milledge, a collaborator of Dame Kathleen Lonsdale, explains very convincingly, that with machines making a

---

* After-dinner talk given on 5 July 1963.

million computations per second one could start with much worse guesses, and leave much more to the machine. I have a feeling though that for a generation at least there will still be a niche for genius in this field.

The second type of scientific application of computers is, as I mentioned, in those problems which would not have been considered important by traditional standards, but whose solution is forced on us by the increased complexity of our civilization. Let me explain what I mean. I do not know what it is now, but the mileage of book-shelves of the British Museum was 75 miles in 1956! This comprises many miles of the descriptive sciences, such as say, botanics or entomology. The material has grown far beyond any human memory. If a man spends all his life reading, he can work his way perhaps through a tenth or at most a fifth of a mile. Only computers, of a type which we do not yet possess, will be able to memorize and to order this immense material, which is growing at a frightening rate. Well-meaning scientists, such as Bernal and Haldane have expressed the belief that there is still a wide field for amateur scientists, or scientific minds of less than the top grade. Bernal has imagined a future world in which 25% of the population are doing research, and Haldane has said that as there are at least a million living species, they could engage a million research workers for a thousand years. But what will happen to the lucky amateur entomologist who, say, discovers a new pattern on the wings of a beetle? Only a giant electronic computer could tell him whether his discovery is new, classify his findings, and give him a certificate of it. The alternative is to consider past descriptive science as perishable material, and considering new additions to it as ephemeral as newspapers.

The third type of application of computers in science is the most unsavoury. It is in the field of problems which formerly were not solvable, which are now solvable, and which *must* be solved because we have computers which must be kept busy. I do not wish to give invidious examples from real life, though I have seen plenty, it will be better to give an imaginary example. Everybody knows that the 3-body problem in astronomy has no general analytical solution. The great mathematicians were satisfied with proving this; at most they gave a few terrible-looking series. But the problem is now solvable, it does not even take a very big machine to give thousands of numerical solutions every day. I hope nobody is doing exactly this on a grand scale, but I am afraid very much of this sort is going on. Once a big machine is installed in an institute, a large staff of programmers must be engaged and research workers who keep the machine busy, quite often forgetting those who would be needed to analyse the result. The outcome is as vicious a Parkinsonian circle as anybody can imagine!

I do not want to close my review of the scientific applications of computers on a too pessimistic note. I can see enormous worthwhile applications in science. Perhaps the greatest of the problems will be the reproduction of biological history by the Monte Carlo method. Ever since Darwin, it has worried many people that homo sapiens has appeared too suddenly on the biological scene to be explicable by random mutations and natural selection. Some thirty years ago, Sir Ronald Fisher believed that he had answered this question in the affirmative, but his argument is now generally considered as unsatisfactory. I do not think that as yet we have got a sufficient knowledge of human genes, but when we shall have, it may be possible to play out millions of Monte Carlo games of the development of man by random mutations and natural selection, and this may then decide the gigantic dilemma whether there was *purpose* in man's development or not.

Coming now to the economic influence of computers, this unfortunately is a highly controversial and somewhat sinister subject. I hasten to say that the sinister side of it concerns less people like you who have learned programming such enormous machines like the *IBM* 7090 or the *ATLAS* because the economic influence of smaller special purpose computers is likely to be many times greater. It is these which are likely to penetrate into industry and business and bring about what may well be a very painful economic and social revolution. A little while ago there appeared in America a much discussed pamphlet by Dr. Donald Michael called 'Cybernation—the Silent Conquest'. Cybernation means the transformations which cybernetics and computers will effect in the social structure. Norbert Wiener, the originator of the term 'cybernetics' has expressed grave doubts on this issue and Dr. Michael has gone even further. Let me quote an abstract of what he wrote:

'Cybernation is regarded as inevitable because of its economic advantages, and to some degree necessary to meet the demands of increasing population; but there are more disadvantages. Unemployment will be widespread in the managerial class and the service industries as well as in the manufacturing industries.

'Unemployment may be also widespread among untrained adolescents. Delinquency will be almost inevitable and thus contribute to further social disruption. Little hope is seen in retraining displaced blue collar workers. Management generally is unwilling to institute retraining programmes.

'No one has seriously proposed what the unemployed in the service industries can be retained to do: "to say nothing of training them for jobs that would pay them high enough wages to make them good consumers of the cornucopia of products manufactured by automation". Shorter hours will clearly not solve the problem when the task is eliminated or new tasks need different talents.

'Public works programmes are regarded as an obvious solution, but the report believes they would not be conducive to maintaining the spirit of a capitalistic economy. The extension of Cybernation in the interest of free enterprise and better profits may be self-defeating.

'Leisure will also be a problem. Boredom might lead many to take part in radical organizations, while family adjustments for those working thirty-two or fewer hours a week will be added to the already inadequate ambiguous and frustrating personal relationships that typify much of middle-class family life.

'The increasing use of computers by government, will inevitably lead to public ignorance of major issues.

'If we do not find the answers to these questions soon we will have a population in the next ten to twenty years more and more out of touch with national and international realities, ever more the victims of insecurity on the one hand and *ennui* on the other, and more and more mismatched to the occupational needs of the day.'

I know that practical people will pooh-pooh these forebodings of Dr. Michael, but not being a practical man, I think they must be taken rather seriously, at any rate in the United States. In this country we are still suffering from old-fashioned economic troubles, productivity is low, and we could not even keep our hospitals and many other public services running without immigration. But in the United States the unemployment is running around five million, and this is to a great part technological unemployment. Between 1947 and 1961 the number of production-line workers has decreased by 7%, while the industrial output has increased in the same time interval by 57%. It is true that the total U.S. working force expanded from 60 million to 70 million, by white-collar services, by a vigorous instinctive application of Parkinson's Law. But this was because rationalization started in the factories and left the offices more or less alone. If there will be a similar efficiency drive in the offices, conditions may well become as serious in the U.S. as prophesied by Donald Michael.

As I said before, if this comes about, only a small part of the responsibility, if any, will fall on the operators of large computers, but a very great part of it on the electronic engineers who are now developing smaller machines for office and factory use. Not so long ago the engineer could have a good conscience if he only did what he was told to do, like a soldier under orders. This is now not good enough. If the electronic crash comes about, we shall be just as little absolved by the future as the German soldiers who acted under orders.

There is no need yet, at any rate in this country, to advocate that electronic engineers shall become conscientious objectors. There is still time, but not very much time, perhaps twenty years. In that time we must either educate a new generation fit to live in leisure, and create an economic system which is in harmony with it, or else we shall have to start suppressing electronic inventions. I hope though that we shall never have to suppress large electronic computers and the FORTRAN or ALGOL systems!